SEEING THE SELF

PHAENOMENOLOGICA

SERIES FOUNDED BY H.L. VAN BREDA AND PUBLISHED
UNDER THE AUSPICES OF THE HUSSERL-ARCHIVES

149

E. ØVERENGET

SEEING THE SELF

HEIDEGGER ON SUBJECTIVITY

Editorial Board:
Director: R. Bernet (Husserl-Archief, Leuven) Secretary: J. Taminiaux (Centre d'études phénoménologiques, Louvain-la-Neuve) Members: S. IJsseling (Husserl-Archief, Leuven), H. Leonardy (Centre d'études phénoménologiques, Louvain-la-Neuve), U. Melle (Husserl-Archief, Leuven), B. Stevens (Centre d'études phénoménologiques, Louvain-la-Neuve)
Advisory Board:
R. Bernasconi (Memphis State University), D. Carr (Emory University, Atlanta), E.S. Casey (State University of New York at Stony Brook), R. Cobb-Stevens (Boston College), J.F. Courtine (Archives-Husserl, Paris), F. Dastur (Université de Paris XII), K. Düsing (Husserl-Archiv, Köln), J. Hart (Indiana University, Bloomington), K. Held (Bergische Universität Wuppertal), D. Janicaud (Université de Nice), K.E. Kaehler (Husserl-Archiv, Köln), D. Lohmar (Husserl-Archiv, Köln), W.R. McKenna (Miami University, Oxford, USA), J.N. Mohanty (Temple University, Philadelphia), E.W. Orth (Universität Trier), B. Rang (Husserl-Archiv, Freiburg i.Br.), P. Ricoeur (Paris), K. Schuhmann (University of Utrecht), C. Sini (Università degli Studi di Milano), R. Sokolowski (Catholic University of America, Washington D.C.), E. Ströker (Universität Köln), B. Waldenfels (Ruhr-Universität, Bochum)

TABLE OF CONTENTS

Acknowledgments	vii
INTRODUCTION	1
I. WHOLES AND PARTS	7
1. Husserl on Wholes and Parts	9
2. Wholes and Parts and Transcendental Phenomenology	13
3. The Presence of the Theory of Wholes and Parts in *Being and Time*	19
4. The Theory of Wholes and Parts in Heidegger's Marburg-Lectures	24
5. The Concreteness of the *Seinsfrage*	27
II. CATEGORIAL INTUITION	34
1. Husserl on Seeing Objects of Higher Levels	35
2. Intentionality and Evidence	36
3. Categorial Intuition	42
4. Heidegger's Analysis of Categorial Intuition	46
5. Intentional Fulfillment	48
6. Intuition and Expression	53
7. Categorial Acts: Synthesis and Ideation	61
8. Constitution	68
III. APRIORISM	72
1. The Phenomenological Sense of the Apriori	74
2. Analytic Description of Intentionality in its Apriori	78
3. Pure Consciousness	84
4. The Being of Consciousness	91
5. Apriori and *Concretum*	98
IV. EXISTENCE	105
1. The Phenomenological Reduction and the Analysis of Dasein	106
2. Dasein as Existence	111
3. Situatedness	116
4. Understanding	120
5. Seeing: Understanding, Interpretation, Assertion	124
6. Being-There: Discourse and Falling	130
7. Care	135

V. SELF-CONSCIOUSNESS — 139
1. Phenomenology and Self-Consciousness — 140
2. Sartre's Critique of Husserl — 145
3. Kant on the Original Synthetic Unity of Apperception — 148
4. Transcendental Apperception and Non-Positional Awareness — 152
5. Heidegger and Egology — 156

VI. CONSTITUTION — 166
1. Being and Constitution — 167
2. Equipment — 174
3. Pre-Ontological Confirmation — 181
4. Reference — 185
5. World — 189
6. Disclosedness and Discoveredness — 193

VII. SELF — 199
1. Arendt on the Human Condition — 200
2. *Poiesis* — 205
3. Inauthenticity — 209
4. The One (*das Man*) — 216
5. *Praxis* — 223

VIII. UNITY — 232
1. The Question of Primordial Totality — 233
2. Anxiety — 236
3. Being-a-whole — 243
4. Death — 246
5. Death and Possibility — 254
6. Authenticity — 258
7. Resoluteness — 266

IX. TEMPORALITY — 270
1. The Traditional Theory of Time and the Temporality of *Praxis* — 272
2. The Temporality of Transcendental Apperception — 276
3. Husserl and the Temporality of Absolute Consciousness — 287
4. Anticipatory Resoluteness — 292
5. Temporality — 297
6. Repeating the Existential Analysis — 304
7. Temporality and Egology — 307

CONCLUSION — 313

Bibliography — 315

Index — 323

ACKNOWLEDGMENTS

I wish to thank The Norwegian Research Council for the Humanities, Fulbright, The American-Scandinavian Foundation and Boston College for generous fellowships. I should also like to thank Richard Cobb-Stevens for all the help, inspiration and support I have received while composing the manuscript of this book. In addition I would like to thank Robert Sokolowski, Jacques Taminiaux, Dagfinn Føllesdal, Hugh O'Beirne, Antonia Galdos, Sarah Glenn, Steinar Mathisen and Lars Fredrik Händler Svendsen for helpful criticisms of various drafts of this book. Sarah Glenn, Antonia Galdos and Steinar Mathisen have also been of considerable assistance in the final preparation of the manuscript. Last, but not least, I would like to thank Johan Frederik Bjelke and Torstein Tollefsen to whom I owe my first introduction to Heidegger's thinking.

This book is dedicated to my parents.

INTRODUCTION

"... die Augen hat mir *Husserl* eingesetzt."[1]

The aim of Twentieth century phenomenology is to provide a non-psychologistic interpretation of subjectivity. Husserl agrees with Frege; to adopt psychologism is to give up truth. But this should not prevent us from investigating the subjective perspective. On the contrary, Husserl thinks that an appropriate rejection of psychologism must be able to show how propositions are correlated to and grounded in subjective intuitions without thereby reducing them to psychological phenomena. Obviously this calls for an interpretation of subjectivity that makes a sharp distinction between the subjective perspective and the psychological realm.

Phenomenology is devoted to the development of a notion of subjectivity that is in accordance with our experience of the world. A fundamental tenet of phenomenology is that philosophy should not dispute this experience but rather account for it. Hence, phenomenology must avoid a notion of subjectivity in which it becomes a problem to account for how a subject can ever hook up with the world. In other words, a phenomenological interpretation of subjectivity must radically disassociate itself from what is often referred to as a worldless, Cartesian subject, a *res cogitans*. But neither can an interpretation of subjectivity consistently advocate a position according to which the human order is described only in the categories appropriate to the physical order. Such an interpretation is obviously not compatible with the phenomenal basis for undertaking this very interpretation, that is, our experience of the world. It simply does not account for experienc*ing*; one cannot coherently claim that doing away with subjectivity is an interpretation of subjectivity. In short, the objective of phenomenology is to rehabilitate the subjective perspective without falling back into psychologism. Its goal is to criticize idealism without falling into objectivism. It seeks to develop a notion of subjectivity that accounts for its fundamental transcendence without thereby psychologizing the world or reducing away subjectivity, that is, without confusing the subjective and

---

[1] M. Heidegger, *Ontologie (Hermeneutik der Faktizität)*, Gesamtausgabe (GA) 63, (Frankfurt am Main: Vittorio Klostermann, 1988), 5.

objective domain.

It is our argument that Heidegger's project of existential analytic is in keeping with this endeavor. In this regard we would like to submit the following thesis: Heidegger's concept of Dasein designates a phenomenological notion of subjectivity. People familiar with Heidegger might find this claim rather peculiar and argue that it goes against many passages in Heidegger's writings where he explicitly precludes interpreting Dasein as a subject. Thus, it is commonly held, and we agree, that Heidegger's aim is to destroy the subject. But there is one thing that must be kept in mind while discussing this issue: what Heidegger seeks to destroy is not subjectivity as such but a specific notion of subjectivity, and he does this by means of reconstructing a notion of subjectivity that is truer to the phenomena. Heidegger challenges the interpretation of the subject as a thing-like entity that is not in the world, but — and this is imperative — by allowing subjectivity back into the world, he is not eliminating subjectivity and thereby treating it like any other thing in the world. In short, while the traditional modern interpretation seems to adhere to a notion of subjectivity as a thing that is not in the world, Heidegger introduces an interpretation according to which subjectivity is a Being-in-the-world that is not a thing.

However, one could still object to our interpretation of Dasein as a subject by pointing out that Heidegger himself never uses this term to refer to Dasein. On Heidegger's account, Dasein is existence, understanding, disclosedness, and mineness, but almost never subjectivity. So how can we justify referring to Dasein as subjectivity? Early phenomenology faced a considerable terminological problem: should this new orientation present itself by making use of a traditional modern philosophical terminology, or should it construct new terms? Husserl represents the former, Heidegger the latter. While Husserl presented his ideas in a common philosophical language, and thus was, and still is, often radically misunderstood, Heidegger adhered strongly to neologisms and was, and still is, often not understood at all. The best way to understand the phenomenology of either is in fact to approach the one from the other. Just as Heidegger often brings out Husserl's ideas better than Husserl ever did himself, so too is it the case that Heidegger's neologisms find a technical foundation in Husserlian terms. For this reason we approach Dasein from essential concepts of Husserl's phenomenology. There are, however, several other reasons for this reading of Heidegger. Firstly, although Heidegger is quite consistent in sticking to his neologisms, there are occasions when he in fact refers to Dasein as a new non-subjectivistic notion of subjectivity. By this we understand that Dasein is a subject, but not by being a worldless ego, but rather as a Being-in-the-world. Secondly, the terms used by Heidegger in order to elucidate the being of Dasein have two things in common: they all suggest that Dasein is essentially related to itself and that it is a condition of possibility for the appearance of entities. The essence of Dasein is existence, existence is understanding, and understanding is a kind of self-understanding through which the world is disclosed. Thus, Heidegger's definition of Dasein does not distance itself radically from the traditional modern definition of subjectivity. In fact, it remains fully within the modern tradition. Where Heidegger transcends the tradition is that the basic principles of phenomenology enable him to locate this subjectivity in the world, and that is by no means a small effort, but the concept of Dasein is still an attempt to soundly rethink the notion of subjectivity.

It is our contention that Dasein not only refers to subjectivity but that this concept in fact designates transcendental subjectivity. Heidegger's concept of Dasein refers to a transcendental subject in the sense that it is a condition of possibility for the appearance of appearances: it appears as that to which appearances appear. In other words, it appears as appearance itself and it is nothing but appearance, whereas a thing always appears *as* this or that entity, transcendental subjectivity does not have any essence other than appearance itself. This is what Heidegger means when he maintains that Dasein has no other essence than existence. If it is indeed the case that transcendental subjectivity is the condition of possibility for appearances in the sense that it appears as that to which appearances appear, it follows that this subjectivity must itself appear, and if it appears it must appear to itself. Hence, we are introduced to the problem of self-appearance or, in a more traditional idiom, self-consciousness. However, the self-appearance of existence is such that Dasein is not thematically aware of itself prior to and independently of its involvement with the world. Existence refers instead to a notion of self-directedness which is not a directedness towards, or consciousness of, a self appearing prior to the world. The self is not given as an object of consciousness but rather is given *with* our consciousness of objects.

The characteristic of Dasein as both constituting and self-directed finds its unity in the description of Dasein as a temporal unity. It is temporality that in the end allows for the being of Dasein as existence and which accounts for this kind of being. Dasein is a non-objective temporal unity, that is, the lifestyle of Dasein is temporality, not spatiality. And its non-objectivity springs from the fact that it has the temporality of that which constitutes objectivity. Dasein has the temporality of action, that is, of a phenomenon that is its own end. To see is also at the same time to have seen, likewise, to understand is to have understood. Thus, the temporal moments of Dasein are non-sequential; Dasein is at once both futural and in the mode of having been.

We argue that Heidegger's existential analytic is a systematic argument geared towards the development of a phenomenological notion of subjectivity. In this inquiry we seek to bring this argument to the fore, beginning with a discussion of the phenomenological basis of his endeavor. In the first three chapters we focus upon the fundamental phenomenological principles upon which the existential analytic rests. Our first chapter is devoted to the most basic of these principles, Husserl's theory of wholes and parts, and its presence in and importance for Heidegger's project. Heidegger never admits to making use of this theory but we nevertheless argue that it structures Heidegger's existential analytic. Firstly, he cannot use the phenomenological principles he in fact admits using — the concept of categorial intuition and the phenomenological sense of the apriori — unless he also incorporates the theory of wholes and parts into his project. Secondly, Heidegger's use of the theory of wholes and parts is consistent with his emphasis on providing every step of the development of an ontology with a phenomenal basis. Thirdly, our analysis makes sense of the very architecture of his magnum opus, *Being and Time*.[2] In our second chapter we shall have a look at the concept of categorial intuition and its importance for Heidegger's existential analytic. We take our departure from Heidegger's analysis of this concept in one of his early lectures and then see how this analysis becomes imperative for his development of the ontology of Dasein. In the third chapter we shall see how the theory of wholes and parts and the concept of categorial intuition together add up to a phenomenological sense of the apriori, and we shall see how important this sense of the apriori is for the development of subjectivity sought by the existential analytic.

The first three chapters will provide a foundation for our interpretation of Heidegger's terminology with regard to his *Daseinsanalytik* and his definition of Dasein as existence. In our fourth chapter we discuss the formal structure of existence, and we introduce the existentials that constitute the being of Dasein. We shall see that these existentials are moments and that they are related to the being of Dasein the way moments are related to a whole. We also see that the elaboration of these essential features of Dasein makes use of the defining method of Husserl's phenomenology: the phenomenological reduction. But we will argue that Heidegger is more faithful to the descriptive nature of phenomenology because he shows how this reduction itself is given in intuition. It is our contention that Heidegger introduces the phenomenon of breakdown in everyday use in order to provide the phenomenological reduction with evidence.

In Chapters V and VI we focus more closely on the nature of existence.

[2] M. Heidegger, *Being and Time*, translated by J. Macquarrie & E. Robinson (Oxford: Basil Blackwell, 1962). Hereafter BT. *Sein und Zeit* (Tübingen: Max Niemeyer Verlag, 1957).

As we have already mentioned, existence designates a kind of self-understanding through which the world is disclosed or constituted. Thus, the concept of existence comprises two essential themes: self-understanding or self-directedness, and disclosedness or constitution. Although these themes are intrinsically related and by no means can appear independently of one another we shall, for systematic reasons, treat them independently in these two Chapters. In Chapter V we discuss self-understanding or self-directedness. We develop our interpretation by confronting Heidegger with Kant and Sartre. Our argument is that Kant's emphasis on the synthetic unity of apperception over the analytic unity of apperception and Sartre's notion of non-positional awareness represents the same kind of egology that is suggested by Heidegger's interpretation of Dasein as existence. In Chapter VI we focus upon the theme of disclosedness or constitution. We show that the priority of Dasein over world does not allow for the appearance of Dasein independently of the world. We shall see that Heidegger takes over the notion of constitution qua categorial intuition (the letting-be-seen in its objectivity) outlined in Husserl's Sixth Logical Investigation. According to this notion, constitution is not fabrication. Dasein's disclosedness must not be understood in terms of fabrication (*poiesis*), where the product appears temporally after the act, but in terms of action (*praxis*) where the end of the act is included in the act itself.

The title of this study is *Seeing the Self* and this endeavor is an elaboration, not only of a notion of *self* or subjectivity, but of a self that is capable of such a *seeing*. This partly culminates in Chapter VII where we discuss more thoroughly the notion of self that is suggested in the prior chapters. The Aristotelian distinction between *poiesis* and *praxis* will play an important role in our discussion. Our objective will be to show how the structure of non-positional awareness is present in Heidegger's existential analytic. We argue that the sight that guides everyday activity is an all-consuming directedness at, or openness to, the environment. But since this sight is also a *praxis*, it follows that it concerns the agent itself.

At this point in the argument Heidegger faces a question that he probably takes more seriously than any other phenomenologist. This concerns the notion of *seeing*. If it is true that Dasein is a non-positional awareness of itself, how can it carry out an existential analytic, that is, how can it reach a positional awareness of this self? In Chapter VIII we investigate how Heidegger deals with this fundamental objection to his project, and we point out how this endeavor accounts for the architecture of the argument carried out in BT. In everydayness Dasein does not focus upon the apriori character of its own existential make-up; the latter is instead a condition of possibility for the former. In everydayness, Dasein is oblivious to its ownmost being—

it is inauthentic. How can Heidegger justify the grasping of Dasein's ownmost being, its being as a whole — which is the pronounced aim of fundamental ontology — if this very being precludes such an endeavor? Heidegger goes about this by calling attention to certain marginal experiences, anxiety and being-towards-death, in which the full meaning of everydayness is given in intuition. Thus, it is our argument that the topics discussed in the first two chapters of Division Two of BT, Being-towards-death, anxiety, conscience, and guilt, play an intrinsic role in the argument of BT. Instead of brushing these discussions aside as excessively speculative or even abstruse, it is imperative that we appreciate them for what they are, namely as that which is to provide a phenomenal basis for the entire project of an existential analytic, whose pronounced objective is to provide an understanding of the being of Dasein as a whole. Only when that is done can Heidegger go on to discuss the full meaning of Dasein. That is why the analysis of temporality is introduced in Division Two of BT, after the analysis of Being-a-whole, and not in Division One.

In our last chapter, Chapter IX, we consider Heidegger's analysis of temporality and its importance for the final understanding of Dasein as a whole. In this chapter several themes are brought together. Just as the themes of self-understanding and constitution find their full ontological meaning in temporality — as does thereby the notion of self as existence — so too does the very seeing of this phenomenon find *its* ontological basis in temporality. Indeed, these themes are all moments of the same whole: Dasein's temporality. The first part of the chapter will focus upon the three important philosophers who influenced Heidegger's discussion of temporality of subjectivity: Aristotle, Kant, and Husserl. Admittedly, of these philosophers, Husserl was the only one to develop a theory of temporality that is immediately related to Heidegger's own theory, but there are concepts in both Aristotle and in Kant that play an important role in the discussion of the temporality of subjectivity. In the second part of our last chapter we investigate Heidegger's temporalization of subjectivity and see how temporality provides the full ontological meaning of the being of Dasein.

CHAPTER I

WHOLES AND PARTS

In the third of his *Logical Investigations*,[1] "On the Theory of Wholes and Parts," Husserl introduces a distinction that stands out as essential to the phenomenological project. His distinction between wholes and parts, and between different kinds of parts, provides Husserl with a formal structure that is crucial to the peculiar approach to philosophical problems that is distinctive for phenomenology. Several scholars have shown the importance of this theory by pointing out how it is operative in Husserl's phenomenology.[2]

The objective of this chapter is twofold. First, we have a closer look at Husserl's theory of wholes and parts and its importance for the phenomenological project as such. We show that it is an essential presupposition for the phenomenological critique of psychologism in that it allows for an apriori necessity rooted in the world. But we also see that the very same theory advocates a kind of non-realism insofar as it precludes the disengagement of any object from the unity of consciousness. It is our argument that the theory of wholes and parts in fact encourages the turn to transcendental phenomenology because it harbors a notion of consciousness as a condition of possibility for the appearance of apriori necessity.

Secondly, we investigate the presence of the theory of wholes and parts

---

[1] E. Husserl, *Logical Investigations*, translated by J.N. Findlay (New York: Humanities Press, 1970). Hereafter LI. Numbers refers to paragraphs in LI. *Logische Untersuchungen* (Tübingen: Max Niemeyer, 1968).

[2] See for instance R. Sokolowski, *Husserlian Meditations* (Evanston: Northwestern University Press, 1974), "The Logic of Parts and Wholes in Husserl's *Investigations*," *Philosophy and Phenomenological Research* Vol. XXVIII, 1968, 537-53, and "The Structure and Content of Husserl's *Logical Investigations*" *Inquiry* Vol. XIV, 1971, 318-47; T. Seebohm, "Reflexion and Totality in the Philosophy of E. Husserl," *Journal of the British Society for Phenomenology*, Vol. 4, No. 1, January 1973, 20-30; B. Smith, *Parts and Moments: Studies in Logic and Formal Ontology* (Munich: Philosophia, 1982); P.M. Simons, *Parts: A Study in Ontology* (Oxford: Clarendon Press, 1982), "The Formalization of Husserl's Theory of Parts and Wholes," in *Parts and Moments: Studies in Logic and Formal Ontology*; J. Lampert, "Husserl's Theory of Part and Wholes: The Dynamic of Individuating and Contextualizing Interpretation," *Research in Phenomenology*, Vol. XIX, 1989, 195-212; K. Fine, "Part-whole," in *The Cambridge Companion to Husserl*, edited by B. Smith and D. Woodruff Smith (New York and Cambridge: Cambridge University Press, 1995).

in Heidegger's thinking and we argue that Husserl's theory of wholes and parts plays an essential role in the phenomenological project Heidegger carries out in BT. In that regard we would like to submit two theses. First, Heidegger not only uses the terminology of the theory of wholes and parts, but he uses it in accordance with the conventions Husserl establishes in the Third Investigation. Second, Heidegger makes use of this theory when he discusses the structural make-up of Dasein, which is, in fact, the epicenter of the fundamental-ontological project as this is carried out in BT.

In this chapter, the treatment of Heidegger will be purely textual; we simply point to the presence of Husserl's theory of wholes and parts in Heidegger's thinking. This approach, however, will prepare for the discussion in the second chapter, Categorial Intuition, and the third chapter, Apriorism. The outcome of these two chapters will be that the presence of the theory of wholes and parts in Heidegger's thinking and its importance for the *Daseinsanalytik* can be attributed to the fact that this theory plays a decisive role in Heidegger's approach to the *Seinsfrage* in BT.

It is commonly argued that although Heidegger started out as a phenomenologist and took as his point of departure what he refers to in the lecture *The History of the Concept of Time*[3] as the fundamental discoveries of phenomenology — intentionality, categorial intuition, and the original sense of the apriori — his overall project was entirely different from that of Husserl. Our claim is that by taking over these fundamental discoveries from Husserl Heidegger relies more extensively on Husserl than one might suspect from a first reading of his texts. He also adopts the formal structure operative in these discoveries and, by so doing, he ensures a structural isomorphism between his project and Husserl's. However, it could be argued that although Heidegger uses the terminology of wholes and parts, this implies by no means such an isomorphism. It is one thing to show that Heidegger takes over a distinction from Husserl and another to claim that he thereby becomes a Husserlian. But, as we shall see, the way the theory of wholes and parts is applied in BT seems to substantiate the claim that the formal structure of Husserl's phenomenology is at work in Heidegger's thinking.

However, Heidegger himself displays a total silence when it comes to this influence. Indeed, there is only one explicit reference to the theory of wholes and parts in BT and that takes place in a footnote in which nothing is said about its importance for his own thinking. Scholars familiar with Heidegger know that he is somewhat reticent about laying bare the sources that influenced BT. Important Husserlian themes, for instance, are in general referred to only in footnotes. Intentionality is mentioned once, in a footnote

---

[3] M. Heidegger, *History of the Concept of Time*, translated by T. Kisiel (Bloomington: Indiana University Press, 1985). Hereafter HCT. *Prolegomena zur Geschichte des Zeitbegriffs*, GA 20 (Frankfurt am Main: Vittorio Klostermann, 1979).

(BT, 414); categorial intuition is mentioned once, in a parenthesis in a footnote (BT, 261); and Husserl's notion of the apriori is mentioned once, again in a footnote (BT, 75). Fortunately the same concepts are given an extensive treatment in one of his lectures,[4] so it is possible for us to trace their influence upon his fundamental-ontology. This is not the case, however, with the theory of wholes and parts. In all of the published lectures from his Marburg period — including the books BT and *Kant and the Problem of Metaphysics*[5] — Heidegger makes only one reference to this theory, apart from the above-mentioned footnote in BT. Heidegger's silence might be responsible for the non-appearance of this theme in the Heidegger-literature.[6]

1. HUSSERL ON WHOLES AND PARTS

Before focusing upon the presence of Husserl's theory of wholes and parts in Heidegger's phenomenology we introduce the theory as it is presented in the Third Investigation of his LI.

In the introduction to the Third Investigation, Husserl claims that the distinction between 'abstract' and 'concrete' contents, which he compares to Stumpf's distinction between dependent and independent contents, is "most important for all phenomenological investigations." This importance is due to the fact that it is not a distinction applying merely to the contents of the psychological sphere. Although it originally arose within the psychological realm — in the field of descriptive psychology or phenomenology of inner experience — it transcends the sphere of inner objects. It is, Husserl claims, a special case of a universal distinction in that it extends beyond this sphere into the "field of objects as such." By distinguishing between independent and non-independent contents (parts), one renders possible an investigation of the latter which is nothing but an investigation of what necessarily belongs to an object (a whole) and the necessary connection between these parts and the other parts that always accompany them. Such an investigation is not an investigation of psychological dispositions but of the essential structure of objects.

Husserl begins the Third Investigation by distinguishing between simple

---

[4] In the Preliminary Part of HCT.

[5] M. Heidegger, *Kant and the Problem of Metaphysics*, translated by R. Taft (Bloomington: Indiana University Press, 1990). Hereafter KPM. *Kant und das Problem der Metaphysik, Vierte, erweiterte Auflage* (Frankfurt am Main: Vittorio Klostermann, 1973).

[6] T. Seebohm, in "Reflexion and Totality in the Philosophy of E. Husserl," discretely suggests the presence of Husserl's theory of wholes and parts in Heidegger by claiming, in a footnote, that through the inquiry into Husserl's theory "we are able to explicate in a quite abstract manner one of the results of the time-analysis of M. Heidegger"(29).

and complex objects or contents. The former are qualified by not having parts, the latter by having parts. A part is, in the widest sense, anything that can be distinguished 'in' an object, but, in a more qualified sense, we must distinguish between two types of parts: independent and non-independent. Independent parts Husserl calls pieces (*Stücke*), non-independent parts he calls moments (*Momente*). Together pieces and moments make up an exhaustive description of parts (*Teilen*). Being a part is to be a part-of, and that *of* which a part is a part is an object. However, the term 'object' should, Husserl claims, in this context always be taken in its widest sense. That is, it should not only be limited to empirical objects but applied to anything that is a whole (*Ganze*).

Husserl distinguishes between pieces and moments in terms of their ability or inability to be presented separately. Pieces are parts that are separately presentable. Husserl uses as an example the head of a horse. It can be presented "'on its own' or 'cut off,' i.e., we can hold it in our fancy, while we allow the other parts of the horse, and its whole intuited setting, to alter and vanish at will" (LI III, #3). Other examples of pieces are the different parts making a house into a whole, such as windows and doors and materials, or the different parts of a plant, such as roots, stem, leafs, etc. In the former example, the parts of the whole are obviously presentable separately because their existence precedes the existence of the house. Before being gathered together in a whole, they were themselves wholes with parts. Likewise, the house can itself become a part of a new whole, a housing estate, but only in the sense of being a piece. Hence, a piece can itself be a whole. In the latter example it is less obvious that the parts are separately presentable since the parts cannot come into being apart from the plant. But its parts can without problem both be imagined and perceived by themselves, either as "cut off" or precisely as a part. Even the human body is a whole whose parts can be separately presented.

'Moment' is Husserl's term for parts that cannot be separately presented. Moments permeate each other in the sense that they cannot be presented apart from each other or from the whole to which they belong. As instances of moments Husserl offers certain examples taken from Stumpf. Husserl notes that Stumpf made powerful observations on this topic, but he distances himself from Stumpf's conclusion. Whereas Stumpf tends to ascribe the necessary interdependency among moments and between moments and a whole to psychological dispositions, Husserl ascribes it to the parts themselves. At this point we find ourselves at the very heart of a phenomenological distinction between the psychological sphere and the subjective perspective. In what follows, we present Husserl's concept of 'moment' in accordance to this distinction. First we see how Husserl develops his non-psychologistic interpretation of moment, then we indicate how the necessity attaching to moments still can have a subjective origin.

The example Husserl sets out to analyze is the relation between *visual quality* and *extension*, and the relation of both of them to the *figure* which bounds them. In a given material object these parts permeate each other in the sense that they cannot be present apart from one another and from the whole of which they are parts. That is, they cannot, like pieces, be detached from their wholes and still exist and be phenomena by themselves. Visual quality necessarily entails a surface, and a surface necessarily entails extension. Surface cannot be presented separately from extension. There is simply no way of imagining a surface without seeing it as a moment of an extended thing. Surface and extension are, as Stumpf puts it, in their natures inseparable. Nor can one imagine brightness apart from color, or color apart from its location on a surface. The very nature of these parts forbids them from being separately presentable. Another example discussed by Husserl is the relation of intensity to quality.

> The intensity of a tone is not something indifferent or so-to-speak alien to its quality. We cannot keep the intensity just as it is, while the quality varies at will, or is allowed to vanish. Eliminate quality and you unavoidably eliminate intensity, and vice versa. Evidently this is no mere fact, but an *apriori* necessity, rooted in the pure essences in question. (LI III, #4)

In other words, the necessity at work here does not have a psychological origin; it springs out of the parts themselves. Moreover, this necessity is called an apriori necessity and it is located in the world. The apriori is, as Heidegger puts it, "a feature of the being of entities" (HCT, 75), and it discloses itself through the composition of moments. The apriori is a rule governing the connection between non-independent parts and the supplements it needs.

It is commonly argued, starting with Heidegger,[7] that Husserl in this way liberates the apriori from the limits assigned to it by Kant. This, however, would imply an excessively psychologistic interpretation of Kant.[8] What Husserl's version of the apriori succeeds in doing is to prevent the apriori from being reduced to a mental content. Of course, this was also Kant's objective. On the other hand, Husserl does not disengage the apriori from the subjective perspective. On the contrary, the apriori discloses itself through the composition of moments, and to be a moment is to be a part that cannot be separately presented to us although we can abstractly consider it apart

---

[7] See HCT, 75.

[8] We shall get back to this in Chapter V, Self-consciousness. We shall see that Kant grants primacy to the synthetic unity of apperception over analytic unity of apperception and in so doing it follows that the apriori can only appear in relation to the world.

from the whole. Hence, it follows that a moment is something that can only disclose itself to the subjective perspective.

Before we continue this discussion, let us first have a look at what Husserl means by inseparability and also introduce his distinction between *abstractum* and *concretum*. Husserl claims that he uses the relation between extension and quality not to prove their mutual inseparability, but rather to define inseparability and non-independence on the one hand, and separability and independence on the other. So, to start with the latter, what does it mean to say that something is separately presentable?

Does this mean, as regards the actually *experienced* contents of the phenomenological sphere, that such a content can be freed from all blending with coexistent contents, can therefore ultimately be torn out of the unity of consciousness? (LI III, #5)

Husserl replies: "Obviously not. In *this* sense no contents are isolable, and the same holds of the phenomenal *thing*-contents in their relation to the total unity of the phenomenon as such" (LI III, #5). Even if a head of a horse can be presented on its own, it is still presented in a context, as a figure against a background. Thus, isolability does not imply the objects capacity to withdraw from perspective or horizon or context.

Isolability means only that we can keep some content constant in idea despite boundless variation — variation that is free, though not excluded by a law rooted in the content's essence — of the contents associated with it, and, in general, given with it. This means that it is unaffected by the elimination of any given arrangement of compresent contents whatsoever. (LI III, #5)

Isolability means that an object could exist through an apriori necessity of essence unaffected by any elimination or altering of compresent objects. As Husserl puts it: "*In the 'nature' of the content itself, in its ideal essence, no dependence on other contents is rooted*; the essence that makes it what it is, also leaves it unconcerned with all other contents" (LI III, #5). Whereas isolability or the ability to be separately presented implies that an object's ideally graspable essence requires that no other essence be interwoven with it, the sense of non-independence lies in its essential dependence. "The content is by its nature bound to other contents, it cannot be, if other contents are not there together with it" (LI III, #5). Hence, the difference between independent and non-independent objects is not that the former has the capacity to exist apart from the subjective perspective and that the latter exist only as mental content. On the contrary, a moment does not have a psychological origin. The fact that surface cannot be presented separately from extension is not due to psychological disposition. Obviously, it reflects a necessity that is grounded in the part itself. Thus, a moment is not reducible to a mental content; it simply discloses a non-independent part of an object to the subjective perspective. And being an independent object — a whole — does not mean not being a phenomenon, i.e., it does not mean that it does not "appear-to." On the contrary, a whole is precisely that which can appear independently to consciousness or perspective, *not* that which can appear independently *of* consciousness or perspective.

At this stage, we have arrived at a point of contact between Husserl's theory of wholes and parts and his later development of transcendental phenomenology that is of particular interest for our argument. It will help us to show how the necessity attaching to moments can have a subjective, although not a psychological, origin. In turn, this can help us to understand how a phenomenological reading of Kant actually would show that Kant did not assign any more limits to the apriori than did Husserl.

2. WHOLES AND PARTS AND TRANSCENDENTAL PHENOMENOLOGY

Although the theory of wholes and parts was developed several years before Husserl introduced his transcendental phenomenology, there is, we argue, an intrinsic relation between the former and the latter. However, before describing this relation let us first provide some textual basis that shows that Husserl makes use of the terminology of wholes and parts when discussing transcendental subjectivity. In order to accomplish this, we shall first have a look at the Husserlian distinction between *abstractum* and *concretum* and at the way in which the latter is employed in describing the foundation arrived at through the transcendental turn.

What Husserl means by 'moments' and 'wholes' can be elucidated by his distinction between '*abstractum*' and '*concretum*' and between '*absolute concretum*' and 'relative *concretum*.' By '*abstractum*' Husserl basically means the same as 'moment,' and a *concretum* is that of which an *abstractum* is a part. To return to a previous example, surface is a *concretum* for color, extension is a *concretum* for surface. Thus, a *concretum* does not necessarily mean a whole. Husserl distinguishes between *concreta* that can be abstract in another direction, and *concreta* that can be abstract in no direction. The former he calls relative *concreta*, the latter absolute *concreta*, and only absolute *concreta* are wholes.

Interestingly enough, these distinctions resurface in the development of Husserl's transcendental phenomenology. In LI, the distinction between pieces and moments was reached through examples of independence and non-independence. Pieces are independent, moments are not. In *Ideas I*[9] the relation and distinction between *absolute consciousness* and the real world is presented along the very same lines. To start with the latter: "Reality, the reality of the physical thing taken singly and the reality of the whole world, lacks self-sufficiency in virtue of its essence (in our strict sense of the word)" (*Ideas I*, 113). In other words, reality is considered to be essentially non-independent. The situation is essentially different in the case of absolute consciousness. "In its *essence* it is independent of all worldly, all natural, being; nor does it need any worldly being for its existence" (*Ideas I*, 116). The difference between independence and non-independence is presented in a way that makes use of the same examples that appear in the Third Investigation.

> If ... consciousness were inconceivable without involvement with nature *in the same fashion* in which colors are inconceivable without extension, then we could not regard consciousness as an absolutely peculiar region by itself in the sense in which we must regard it.[10]

Hence, just as color is a moment or *abstractum* of extension, so reality is a moment or *abstractum* of consciousness and, conversely, consciousness is the *concretum* for reality. However, Husserl distinguishes between two kinds of *concreta*, those that can be abstract in another direction (in the way surface is a *concretum* for color, but an *abstractum* of extension) and those that can be abstract in no direction. Obviously, consciousness belongs to the latter in that it "need[s] [no] worldly being for its existence." For this reason Husserl refers to transcendental subjectivity as "*the only absolute concretion*,"[11] and likewise, to the world as a moment within pure subjectivity.[12]

The very fact that Husserl makes use of this terminology of wholes and parts while introducing his transcendental phenomenology, along with his own claims regarding the importance of the theory, suggests an intrinsic

---

[9] E. Husserl, *Ideas Pertaining to a Pure Phenomenology and to a Phenomenological Philosophy*. Book I. Translated by F. Kersten (The Hague: Martinus Nijhoff, 1982). *Ideen zu einer reinen Phänomenologie und phänomenologischen Philosophie*. Buch I. Edited by K. Schuhmann, Husserliana III (The Hague: Martinus Nijhoff, 1976).

[10] *Ideas I*, 115.

[11] *Cartesian Meditations, An Introduction to Phenomenology*, translated by D. Cairns (The Hague: Martinus Nijhoff, 1960), 84. Hereafter referred to as CM. *Cartesianische Meditationen und Pariser Vorträge*, edited by S. Strasser, Husserliana I (The Hague: Martinus Nijhoff, 1950).

[12] *Erste Philosophie*, Band II. Edited by R. Boehm, Husserliana VIII (The Hague: Martinus Nijhoff, 1959), 448. "Now the world is reached within pure subjectivity, as a moment within it (although not as a lived experience within it)."

relation between them.[13] In the foreword to the Second Edition of the LI, Husserl claims that the Third Investigation is "all to little read" (LI III, 49), and that it is "an essential presupposition for the Investigations which follow" (LI III, 49). Although what Husserl has in mind probably is the Fourth, Fifth, and Sixth Investigation of LI, it is not unreasonable to suggest that his comment also applies to all of the phenomenological investigations which follow, including those of transcendental phenomenology. We should not forget that the foreword to the Second Edition was written in 1913, that is, after his transcendental turn. Moreover, it is highly unlikely that Husserl would at the same time use the terminology of the theory of wholes and parts in presenting his transcendental phenomenology if this theory was not also an essential presupposition for this transcendental turn.

Hence, the fact that Husserl uses the terminology of the theory of wholes and parts in presenting his transcendental phenomenology indicates that, although the latter goes beyond the scope of LI, it does not thereby follow that Husserl's transcendental turn is incompatible with his earlier phenomenological project. On the contrary, the continuity is reflected in his very terminology. Thus, it is our argument that Husserl's transcendental turn does not really introduce something completely new into his phenomenology, but rather radicalizes what is already there. Husserl's transcendental turn is not a turn from one kind of philosophy to another, it is a change of focus within phenomenology; from a focus on appearances to that to which appearances appear.

Admittedly, the very presence of the terminology of the theory of wholes and parts in Husserl's transcendental phenomenology does not itself do more than just suggest a relation. We have yet to exhibit what the intrinsic relation consists in. In what follows we attempt to do so. Our argument is that the logic of wholes and parts in fact invites the transcendental turn, in the sense that such a turn unfolds the full meaning of the whole-part relationship. However, we do not intend to carry out an in-depth analysis of Husserl's transcendental turn. Our intent is to indicate the importance of the theory of wholes and parts for this turn and also to argue that this logic reinforces such a turn. This latter claim makes sense of Husserl's assertion that failing to

[13] In *Husserlian Meditations*, Sokolowski uses the concept of absolute *concreta* in order to define the difference between the natural attitude and the phenomenological attitude and thus to define the nature of transcendental phenomenology. He says: "After Husserl makes the turn into transcendental phenomenology, the final *concretum* turns out to be transcendental subjectivity because, speaking phenomenologically, it is the only whole which has no reference to anything beyond itself, while all other wholes are to be taken as constituted by subjectivity. In the natural attitude, however, the world is taken as an absolute *concretum* and consciousness is a part within it. The natural attitude and the phenomenological attitude are defined by what each takes to be the final concrete whole: the world or transcendental subjectivity." (10)

execute the transcendental reduction is in fact a violation of the phenomenological maxim *Zu den Sachen selbst*. As shown above, the theory of wholes and parts is what constitutes the peculiar phenomenological approach to philosophical problems; indeed, it is the very move *Zu den Sachen selbst*. Evidently, Husserl saw this move, the logic of wholes and parts, being violated in any philosophy that fails to effect the transcendental turn. This will be important in our treatment of the presence of Husserl's theory of wholes and parts in Heidegger. If this theory does indeed reinforce the transcendental turn, we can argue that, if Heidegger makes use of this theory, he himself is already committed to carrying out such a turn.

So far we have pointed out the presence of the terminology of the theory of wholes and parts in Husserl's transcendental phenomenology and we have indicated that the latter transcends the scope of his early phenomenology. We nevertheless argue that there are certain transcendental "seeds" present in the Third Investigation of LI. In presenting 'moments' and 'pieces,' Husserl makes use of terms like inseparability and non-independence and, conversely, separability and independence. Moreover, in discussing the nature of the latter recall the following question:

Does this mean, as regards the actually *experienced* contents of the phenomenological sphere, that such a content can be freed from all blending with coexistent contents, can therefore ultimately be torn out of the unity of consciousness? (LI III, #5)

As we remember, the answer is "[o]bviously not. In *this* sense no contents are isolable, and the same holds of the phenomenal *thing*-contents in their relation to the total unity of the phenomenon as such" (LI III, #5). This statement exhibits a transcendental position; no object can be torn out of the unity of consciousness. This is indeed a startling anticipation of claims made in *Ideas I* about the reality of a physical thing lacking self-sufficiency. It also invites an interpretation of consciousness that suggests its essential independence. If no object is independent in the sense that it can be torn out of the unity of consciousness, it follows that it cannot exist apart from consciousness and, conversely, that consciousness does not need "any worldly being [object] for its existence" (*Ideas I*, 116). Hence, consciousness is, as Husserl later puts it in the CM, "*the only absolute concretion*" (CM, 84).

Phenomenology is a science of essences, and eidetic insight is achieved through eidetic intuition. Eidetic intuition takes place through what Husserl refers to as free variation. Out of the free or imaginative variation emerges an eidetic necessity that discloses itself through the composition of moments. According to this eidetic necessity moments are ordered in a hierarchy of *abstracta* and *concreta*. Surface is a *concretum* for color and color is an *abstractum* of surface. Surface is, in relation to color, a *concretum*, that is, independent, but it is not thereby a whole because it is abstract in another direction. Extension is a *concretum* for surface. However, this order is not a contingent one. Rather it is, as Husserl puts it, "an *apriori* necessity, rooted in the pure essences in question" (LI III, #4). Pieces, on the other hand, exhibit no essential relationship. A finger, for instance, can be thought as either a part of the hand or the arm or the body.

The hierarchy of *abstracta* and *concreta* has an inner dynamic eventually leading back to a *concretum* that is abstract in no direction. For such an object it holds, Husserl claims, that "the essence that makes it what it is, also leaves it unconcerned with all other contents [objects]" (LI III, #5). In LI this absolute *concretum* seems to be individual objects.

A thing or a piece of a thing can be presented by itself — this means it would be what it is even if everything outside it were annihilated. If we form a presentation of it, we are not necessarily referred to something else... We can imagine it as existing by itself alone, and beyond it nothing else. (LI III, #6)

Although this passage reveals an orientation towards realism, one should remember that the kind of isolability described in this passage is not the capacity to withdraw from "the unity of consciousness" (LI III, #5). "In *this* sense," Husserl claims, "no contents are isolable" (LI III, #5). In other words, this affirmation of the independent existence of the individual object does not qualify as realism given the fact that these objects are not independent of the phenomenological sphere, that is, of consciousness. But it does not thereby qualify as idealism either, if one by idealism means empirical idealism. According to the phenomenological doctrine of intentionality objective correlates are other than consciousness.

When Husserl makes the transcendental claim that no object is isolable in the sense that it could be torn out of the unity of consciousness, he does not contradict the notion that individual objects are absolute *concreta*. Husserl is a realist in the sense that the notion of the intentionality of consciousness affirms the objectivity of its correlates. However, this phenomenological realism implies a non-realism on the transcendental level. The very notion of an objective correlate affirms not only that the correlate is an object, but also that the object is a correlate (of consciousness).

So far we have used the term 'transcendental' somewhat indiscriminately. But let us now quote a passage from Kant in order to indicate specifically what we mean by this term.

I entitle *transcendental* all knowledge which is occupied not so much with objects as with the mode of our knowledge of objects in so far as this mode of knowledge is to be possible *apriori*. A system of such concepts might be entitled transcendental philosophy.[14]

Thus, transcendental knowledge cannot be characterized as a knowledge of objects, whether these objects are the typical objects of the natural sciences, i.e., spatiotemporal objects, or ideal objects such as state-of-affairs and essences. Husserl's LI is therefore strictly speaking not a full-fledged transcendental project. Although the knowledge sought in this work is not a knowledge of the objects of the natural sciences, its focus is directed primarily on the objective status ideal objects. Thus, the LI is first and foremost occupied with objects and not with our mode of knowledge of objects. Of course, to argue in favor of the objective status of ideal objects in a phenomenological manner does imply bringing into view the subjective mode of knowledge. But in LI Husserl does not systematically discuss our mode of knowledge.

Now, as we have mentioned above, it is often argued that Husserl liberates the apriori from the limits assigned to it by Kant. This view is often accompanied by the view that Husserl's later transcendental turn is a relapse into a kind of idealism incompatible with the phenomenology introduced in the LI. This, we argue, is a misconception. The fundamental structure of Husserl's early phenomenology invites a transcendental turn which brings out its full implications.

The main target of LI is psychologism. And Husserl makes use of the theory of wholes and parts in order to show that the reduction of ideal objects such as essences to psychological phenomena is fundamentally mistaken. But to claim that ideal objects are not reducible to psychological phenomena is not to say that they do not have a subjective origin. In what follows, we argue that the very theory used in order to undermine psychologism in fact shows that the apriori cannot be disengaged from the subjective perspective.

The development of the theory of wholes and parts takes place through the distinction of different kinds of parts. The distinction of different kinds of parts is, in turn, carried out by applying concepts such as independent and separable and non-independent and inseparable. However, conceptually speaking, the very distinction between different kinds of parts into independent and non-independent presupposes the concept of appearance. Pieces and moments are independent and non-independent, respectively, in so far as they *appear* as independent and non-independent. Thus, even if pieces are essentially independent, this independence is dependent upon their appearance; they appear as independent. Given the fact that to appear is to appear-to (consciousness), we are right back to Husserl's claim that no object can be

---

[14] Kant, *Critique of Pure Reason*, translated by N. K. Smith (Toronto: Macmillan, 1965), B25. Hereafter referred to as Kant. *Kritik der reinen Vernunft* (Hamburg: Felix Meiner Verlag, 1956).

torn out of the unity of consciousness. In other words, the formal structure that is effective in the peculiar approach to philosophical problems that is distinctive for phenomenology (the theory of wholes and parts) harbors a notion of consciousness as the only absolute concretion. For this reason it is perfectly understandable that the terminology of this theory should resurface in Husserl's discussion of transcendental subjectivity after the transcendental turn.

Having underscored the fundamental importance of the theory of wholes and parts for the phenomenological project and having also elucidated its inherent transcendentalism, let us now move on to a consideration of the presence of this theory in Heidegger's phenomenology.

3. THE PRESENCE OF THE THEORY OF WHOLES AND PARTS IN *BEING AND TIME*

In this section we show that Heidegger makes use of the terminology of the theory of wholes and parts in BT, that he uses it in a technical sense and in accordance with Husserl's conventions, and that he makes use of it while discussing the structural composition of Dasein. In a footnote in Division Two of BT Heidegger makes the following claim:

> The distinction between a whole and a sum, ολον and παν, *totum* and *compositum*, has been familiar since the time of Plato and Aristotle. But admittedly no one as yet *knows* anything about the systematics of the categorial variations which this division already embraces, nor have these been conceptualized. As an approach to a thorough analysis of the structures in question, cf. Edmund Husserl, *Logische Untersuchungen*, vol. II, *Untersuchung* III: "Zur Lehre von den Ganzen und Teilen." (BT, 288n)

This footnote occurs in Heidegger's discussion of the "not-yet" character of Dasein's structural make-up in which he draws heavily upon the Husserlian distinction between pieces and moments, though he does not explicitly admit it. Moreover, this footnote is Heidegger's only explicit reference to Husserl's theory of parts and wholes in BT. Our objective is to show that Heidegger nevertheless makes extensive use of this theory while discussing Dasein's structural composition, and that he could not have succeeded in developing his *Daseinsanalytik* without it.

Let us first consider Heidegger's use of the term 'piece' (*Stück*). In a very interesting passage discussing the nature of the existential structures of Dasein Heidegger says that,

> [t]hese existential characteristics are not pieces [*Stücke*] belonging to something composite, one of which might sometimes be missing; but there is woven together in them a primordial context which makes up that totality of the structural whole

which we are seeking. (BT, 235-6)

It seems obvious that Heidegger here uses the term 'pieces' in accordance to the convention Husserl establishes in the Third Investigation. Pieces are parts of a composite, a whole, that are not necessarily tied to this whole; they can sometimes be missing. Pieces, according to Heidegger, have a certain independence in that, unlike existential characteristics, there is not "woven together in them a primordial context." One can, of course, argue that Heidegger is not here assigning the term 'pieces' the same technical sense given to the term by Husserl. For instance, he does not explicitly say that pieces are separately presentable. However, his use of 'pieces' displays a striking resemblance to Husserl's use of the same term, and it seems evident that he would hold that a piece is a piece even if it is missing. This is further substantiated by another passage where he talks about a "joining together of ... pieces [*Stücke*] into a single edifice" (BT, 43). Finally, in discussing the phenomenon of the 'as'-structure he claims that it is "not to be dissolved or broken up into pieces [*in Stücke*]" (BT, 192). On the basis of these examples we can at least conclude that there is a coherence between Heidegger's use of the term 'piece' and the conventions Husserl establishes in LI. Moreover, in BT there is not one instance of a use of this term that conflicts with Husserl's. However, in what follows we marshall evidence in favor of a stronger claim, namely that Husserl's theory of parts and wholes plays the role of a formal structure in BT and that Heidegger, accordingly, uses the terminology of this theory in a technical sense.

Let us begin this discussion with a note on the terminology of the English translations of the terms '*Stück*' and '*Moment*' in Husserl and Heidegger. In his translation of Husserl's LI, Findlay solves the problem of distinguishing between two kinds of parts by consistently employing only the terms 'piece' and 'moment.' While the latter is a straightforward translation of the German '*Moment*,' the former could also have been replaced with 'part' — but that would of course have led to terminological difficulties. In Macquarrie's and Robinson's translation of Heidegger's BT the situation is somewhat different. Although Heidegger does not explicitly introduce a theory of wholes and parts and therefore should not be held to such precision in his terminology, he nevertheless consistently uses the terms '*Stück*' and '*Moment*' in the same way as Husserl. Macquarrie and Robinson do translate '*Stück*' with 'piece,' but for the German term '*Moment*' they tend to use the English term 'item.' This is a striking choice given the fact that, according to for example *The Oxford Duden German Dictionary*, the term 'item' is not listed as a possible translation of the German '*Moment*.' The terms listed are 'moment,' 'factor,' and 'element.' Although the English translation of BT precedes the English translation of LI by eight years — and for that reason cannot be expected to conform to the translation of Husserlian terms — this does not exempt the translators from taking notice of the fact that Heidegger follows Husserl in his use of *'Stück'* and *'Moment'* in BT. They should at least have noted the fact that these terms are the subject-matter discussed in Husserl's Third Investigation. Even if they were to use the term 'item' as a translation of 'moment,' they should have observed that this is a translation of a term that is an important technical term in Husserl.

In English translations of Heidegger made after Findlay's translation of LI one would expect more consistency. It would be appropriate for translators either to stick to Findlay's translation, or to deviate, but with a note stating that Heidegger is here using a Husserlian technical term. *'Moment'* is usually translated 'moment,' but there are enough deviations to suggest that the consistency is accidental rather than a reflection of a technical use in Heidegger. In HCT, for instance, in the glossary of German terms, the translator exhibits a general ambiguity in using both 'moment' and 'part,' along with 'element,' 'factor,' 'feature,' as possible translations of 'Moment.' Moreover, none of the English translations of Heidegger's Marburg lectures make a note of the fact that the term in question is a technical Husserlian term.

In what follows we have a look at most of the instances where Heidegger makes use of the term *'Moment'* in BT.[15] Let us begin with one of the most interesting cases in which the term *'Moment'* is applied. In the introduction to Division One of BT — the Preparatory Fundamental Analysis of Dasein — Heidegger makes the following claim after stating that the question of the meaning of being must be preceded by an analysis of the structure of human being or Dasein.

> In the interpretation of Dasein, this structure is something 'apriori;' it is not pieced [*zusammengestückte*] together, but is primordially and constantly a whole. It affords us, however, various ways of looking at the items which are constitutive [*konstituierenden Momente*] for it. The whole [*Ganzen*] of this structure always comes first; but if we keep this constantly in view, these items [*Momente*], as phenomena, will be made to stand out. (BT, 65)

Here Heidegger makes several interesting claims. Firstly, the structure of Dasein is apriori, and it is so by virtue of being primordially and constantly a whole. Secondly, it can be such a whole only because the parts of which it consists, its constitutive items/moments, are not pieced together. Thus, only a manifold of moments can make up a primordial whole, a unity. Thirdly, if we keep this whole in view, that is, if we focus on the condition of the

---

[15] This term is used 29 times, in different grammatical variations: *'Moment'* 4 times; *'Momente'* 21 times; *'Momenten'* 2 times; and *'Momentes'* 2 times. Not one of these instances exhibits a use that is in conflict with the conventions established by Husserl.

possibility of relating to being, the constitutive moments can be made to appear.

In this passage Heidegger obviously makes use of Husserl's theory of wholes and parts. Not only is he using the very same terminology, but he is also using it in accordance with Husserl's conventions. 'Moments' or 'constitutive moments' are what they are by belonging to a whole and by doing so in a non-pieced-together manner. The very fact that Heidegger refers to parts which are not pieces as moments should, given his extensive knowledge of and high regard for Husserl's LI, provide evidence to support the claim that he is under the influence of Husserl's Third Investigation. Another striking element in this quote is the connection between the apriori and the whole consisting of a manifold of moments. This also has an unmistakable Husserlian flavor to it. And lastly, in advocating the necessity of reflecting on the conditions of its own possibility (to relate to being) in order to make constitutive moments appear, Heidegger seems to take over the method of transcendental phenomenology.

In the following pages Heidegger keeps referring to the constitutive moments of the whole Being-in-the-world.[16] He thematizes the non-independence of the constitutive moments by emphasizing the "phenomenon of equiprimordiality of [the] constitutive moments" (BT, 170; translation altered). To keep the whole constantly in view as primordially and constantly a whole entails the view that none of its parts can be presented separately from one another or from the whole. And this, Heidegger claims, "has often been disregarded in ontology, because of a methodological unrestrained tendency to derive everything and anything from some simple 'primal ground'" (BT, 170). The objective of BT, Heidegger maintains, is not that of "perceptually tracking down and inspecting a point called the 'Self,'" but rather

one of seizing upon the full disclosedness of Being-in-the-world *throughout all* the constitutive moments [*Verfassungsmomente*] which are essential to it ... In existing, entities sight 'themselves' [*sichtet 'sich'*] only in so far as they have become transparent to themselves with equal primordiality in those moments which are constitutive [*konstitutiven Momente*] for their existence... (BT, 187; translation altered)

Here again we see how closely linked the terminology and the theory of wholes and parts is to Heidegger's project. Moreover, in the concluding chapter of the first division of BT Heidegger nails down the importance of this theory by making use of it in his description of the phenomenon of care.

"Care" cannot stand for some special attitude towards the Self; for the Self has

[16] See BT, 149, 169, 181, 206.

already been characterized ontologically by "Being-ahead-of-itself," a characteristic in which the other two moments in the structure of care [*strukturalen Momente der Sorge*] — Being-already-in...and Being-alongside... — have been *jointly posited* [*mitgesetzt*]. (BT, 237; translation altered)

Having investigated Heidegger's use of the theory of wholes and parts in Division One of BT, let us now move on to Division Two and have a look at the use of the theory from the point of view of the new and broader scope of this division. The introduction to this Division is entitled "The outcome of the Preparatory Fundamental analysis of Dasein, and the Task of a Primordial Existential Interpretation of this Entity." Heidegger sums up the outcome of Division One in the following manner:

The totality of Being-in-the-world as a structural whole has revealed itself as care ... By working out the phenomenon of care, we have given ourselves an insight into the concrete constitution of existence. (BT, 274)

He points out that the objective of Division two is to "exhibit its [care's] concrete temporal constitution" (BT, 384). At this point the theory of wholes and parts, especially the concept of 'moment' plays an essential role.

Through the unity of the moments which are constitutive for care [*konstitutiven Momente der Sorge*] — existentiality, facticity, and fallenness — it has become possible to give the first ontological definition for the totality of Dasein's structural whole. (BT, 364; translation altered)

In Division Two Heidegger reformulates the structural moments of Dasein as temporal moments in order to account for their possibility of creating a unity.[17] Let us consider a passage in which Heidegger sums up the interconnection between temporality, unity, and the moments of care:

Temporality makes possible the unity of existence, facticity, and falling, and in this way constitutes primordially the totality of the structure of care. The moments of care [*Die Momente der Sorge*] have not been pieced together [*zusammengestückt*] cumulatively... (BT, 376; translation altered)

In these passages Heidegger spells out what is the objective of the second division, namely to ensure the wholeness of the phenomenon we know as Dasein. To do that we must be able to see the unity of the structural moments that constitutes Dasein's essence. Note that Heidegger again introduces the terminology of wholes and parts (moments) into the very heart of his philosophical enterprise. Is he still using this terminology in accordance to Husserl's convention? He is. Firstly, it would be rather strange if Heidegger suddenly started ascribing new meaning to these terms and, secondly, he is

[18] We will return to this in Chapter IX, Temporality.

about to discuss how a manifold can constitute a whole without exploding the unity. In other words, he intends to provide a closer description of what distinguishes moments from pieces.

In this section we have limited ourselves to calling attention to the presence of Husserl's theory of wholes and parts in Division One and Two of BT. We have ascertained that Heidegger makes use of this theory in the sense that he uses its terminology in accordance with Husserl's conventions, and we have indicated its importance by pointing to the fact that he makes use of it while discussing the structural composition of Dasein. Let us now further substantiate our claim by showing the presence of Husserl's theory of wholes and parts throughout Heidegger's Marburg period.

4. THE THEORY OF WHOLES AND PARTS IN HEIDEGGER'S MARBURG LECTURES

Heidegger's use of the theory of wholes and parts does not only take place in BT, but also in his lectures from the Twenties. In a lecture from the summer-semester 1925, HCT, Heidegger makes the following claim while discussing the basic constitution of Dasein as Being-in-the-world and the nature of the three aspects.

What the aspects bring out in each case are not pieces, detachable moments out of which the whole may first be assembled. Bringing out the individual structural moments is a purely thematic accentuation and as such always only an *actual apprehension of the whole structure in itself.* (HCT, 157)

Although he seems to display a slight inconsistency in this quote by the term 'detachable moments' it is nevertheless evident that he distinguishes structural moments from pieces by claiming that the former cannot be given apart from the whole. Throughout this lecture he speaks of the structural moments of Dasein;[18] the structural moments of language (*Rede*), which are structures that are given because language itself is a possibility of the Being of Dasein;[19] the structural moments of fear;[20] and the structural moments of care and their relation to time.[21]

In the lecture *Logik. Die Frage nach der Wahrheit*[22] from the winter-semester 1925/26 we find the only other explicit reference to Husserl's Third Investigation (in the Marburg period) apart from the footnote in BT. In

---

[18] See HCT, 233, 256.
[19] See HCT, 263-4.
[20] See HCT, 285-7.
[21] See HCT, 293, 295-6.
[22] GA 21 (Frankfurt am Main: Vittorio Klostermann, 1976).

discussing Kant's transcendental aesthetic, Heidegger claims that

> the difficulties of providing an accurate determination of these phenomena rest in seeing the general relation between wholes and parts ... Up till today an analysis of even the most elementary structures of these basic concepts has been lacking. The first productive and independent advance is also here made by Husserl; *Logical Investigations*, Vol. II, III. Investigation: On the Theory of Wholes and Parts.[23]

Heidegger does not say anything about the theory's importance for his own endeavor, but at least we know that he considers Husserl's analysis of wholes and parts the first productive advance into the topic.[24] This means that if we can locate a discussion of wholes and parts in Heidegger, we have reasons to believe that it is at least influenced by Husserl's Third Investigation. This takes us on to the lecture *Grundbegriffe der antiken Philosophie*[25] from the summer-semester 1926. Here Heidegger sums up his view on wholes and parts in a short passage.

> The parts of a whole have a quite different way of being connected than do the parts of a sum. To differentiate: A sum and a whole both have the formal character of "togetherness." A "togetherness" consists of or covers parts. Kinds of "togetherness:" a) Sum, composite. Parts: Pieces; the adding together of pieces = sum. b) Whole, totum. The part-character corresponding to the whole is to be grasped as moment.[26]

---

[23] GA 21, 303 (our translation). The original reads: "die Schwierigkeiten einer genaueren Bestimmung der Phänomene liegen, nämlich darin, zu sehen, wie überhaupt Ganzheit zu Teilheit steht ... Es fehlt bis heute an der Herausarbeitung auch nur der elementarsten Strukturen dieser Grundbegriffe. Den ersten produktiven und selbständigen Vorstoss hat auch hier wieder Husserl gemacht; *Logische Untersuchungen*, Bd. 2, III. Untersuchung: Zur Lehre von den Ganzen und Teilen." This echoes a claim Heidegger made in 1915 in the *Habilitationsschrift "Die Kategorien-und Bedeutungslehre des Duns Scotus."* We quote: "In der Gegenwart hat besonders Husserl dem Unterschied von selbständigen und unselbständigen Gegenständen seine Aufmerksamkeit geschenkt, ihn in möglichster theoretischer Reinheit herausgestellt und die daraus sich ergebenden Wesensgesetzlichkeiten entwickelt. Das Wesen selbständiger Gegenstände 'fordert durch sich selbst, also a priori, kein mitverflochtenes anderes Wesen'; der unselbständige Inhalt (Gegenstand) ist seinem Wesen nach an andere Inhalte gebunden." [Footnote: *Logische Untersuchungen*. 2. Aufl. III. Unters. Zur Lehre von den Ganzen und Teilen. bes. S. 236]. GA 1 (Frankfurt am Main: Vittorio Klostermann, 1978), 343-4

[24] We also see Heidegger using the terminology of the theory of wholes and parts in this lecture. In discussing Dasein's constitution he says that "Diese einheitliche Grundstruktur, die mit 'als' ausgedrückt wird, nicht auflösbar in Stücke, sondern lediglich als ganze in ihrer Ganzheit ursprünglicher zu interpretieren" (GA 21, 151). In discussing temporality he refers to "die einzelnen Momente der Zeit, Vergangenheit, Gegenwart und Zukunft" (GA 21, 250).

[25] GA 22 (Frankfurt am Main: Vittorio Klostermann, 1993).

[26] GA 22, 280 (our translation). The original reads: Die Teile eines Ganzen haben einen ganz anderen Bezug zum Zusammen als die Teile einer Summe. Zu unterscheiden: Summe und Ganzes haben beide den formalen Charakter des Zusammen. Zusammen besteht aus oder ist bezogen auf Teile. Arten von Zusammen: a) Summe, compositum. Teile: Stücke; Zusammenzählung von Stücken = Summe. b) Ganzes, totum. Der Teilcharakter, der dem

Although Heidegger in this passage obviously is influenced by Husserl's Third Investigation he does not refer to Husserl. Instead he refers to Plato. This is curious given the fact that the preceding winter he held that Husserl had made the first productive advance into this problem. We shall not, however, dwell on this incident but simply conclude that just before finishing BT Heidegger considered Husserl's analysis of wholes and parts to be the "first productive and independent advance," and that just after BT was concluded he makes a claim that in fact sums up the position taken in Husserl's Third Investigation and uses the very same terms. As in the prior lectures Heidegger also makes use of the theory of wholes and parts when addressing different topics in the *Grundbegriffe*. For instance, he refers to certain phenomena as being "[n]ot next to one another, rather these moments are detectable in the unity of the being thought of."[27] Again, he says, "The whole object is what is primarily given to me, out of which I can free the individual moments."[28]

In the lecture *Basic Problems of Phenomenology*[29] from the summer-semester of 1927 Heidegger once again makes extensive use of the term 'moment' when addressing the fundamental issues of his project. He speaks of the moments of the existential structure of Dasein,[30] their relation to time,[31] and the structural moments of time.[32] In the lecture *Phänomenologische Interpretation von Kants Kritik der reinen Vernunft*[33] from the winter-semester 1927/28, Heidegger again makes a claim that reflects the theory of wholes and parts. In discussing the relation between synthesis and unity he says that "synthesis presupposes unity, unity presupposes synthesis, here reigns an original correlation according to which one moment cannot be diverted from another, instead both have a common root."[34] In other words, synthesis and unity are non-independent parts of a whole, i.e., moments.

Ganzen entspricht, ist als Moment zu fassen.

[27] GA 22, 122 (our translation). The original reads: "Nicht nebeneinandergesetzt, sondern *aus der Einheit des gedachten Seienden* her sind diese Momente ablesbar."

[28] GA 22, 270 (our translation). The original reads: "Primär ist mir der *ganze* Gegenstand gegeben, aus dem ich dann die einzelnen Momente herauslösen kann."

[29] M. Heidegger, *Basic Problems of Phenomenology*, translated by A. Hofstadter (Bloomington: Indiana University Press, 1988). Hereafter BP. *Die Grundprobleme der Phänomenologie*, GA 24 (Frankfurt am Main: Vittorio Klostermann, 1975).

[30] See BP, 170.

[31] See BP, 301.

[32] See BP, 260, 261, 262, 263, 264, 268, 271, 302.

[33] GA 25 (Frankfurt am Main: Vittorio Klostermann, 1977).

[34] GA 25, 424 (our translation). The original reads: "Die Synthesis fordert Einheit, die Einheit fordert Synthesis, hier herrscht eine ursprüngliche Korrelation, die besagt, dass nicht ein Moment aus dem anderen abzuleiten ist, sondern dass beide eine gemeinsame Wurzel haben."

Hence, we may conclude, then, that Heidegger makes use of Husserl's theory of wholes and parts in several of the lectures from his period in Marburg.

5. THE CONCRETENESS OF THE *SEINSFRAGE*

So far we have underscored the presence of Husserl's theory of wholes and parts in Heidegger's *Daseinsanalytik*. We have also indicated the importance of this theory by pointing to the fact that Heidegger makes use of it when discussing the structural composition of Dasein. In this section, we argue that the importance of Husserl's theory of wholes and parts for the *Daseinsanalytik* can be attributed to the fact that this theory plays a decisive role in the peculiar approach to the *Seinsfrage* that is distinctive for BT. In what follows, we substantiate this claim by showing how Heidegger's commitment to this theory is reflected in the very design of BT.

On the first page of BT Heidegger states that "[o]ur aim in the following treatise is to work out the question of *Being* and to do so concretely" (BT, 19). A couple of pages later he refers to the being question as "the most concrete" (BT, 29), and to his own project as a "concrete ontological research" (BT, 40). Then, he continues, "[i]n the exposition of the problematic of temporality the question of the meaning of being will first be concretely answered" (BT, 40). The reference to the question of Being — and the working out of its answer — as concrete seems to go against any ordinary use of 'concrete.' The question of Being, should, by ordinary standards, be labeled an extremely abstract question. But Heidegger does not adhere to an ordinary use of 'concrete.' For him this is obviously a technical term. Now given the fact that 'concrete' is a technical term in Husserl's theory of wholes and parts, a theory whose presence has already been ascertained in Heidegger's BT, it is at least tempting to suspect that Heidegger also uses *this* term in accordance with Husserl.[35] In what follows, we argue that this is the case. Although Heidegger does not explicitly admit taking over a Husserlian notion of 'concrete,' we shall see that he uses the term 'concrete' in the sense of being a whole, i.e., in the sense of an absolute *concretum*. We shall also see that he speaks of a difference between ontical concreteness and ontological

[35] In the lecture *Phänomenologische Interpretationen zu Aristoteles, Einführung in die phänomenologische Forschung* from the Winter-semester 1921/22, GA 61 (Frankfurt am Main: Vittorio Klostermann, 1985), Heidegger discusses the term 'concrete' in a way that testifies to a Husserlian influence on his use of this term. We quote: "Was heisst *konkret*? ... Das Konkrete, genauer das 'konkret' Genannte, ist das, was in der Verdichtung und aus der Verdichtung, im Zusammenwachsen wird und ist. Sofern ein Gegenstand konkret im Haben ist, ist das Haben so am Gegenstand, dass es dessen Bestimmtheiten voll und in ihrem vollen Fügungs- und Verdichtungszusammenhang erfasst, d.h. eigentlich erfasst den (letzten) Struktursinn des vollen Gegenständes in der Fülle seiner Was-Wie-Bestimmtheiten." (27-8)

concreteness, and that the objective of his approach is the determination of ontological concreteness.

According to Heidegger, before we can work out the question of Being concretely, we must work out the question of human being. We must, as he puts it, "make a being — the inquirer — perspicuous in his own Being" (BT, 27). The goal of the two divisions that make up BT is to seek an adequate understanding of Dasein. Throughout BT, Heidegger refers to the understanding of Dasein as concrete. In some places he speaks in terms of "a concrete understanding of the basic constitution of Dasein" (BT, 168), or of a "concrete disclosure of Dasein" (BT, 446). In other places he concludes that he has "[c]oncretely worked out the structure of Dasein's being" (BT, 358), or has reached an "insight into the concrete constitution of existence" (BT, 274). In other words, the concrete working out of the question of Being must be preceded by a concrete analysis of Dasein. In Division One of BT, Heidegger begins this concrete analysis of Dasein with an analysis of Being-in-the-world. About this expression he says that

> [t]he compound expression 'Being-in-the-world' indicates the very way we have coined it, that it stands for a *unitary* phenomenon. This primary datum must be seen as a whole. But while Being-in-the-world cannot be broken up into contents which may be pieced together [*zusammenstückbare Bestände*], this does not prevent it from having several constitutive moments in its structure [*konstitutiver Strukturmomente*]. (BT, 78; translation altered)

Again we see that Heidegger makes use of the term 'moment' when he is about to describe the parts of a complex whole or a unitary phenomenon. We also see that the concrete analysis of the basic state of Dasein, Being-in-the-world, is a matter of seeing the whole as a whole. Hence, it seems evident that Heidegger's use of 'concrete' is closely related to the Husserlian term 'absolute concrete.' In what follows, we shall see that this is not a mere terminological agreement but that Heidegger's distinction between ontical and ontological concreteness is structurally related to Husserl's distinction between the final concrete whole as taken by the natural attitude and as taken by the phenomenological attitude.

Let us now briefly indicate the way in which the theory of wholes and parts is present in Heidegger's treatment of Dasein as Being-in-the-world. This, however, is just to set the stage for the more thorough discussion which will take place in Chapters IV through IX. Heidegger starts out with an analysis of the first structural moment in the basic state of Dasein: the phenomenon of the world. What he seeks is a "concrete working-out of the world-structure" (BT, 418). The concretion which lies closest to Dasein is the everyday encounter with equipment (*Zeug*). But although a piece of equipment is an ontically concrete object (i.e., a whole), there is, Heidegger claims, phenomenologically speaking, no such thing as one piece of equipment given alone. "Taken strictly there 'is' no such thing as *an* equipment. To the being of any equipment there belongs a totality of equipment in which it can be this equipment that it is" (BT, 97). The individual piece of equipment cannot itself account for the serviceability by which it is constituted. Ontical concreteness, the givenness of a piece of equipment, presupposes an ontological attribute of equipment as equipment. The concreteness of a definite kind of equipment becomes possible by reason of its being a part of a totality of equipment (*Zeug-Ganzheit*). This equipmental totality makes up a referential whole (*Verweisungsganzheit*) wherein one tool refers to another. This whole, in turn, cannot account fully for itself. The referentiality of equipment depends upon its relevance in purposive activity.

[W]ith this thing, for instance, which is available, and which we accordingly call a "hammer," there is an involvement in hammering; with hammering, there is an involvement in making something fast; with making something fast, there is an involvement in protection against bad weather; and this protection "is" for the sake of providing shelter for Dasein — that is to say, for the sake of a possibility of Dasein's being. (BT, 116)

Thus, the hierarchy of means and ends terminates in a towards-which which is itself not for anything. What structures the entire framework of means/ends relations is an end that is not itself a means to anything else. The last assignment in this teleological chain stretching beyond a tool's "towards-which" is some possible way for Dasein to be itself.

What Heidegger has done here is to show that what are usually taken as independent wholes, things in the world (and in the last resort, world itself), are from a phenomenological point of view in fact non-independent parts of a whole. Although our everyday (ontical) encounter with things in the world discloses them as independent wholes, this must not lead us to conclude that they are ontologically independent wholes, i.e., that they can appear independently of subjectivity. This is Heidegger's critique of transcendental realism.[36]

In the investigation of the second structural moment of the basic state of Dasein, the entity which in every case has Being-in-the-world as the way in which it is, Heidegger presents his critique of empirical idealism. In the lecture *The Metaphysical Foundations of Logic*,[37] he makes a claim that is

---

[36] In Chapter VI, Constitution, we provide a more thorough argument in favor of this interpretation.

[37] M. Heidegger, *The Metaphysical Foundations of Logic*, translated by M. Heim (Bloomington: Indiana University Press, 1984). Hereafter referred to as MFL. *Metaphysische Anfangsgründe der Logik im Ausgang von Leibniz*, GA 26 (Frankfurt am Main: Vittorio

very illuminating for his entire project.

> The world is only insofar as Dasein exists. But then is the world not something "subjective"? In fact it is. Only one may not at this point reintroduce a common, subjectivistic concept of "subject."[38]

Thus, Heidegger does not seek to do away with subjectivity as such. On the contrary, he seeks to use the basic state of Dasein in order to redefine the notion of subjectivity. The guideline for this approach is to keep the whole in view as a whole.

In responding to the question concerning the "who" of Dasein, Heidegger again warns against misconstruing an *abstractum* as a *concretum*. Although it is ontically obvious, he claims, that each "I" is Dasein, this must not lead us into believing that Dasein is a bare subject without a world. Here we can see that Heidegger indicates a distinction between the subject ontically and ontologically conceived, the former being the psychological or private sphere, the latter being the subjective perspective. When Heidegger attacks the Cartesian tradition, his target is in fact its ignorance of this distinction and

Klostermann, 1978).

[38] MFL, 195. Similar claims are made in BP: "We tried to make clear that world is nothing that occurs within the realm of the extant but belongs to the subjective, is something subjective in the well-understood sense " (BP, 174); "If there are no subjects, taken in fact in the well-understood sense of the existent Dasein, then there is neither truth nor falsehood" (BP, 219). These passages seem to challenge an interpretation of Dasein according to which it is not a subject. W.J. Richardson emphasizes "the insistence which Heidegger lays on the fact that There-being [Dasein] is not to be understood as a subject," *Heidegger — Through Phenomenology to Thought* (The Hague: Martinus Nijhoff, 1963), 154. Richardson is right if by 'subject' he means a worldless *res cogitans*, but he seems not to pay attention to the fact that Heidegger does refer to Dasein as a subject. Richardson's claim that Dasein refers to "a pre-subjective self that precedes the dichotomy of subject and object and renders this dichotomy possible" (154) suggests that Dasein designates something pre-subjective. It is correct that Heidegger seeks to account for the subject-object relation (i.e., for intentionality), but this endeavor does not introduce something pre-subjective. Rather, it introduces a new way of seeing the subject. It introduces "something subjective in the well-understood sense" (BP, 174). Phenomenological grounding does not go beyond what is given, rather it *accounts* for it. However, in his interpretation of BT, Fr.-W. von Herrmann bases his rejection of referring to Dasein as a subject on a claim suggesting the opposite, i.e., that the endeavor of phenomenological grounding does away with what it grounds. He rejects that "die Bestimmung und Auslegung des Menschen als Dasein sei nichts anderes als eine Neubestimmung der Subjektivität des Subjekts," *Subjekt und Dasein* (Frankfurt am Main: Vittorio Klostermann, 1974), 10. Rather, he maintains that the subjectivity of the subject is grounded in Dasein, and he says that "Dasein ist *keine Neubestimmung der Subjektivität*, sondern *ihre Verabschiedung*" (10). It is our contention that Richardson and von Herrmann are not sufficiently sensitive to the nature of phenomenological grounding. We base this claim on an investigation of the principles by which Heidegger approaches the subjectivity of the subject. This investigation will be carried out in Chapters II, III, IV, and V.

thus of the order of the whole-part relation between these two phenomena.[39]

It falls beyond the scope of this section to present an in-depth analysis of Heidegger's argument in this important chapter,[40] but his general point is that the ontical obviousness of the fact that it is I who in each case is Dasein should not lead us to infer the ontological primordiality of the psychological sphere (in the meaning of a bare subject without a world). This is due to the fact that even the ontical obviousness of the givenness of the psychological "I" is questionable. "It could be," Heidegger claims, "that the 'who' of everyday Dasein just is *not* the 'I myself.'"[41] Hence, ontologically speaking (at least), the psychological sphere is not a whole in itself, an absolute *concretum*. Rather, it is a non-independent part of the basic state of Dasein — the unitary phenomenon we know as Being-in-the-world.

As already mentioned, Heidegger argues that traditional ontology failed to keep the whole constantly in view as primordially and constantly a whole, "because of a methodological unrestrained tendency to derive anything from some simple 'primal ground'" (BT, 170). This echoes Husserl's claim that the principal philosophical mistake is to force an *abstractum* into being an absolute *concretum*, a phenomenon. This consideration permeates Heidegger's analysis of Dasein. Throughout BT, he is very particular about the fact that the compound expression Being-in-the-world stands for a unitary phenomenon.

> Emphasis upon any one of these constitutive moments [*Verfassungsmomente*][of Being-in-the-world] signifies that the others are emphasized along with it; this means that in any such case the whole phenomenon gets seen. (BT, 79; translation altered)

We have seen how this emphasis on the whole has found expression in Heidegger's treatment of two of the constitutive moments of Being-in-the-world. Now we shall see that this consideration is also very much present in

---

[39] A traditional mistake has been to overlook this distinction and, in order to uphold the subjective perspective, thereby reduce reality to psychological phenomena. Then, in order to avoid the absurdities of such an approach some have attempted to describe the human order only in the categories appropriate to the physical order. However, Heidegger rejects the Cartesian subject-object dichotomy both in its subjective and its objective garb. He does not see the modern shift in emphasis away from *res cogitans* to *res extensa* — with the result that subjectivity is virtually ignored as a significant area of investigation in its own right — as any more tenable, or less Cartesian than the traditional emphasis on a mental reality. Heidegger seeks to get beyond the entire dichotomy and aims at rehabilitating the subjective perspective without reducing it to the psychological sphere.

[41] This theme will be explored in detail in Chapter VII, Self.

[41] BT, 150. Here Heidegger introduces the concept of the 'One' (*das Man*) as the answer to the question who Dasein is in its everydayness. For reasons stated below (in Chapter VII) we use the term 'the One' as a translation of the German '*das Man*' instead of the term 'the they' used in the English translation.

Heidegger's discussion of the third structural moment of the basic state of Dasein, the *Being-in* and in the constitution of "inhood" (*Inheit*) itself. According to Heidegger, "*'Being in' is ... the formal existential expression for the Being of Dasein, which has Being-in-the-world as its essential state*" (BT, 80). Thus, in investigating the *Being-in*, Heidegger focuses upon the ontological structure which makes Being-in-the-world a whole. Again we shall see that he emphasizes the phenomenological thesis of turning to the phenomena themselves. As the structural moments of the basic state of Dasein cannot be detached from this whole, so the structural moments of Dasein's existence belong equiprimordially to the essence of Dasein. When discussing these *existentialia*, Heidegger is very much aware of the fact that they are individually abstract and that they cannot be presented separately.

In *understanding* and *situatedness* [*Befindlichkeit*], we shall see the two constitutive ways of being the "there"; and these are equiprimordial. If these are to be analyzed, some phenomenal confirmation is necessary; in both cases this will be attained by Interpreting some concrete mode which is important for the subsequent problematic. Situatedness and understanding are characterized equiprimordially by *discourse* [*Rede*]. (BT, 171-2; translation altered)

For Heidegger, then, to "work out these *existentialia* concretely" (BT, 188) means to treat them always as non-independent parts of a whole.[42]

The objective of this chapter was twofold. First we introduced Husserl's theory of wholes and parts in order to indicate its importance for the phenomenological project. We have argued that it is an essential presupposition for a critique of psychologism in that it allows for an apriori necessity rooted in the world. We have also seen that this theory advocates a kind of non-realism in that it precludes the disengagement of any object from the unity of consciousness. Secondly, we have investigated the presence of this theory in Heidegger and we have seen that Heidegger not only uses the terminology of the theory of wholes and parts, but that he also uses it in accordance with the conventions Husserl establishes, and that Heidegger makes use of this theory when he discusses the structural make-up of Dasein.

In the last section we have also argued that the presence of Husserl's theory of wholes and parts in Heidegger's *Daseinsanalytik* can be attributed

---

[42] In Chapter IV, Existence, we discuss this more thoroughly and the objective is to show that Dasein, qua being-in, has apriority in relation to the world without thereby appearing prior to and independently of the world. In the last chapter, Temporality, we shall see that the final ground for the determination of Dasein as a whole is to be found in temporality. "Our existential analytic of Dasein ... starts with the 'concretion' of factically thrown existence itself in order to unveil temporality as that which primordially makes such existence possible"(BT, 486). It is our contention that when Heidegger sets out to "give a concrete demonstration of the temporality of the Being-in-the-world"(BT, 408), he is in fact showing the temporal basis for the unity of the whole.

to the fact that this theory plays a decisive role in Heidegger's attempted reappropriation of the *Seinsfrage*. We have indicated this by showing that Heidegger's commitment to this theory is reflected in the very design of BT.

Although several key terms have not yet been introduced, we can nonetheless offer the following anticipatory sketch of our argument. A concrete understanding of Being presupposes a concrete understanding of Dasein. A concrete understanding of Dasein presupposes seeing the unitary phenomenon Being-in-the-world as a whole. In Division One this takes place through a working out of the phenomenon of care (see Chapter IV) in which Heidegger makes extensive use of the theory of wholes and parts in order to honor his commitment to relate to Dasein as a whole. The only way he can interpret a composite like Dasein as a whole is to treat the parts of the composite as moments. This, however, presupposes the very possibility of bringing Dasein into view as a whole (see Chapter VIII). We must have what Heidegger refers to as a "pre-ontological confirmation." This takes place in two steps. First, anxiety discloses Dasein's being as care. The possibility of referring to Dasein as this kind of a structural composite is therefore warranted by anxiety. At this point Heidegger is on his way to show that the notion of 'moment' is not merely a logical tool, it also has an ontological status. But he is not there yet. This brings us to the second stage of Heidegger's pre-ontological confirmation. He must justify the possibility of referring to this structural composite as a whole. This he does by calling attention to death, or Being-towards-death. Being-towards-death brings the structural composite called Dasein into view as a whole. When this is achieved Heidegger can go on to unveil temporality as that which makes possible the unity of a composite and thus the being of moments (see Chapter IX). Thus, in many ways, BT can be looked upon as a systematic argument in favor of the ontological status of moments and, subsequently, the ontological status of apriori necessity, of essence. After all, BT is an investigation of essence, of Dasein's essence.

CHAPTER II

CATEGORIAL INTUITION

In his last seminar, held in Zähringen in 1973, Heidegger emphasizes the importance of Husserl's concept of categorial intuition for his own approach to the *Seinsfrage*. Although he denies that there is actually a *Seinsfrage* for Husserl, he adds that Husserl nevertheless "touches upon, grazes ever so lightly, the question of Being in the sixth chapter of the Sixth *Logical Investigation* with the notion of categorial intuition."[1] Likewise, in "My Way to Phenomenology"[2] he claims that when he started to practice phenomenological seeing, teaching and studying at Husserl's side in Freiburg, his interest was drawn again to *Logical Investigations*. This work had played a major role in the young Heidegger's philosophical development, but what captured his interest this time was mainly the Sixth Investigation of the First Edition. "The difference between sensuous and categorial intuitions, worked out in that *Investigation*, revealed to me its importance for the determination of the 'manifold meaning of Being'" (MWP, 78). According to Heidegger, this renewed focus on LI took place as he was experimenting with a new understanding of Aristotle in seminars that were held from the summer semester 1921 through the winter semester 1922-23. This was exactly the period in which Heidegger started to contemplate the ideas that were to emerge as BT. Just two years later, after having moved on to Marburg, Heidegger gave a lecture entitled *Prolegomena zur Geschichte des Zeitbegriffs* (HCT). In this lecture, he refers to Husserl's notion of categorial intuition as one of the three fundamental discoveries of phenomenology; it is moreover the one to which he devotes the most lengthy discussion.

Though Heidegger points to the influence of categorial intuition when retrospectively commenting upon his formulation of the *Seinsfrage*, this influence is by no means textually substantiated in BT. BT contains no explicit references to the analysis of categorial intuition that was carried out

---

[1] Heidegger, "Seminar in Zähringen 1973" in *Vier Seminare* (Frankfurt am Main: Vittorio Klostermann, 1977), 111. Translation from J. Taminiaux "Heidegger and Husserl's Logical Investigation" in *Dialectic and Difference: Finitude in Modern Thought*, translated by R. Crease and J. Decker (Atlantic Highlands, N.J.: Humanities Press International, 1985), 99.

[2] Heidegger, "My Way to Phenomenology," in *On Time and Being*, translated by J. Stambaugh (New York: Harper & Row, 1972). Hereafter MWP.

in the preliminary part of HCT, nor any comments on the importance of this notion for his project in general. On the contrary, in BT Heidegger displays total silence when it comes to the role of the notion of categorial intuition in his project. As a matter of fact, he uses the term only once and then in a parenthesis in a footnote where the phrase "*Über sinnliche und kategoriale Anschauungen*" (BT, 261n) is meant merely as a reference to the Sixth Investigation of LI.

In this chapter we take seriously the later Heidegger's emphasis on the importance of the notion of categorial intuition for his own formulation of the *Seinsfrage* and investigate the nature of this Husserlian influence upon his project. We argue that Husserl's distinction between sensuous intuition and categorial intuition — along with the notions of intentionality[3] and apriori (there is a mutual state of dependence between these distinctions) — furnishes a ground that is of capital importance for the peculiarly Heideggerian approach to the *Seinsfrage*. Without this distinction Heidegger would have had no access to the appearance of Being and thus no way of distinguishing it from the appearance of beings. In short, what will later be known as the *ontological difference* (a term hardly employed in BT but which nevertheless is to be found in the marginal notes in Heidegger's own copy) springs out of Husserl's distinction between sensuous and categorial intuition.

We proceed in the following manner. In the first section we present Husserl's distinction between sensuous and categorial intuition as this is outlined in chapter six of the Sixth Investigation. The objective of this section is not to provide an in-depth analysis of this Husserlian distinction, but is meant merely to introduce Heidegger's thinking. In the second section lay hold of Heidegger's interpretation of this distinction in the preliminary part of HCT.

1. HUSSERL ON SEEING OBJECTS OF HIGHER LEVELS

In the Sixth Investigation of LI Husserl makes the following claim:

It is said of every percept that it grasps its object *directly*, or grasps this object *itself*. But this grasping has a different sense and character according as we are concerned with a percept in the narrower or the wider sense, or according as the directly grasped object is *sensuous* or *categorial*. Or otherwise put, according as it is a *real* or an *ideal* object. Sensuous or real objects can in fact be characterized as *objects of the lowest level of possible intuition*, categorial or ideal objects as *objects of higher levels*. (LI VI, #46)

---

[3] 'Intentionality' is another Husserlian term that Heidegger in HCT considers a decisive discovery but which in BT is mentioned only once, in n. xxiii, 414.

In this section Husserl introduces several distinctions in order to shed light on the nature of categorial intuition. He distinguishes between a narrow and a wide sense of perception, between sensuous and categorial objects (a distinction which corresponds to the distinction between real and ideal objects), and between objects of the lowest level of possible intuition and objects of higher levels. Whereas the narrow sense of perception refers to the direct grasping that takes place on the lowest level of possible intuition, the wide sense of perception refers to the grasping that takes place on higher levels. The former yields sensuous objects, the latter categorial.

The aim of this section is to interpret Husserl's notion of categorial intuition by carrying out an investigation of these fundamental distinctions. However, we do not intend to carry out an in-depth analysis of the entire Sixth Investigation nor do we intend to provide an accurate determination of all aspects of the concept of categorial intuition. Our intention is simply to lay bare the source of the influence of this concept upon Heidegger's thinking. We shall, therefore, restrict ourselves to a description of certain elements from chapter six of the Sixth Investigation. First we briefly discuss Husserl's concept of perception and his distinction between empty and fulfilled intentions. Then we have a closer look at his distinction between sensuous or real and categorial or ideal objects — from which we proceed to discuss what Husserl calls supersensuous perception and try to interpret the concept of categorial intuition.

Husserl discusses two kinds of categorial acts, acts of synthesis and acts of ideation. However, the importance of the following is not first and foremost to establish the difference between the two kinds of categorial acts but to introduce and investigate the concept of categorial intuition as such. Before going on to Heidegger's interpretation we shall qualify acts of synthesis and ideation by relating them to other philosophical positions. We shall see that the concept of categorial intuition enables phenomenology to maintain that apriori structures are intuited rather than deduced without thereby having to lapse into a free-floating grasp of the non-sensory and ideal.

2. INTENTIONALITY AND EVIDENCE

A guiding principle in Husserl's phenomenology is that perception grasps the object itself. He rejects any talk about things-in-themselves as inaccessible to the human intellect and introduces an account of consciousness which defines it as intentional. Generally speaking, the term intentionality is used to suggest a movement towards something, a directedness. To refer to consciousness as intentional is another way of saying that consciousness is always directed towards an object. Quite simply, consciousness is always consciousness-of something.

A fundamental tenet of the phenomenological notion of intentionality is the emphasis on the transcending nature of consciousness. However, even 'transcending' is somewhat misleading because it can be taken to indicate that consciousness is something in need of transcending, like, say, an inner cabinet estranged from the world which has to be transcended in order to reach out to reality. But the definition of consciousness as consciousness-of underscores this view as a misconception. According to the concept of intentionality, consciousness is not an inner sphere trapped in its own immanence, nor does it have to escape its own nature to direct itself towards something. Intentionality is an exhaustive description of consciousness because there is no residue of consciousness withheld from intentionality and by which intentionality is a means to get out to the world. There is no consciousness apart from consciousness-of; consciousness is simply a relational directedness. Thus, consciousness does not have to escape its own confines in order to direct itself towards something. No transcending is needed. In other words, emphasis on the transcending nature of consciousness should not be taken to suggest that consciousness is something that transcends. Transcendence is not something consciousness has or needs; transcendence is what consciousness is. Thus, Husserl rejects any philosophical attempt to build a bridge between the interiority of the subject and the world of transcendent objects as fundamentally mistaken. If we leave all the traditional apparatus of philosophy and proceed *zu den Sachen selbst*, we will, Husserl claims, find that there is no need for such a bridge, simply because consciousness is relational and its very life is expressed in relation to the world.

When we perceive, say, a car, we are thing-directed and we grasp this sensuous object directly. This is what Husserl calls straightforward perception or sense-perception.

In *sense*-perception, the 'external' thing appears 'in one blow,' as soon as our glance falls upon it. The manner in which it makes the thing appear present is straightforward: it requires no apparatus of founding or founded acts. (LI VI, #47)

When we perceive a car or a tree or a house or any other 'external' thing, we perceive the thing itself, not a mental picture or any kind of subjective construct.

However, due to the peculiar directedness of consciousness, one can also intend an object without perceiving it. While at work one can think about one's apartment and, although one is not perceiving it, one does intend this apartment, not something else. The only difference between this intention and one in which one actually perceives an object is that the latter is a filled or saturated intention, while the former is empty. However, when coming home from work the empty intention of the apartment will be filled by the fulfilled intending of the same object.

An empty intention is fulfilled in intuition whenever its intended correlate is manifest. This manifestation of the intended correlate is known as evidence (*Evidenz*) in phenomenological terminology. We speak, Husserl says, "somewhat loosely of evidence wherever an assertive intention (a statement in particular) finds verification in a corresponding, fully accommodated percept" (LI VI, #38). As this indicates, there are different levels and degrees of evidence. Husserl distinguishes between evidence in the loose and strict sense (LI VI, #38), and in the subsequent section he discusses the relation between evidence and truth. At this stage we choose not to enter this closer discussion of evidence, but we will return to it in our discussion of Heidegger's treatment of intentional fulfillment. What is of interest for us at this point is the fact that evidence is the manifestation of the intended correlate — an object — and that it does not matter "whether one is dealing with an individual or a universal object, with an object in the narrower sense or with a state of affairs" (LI VI, #38).

A manifestation of the intended correlate can take place on a nominal level when there is something in what we perceive that corresponds to a name, say, Socrates, or on a propositional level when there is something in what we perceive that corresponds to, say, the sentence "The car is red." In what follows, we focus on the latter, i.e., the manifestation of the intended correlate of objectifying propositional acts.[4] In the case of such acts, Husserl emphasizes that "not only the inwrought nominal presentations are fulfilled: the whole sense of the statement finds fulfillment through our underlying percept" (LI VI, #40). Thus, according to Husserl, the entire statement "The car is red" or "The paper is white" finds fulfillment. In other words, we perceive not only something that can correspond to 'car' and 'red,' 'paper' and 'white,' but also to the 'is;' it too must be fulfilled in perception. Thus, there must be objective correlates for all the formal words which make up the propositional form as such.

Although the terms 'car' and 'red,' 'paper' and 'white' find their fulfillment in ordinary sensory intuition, this is not the case with the car's *being* red or the paper's *being* white. We do not intuit the car's *being* red in straightforward perception. The 'is' and other formal components of propositions, the

---

[4] Although it falls beyond the limit of the focus of this study we would like to add that the identity-synthesis that occurs in nominal acts is not without problems. This is due to the fact that, according to Husserl, a name names its object in so far as it means that object and it might be that this meaning involves a propositional content.

categorial forms, introduce a surplus of meaning which finds no fulfillment in sense perception. Therefore Husserl claims that the

> intention of the word 'white' only partially coincides with the color-aspect of the apparent object; a surplus of meaning remains over, a form which finds nothing in the appearance itself to confirm it. (LI VI, #40)

Thus, although he says that the whole sense of the statement "The car is red" finds fulfillment through our underlying percept, Husserl nevertheless maintains that "we should look in vain for their [the categorial forms] objective correlates in the sphere of *real* objects" (LI VI, #43).

> I can see color, but not *being*-colored. I can feel smoothness, but not *being*-smooth. I can hear a sound, but not that something *is* sounding. Being is nothing *in* the object ... But being is also nothing attaching *to* an object: as it is no real (*reales*) internal feature, so also is it no real external feature, and therefore not, in the *real* sense, a 'feature' at all. (LI VI, #43)

Given the fact that being does not reside in the realm of what is real, it must obviously be sought elsewhere. At this point we see the first glimpse of the radical nature of phenomenology: objectivity is not exhausted by reality; it is much richer than the reality of a thing. An object is still an object even if it is not real.

According to Husserl, "the objective correlates of categorial forms are not 'real' (*realen*) moments" (LI VI, #43). This sentence raises two questions: what is an object if it is not real, and what does it mean for something to be a moment? Let us first consider the latter question and begin by summing up Husserl's analysis of the logic of wholes and parts as this notion was presented in the previous chapter. There are two kinds of parts, independent and non-independent, that is, pieces and moments, respectively. Moments are parts that cannot be separately presented to us though we may consider them abstractly apart from the whole. Thus, to refer to categorial forms as moments implies that their objective correlates cannot be presented separately from the whole, i.e., objects of the lowest level of possible intuition. This is what Husserl means when he says that "the sense of the statement finds fulfillment through our underlying percept" (LI VI, #43). Abstractly we can think and speak about these forms as if they were independent wholes, i.e., individual categorial objects, but their ontological status is more like that of an Aristotelian secondary substance.

In LI Husserl distinguishes between real and ideal objects. Both are objects, but while the former possess temporal properties, the latter do not. Ideal objects have no coordinates in time; they are atemporal and can neither come into existence nor go out of existence. The real objects are those objects grasped in straightforward perception. Their sphere is, Husserl claims, "in fact no other than the sphere of *objects of possible sense-perception*" (LI VI, #43). Ideal objects, on the other hand, cannot be grasped by ordinary sense-perception. According to Husserl, the distinction between real and ideal objects coincides with the distinction between sensuous and categorial objects. Ideal or categorial objects are what he calls objects of higher levels of possible intuition, that is, they are not graspable by ordinary sense-perception.

By saying that the objective correlates of categorial forms are not real moments Husserl claims that the objective correlate of, say, being cannot be grasped by sense-perception. But this sentence still yields an ambiguity: does Husserl mean that the objective correlate of categorial forms are not real moments, i.e., that they are not really moments, or that they are moments that are not real? Obviously, in this sentence Husserl uses 'real' (*realen*) in a technical sense, and what he says is that correlates of categorial forms, qua non-real, cannot be grasped by sense-perception but that they, qua moments, are not presented to us as independent wholes either. In other words, correlates of categorial forms are non-real and non-independent parts of the whole.

However, by claiming that the objective correlate of categorial forms are not real moments, Husserl appears to contradict himself. On the one hand he says that these objects cannot be grasped by sense-perception, on the other hand he says that they are not presented to us apart from the objects of sense-perception. To resolve this apparent contradiction one must take a closer look at the objective correlates of categorial forms.

The objective correlate of 'being' in the statement "The car is red" is not an object in the usual sense of this word. It is not sensuous and it is not an individual being. It is not an object at all if by 'object' one means real object. The objective correlate of 'being' in "The car *is* red" is not *a* being the way car is. It refers instead to the being of an object: the car's *being* red. Surely, that cannot be a real object. The being of a being cannot be a being. But — and this is paramount for Husserl's phenomenology — it is still an object; it is a correlate of an act of objectification. One might now ask, why this terminology? Why does Husserl talk about categorial objects as objects if they are not real objects? This brings us back to our initial statement about objectivity not being exhausted by reality. The correlate to the categorial form 'being' in the statement "The car is red" is objective in the sense that it refers to a *relation* within the thing itself. Against empiricism Husserl claims that categorial objects do not refer to ideas of reflection or to relations of ideas in thought alone. However, although having an objective status, Husserl precludes seeing ideal objects as independently existing entities; they are moments of the correlates of straightforward acts of perception.

To account for our seeing of categorial objects, Husserl calls attention to a distinction between a wide and a narrow sense of perception present in our everyday use of words like 'perceiving' and 'seeing.' In the narrow sense of perception we perceive, Husserl claims, "everything objective that we see with our eyes, hear with our ears or can grasp with any 'outer' or even 'inner' sense" (LI VI, #43). In this sense of perception the word 'being' can find no possible objective correlate. But although categorial objects are not grasped by sense-perception, Husserl nevertheless claims that the surplus of meaning that is introduced by the categorial forms finds fulfillment through an underlying percept. "It is well-known that one also speaks of 'perceiving,' and in particular of 'seeing,' in a greatly widened sense, which covers the grasping of whole states of affairs" (LI VI, #43). In other words, Husserl is calling attention to a wider kind of seeing that takes place, not isolated from or outside of straightforward perception, but within it.

Plainly the connection between the wider and the narrower, the supersensuous (i.e., raised above sense, or categorial) and *sensuous concept of perception*, is no external or contingent matter, but one rooted in the whole business on hand. It falls within the great class of acts whose peculiarity it is that in them something appears as 'actual,' as 'self-given.' (LI VI, #45)

Thus, although not reducible to sense-perception, supersensuous perception cannot be considered apart from sense-perception. Far from being merely the expression of an autonomous formative power or the active arrangement of passively received material, categorial acts are rooted in perceptive life.

Supersensuous seeing is not a pure, abstract seeing. Any appeal to separate acts of seeing objects of a higher order belonging to a separate world of thought is incompatible with the nature of Husserl's thinking.[5] What Husserl has in mind when distinguishing between sensuous and categorial perception is not two separable sets of acts but rather two aspects of one and the same act. He says, "these two acts are not merely performed together, or after one another, in the manner of disjoined experiences; rather they are bound together in a single act" (LI VI, #48). According to Husserl, categorial acts are founded acts. They do nothing more than explicate the articulations of the world of perceptive life. A categorial act is an act of grasping a moment that belongs constitutively to what is grasped in straightforward perception. In straightforward perception we grasp something as a whole, at one "blow," as Husserl says. But when we see a red car, we grasp not only the

---

[5] See for instance LI 2 (#7), where Husserl rejects as a metaphysical hypostatization the assumption that species really exist externally to thought.

car and the red but also the car's *being* red.[6] This is a relation within the thing itself, a state of affairs. Founded upon straightforward perception there is a second act of perception, Husserl claims,[7] which focuses upon a moment that belongs constitutively to the whole. This moment is the *presencing* of the objective correlate of straightforward perception.

Thus, the founded character of categorial intuition is due to the fact that the objective correlate of categorial acts is the presencing of the objective correlate of straightforward acts of perception. Husserl makes this clear in a twofold manner by saying that a categorial act is founded upon a straightforward act of perception, and that the objective correlate of a categorial act is a moment of the objective correlate of a straightforward act of perception.

Now that we have made it clear that Husserl's notion of supersensuous perception does not refer to something that takes place isolated from straightforward sense-perception and that its objective correlate is not something that can be sought in a higher order of reality or that belongs to the transcendental structure of human cognition, it is now time to give a closer description of Husserl's notion of seeing objects of higher levels.

3. CATEGORIAL INTUITION

So far we have seen that although categorial acts are founded upon sense-perception, they cannot be reduced to these straightforward acts of perception. What is given in a categorial intuition is a surplus in the sense that it exceeds the sensory givens. This surplus makes itself manifest in a perceptual judgment.

Though a perceptual judgment is nothing but an "expression" of a perception, it goes beyond perception. This is because it contains syntactical forms and other formal components of propositions which do not have their correlates in straightforward sense-perception. Thus, categorial intuition is necessary in order to justify the truth of a perceptual judgment, that is, to ensure its intuitive fulfillment.

A categorial intuition is usually an act explicitly establishing the relations implied in perceptions. It can be an act of synthesis, i.e., a predicative judgment which establishes and affirms a relation of unity (or identity) between sensible givens, or an act of ideation, i.e., an act establishing an ideative relation between a sensible object and its concept. Acts of ideation

---

[6] As Sokolowski puts it: "Not only do we have a thing and its feature presented to us, but we also have the presencing of the thing in its feature presented to us. Presencing is also presented, as well as that which is presented." R. Sokolowksi, "Husserl's Concept of Categorial Intuition" *Phenomenology and the Human Sciences*, vol. 12, 1981, 129.

[7] cf. LI, #48.

are distinguished from categorial acts of synthesis by excluding rather than containing the sensuous acts on which they are founded. Although we primarily focus upon the former in this section we also make some comments on the latter in order to prepare for Heidegger's treatment of acts of ideation in the next section.

The presence of a categorial surplus within the experience of simple entities appears as soon as we start to compare things, to assemble things into a group, to take entities as such and such and to place them in some sort of order. Whenever one of these relations is explicitly posited, a categorial act of synthesis is performed and a categorial object is given. A typical example of a categorial act of synthesis is a predicative judgment which establishes and affirms a relation of unity between the givens of straightforward sense-perception. Take for example the assertion "The car is red." Everything in the assertion is already found in straightforward perception; the car and the color, everything but this *being* red which is the key to the assertion. Although Husserl claims that in a judgment the 'is' functions as a part of the meaning just as 'car' and 'red,' he goes on to claim that there is an important difference: it does not thereby refer to a third real object perceived but, as we shall see, to the unity of what is perceived.

> The *is* itself does not enter into the judgment, it is merely meant, signitively referred to, by the little word 'is.' It is, however, *self-given*, or at least putatively given, in the *fulfillment* which at times invests the judgment, the *becoming aware* of the state of affairs supposed. (LI VI, #44)

Considered separately this 'is' has little meaning. Its meaning is related to the formal role it plays in the composition of a proposition. The 'is' or the 'being' is not the car and not the red and not a third object, a something in itself; it is the car-being-red: a state of affairs made present in articulation. The state of affairs, Husserl claims, is not in the judgment itself but is the objective correlate of a complete judgment. "As the sensible object stands to sense-perception so the state of affairs stands to the 'becoming aware' in which it is (more or less adequately) given" (LI VI, #44). In other words, in a categorial intuition an articulated fact, e.g., the fact that the car is red, is made present to us. A categorial intuition can thus refer to the act of synthesis that takes place in a predicative judgment which establishes a relation of unity between sensible givens, but it can also refer to another set of categorial acts, namely acts of ideation.

According to Husserl, acts of ideation are a kind of categorial intuition in which we apprehend universal objects, that is, essences or ideas. These acts belong to what Husserl calls the field of universal intuition, which refers to a kind of abstraction that works on the basis of primary intuitions. Through the universal intuition a new kind of objectivity becomes apparent, namely the objectivity of the universal. However, in order to safeguard against interpreting his notion of universal intuition as yielding a self-contradictory claim, he immediately qualifies his use of the term 'abstraction.'

Naturally I do not here mean 'abstraction' in the sense of a setting-in-relief of some non-independent moment in a sensible object, but Ideational Abstraction, where no such non-independent moment, but its Idea, its Universal, is brought to consciousness, and achieves *actual givenness*. (LI VI, #52)

The description of the ideational abstraction through which the universal achieves actual givenness seems, however, to call attention both to what we must presuppose and to what takes place. On the one hand Husserl says that we "must presuppose such an act in order that the Very Sort, to which the manifold single moments 'of one and the same sort' stand opposed, may itself come before us *as one and the same*" (LI VI, #52). This claim seems to echo claims made in the Second Investigation stating that universal identity is a condition of possibility for particular alikeness. On the other hand he goes further and says that

we become aware of the identity of the universal through the repeated performance of such acts upon basis of several individual intuitions, and we plainly do so in an overreaching act of identification which brings all such single acts of abstraction into one synthesis. (LI VI, #52)

The argument he is making here seems to be parallel to the one he made when discussing categorial acts of synthesis: he calls attention to an overreaching or exceeding aspect of our individual intuitions which cannot find its fulfillment in the sphere of particulars. Just as the objective correlate of a categorial act of synthesis is the actual givenness of a unity, the objective correlate of a categorial act of ideation is the actual givenness of an universal.[8] In an extremely interesting passage Husserl makes the following claim: "The unity of perception does *not* therefore arise through *our own synthetic activity* [rather] the unity of perception comes into being as a straightforward unity" (LI VI, #47). In the following we interpret this claim in order to shed further light on the notion of categorial intuition and the role it is to play in Husserl's phenomenology.

The term 'unity of perception' brings to mind Kant, and Husserl obviously employs this term in a way analogous to Kant's usage. But there is one major difference: whereas Kant claims that the unity of our perception cannot itself be given in experience and therefore must owe its existence to our synthetic activity, Husserl claims that it "comes into being as a straightforward unity"

---

[8] See J. Taminiaux, *Dialectic and Difference: Finitude in Modern Thought*, 105.

(LI VI, #47). Given the fact that, for Husserl, the term 'straightforward' means that the unity appears 'in one blow' in sense perception, this statement seems to be diametrically opposed to the claim made in this famous passage from Kant's Transcendental Deduction: "[T]he combination of a manifold in general can never come to us through the senses, and cannot, therefore, be already combined in the pure form of sensible intuition" (B129). To this Husserl would say both yes and no. He would agree in the sense that the unity itself does not belong to the sphere of real (*realen*) objects,[9] but he would disagree with the conclusion Kant draws from this fact:

For it is an act of spontaneity of the faculty of presentation; and all combination ... is an act of the understanding. To this act the general title 'synthesis' may be assigned, as indicating that we cannot present to ourselves anything as combined in the object which we have not previously combined, and that of all presentation, combination is the only one which cannot be given through objects. (B130)

For Husserl, even if the unity itself does not belong to the sphere of real objects, it is nevertheless given to us through an underlying percept.[10] For a Kantian, this would seem an impossible position or at best a sophisticated version of transcendental realism, but according to Husserl's notion of categorial intuition it is a sound position.

In order to account for the soundness of this position one must first call attention to the self-transcending mode of being attributed to consciousness by the phenomenological doctrine of intentionality. Because of the relational character of consciousness human perception grasps things themselves, not mental pictures, and further, it grasps them "in one blow." Thus, in sense perception a thing and its feature are given as a unity, not as a heap of components in need of being synthesized into a unity.

When we see a red car we do not perceive a particular car and a particular red. We simply perceive a red car. A predicative judgment such as "The car is red" articulates the mode of "belonging to," the unity, between the thing and the feature, not a synthesis of intramental contents. If we accept that perception grasps the thing in itself, it would be a mistake to ascribe the unity of a given thing and its feature to the expression of our own synthetic activity.

However, although the unity comes with the object, it would lead to an infinite regress to consider the unity of a thing and its feature as either a thing or a feature or both. To solve this problem without making an appeal to an autonomous formative power, Husserl distinguishes between founding and founded acts with different kinds of objective correlates. Both kinds of acts

[9] cf. LI, #43.
[10] cf. LI, #40.

have correlates that are objective, but whereas the objective correlate of straightforward sense-perception is a unitary real object, the objective correlate of a categorial act is the *unity* of the unitary real object. Although the latter is founded upon the former, it cannot be reduced to it.

4. HEIDEGGER'S ANALYSIS OF CATEGORIAL INTUITION

The subtitle of the lecture HCT reads "Prolegomena to the Phenomenology of History and Nature." Heidegger's objective, however, is not to investigate nature and history as they appear as objects for the sciences. On the contrary, his aim is to disclose a more original domain which is "reality as it shows itself before scientific inquiry, as the reality which is already given to it" (HCT, 2).

History and nature make up the domain that is investigated by the two main groups of empirical sciences: historical sciences and natural sciences, respectively. According to Heidegger, these sciences tend to dictate the way we understand history and nature with the result that they are "accessible only insofar as they are objects thematized in these sciences" (HCT, 1).

It might well be that something essential necessarily remains closed to the potentially scientific way of disclosing a particular field of subject matter; indeed, must remain closed if the science wishes to perform its proper function. (HCT, 1)

The separation between the two domains investigated by the empirical sciences may hide an undivided subject matter. However, it would prove futile to try to restore this original undividedness by taking as a point of departure the very division brought about by the sciences. This would imply an acceptance of the division as an original separation between nature and spirit. One cannot disclose anything essential by bringing together entities that do not originally belong together. The principal mistake of the modern philosophical tradition is to accept the scientific separation between nature and spirit as original and then attempt to somehow bring the two together. There is, Heidegger claims, nothing wrong with this separation. Indeed, it may even be necessary if science "wishes to perform its proper function." Heidegger's argument is instead that the separation is not an original one, but rather a product of the sciences for whom history and nature are reduced to the level of domains of objects.

What Heidegger seeks is not an investigation of the sciences of history and nature, nor an investigation of the objects of these sciences but, as he puts it, "a phenomenological disclosure of the original kind of being and constitution of both" (HCT, 1). Thus, while the empirical sciences are directed towards objects, phenomenology is directed towards the constitution and being of objects. Hence, the phenomenological investigation Heidegger intends to carry out is essentially an investigation of being.

However, the HCT is meant as a prolegomenon to a phenomenology of nature and history. It is not itself supposed to be such a phenomenological investigation. As a prolegomenon it is supposed to lay the ground and to provide the necessary foundation for carrying out a phenomenology of history and nature. In our treatment of this lecture we concentrate upon the preliminary part, "The Sense and Task of Phenomenological Research," which Heidegger refers to as "a short introductory orientation regarding the general character of the investigations." We focus upon chapter two, "The Fundamental discoveries of Phenomenology, Its Principle, and the Clarification of Its Name." Of the three fundamental discoveries of phenomenology Heidegger refers to in this chapter, we have a close look at his analysis of categorial intuition. However, in doing so we are by no means refraining from treating Heidegger's investigation of the two other decisive discoveries of phenomenology: intentionality and the original sense of the apriori. On the contrary, an accurate appreciation of these notions presupposes a correct grasp of the notion of categorial intuition. Heidegger's treatment of categorial intuition is at the same time a treatment of intentionality in the sense that the correct grasp of the categorial "is at once linked to the discovery of intentionality" (HCT, 59). Although categorial intuition is "just a concretion of the basic constitution of intentionality" and thus "possible only on the basis of the phenomenon of intentionality" (HCT, 72), Heidegger nevertheless holds that only through analysis of categorial intuition can we comprehend the full meaning of intentionality. Furthermore, Heidegger claims, "as a result of this discovery [of categorial intuition], philosophical research is now in a position to conceive the *apriori* more rigorously and to prepare for the characterization of the sense of its being" (HCT, 72). Hence, it follows that the intelligibility of the phenomenological notions of intentionality and apriori presupposes the concept of categorial intuition. This also makes sense of Heidegger's emphasis on the importance of the notion of categorial intuition for his own approach to the *Seinsfrage*.[11]

The Preliminary Part of HCT contains Heidegger's most in-depth and extensive treatment of fundamental themes of Husserlian phenomenology. It allows us to see how these themes provide Heidegger with a ground for his approach to the *Seinsfrage*. Heidegger interprets the Husserlian analysis of categorial intuition as the liberation of being from its connection to judgment alone. This opens up an entirely new approach to being. Firstly, being is not something that occurs only in the judgment itself. That is, it is not a mere

---

[11] We return to this theme in the next chapter, Apriorism.

logical concept without ontological status. Indeed, being is not *in* the judgment at all but is a correlate to an act. And, secondly, it is a correlate, not to judgment only, but to all acts which give their objects.

In the introduction to his treatment of categorial intuition Heidegger starts out by qualifying the term 'intuition.' "Intuition means," he claims, "simple apprehension of what is itself bodily found just as it shows itself" (HCT, 47). Heidegger adds that this is an exhaustive definition of the term 'intuition.' This means, firstly, that the term 'intuition' is indifferent as to whether sense perception is the only or the most original form of intuition or whether there are other ways of apprehending the bodily given as it shows itself. Secondly, intuition does not mean anything other than this. There is nothing mystical about intuition. Intuition simply means the apprehension of what is itself bodily found just as it shows itself. "Intuition in the phenomenological sense implies no special capacity, no exceptional way of transposing oneself into otherwise closed domains and depths of the world" (HCT, 47). Heidegger rejects the notion that the phenomenological concept of intuition has anything to do with the kind of intuition employed by Bergson or with any kind of modern intuitionism.

Having thus qualified the term 'intuition,' Heidegger next focuses upon the concept of categorial intuition. The discovery of this notion demonstrates that there is a simple apprehension of the categorial and that "this apprehension is invested in the most everyday of perceptions and in every experience" (HCT, 48). The objective of his analysis is, however, not merely that to clarify the meaning of the term but also to elucidate this kind of intuition itself, that is, "to make clear *what* is intuited in it and *how*" (HCT, 48).

Heidegger proceeds in the following manner. Before starting to discuss the themes acts of synthesis and acts of ideation he focuses on what he calls intentional presuming, intentional fulfillment, and intuition and expression. We follow Heidegger's analysis of these four themes closely and we shall add a fifth theme called constitution. Here we indicate a theme that is paramount for our own project: the notion of categorial acts as non-creative, non-fabricating, constituting acts.

5. INTENTIONAL FULFILLMENT

The first stage in Heidegger's analysis of categorial intuition discusses the concepts of intuition and evidence. The central issue is the development of a non-psychologistic notion of evidence according to which evidence is a property of intentionality rather than a psychic datum. Evidence is simply the manifestation of the intended correlate. From this it follows that evidence is both regional and universal. This theme makes possible a new approach to truth and being.

Heidegger distinguishes between empty intending and different levels of intuitive fulfillment. "Fulfillment means having the entity present in its intuitive content so that what is at first only emptily presumed in it demonstrates itself as grounded in the matters" (HCT, 49). What is intended can be given in greater or lesser fullness, but no fullness is greater than the one given in sense perception. Sense perception is what gives the entity in its originality. But originality does not mean total fullness. Fullness given in sense perception gives the entity originarily, but only from one side. Thus, original and complete fullness does not mean total non-perspectival fullness; fullness is always perspectival.

What happens in the passage from an empty intention to a demonstrative fulfillment is a bringing-into-coincidence of the emptily intended and the originarily intuited. This, Heidegger claims, is an act of identification. And, he continues, "[t]he intended identifies itself in the intuited; selfsameness is *experienced [erfahren]*" (HCT, 49). But, and this is a crucial point in phenomenology, in the act of identification what is apprehended is not the *identity* itself but rather the *identical*. An act of identification is accomplished as the originarily intuited is brought into coincidence with the emptily intended. The originarily intuited is bodily originary, it is the entity itself. Thus, it would entail a mistake to claim that the objective correlate of an act of identification is identity. What is apprehended in this act of identification is the thing itself as it is given to sense perception — through which the selfsameness of the emptily intended and the originarily intuited is experienced.

The phenomenological interpretation of evidence arises out of this interpretation of fulfillment as an act of identification of the entity itself. "[F]ulfillment as an act of identification includes obtaining insight into the grounding of what is presumed in the matter. This act of obtaining insight, as identifying fulfillment, is called *evidence*" (HCT, 50). According to Heidegger, Husserl was the first to develop this notion of evidence which he considers an essential advance beyond the psychologistic notions of evidence prevailing in the tradition of logic and epistemology. Although he admits that it has not yet had much of an effect, this account of evidence represents an important break from the traditional interpretation of evidence. Heidegger specifically takes issue with what he refers to as Rickert's notion of "feeling of evidence" according to which evidence is considered a psychic process announcing that there is something real corresponding to our judging. Heidegger rejects this interpretation of evidence because it is governed by a phenomenologically unsound distinction between transcendence and immanence. Instead, Heidegger emphasizes that the Husserlian notion of evidence is one that springs out of a distinction between transcendence and immanence which has been revised by the phenomenon of intentionality. "[I]f we see that the acts of identifying apprehension are defined by intentionality, then we do not resort to the mythological account of evidence as psychic feeling or psychic datum" (HCT, 50). The distinction between transcendence and immanence is simply not the kind that necessitates evidence in the sense of a psychic datum announcing the correspondence between judgment and reality. Evidence, Heidegger claims, is of a totally different nature. Evidence is a specific intentional act which identifies the intended and the intuited. The objective correlate of this act is the thing itself as it is given to sense perception and through which the identity of the emptily intended and the originarily intuited is experienced.

According to Heidegger, this phenomenological interpretation of evidence yields a fundamental insight of great significance, namely that evidence is both regional and universal. It is regional, Heidegger argues, because "all evidence is in its sense geared to a corresponding region of subject matter" (HCT, 50). In other words, each region of subject matter generates its own peculiar evidence. And for this reason "it is absurd to want to transpose one possibility of evidence ... into other kinds of apprehension" (HCT, 50). Heidegger adds that it is equally important to note that a phenomenological interpretation of evidence also emphasizes the universal character of evidence. Evidence is universal in not being restricted to specific acts. That is, "*[e]vidence is a universal function, first, of all acts which give their objects, and then, of all acts*" (HCT, 51). Thus, Heidegger argues, whereas in traditional theory of knowledge evidence appears only in relation to assertions, predications, and judgments, the phenomenological emphasis on evidence as a property of intentionality underscores the universal character of evidence.

Heidegger considers the discovery of evidence as being at once regional and universal to be a phenomenological interpretation of the scholastic definition of truth as *veritas est adaequatio rei et intellectus*. "Definitive and thoroughgoing fulfillment means commensuration (*adaequatio*) of what is presumed (*intellectus*) with the intuited subject matter itself (*res*)" (HCT, 51). However, the strength of the phenomenological interpretation of the scholastic definition of truth lies in the fact that it more adequately appreciates the full meaning of this definition. Heidegger elucidates this point by proposing a threefold designation of the concept of truth and by discussing corresponding concepts of being. According to Heidegger, the regional character of evidence represents a concretization of the scholastic definition of truth that brings into view the double meaning of *adaequatio*. From this concretization we can obtain two concepts of truth, one designating the being-identical of the intended and the intuited, and one designating the *intentio*, that is, not the content of the act but the act itself.

We obtain, Heidegger argues, the first concept of truth by "referring to the correlate of the act of identification: subsistence of the identity of presumed and intuited" (HCT, 52). However, concerning this correlate Heidegger notes the necessity of distinguishing between apprehension and experience. In the act of identification one is thematically directed towards the thing itself, not towards its identity with the emptily intended. What is apprehended is the identical object through which the identity of the emptily intended and the originarily intuited is experienced.

> The correlation is peculiar in that *something is experienced but not apprehended.* So it is really only in apprehending the object as such, which amounts to not apprehending the identity, that this identity is experienced. (HCT, 52)

In other words, this first concept of truth designates, not the identity, but the *res*, the *intentum*.

Whereas the first concept of truth is the being-identical of the intended and the intuited, the second one designates the *intentio*, that is, this concept of truth designates "*the act-structure of evidence itself as this coincident identification*" (HCT, 53). The latter conception emphasizes truth as a specific correlation of acts. However, Heidegger maintains that both of these concepts of truth are incomplete. "Neither the one oriented towards the state of affairs nor the one oriented towards the act captures the original sense of truth" (HCT, 53). According to Heidegger, both positions presuppose a more original sense of truth. Truth cannot be reduced to either *intentum* or *intentio*; it is the *concretum* of both. Truth is most properly attributed to intentionality. Original truth "is what *makes* knowledge *true* [i.e., the true-making matter, the entity itself as an intuited matter]" (HCT, 53). Original truth, Heidegger claims, is *being*, and this notion of truth goes back to early Greek philosophy. However, before elaborating on this notion of truth and being we first consider the concepts of being which correspond to the two first concepts of truth.

Corresponding to the first concept of truth there is, Heidegger argues, a "specific sense of being; being in the sense of being-true" (HCT, 53). As an example Heidegger uses the assertion "The chair is yellow." Emphasizing the being of *being*-yellow leaves us with a concept of being based on the fact that a judged state of affairs truly is. "Underscoring being means that the truth-relation just discussed subsists, an identity between presumed and intuited subsists" (HCT, 54). Thus, the first concept of being springs out of an interpretation of truth as the subsistence of identity. In this sense Being means being-real.

To the second concept of truth there corresponds a concept of being that arises out of an interpretation of truth as a specific correlation of acts. Heidegger starts out from the same example but this time he underscores the opposite pole, that is, the being-*yellow*.

> This time I do not want to say that the judged state of affairs truly is, but to express the being-P of S [being-yellow of the chair], the pertinence of the predicate to the subject. In other words, in the emphasis of being-*yellow* 'being' refers to the *being of the copula* — The chair *is* yellow. (HCT, 54)

And, he continues, "[t]his second concept of being does not refer to the subsistence of the truth-relation ... but to a *structural moment* of the state of affairs itself" (HCT, 54; our emphasis). Thus, the second concept of being refers to the being of the copula which is a structural moment of the state of affairs itself. This is a very interesting claim in that it is closely related to Husserl's discussion of the copula in the Sixth Investigation of LI. According to Heidegger, although the copula is situated in the assertive act, it refers not to ideas of reflection or any kind of mental activity, but to the state of affairs itself. We are thing-directed when we say "The chair is yellow." The "is" refers to something in the chair in the sense that we find the chair *being* yellow. But this should not be taken to imply that the "is" refers to a feature of the chair like shape or color. The objective correlate of the copula is not to be considered a predicate of the chair, just as it is not to be considered a predicate of the mental activity that takes place when we make a judgment. Hence, the objective correlate of the copula is not a real predicate; rather it is a structural moment of the state of affairs itself. It is not a real moment in the sense that the origin of this concept of being lies in the realm of sense-perception. By claiming that the origin of this sense of being is neither the realm of sense-perception nor the realm of inner perception, i.e., introspection, Heidegger points ahead to the concept of categorial intuition as a way of accounting for where we find and how we experience what is expressed by the copula.

Thus far Heidegger has given an interpretation of two aspects of truth, and the corresponding concepts of being, neither of which alone defines truth or being and neither of which appears independently of the other.

> In the expression "The chair is yellow" both meanings of being are meant — *being as a relational factor of the state of affairs as such and being as a truth-relation*, or more accurately, *the subsistence and the stasis* [*Bestand und Stehen*] of the state of affairs in the truth-relation. (HCT, 54)

In other words, the first and the second concept of truth and being are moments of a whole. To reduce the concept of truth to either the *intentio* or the *intentum* would be to force one of these two moments into being a whole, that is, to force an *abstractum* into being a *concretum*. "The term 'truth' is originally and properly attributed to intentionality, but this is done on the basis of its being composed of both the *intentio* and the *intentum*" (HCT, 55). With his introduction of the third concept of truth Heidegger moves towards an analysis of truth that takes into account both aspects of truth discussed above. This takes us beyond the realm of being-identical and beyond the very act of bringing into coincidence. As Heidegger puts it, this takes us into the realm of "that which *makes* knowledge *true*" (HCT, 53).

While the first two concepts of truth are based on the concretization of the *adaequatio* that follows from the discovery of the regional character of evidence, Heidegger finds that the universality of evidence represents a radicalization of the scholastic definition of truth. This radicalization arises from the fact that evidence is no longer restricted to the realm of assertions, predications, and judgments, but is "*a universal function, first, of all acts which give their objects, and then, of all acts*" (HCT, 52). As a result, Heidegger argues, "phenomenology thus breaks with the restriction of the concept of truth to relational acts, to judgments. The truth of relational acts is only one particular kind of truth for the objectifying acts of knowing in general" (HCT, 55).

While truth is traditionally linked to the relational acts of judgment, the term 'being' is readily attributed to the correlate of non-relational, single-rayed acts, as a specification of the object, of the subject matter itself. But just as truth must undergo a 'widening,' so too must 'being,' a widening not only from the subject matter but from the state of affairs — being and being-such-and-such. (HCT, 55)

At this point we are moving towards an understanding of the nature of categorial intuition. While the first concept of truth emphasized the traditional notion of truth as the subsistence of identity of presumed and intuited and its corresponding concept of being as being-real, the second concept of truth has a more phenomenological flavor to it. Here we find an emphasis on the *expression* being-P of S in which the copula is considered a structural moment of the state of affairs itself. With this second concept of truth Heidegger indicates the direction in which he is moving. But this view is still too narrow in that it focuses upon traditional acts of judgment. If we add the universality of evidence to this view, we are in position to initiate an analysis of the concept of categorial intuition.

6. INTUITION AND EXPRESSION

In his introduction to the treatment of categorial intuition, Heidegger claimed that the discovery of this notion is the demonstration that the apprehension of the categorial is "invested in the most everyday of perceptions and in everyday experience" (HCT, 48). He stresses, however, that in order to see the categorial intuition in straightforward perception we must be adequately prepared. The first step of this preparation is described in the above section dealing with the concepts of intuition, evidence, and truth. The second step takes place in the discussion of the link between intuition and expression in this section.

According to Heidegger, the analysis of the relation between intuition and expression is meant to clarify the sense in which categorial intuition is included in every experience. However, we shall see that his analysis extends beyond this inclusion to the phenomenological concept of categorial intuition itself. What is new with this notion of categorial intuition is not the idea of apprehending the categorial; it is instead the fact that this does not call for a special capacity, but that it is to be found in every experience.

Heidegger's emphasis on the universal nature of evidence surfaces in this section as the subordination of assertions to expressness and the qualification of expressness as the expression of lived experiences or comportments through meaning. As evidence in favor of this claim Heidegger points to the fact that "our comportments are in actual fact pervaded through and through by assertions, that they are always performed in some form of expressness" (HCT, 56). It is, he continues, "also a matter of fact that our simplest perceptions and constitutive states are already *expressed*, even more, are *interpreted in a certain way*" (HCT, 56). Heidegger does not here engage in a discussion of which is primary — expression or interpretation — but he emphasizes the fact that perception is not independent of either. It is, he claims, "not so much that we see the objects and things but rather that we first talk about them. To put it more precisely: we do not say what we see, but rather the reverse, we see what *one says* about the matter" (HCT, 56). The claim that perception is always an expression of perception is Heidegger's way of saying that the categories are at work even on the simplest level of perception. At the same time, however, they introduce an intentional surplus whose fulfillment cannot be achieved in perception.

Heidegger begins his analysis with a discussion of expressions of perceptions. When one gives expression to a perception with an assertion, there are, Heidegger claims, two ways in which to understand 'expression.' First it may sometimes simply refer to an announcement of a perception.

> Giving expression in this first sense is therefore announcing the presence of an act, my being animated by it. To give expression to a perception then means something like the following: I now communicate that I hear the sound of a car below. (HCT, 56)

However, when we give expression to a perception with the assertion "This chair is yellow and upholstered," this is not a matter of giving notice of the act but of "the *communication* of what is perceived in the act" (HCT, 57). As Heidegger emphasizes, "a perceptual assertion is a communication about the entity perceived in perception and not about the act of perception as such" (HCT, 57). But if the assertion "This chair is yellow and upholstered" is a communication about the entity perceived in perception, then we must address the question of the nature of fulfillment in such a case. We must ask whether the assertion finds a complete fulfillment in what is perceived. "Is every intention within the full intending and asserting perceptually demonstrable in the subject matter? In short, is the perceptual assertion which gives expression to perception demonstrable perceptually?" (HCT, 57). The question remains: "Are the 'this,' the 'is,' the 'and' perceptually demonstrable in the subject matter?" (HCT, 57). Heidegger answers that

I can see the chair, its being-*upholstered*, and its being-*yellow* but I shall never in all eternity see the 'this,' 'is,' 'and' as I see the chair. There is in the full perceptual assertion a *surplus of intentions* whose demonstration cannot be borne by the simple perception of the subject matter. (HCT, 57–8)

Heidegger first asks whether such a demonstration "is still possible in the less complicated expression of simple naming, a so-called nominal positing of the kind 'the yellow upholstered chair'" (HCT, 58). But he then rejects this possibility by pointing out that even on this level there is a surplus of intentions. The surplus is not something that is added at a certain level of sophistication, it is present even on a nominal level. Thus, according to Heidegger, the way to solve this problem is not to break a complicated assertion down into a set of less complicated nominal statements, each of which can be fulfilled through simple perception. Even if that were possible, one would still have to account for the addition of the surplus at a certain level.

In what follows Heidegger recalls a Kantian insight, repeated by Husserl, that further underscores the fact that being is neither sensory nor real, and, subsequently, that there is "no adequation between what is expressed and what is perceived" (HCT, 58).

'Being' is not a real moment in the chair like the wood, the weight, hardness, or color; nor is it something on the chair like the upholstery and screws. 'Being,' Kant already said, whereby he meant *being-real, is not a real predicate of the object.* (HCT, 58)

If it is the case that perceptual statements are directed towards the entity perceived in perceptions *and* that the assertion expresses something which does not find perceptual fulfillment, it seems to follow, Heidegger notes, "that we must give up the idea of an adequate fulfillment of assertions and the idea of truth associated with it" (HCT, 58). One way to cope with the problem of there being components of the assertion that are in excess of what is given in perception is to claim that the origin of these components lies somewhere else. In this regard Heidegger points to the argument of the tradition of British Empiricism since Locke, and he recapitulates this argument as follows:

While the real is regarded as the objective, as a structure and moment of the object, the non-sensory is equated with the mental in the subject, the immanent. The real is given from the side of the object, the rest is thought into the subject. (HCT, 58)

According to this tradition, Heidegger argues, "the origin of these non-sensory moments lies in *immanent* perception, in the reflection upon consciousness" (HCT, 58). He takes issue with this argument which, he claims, has its origin in Descartes and which is also present, though in a modified version, in Kant and in German Idealism.

Heidegger's guiding question is "[w]ill I find 'being,' 'unity,' 'plurality, 'and,' 'or' in inner perception?" (HCT, 58). His answer is that "the non-sensory and ideal cannot without further ado be identified with the immanent, conscious, subjective" (HCT, 58). This is, he claims, demonstrated by phenomenology. Phenomenology does not oppose a turn towards consciousness in order to account for non-sensory concepts.

Because the 'is,' 'being,' 'unity,' 'thisness' and the like refer to the non-sensory, and the non-sensory is not real, not objective, hence is something subjective, we must look to the subject, to consciousness. (HCT, 58-9)

What phenomenology rejects is the consideration of consciousness without taking into account intentionality which, Heidegger maintains, "was the typical way of considering it before" (HCT, 59). If acts of consciousness are understood only as psychic processes, then the discussion of non-sensory concepts in terms of consciousness entails a return to British Empiricism. But, Heidegger argues, phenomenological consistency requires a further qualification of the acts of consciousness. One can approach these acts as immanent psychic events, i.e., as objects, and in this case, Heidegger says, "I always find only the sensory and objective, which I must take as an 'immanently real' [*reelles*] component of the psychic process, but I never find anything like 'being,' 'this,' 'and'" (HCT, 59). However, if one investigates consciousness in the light of the phenomenological doctrine of intentionality, one instead approaches the objects of these acts. In that case the situation is different. Here Heidegger recalls Husserl by quoting a section from LI:

It is not in the reflection upon judgments nor even upon fulfillments of judgments but rather in these fulfillments themselves that we find the true source of the concepts State of Affairs and Being (in the copulative sense). Not in these *acts as objects*, but in *the objects of these acts*, do we have the abstractive basis which enables us to realize the concepts in question. (LI VI, #44)

From this Heidegger concludes: "The category 'being,' 'and,' 'or,' 'this,' 'one,' 'several,' 'then' are nothing like consciousness, but are correlates of certain acts" (HCT, 59). And, he continues,

I find the categorial of identity not in the reflection upon consciousness and the subject as a process of ideating comportment, but in the reference to what is intended in this comportment as such. (HCT, 59)

Hence, the concepts 'subjective,' 'consciousness,' 'immanence' have different meanings depending upon whether one focuses on subjective, conscious, immanent acts qua objects or upon the objective correlate of these acts. In order to distinguish these two meanings of subjectivity, we call the former the psychological sphere, and the latter the subjective perspective. Although 'being' does not belong to the psychological sphere, it is nonetheless subjective in the sense that it appears to the subjective perspective. Being is a correlate of an act of consciousness. According to Heidegger, the traditional mistake is to overlook this distinction, thus identifying non-sensory with immanent in the sense of psychological sphere. But, Heidegger claims, although non-sensory and ideal concepts express something which cannot be found perceptually, they "are nothing like consciousness, nothing psychic, but a special kind of objectivity" (HCT, 59).

Having shown that the non-sensory and ideal are correlates of certain acts, Heidegger goes on to discuss the nature of the non-sensory perception to which they are given. These acts, Heidegger claims, give "something which does not have the character of a real sensory thing-like object or a part or a moment of such an object" (HCT, 60).

These moments are *not demonstrable through sense perception*. But they are demonstrable by way of an essentially *similar type of fulfillment* ... Since 'allness,' 'number,' 'subject,' 'predicate,' 'state of affairs,' 'something' are objects, we will correspondingly have to understand as intuitions the acts which originally demonstrate them. (HCT, 60)

Heidegger distinguishes between sense perception and non-sensory perception. The latter gives fulfillment to the moments in the assertion which do not find fulfillment through the former. Heidegger thus equates non-sensory perception with categorial intuition.

"The categorial," Heidegger says, "are the moments of the full assertion whose mode of fulfillment has not yet been clarified" (HCT, 60). In order to obtain a clarification of their mode of fulfillment, we must "sharpen the distinction between two kinds of intuition" and thus "define more precisely categorial acts as such" (HCT, 60). These two kinds of intuition are simple and multi-level intuition. Simple perception refers to what Husserl calls straightforward sense perception. This perception "does not bring about the fulfillment of all the intentions of the assertion" (HCT, 60). In order to grasp the difference between simple and categorial intuition, we must first characterize the nature of straightforward sense perception more thoroughly. The clarification of simplicity will "lead to the clarification of the sense of the founding and being founded of categorial acts" (HCT, 60). Simple perception founds multi-level acts. Thus, the distinction between simple and multi-level acts is a distinction between founding and founded acts. This implies that the two different kinds of acts do not appear independently of each other. Simple acts are pervaded by multi-level acts.

Although sense perception is simple there is still a high degree of complexity in the structure of such an act. So far we have established that in simple perception "the object is bodily given and persists in this state as the same object" (HCT, 60). Through a continuous sequence of perceptions of the same thing, one sees the object as identically the same. The continuity of this sequence is not a result of a subsequent drawing together of temporally continuous acts into one perception. On the contrary, Heidegger argues, "it can be phenomenologically established that every single phase of perception in the whole of the continuous sequence is in itself a full perception of the thing" (HCT, 60–1). This is because sense perception gives the entity in its originality. Since fullness of sense perception gives the entity originarily, it would be a contradiction to claim that there is something like a single phase of perception that is not a full perception of a thing, but which could be combined with other phases to form a full perception. Thus, in the case of simple perception, Heidegger notes, "the continuum of the perceptual sequence is not instituted supplementally by a supervening synthesis, but what is perceived in this sequence is there at *one* level of act" (HCT, 61). He adds that "the perceptual continuity is a single perception, merely extended" (HCT, 61). What this means is that on the level of simple perception, of simplicity, there are no additional unifying or mediating acts included in our apprehension of objects. Here Heidegger recalls Husserl's thesis that single perception "presents its object in a straightforward and immediate way" (HCT, 61). He says, "*[s]implicity means the absence of multi-level acts, which institute their unity only subsequently*" (HCT, 61). However, this claim must be further qualified by an important distinction that Heidegger makes between the *way of apprehending* and the *act-structure*. In this context, simplicity refers to a feature of intentionality, to a way of apprehending an object, and in this sense it means the absence of multi-level acts. But if we focus back on the structure of the act itself we will find that sense perception displays a high degree of complexity. Thus, considered as a way of apprehending sense perception is simple in that it presents its object in a straightforward and immediate way, but it does not follow that the structure of this act is thereby simple. "Simplicity of perception ... does not mean simplicity of the act-structure as such. Conversely, the multi-level character of categorial acts does not exclude the simplicity of these acts" (HCT, 61). To claim that simplicity in the way of apprehending an object entails the simplicity of the structure of the act would reintroduce the empiricist argument. If simplicity excludes complexity in the structure of the act we would have to appeal to the notion of simple, non-complex impressions. In other words, without complexity on the act-side there can be no complexity on the correlate-side. Moreover, without the latter there is no way of claiming that the non-sensory and ideal are correlates of acts. Thus, one would have no choice but to identify the non-sensory and ideal with the psychological sphere if one does not allow for a notion of unfounded categorial acts.

This is further underscored in Heidegger's interpretation of the real object that follows from the single level character of apprehension in sense perception. Again Heidegger recalls Husserl's teaching. According to Husserl, Heidegger claims, "a real object is by definition a possible object of simple perception" (HCT, 61). But being an object of simple perception is not the same as being a simple object in the technical sense of 'simple.' 'Simple,' according to Husserl's theory of wholes and parts, means an object without parts. To be an object of possible sense perception is not to be an object without parts. On the contrary, to be an object of possible sense perception is to have the capacity to appear to a perspective, and by appearing to a perspective the object appears originarily, but only from one side. In other words, what appears to sense perception is the whole object and, by the same token, a part of it, a moment. Thus, to be an object of possible sense perception is to have parts. To be a real object is to be a complex object. Even if the totality of the object were given in simple apprehension, the object would still not thereby be simple in the sense of having no parts. On the contrary, the parts are there, although implicitly.

In simple apprehension the totality of the object is explicitly given through the bodily sameness of the thing. The parts, moments, portions of what is at first simply perceived, by contrast, *are there implicitly, unsilhouetted — but still given so that they can be made explicit.* (HCT, 61–2; our emphasis)

Since the parts and moments are given in such a way that they can be made explicit to simple apprehension, it follows that simple apprehension founds the possibility of doing just that.

> This simple perception ... can of course on its part now become the *basis for acts which are built upon it in its specific intentionality as correlate of its objectivity*, and so claim it as the foundation for the construction of new objectivities. (HCT, 62; our emphasis)

The notion of simplicity as the unsilhouetted inclusion of parts and moments renders a more accurate appreciation of the full meaning of the founded nature of categorial acts. This notion entails the rejection of a notion of unfounded categorial acts, i.e., of a free-floating apprehension of the non-sensory and ideal, of being. Categorial acts presuppose actual perceptions upon which they depend, and they do so because they make explicit the parts and moments given to simple apprehension. Not only are there no unfounded categorial acts, there are also no unfounding simple acts. Simple apprehension "is already intrinsically pervaded by categorial intuition" (HCT, 60). Thus, against empiricism phenomenology claims there is no such thing as a simple act of perception, and for this reason it can uphold a notion of the non-sensory and ideal as correlates of acts. Against extreme rationalism it can uphold this notion without thereby advocating a notion of unfounded categorial acts.

According to Heidegger, multi-level acts can be made explicit in the construction of new objectivities. This has already been indicated above in the treatment of the possible fulfillment of the full assertion. But, Heidegger claims, this "preliminary suggestion of a mode of intuition giving such objects" (HCT, 62) must be further elucidated by focusing on the connection between simple and multi-level acts.

> Now it is a matter of seeing the connection of this new objectivity with that of the real objects, the objectivity of the basic level, in other words, of seeing the structural and constructional relationships of the intentions themselves. (HCT, 62)

However, Heidegger quickly adds that even if this leaves us with two objectivities, the objectivity of the basic level and the new constructed objectivity of the multi-level acts, these "two objectivities cannot be separated" (HCT, 62). That is because these objectivities are correlates of acts that cannot be separated. They are structural moments making up the basic constitution of intentionality.

Heidegger specifically criticizes the psychologistic interpretation of the connection between the two objectivities and the acts of which they are correlates.

When we now speak of connections between acts, like those at the ground level and those built upon it (simple and founded acts), we are not thereby directing our attention to psychic events and their coupling in the manner of temporal succession. (HCT, 62)

The connection between simple and founded acts is not a product of a "bringing together." These acts belong to the realm of intentionality as "structures of the particular directedness towards the objects appropriate to each type" (HCT, 62). They are originarily connected, but in a way that prohibits an objective correlate of multi-level acts to be accessible in simple acts. This means, Heidegger argues, "that categorial acts make the objectivity upon which they build, the simply given, accessible in a new kind of object" (HCT, 62). From these considerations on the nature of the relationship between simple and multi-level acts it follows that categorial acts, qua founded, are "directed towards the objectivities co-posited in them from the simple acts" (HCT, 62), but are not thereby a formal repetition of the founding acts. Since these co-posited objectivities are not accessible in simple acts, it follows that the intentionality of the categorial acts differ from that of the simple acts. This implies, Heidegger concludes, "that the founded acts *disclose* the simply given objects *anew*" (HCT, 62). By virtue of the categorial acts the objects of simple perception "come to explicit apprehension precisely in what they are" (HCT, 62). For instance, the chair comes to explicit apprehension as being yellow through a categorial act.

7. CATEGORIAL ACTS: SYNTHESIS AND IDEATION

Like Husserl, Heidegger distinguishes between two groups of categorial acts, acts of synthesis and acts of ideation. These make up an exhaustive description of categorial intuition. Heidegger considers these categorial acts in a threefold way by looking at their founded character, their character as intuitions, i.e., as acts that give objectivity, and by focusing upon how the objectivity of simple acts is given with them.

Before Heidegger discusses acts of ideation, he analyzes acts of synthesis. This order is not accidental but reflects the necessity of approaching founded acts step by step. In this context this means that we must start with the founded acts of synthesis which cointend their founding objectivity and then proceed to acts of ideation which, although founded, do not actually cointend the founding objectivity. In order to grasp the nature of the latter without falling back into empiricism or extreme rationalism it is paramount to accurately understand the nature of founded acts.

In presenting acts of synthesis, Heidegger starts out from simple perception in a Husserlian manner. Just as Husserl claims that in sense perception the thing appears "in one blow," Heidegger calls attention to the fact that in simple perception the entity is "there simply [in 'onefold' as it were] without complication" (HCT, 63). What both mean is that sense perception is simple because in it things appear in a straightforward and immediate manner. In other words, the simple way of apprehending a thing does not presuppose an apparatus of founding and founded acts. And, correlatively, the object appears as a unity. But, as we have already made clear, the simple way of apprehending does not entail a simple act-structure, nor is the correlate of simple apprehension a simple object in the sense of having no parts. On the contrary, "simplicity means that the real parts and moments *included in it* do not stand out in relief" (HCT, 63; our emphasis). Since they are included in the unity of the object, parts and moments can, Heidegger concludes, be brought into relief through special acts of explication.

At this point it seems appropriate to ask what it means to claim that, on the one hand, categorial intuition is found in every and everyday experience and, on the other hand, that the bringing into relief of the categorial calls for special acts of explication? A first response to this question might be that just as parts and moments are included in the object of sense perception, so categorial acts are included in sense perception itself. That is, these new and special acts of explication are merely a bringing into relief something which is already there in simple perception. But this is not entirely correct. Categorial acts are not included in simple perception as acts, the intentionalities of these acts do not coincide, nor are the parts and moments present as correlates before being brought into relief. As a way of apprehending, sense perception is simple and its correlate presents itself as a whole. An object does not appear as complex to sense perception. It appears as a unity. Hence, we must have a closer look at the structure of acts of synthesis.

Heidegger takes as his point of departure the example of the "yellow chair." The accentuation of 'yellow' in the perceived chair is a drawing out of a specific property from the perceived subject matter. This makes present something which was not present in the simple perception of the thing. But, Heidegger continues, accentuating yellow as something that is in the chair is at the same time an accentuation of the chair as the whole containing the yellow. "Accentuating q as a part of the whole and accentuating the whole which contains q as a part are one and the same act of accentuating S as a whole" (HCT, 63). Thus, the accentuation of the property yellow is an accentuation of the relationship of yellow and chair. Heidegger continues, "the being-yellow of the chair, the previously unarticulated subject matter, now becomes visible through the articulation, through the arrangement which we call the state of affairs" (HCT, 63). About this articulation Heidegger makes several observations. First, he makes it clear that the articulation of the state of affairs is not a putting together of pre-given pieces.

[W]hat is primary is not first drawing q out, then S as the whole, and finally taking them together, as if the relationship of the state of affairs were assembled from elements already given. (HCT, 64)

It is of pivotal importance for Heidegger to show that the new objectivity, the state of affairs, is not a product of a putting together objects of sense perception. If it were, he would have to allow for a notion of simple objects, and thus there would be no way for him to maintain his thesis concerning the inclusion of categorial intuition in every and everyday experience. If this were the case, the justification for Heidegger's approach to the *Seinsfrage* would be missing.

Synthesis is not a matter of adding together elements which are at first separate. Indeed, in order to understand the true nature of synthesis, the primary thing is not to focus on parts being brought together. What is primary, Heidegger claims, "is the relating itself, through which the members of the relation as such first become explicit" (HCT, 64). In other words, Heidegger warns against falling back on the traditional conception of synthesis as a production of new objects out of given pieces, out of building blocks given in the form of simple impressions. In order to avoid this, he emphasizes the necessity of sticking to a description of the objectifying acts themselves. He observes that the relation of the state of affairs can be taken in two ways. The direction can go from part to whole or it can go the other way, from simple apprehension of the whole to the part. This double direction, Heidegger claims, "belongs to the very sense of the structure of a state of affairs" (HCT, 64). "The acts of accentuating and giving the relationship are not next to and after one another but are unified in the unity of intending the very relation of the state of affairs" (HCT, 64). Thus, in a response to our question we can state that there is no tension between maintaining the inclusion of categorial intuition in every and everyday experience and claiming that the bringing into relief of the categorial calls for special acts of explication. Simple apprehension and categorial intuition are "unified in the unity of intending the very relation of the state of affairs" (HCT, 64). Simple perception and categorial intuition are structural moments of the act of relating. "They constitute an original unity of acts which, as an overarching unity, brings the new objectivity, more precisely, the entity in this new objectivity, to givenness" (HCT, 64). Let us now consider how this unity manifests itself. The act of synthesis brings into relief a property of a given thing. In this sense synthesis involves an analysis of this thing. It brings into relief a moment included in the unity of the whole object. Accentuating the new objectivity is then in fact a double act that involves both synthesis and analysis, both taking together and laying apart. Hence, the bringing into relief of moments is at the same time a return to the whole object given to simple apprehension. It thus follows that "synthesis is not so much a matter of connecting two parts which are at first separated, as we glue them together and fuse them" (HCT, 64). According to Heidegger, "synthesis is not a connecting of objects, but *synthesis* and *dihairesis* give objects" (HCT, 64). Synthesis discloses the simply given object anew in that *it brings it into view as complex*. Something new becomes visible about the given matter, e.g., the chair's *being* yellow and upholstered. This, Heidegger claims, is "a form of more authentic objectification of the given matter" (HCT, 63). It is more authentic because the chair becomes expressly visible in what it is, namely yellow and upholstered. The kind of categorial objectification that takes place through an act of synthesis makes explicit a relation within the thing itself. This relation, being a correlate to objectification, is an object, a categorial object, but it is not real. Although the articulation is grounded in the perceived subject matter, its outcome, the state of affairs itself, is not "a real part or portion of this matter" (HCT, 63). "The being-yellow of the chair, this state of affairs as such, is *not a real moment* in the chair ... This state of affairs is rather of an ideal nature" (HCT, 63; our emphasis). This statement echoes Husserl's claim that "the objective correlates of categorial forms are not 'real' (*realen*) moments" (LI VI, #43). Note also that this further underscores Heidegger's use of Husserl's theory of wholes and parts. Heidegger's analysis is totally dependent upon the concept of moment as presented by Husserl. Like Husserl, he ascertains that the non-real character of the state of affairs does not imply its non-objectivity. Although the expressed state of affairs is not a real part of a given thing, it is a correlate to an act of objectification. It is a relation within the thing itself intuitively grasped through the act of synthesis. Thus, the terms 'real' and 'objective' cannot be used interchangeably.

Rather, by way of understanding what is present in categorial intuition, we can come to see that the objectivity of an entity is really not exhausted by this narrow definition of reality, that objectivity in its broadest sense is much richer than the reality of a thing, and what is more, that the reality of a thing is comprehensible in its structure only on the basis of the full objectivity of the simply experienced entity. (HCT, 66)

In other words, real objectivity only not does not exhaust objectivity in its broadest sense, it is also comprehensible only on the basis of a full sense of objectivity. *It can only be grasped within the framework of ideal objecti-*

vity.

Having investigated the nature of acts of synthesis, let us now turn to the other kind of categorial acts. Acts of ideation are, qua categorial acts, founded acts, but they differ from acts of synthesis in that they do not intend the founding objectivity on which they are based. Whereas an act of synthesis cointends the S and the p when raising the "S is p" into a new objectivity, "the founding objectivity is *not* taken up into the content of what is intended in ideation" (HCT, 67). An act of ideation is the intuition of the universal. This categorial act presents an object and the object thus given is the *idea* or, in Latin, the *species*. The concept of categorial intuition leads us into a philosophical discussion of the nature of universals. Indeed, the very term *intuition* seems to testify to a pre-modern influence on phenomenology. However, we shall see that this pre-modernity is not a product of a philosophical nostalgia but is based on a phenomenological interpretation of modern philosophy. Heidegger's analysis of ideation demonstrates that phenomenology is, in fact, a radical empiricism.[12] Phenomenology agrees that a theory of universals must be based on impressions as long as one remembers that we see more than the empiricists claim we do.

When I perceive simply ... when I see houses, for example, I do not first see houses primarily and expressly in their individuation, in their distinctiveness. Rather, I first see universally: this is a house. This "as-what," the universal feature of house, is itself not expressly apprehended in what it is, but is already coapprehended in simple intuition as that which to some extent here illuminates what is given. (HCT, 67)

When he claims that one sees universally, Heidegger emphasizes that this does not mean that the universal is apprehended in simple intuition. The species is not given in simple intuition but rather is coapprehended. The species is first given as a correlate to an act of ideation, that is, through ideating abstraction "the species house is brought into relief within the multiplicity of individual houses" (HCT, 67). This eidetic abstraction is a founded act in the sense that it starts out from individuations. Heidegger says, "from a multitude of individuations of red I see *the* red" (HCT, 67). Thus, there is no such thing as a free-floating unfounded grasping of the universal. Eidetic abstraction must "be based upon an already given apprehension of individuation" (HCT, 67). At this point one might object that eidetic abstraction exhibits nothing but a psychological disposition. Although we utilize concepts such as 'red,' 'house,' and 'man,' it does not follow that these concepts refer to things in the world. These concepts might be just names we came up with in order to economize communication. Their usage might be

---

[12] This term was originally coined by W. James, but there is a strong affinity between James' radical empiricism and Husserlian phenomenology. See for instance R. Stevens, *James and Husserl: The Foundations of Meaning* (The Hague: Martinus Nijhoff, 1974), 10–21.

nothing but a preserver of habit and custom. We would thus be advocating the position of nominalism: ideas have no ontological status; an idea has no existence except as a word.

Phenomenology agrees with the fact that a concept such as 'red' does not refer to a real object. 'Red,' 'house,' and 'man' refer to the non-sensory, and the non-sensory is not real. But, as we concluded in presenting acts of synthesis, objectivity in its broadest sense is much richer than the reality of a thing. Thus, although the non-sensory is non-real, it does not follow that it is non-objective. Although non-real, ideas might very well enjoy a special kind of objectivity.

To give an adequate account of eidetic abstraction one has to look towards consciousness. After all, eidetic abstraction is an act. But that does not imply that the non-sensory — in this case the universal — should be equated with the mental and thus be given a psychological origin. Phenomenology rejects the tendency to consider consciousness without taking into account the notion of intentionality. If one investigates consciousness according to this notion, one does not approach acts as immanent psychic events, i.e., as objects. Instead one approaches the objects of these acts. Being an objective correlate of an act is being other than consciousness. As a matter of fact, consciousness, qua intentional, does not have an interiority or a circumscribed sphere. Taken as intentional, there is nothing "inner" about consciousness; it is a perspective, an act. Surely, an act considered as an object is an immanent psychic event, but the object of the act is not reducible to an immanent event. The objective correlate of an act directed towards an act is obviously a psychic event, but it would be absurd to claim that the objective correlate of an act directed towards a house, i.e., the house, is an immanent psychological event. Considered as correlates, an act and a house have in common that they are objects, but while the latter has coordinates in space and time, the former has coordinates in time only. The latter is a transcendent object, the former is an immanent object.

What, then, about ideal objects? They have no coordinates in space, neither do they possess temporal properties. They are atemporal and can neither come into existence nor go out of existence. Thus, ideal objects are by definition indifferent to the distinction of immanent and transcendent. This distinction applies to real objects only. But that does not imply indifference to the distinction of objective and non-objective. An ideal object is an object by virtue of being the correlate of an act of ideation.

Whereas an act of synthesis establishes and affirms a relation of unity between sensible givens, acts of ideation establish an ideative relation between a sensible object and its concept. However, for both kinds of categorial acts, the correlate is not a philosophical construct but rather a special kind of objectivity. An act of synthesis makes explicit a relation within the thing itself, that is, it discloses a state of affairs. In so doing it does not construct unity but discloses the simply given object anew as it brings the object into view as complex. Likewise, an act of ideation does not construct the idea; it instead reveals the idea implicitly included in simple apprehension. An act of ideation is, qua founded, by definition not creative. It must be based upon an already given apprehension of individuation. Hence, it does not create something new; rather it allows us to see *anew* the idea itself.

The founded character of acts of ideation differs from the founded character of acts of synthesis in that the former do not cointend the founding objectivities. Thus, being founded does not necessarily presuppose that the founding objectivity is taken up into the content of what is intended in a founded act. But — and this is a crucial point in phenomenology — the key word in the context of foundedness is not the cointention of founding objectivity, but the *disclosing anew* as complex the object given to simple apprehension so that the implicit parts and moments are made explicit. In acts of synthesis this disclosing anew necessarily presupposes the cointention of the founding objectivity. Both the S and the p must be cointended if the "S is p" is to be raised up into a new objectivity. In the case of ideation, the disclosure is based upon a multitude of individuations, of simple apprehensions. The objective, Heidegger states, is "the identical unity red: this objective is not the individuation, this particular red" (HCT, 67). Heidegger offers the following example. Simple apprehension can intend a "this-here or a multiplicity of them in a particular regard: these red balls insofar as they are alike" (HCT, 67). And he continues, "this being-alike can be seen at a glance or can be established in a comparative survey of the balls. But in all these cases the likeness as such is not thematically objective" (HCT, 67). Thus, when simple apprehension intends several red balls insofar as they are alike the "that in-itself with regards to which the balls are compared" (HCT, 67) is not itself expressly apprehended. According to Heidegger, "the to-which of the regard is the ideal unity of likeness as such and not the likeness of the balls as real objects" (HCT, 67). Hence, simple apprehension includes "the ideal unity of likeness as such" in a non-thematic manner.

Each concrete apprehending thus also already includes the ideal unity of the species, although not explicitly as that towards which the regard of comparative consideration looks. (HCT, 67)

This ideal unity of species towards which one looks in such a comparative consideration can be apprehended in its own right through an act of ideation. Thus, an act of ideation is founded in the sense that it needs the foundation of simple apprehension to get started. But the act itself does not have to cointend this founding objectivity simply because the extent of the concrete individuations is arbitrary. "As far as the content of the idea is concerned, it makes absolutely no difference in which concrete objects, in which nuances the red is realized in the particular individuations" (HCT, 67). Even if an act of ideation, qua categorial act, necessarily needs founding objects, it does not itself intend them.

To sum up, then, acts of synthesis and acts of ideation are both founded categorial acts. Each discloses a new objectivity, or more accurately, discloses the given objects anew. Acts of synthesis disclose a state of affairs, a relation within the thing itself, and acts of ideation disclose generality.

8. CONSTITUTION

The founded character of categorial acts opens up a new approach to the concept of constitution. We shall see that this phenomenological concept of constitution has a decidedly Aristotelian flavor to it. It may sound rather strange to relate a modern term like constitution to Aristotle and, of course, we do not claim that Aristotle maintained a concept of constitution. Nevertheless, Heidegger emphasizes the fact that the founded character of categorial acts assures a non-creative notion of constitution which is indifferent to the realism-idealism debate and that is quite compatible with Aristotle's account of knowing.

After qualifying the notion of founded acts by claiming that everything categorial ultimately rests upon sense intuition without thereby being interpretable as sensory, Heidegger makes the following statement:

Everything categorial ultimately rests upon sense intuition, no objective explication floats freely but is always an explication of something already given. The thesis that everything categorial ultimately rests upon sense intuition is but a restatement of the Aristotelian proposition: "The soul can presume nothing, apprehend nothing objective in its objectivity, if nothing at all has been shown to it beforehand." (HCT, 69; Heidegger's own translation of Aristotle's *De Anima*, 431a16f)

Thus, the founded character of categorial acts makes for a notion of the categorial without advocating unfounded or pure grasping of the non-sensory and ideal. The simplicity of simple apprehension and the founded character of categorial acts allows for a notion of the non-sensory and ideal as correlates to acts. Thus, an idea, an essence, has an ontological status; it does not exist merely as a word, but rather as an implicit moment of an objective correlate of simple apprehension that can be made explicit through an act of ideation. There is indeed a certain Aristotelian ring to this notion.

Interestingly enough, Heidegger follows the above reference to Aristotle's

De Anima with a quote from Husserl's LI. "The idea of a 'pure intellect' could only be conceived '*before* an elementary analysis of knowledge in the irrevocable evidence of its composition'" (HCT, 69/LI VI, #60). By thus invoking Husserl, Heidegger maintains that any talk about an unfounded categorial act is simply phenomenologically unsound.

Phenomenology not only rejects traditional empiricism, psychologism, and nominalism; it also disqualifies extreme rationalism as a sound philosophical position. A major problem, however, is that these positions, although in a variety of nuances, were thought to comprise an exhaustive description of possible stances with regard to epistemological questions. They were also thought to be mutually exclusive.

Phenomenology rejects both the exhaustiveness and the mutual exclusiveness of these positions. What characterizes the former is the belief that the simplicity of simple apprehension excludes the complexity of the structure of such an act. According to this position, the objective correlate of simple apprehension is a simple object in the technical sense of not having parts. For this reason it rejects the notion of the non-sensory and ideal as correlates of acts in favor of a notion of its psychological origin. What characterizes the latter, the position of extreme rationalism, is not radically different. If the objective status of the non-sensory and ideal is taken for granted and simple apprehension is considered as nothing but the passive reception of simple objects, it follows that one must stress the importance of unfounded categorial acts. What both positions have in common is a certain way of interpreting sensuousness as *the passive reception of simple objects, of discrete atomic impressions.* The former yields a perverted idealism, the latter a perverted realism.

Phenomenology refuses to take part in the realism-idealism debate. It rejects both positions. Against the former it holds that the world is constituted, against the latter it makes it clear that this does not mean that the world is constructed, made, or fabricated by subjectivity. According to Heidegger, the basis for this position is a phenomenological notion of sensuousness.

Sensuousness is a formal phenomenological concept and refers to all material content as it is already given by the subject matter themselves ... *Sensuousness is therefore the title for the total constellation of entities which are given beforehand in their material content* ... This broad concept of sensuousness is really at the bottom of the distinction of sense and categorial intuition. (HCT, 70)

However, this must not lead one to confuse phenomenology with phenomenalism and sensualism. What Heidegger has in mind when he claims that sensuousness is the title for the total constellation of entities is not sense data. His broad concept of sensuousness is precisely a refutation of the basis of phenomenalism. Heidegger's point is that sensuousness embraces more than what is meant by the concept of sense data. Sensuousness presents objectivity in its broadest sense, a sense that is much richer than the reality of a thing. Moreover, since the reality of a thing is comprehensible only on the basis of this full objectivity, it follows that there is no such thing as a sense datum if by this term one means something like a simple atomic impression.

If one, however, takes it for granted that sensuousness is a matter of passively receiving simple atomic impressions — that is, if one presupposes that the simplicity of simple apprehension entails simple objects — one is forced back into the classical contrast of sense and understanding. And, Heidegger notes, "if one adds to this the conceptual pair of *form* and *matter*" (HCT, 70), one gets the following:

Sensuousness is characterized as receptivity and understanding as spontaneity (Kant), the sensory as matter and the categorial as form. Accordingly, the spontaneity of understanding becomes the formative principle of a receptive matter, and in one stroke we have the old mythology of an intellect which glues and rigs together the world's matter with its own forms. (HCT, 70)

As long as philosophers construe sensuousness as the passive reception of mere sense data, they will, Heidegger claims, fall back on a notion of the non-sensory and ideal categorial forms as constructs of acts. However, a proper analysis of the basic structure of acts and correlates reveals that states of affairs and generality "are not constructs of acts but objects which manifest themselves in these acts" (HCT, 70). "They are not made by the subject and even less something added to the real objects ... Rather, they actually present the entity more truly in its 'being-in-itself'" (HCT, 70). The fact that categorial acts constitute new objectivities must be understood intentionally. What that means can be summed up in the following passage: "'*Constituting*' does not mean producing in the sense of making and fabricating; it means *letting the entity be seen in its objectivity*" (HCT, 71). Thus, categorial acts are not creative; they cannot create anything new. They can only disclose anew something already apprehended. This is because they are founded acts. But they are acts and should be treated accordingly.

The objective of this chapter was to take seriously the later Heidegger's emphasis on the importance of Husserl's concept of categorial intuition for his own reappropriation of the *Seinsfrage*. Husserl's distinction between sensuous intuition and categorial intuition furnishes Heidegger with a ground that is of capital importance for his project. Without this distinction he would have had no access to the appearance of being and thus no way of distinguishing it from the appearance of beings. Hence, there would be no way of establishing the key notion of ontological difference.

In the concluding remarks of the previous chapter we indicated that the investigation of the concept of categorial intuition would reveal how the theory of wholes and parts found its way into Heidegger's phenomenology. At this point we are in a position to conclude that the very foundation of Heidegger's reappropriation of the *Seinsfrage* in fact presupposes an even more foundational distinction, the theory of wholes and parts. There is simply no way of utilizing the concept of categorial intuition without also accepting this theory.

We have seen how the systematic discussion of the concept of categorial intuition leads us to a notion of constitution that is of pivotal importance for seeing the development from Husserl to Heidegger. This ties in with our section on the relation between the theory of wholes and parts and transcendental phenomenology. In the chapters to follow the concept of constitution will be continually discussed, either in relation to the appearance of the constituting entity (in Chapter V) or in relation to the constituted world (Chapter VI). However, before we do that we proceed from the concept of categorial intuition to the phenomenological sense of the apriori. Once again, we shall see that the theory of wholes and parts plays an essential role.

CHAPTER III

APRIORISM

In one of the few explicit references to Husserl's notion of apriori in BT Heidegger makes the following claim:

Edmund Husserl has not only enabled us to understand once more the meaning of any genuine philosophical empiricism; he has also given us the necessary tools. *'A-priorism'* is the method of every scientific philosophy which understands itself. (BT, 75n)

This method is not something new or unrelated to the phenomenological discoveries already discussed. There is an intrinsic relation between apriorism and these discoveries. However, the notion of the apriori introduces a new perspective. Whereas intentionality and categorial intuition refer to the structure of consciousness, apriorism is more of a method than a structure. According to Heidegger, this method belongs to "every scientific philosophy which understands itself." By linking apriorism to the self-understanding of philosophy, Heidegger seems to refer not to phenomenology but to a phenomenology of phenomenology. Apriorism refers to the metaphenomenology carried out when phenomenology reflects on the conditions of its own possibility. That is exactly what marks the transcendental turn in Husserl and in all transcendental philosophy in the Kantian tradition. Recall Kant's characterization of transcendental knowledge as "all knowledge which is occupied not so much with objects as with the mode of our knowledge of objects in so far as this mode of knowledge is to be possible *a priori*" (B25). Though the move from phenomenology to metaphenomenology involves a change of perspective, it is not a radical shift from one kind of philosophy to another. In fact, it is phenomenological analysis itself that necessitates a transcendental turn. A phenomenological analysis of consciousness leads to a concept of constitution which in turn shows that the framework of acts and correlates cannot account for itself but in fact points to a new dimension, to transcendental subjectivity. In other words, through apriorism the fundamental significance of intentionality is disclosed.

As categorial intuition is possible only on the basis of the phenomenon of intentionality having been seen before it, so the *third discovery* [the apriori] to be discussed now is intelligible only on the basis of the *second* and accordingly only on the basis of the *first*. It is first in this way that the sequence of discoveries accounts for itself, and the first manifests its fundamental significance step by step. (HCT, 72)

Hence, whereas categorial intuition is a concretion of the basic constitution of intentionality, apriorism refers to its self-understanding.

Apriorism, we argue, is the unfolding of the theory of wholes and parts in its full range. Undoubtedly, phenomenological apriorism is anchored in the Kantian transcendental tradition in the sense that what it discloses — the apriori — refers not to knowledge of objects, but to the nature of that to which appearances appear. But the vehicle of phenomenological apriorism is not conceptual analysis; it is the theory of wholes and parts. Whereas phenomenology consists in seeing the proper relation between wholes and parts among objective correlates, phenomenology of phenomenology traces the hierarchy of wholes and parts, *abstracta* and *concreta*, to its very origin. This process does not construe the apriori, it discloses it. Thus, Heidegger maintains, "to disclose the *apriori* is not to make an '*a-prioristic*' construction. There is nothing constructivistic about it" (BT, 75n).

We conclude this line of reasoning with the claim that phenomenological apriorism is a method that leads us back to a notion of transcendental subjectivity which is compatible with the notion of constitution as non-creative. Transcendental subjectivity is non-creative because it does not appear temporally prior to what is constituted, like a creator in relation to what is created, but instead it appears *in* constituting activity. A whole does not appear temporally prior to its parts; it appears with the parts. But the whole is still prior in the sense that its parts depend upon it for their being. In other words, it is ontologically prior.

Before considering the full implications of this notion, let us first analyze in more detail the notion of apriorism. We shall first see how Heidegger contrasts the phenomenological sense of the apriori with the traditional sense of this concept. We shall stress how he interprets the apriori, specifically intentionality in its apriori, as *the* topic of phenomenology. This will lead us to the second task of this chapter, which is to reflect on Heidegger's interpretation and critique of Husserl's notion of the phenomenological reduction. We argue that Heidegger makes use of the theory of wholes and parts in his presentation of phenomenological apriorism. We contend that he thus introduces a phenomenon structurally related to what Husserl reaches through the reduction, and hence that his critique of Husserl is mistaken. It disregards a fundamental phenomenological principle emphasized by Heidegger in a different context: the founded character of categorial acts.

1. THE PHENOMENOLOGICAL SENSE OF THE APRIORI

In HCT, under the title *The Original Sense of the Apriori*, Heidegger sets out to characterize more clearly the original meaning of apriorism. He acknowledges the fact that his previous analysis of categorial intuition suggests that phenomenological apriorism is intelligible only on the basis of categorial intuition. However, he still finds it necessary to focus on the apriori itself. One reason for this emphasis is the fact that this term is so "intertwined with traditional lines of inquiry" (HCT, 72); another, and more important one is that "the clarification of its sense really presupposes the understanding of what we are seeking: *time*" (HCT, 72). "The apriori is a term which implies a time sequence [the idea of before and after], although this is left quite vague, undefined, and empty" (HCT, 73). The term 'apriori' clearly refers to something prior. Is this priority to be understood in terms of one object appearing temporally prior to another object, or is the "earlier" of the apriori of a different nature? We shall see that Heidegger argues in favor of the latter and that he discusses the apriori, not as the priority of one object over another, but as the priority of the objectivity over objects or, in his language, of being over beings. In other words, the phenomenological concept of the apriori is closely related to what will later be referred to as Heidegger's notion of ontological difference. However, before investigating Heidegger's own notion of the apriori, let us consider his analysis of the concept of apriori in earlier philosophy.

One way to determine the apriori is to approach it along the lines of what Heidegger refers to as the Cartesian-Kantian tradition. According to this tradition, he claims, "the term apriori has been attributed first and foremost to knowing" (HCT, 73), specifically to a kind of knowing prior to or independent of experience.

> From the interpretation of knowing given by Descartes, apriori knowledge is accessible first and only in the subject as such, insofar as it is self-enclosed and remains within its own sphere. Apriori knowledge is in this way always already included in all knowledge of the real, in all transcendent knowledge. (HCT, 73)

Thus, as Heidegger sees it, the apriori according to this tradition is a knowledge that is prior to or before knowledge of the object. The latter is known as a posteriori knowledge, that is, the knowledge that comes "after the earlier and pure subjective knowing" (HCT, 73). Heidegger concludes these brief comments by characterizing the traditional concept of the apriori as follows: "This concept of the apriori can be broadened to include any subjective comportment as such — whether it be knowing or any other comportment — *before* it oversteps the bounds of its immanence" (HCT, 73).

Obviously, such an interpretation of the apriori is at odds with the fundamental phenomenological position which advocates that the correlate of any kind of subjective comportment is something other than the act. Indeed, according to the phenomenological notion of intentionality, a subjective comportment does not even have an immanence in the sense of an interiority, that is, it is not a container-like entity with bounds that one can step over. Rather, the comportment is the very overstepping itself, so to speak.

Hence, interpreting the 'earlier' of the apriori as a pure subjective knowing prior to knowledge of the world is simply inconsistent with phenomenology. Such a position would presuppose a non-intentional interpretation of consciousness, or at least the hypostatization of a residue of consciousness which would remain non-intentional. These interpretations are effectively precluded by the definition of consciousness as essentially intentional. Thus, although the concept of apriori is of paramount importance for phenomenology, it cannot be understood as earlier in the sense of the appearance of inner knowledge temporally prior to transcendent knowledge. For the same reason, it cannot imply the appearance of transcendent objects prior to subjective acts. Both positions violate fundamental tenets of phenomenology. In phenomenology, the concept of apriori does not imply a classification of appearances into prior and posterior. Rather, as we shall see, it involves a difference between appearances and that to which appearances appear. The prior-character of the apriori is structurally related to the latter. However, before we elaborate on this topic, let us first have a brief look at Heidegger's comments on Kant's use of the apriori.[1]

In spite of his preliminary references to Descartes, Heidegger seems to appoint Kant as the foremost representative of traditional apriorism.

The apriori in Kant's sense is a feature of the subjective sphere. This coupling of the apriori with the subjectivity became especially pertinacious through Kant, who joined the question of the apriori with his specific epistemological inquiry and asked, in reference to a particular apriori comportment, that of synthetic apriori judgments, whether and how they have transcendent validity. (HCT, 73-4)

To counter Kant, Heidegger refers to categorial intuition as something that liberates the apriori from the limits (allegedly) assigned to it by Kant:

Against this [the "Kantian" view delineated above], phenomenology has shown that the apriori is not limited to the subjectivity, indeed that in the first instance it has primarily nothing at all to do with subjectivity. The characterization of ideation as a

---

[1] These comments reflects an interpretation of Kant with which we do not entirely agree. We shall, however, confine our comments on Kant to one section in the following chapter. There we attempt to show that there are reasons to believe that Kant in fact holds the position Heidegger advocates.

categorial intuition has made it clear that something like the highlighting of ideas occurs both in the field of the ideal, hence of the categories, and in the field of the real. (HCT, 74)

Here Heidegger appeals to what was underscored in the treatment of categorial intuition, i.e., to the objective status of ideas. He distinguishes between ideas in the field of the ideal, which was mainly our focus in our investigation of ideational acts, and ideas in the field of the real. The former refer to traditional categories, while the latter refer to sensory universals. About the latter Heidegger claims that

[they] are sensory ideas, ideas whose structure comes from the subject matter's content (color, materiality, spatiality), a structure which is already there in every real individuation and so is apriori in relation to the here and now of a particular coloration of a thing. (HCT, 74)

Both traditional categories and sensory universals are apriori in the sense of being structurally earlier than real appearances. They are not, however, earlier in the sense of appearing temporally prior to real appearances, that is, to transcendent objects. The apriori is not a kind of mental object present in the subject temporally prior to its involvement with the world; that would be incompatible with the fact that ideas are correlates of acts of ideation. But for the same reason the apriori is not a set of structures present temporally prior to subjective involvement. Therefore, Heidegger claims, "the apriori is not only nothing immanent, belonging primarily to the sphere of the subject, it is also nothing transcendent, specifically bound up with reality" (HCT, 74). The priority of the apriori does not concern what objects appear first, immanent or transcendent; it concerns the being or objectivity of the object. Thus, Heidegger argues, "the apriori phenomenologically understood is not a title for comportment but a *title for being*" (HCT, 74).

In order to elucidate these remarks on the apriori let us for a moment go back to our treatment of categorial intuition in the previous chapter. When Heidegger claims that the apriori is a title for being and not for comportment he in fact claims that the apriori can be reduced neither to the *intentio* nor the *intentum*. The apriori is a feature neither of the acts nor of the entities themselves, it is "a feature of the being of the entities" (HCT, 75). Thus, the concept of the apriori takes us beyond the realm of being-identical and beyond the acts of bringing-into-coincidence, to use Heidegger's terms, into the realm of "that which *makes* knowledge *true*" (HCT, 53).

According to Husserl, "the objective correlates of categorial forms are not 'real' (*realen*) moments" (LI VI, #43). Heidegger makes a similar claim when he says that "[t]he being-yellow of the chair, this state of affairs as such, is not a real moment in the chair ... [but] is rather of an ideal nature" (HCT, 63).

However — and this is paramount — the fact that the correlates to categorial acts are not real does not mean they are not objective. Although they are not real parts of a given thing, they are correlates to acts of objectification. Hence, we must again emphasize the distinction between what is real and what is objective. As Heidegger puts it, "by way of understanding what is present in categorial intuition, we can come to see that the objectivity of an entity is really not exhausted by this narrow definition of reality" (HCT, 66). Real objectivity does not exhaust the definition of objectivity in its broadest sense. Categorial intuition shows that "objectivity in its broadest sense is much richer than the reality of a thing" (HCT, 66), so much so that the latter is comprehensible only one the basis of the former, i.e., of full objectivity. According to Heidegger, "the reality of a thing is comprehensible in its structure only on the basis of the full objectivity of the simply experienced entity" (HCT, 66). Hence, real objectivity is a "subset" of the full objectivity given in categorial intuition, that is, full objectivity is prior to real objectivity; it is apriori. We may conclude, then, that the phenomenological sense of the apriori is associated with the full objectivity disclosed in categorial intuition. From this it follows that the apriori is not something subjective in the sense of being a psychological phenomenon. It does not refer to mental content.

We must make it clear that subjective origin does not imply a psychological phenomenon and that the terms 'subjective' and 'psychological' cannot be used interchangeably. While the latter refers to a certain kind of objects, mental or inner objects, the former refers to that to which objects appear. Thus, although a psychological phenomenon is necessarily subjective in the sense that it is an appearance, it would be a category mistake to claim the opposite, i.e., that the subjective sphere is psychological. This is exactly the kind of mistake Husserl accuses the empiricists of making.

The phenomenological sense of the apriori not only reacts to empiricism but also takes aim at rationalism. Just as it is fundamentally mistaken to reduce what is subjective to psychological phenomena, so is it equally wrong to try to disengage the apriori from subjectivity in fear of turning it into a psychological phenomenon. Thus, deep down empiricism and rationalism are not as opposed to each other as one is often led to believe. They both fail to see the correct distinction between subjectivity and the psychological sphere. This occasions a distorted notion of a category as a kind of object, either an immanent object in the sense of a psychological phenomenon or a transcendent object disengaged from subjectivity. Whereas the former refer to a kind of object whose aprioricity is that of appearing prior to the world, the latter refer to objects that appear prior to subjectivity. However, as we have already pointed out, the phenomenological sense of the apriori does not refer to any kind of an object but to the appearance of the object, i.e., to that to which objects appear. In order for something to appear, it follows that that to which it appears must also appear, and it is the latter to which the term 'apriori' refers.

At this point we must address the following question: in what way is that to which appearances appear prior to that which appears? A first response based on the above remarks is that it is not prior to that which appears as one object is prior to another. This is, however, hardly anything but a merely negative determination of the phenomenon in question. In what follows, we undertake a more positive description of the prior-character of the apriori, but this requires some preliminary work. First, we have a look at Heidegger's emphasis on the intrinsic relation between intentionality and the phenomenological sense of the apriori and determination of phenomenology as the analytic description of intentionality in its apriori. Second, we delineate Heidegger's interpretation and critique of Husserl's notion of phenomenological reduction. Third, we will accentuate the importance of the theory of wholes and parts for Heidegger's notion of the apriori. At this point we may begin by focusing on the prior-character of the apriori.

2. ANALYTIC DESCRIPTION OF INTENTIONALITY IN ITS APRIORI

Heidegger emphasizes that the phenomenological maxim "*to the matters themselves*" is a reaction against "construction and free-floating questioning in traditional concepts which have become more and more groundless" (HCT, 76). As we may recall, in discussing the fundamental discoveries of phenomenology, Heidegger accentuates the founded character and non-constructive nature of traditional philosophical concepts. For instance, what is new in the phenomenological concept of categorial intuition is not the idea of apprehending categories but that such acts are founded acts. These acts are not free-floating in the sense that they call for a special capacity. On the contrary, they are to be found in every experience. Likewise, the concept of constitution that arises out of reflections on categorial intuition is not a constructive or creative notion of constitution. The phenomenological return to the matters themselves is a "battle cry against free-floating thought" (HCT, 76). It is not an attempt to do away with traditional philosophical concepts, but rather to provide them with the necessary ground. In this sense the phenomenological maxim is "the principle of *all* scientific knowledge" (HCT, 76). But in order to attempt to lay the foundation for philosophy one must necessarily know the subject matter: "what are these matters to which philosophy must return if it ever is to be scientific" (HCT, 76). According to Heidegger, the phenomenological maxim harbors a double demand.

1) to do research that is autochthonously demonstrative, to provide demonstrations rooted in native ground ... then 2) to arrive at and to secure this ground once more, which is the way Husserl understood his philosophical efforts. (HCT, 76)

While the former is the demand to do demonstrative work, the latter "is the demand to lay the foundation, and so includes the first" (HCT, 76). Hence, as Heidegger sees it, in advocating the necessity of demonstrative work, the phenomenological maxim yields a demand to lay the foundation of this work. The latter is somehow prior to the former in the sense that it includes it. In other words, while the demonstrative work concerns the approach to and knowledge of objects, Heidegger underscores that this presupposes a more fundamental demand of investigating the conditions of doing so. What he in fact is claiming is that the phenomenological maxim demands that phenomenology reflects on the conditions of its own possibility. This claim bears a striking resemblance to a transcendental approach as it is delineated by Kant.

Although the question concerning the subject matter ties in with the traditional way of doing philosophy, Heidegger does not want to address it from a preconceived notion of philosophy. Instead he looks at what phenomenology brings to this topic by examining how "phenomenology and its discoveries have laid open a field of research within contemporary philosophy" (HCT, 76). He concedes that his approach to the phenomenological maxim will contain no deductions from the idea of phenomenology. Instead he will be *"reading the principle from its concretion in the research work"* (HCT, 77).

The concretion is characterized by the discoveries, and now it is only a question of the extent to which they supply content to the formal sense of the research principle: *What field of subject matter, what regard toward it and what mode of dealing with it* are intended? (HCT, 77)

Instead of starting out from an idea of phenomenology, Heidegger intends to specify the phenomenological maxim by investigating the maxim in its concretion. The occurrence of the term 'concretion' in this context is extremely interesting. Is Heidegger using it technically — and, furthermore, in coherence with Husserl's theory of wholes and parts — or is he using it in a looser, more everyday sense? Both, it seems. When Heidegger claims that he will investigate the phenomenological maxim from its concretion in the research work, he is certainly approaching it by focusing upon how it actually appears in this work. On this interpretation, it would seem that Heidegger uses the term 'concretion' in a non-technical and more everyday sense. After all, the phenomenological maxim *to the matters themselves* cannot be investigated any other way than by actually turning to these matters. However, there are also reasons to believe that Heidegger at the same time uses 'concretion' in a technical sense. One reason for making such a claim is the fact that this term is a fundamental technical term in the Husserlian phenomenology which Heidegger discusses on these very pages. Given its importance for Husserl's phenomenology, it would be reasonable to assume that Heidegger would have chosen another term if he did not also have a technical meaning in mind. Furthermore, if he were using it technically but with a different meaning from that of Husserl, it would be equally reasonable to assume that he would call attention to this.

Another and more convincing reason emerges from the way this concrete investigation actually unfolds. Heidegger's reading of the phenomenological maxim from its concretion in research work in fact ends up introducing a *concretum*. His concrete investigation is an endeavor that starts out by investigating how something actually appears and then gradually moves towards an emphasis on the ontological priority of an absolute *concretum*. Heidegger begins with the first sense of the phenomenological maxim and he asks "toward what matters does phenomenology tend?" (HCT, 77). He notes that phenomenology was initially directed towards logic and epistemology but concludes that the important question is the following one:

Do the discoveries — the elaboration of intentionality, of the categorial and the way of access to it, and of the apriori — give us the ground on which the matters of logic can be located and demonstrated? (HCT, 77)

Logic concerns the law of thought, but Heidegger quickly points out that the topic is not thinking taken as a psychic occurrence but thinking as "lawfulness of the object" (HCT, 77). This is fully consistent with Husserl's characterization of phenomenology as the investigation, not of acts as objects, but of the objects of acts. These objects are, Heidegger notes, "meaning, concept, assertion, proposition, judgment, state of affairs, objectivity, fact, law, being, and the like" (HCT, 77). About these objects he asks a series of questions which all point towards a specific conclusion. His first question, "where and as what can and must such objects [the objects of logic] become accessible?" (HCT, 77) sets the tone for the rest. Obviously, from a phenomenological point of view, objects are appearances and an appearance must necessarily have something to which it appears. Like any objects, logical objects become accessible by appearing, and the *where* of their becoming accessible is precisely in the field of appearances. The rest of the questions exhibit the same rhetorical emphasis on the fundamental nature of phenomenology by indicating, as Heidegger puts it, "the real direction of the line of questioning in search for a scientific logic" (HCT, 48). In a conclusion to the series of questions, Heidegger states that "[i]ntentionality now is nothing other than *the basic field* in which these objects are found. [As *intentio* and *intentum*, it is] the totality of comportments and the totality of entities in their being" (HCT, 48). Hence, the investigation of the concerns of phenomenology culminates in the conclusion that intentionality is the basic field in which the objects of phenomenology are found. The apparent circularity of this argument is instructive. It reveals the unfolding of the self-understanding of phenomenology.

As the quest for a return to the matters themselves is made concrete in research work, a notion of intentionality as an absolute *concretum* for its objects emerges. Intentionality is the basic field where these objects are found. They are non-independent parts of this field in the sense that they do not appear outside or independently of it. This is further underscored as Heidegger continues his investigation.

> Now the question is: In the two directions of *intentio* and *intentum*, when the given is either the comportment or the entity in regard to its being, what is it that is structural, what is already there in the given as a structural composition, what is to be found in it as that which constitutes its being? (HCT, 78)

Intentionality is a whole, a *concretum*, for both the *intentio* and the *intentum*. Thus, neither *intentio* nor *intentum* can appear prior to or independently of intentionality. For any given act or object it follows that intentionality is already there. That is, there is something about intentionality that gives the latter an "already-there" character; given *intentio* or *intentum*, intentionality is already there. However, intentionality cannot be prior to *intentio* and *intentum* in the sense that it appears temporally prior to them. That would be absurd. But intentionality still enjoys a status of priority in relation to *intentio* and *intentum*. The latter are what they are because of intentionality. Moreover, neither *intentio* nor *intentum* can provide an exhaustive definition of intentionality. According to Heidegger, it is the nature of this priority that is the true subject matter for phenomenology. That is, "the field of matters for phenomenological research is accordingly *intentionality in its apriori*, understood in the two directions of *intentio* and *intentum*" (HCT, 78). Thus, even if phenomenological investigations were initially investigations in logic and epistemology, the subject matter for phenomenology ends up radically exceeding this framework. A thorough examination puts the matters in the right perspective and shows that a phenomenological investigation does not find its conclusion in comportments and correlates. These structures merely point to a prior whole which is the true foundation of phenomenology. And if the field of investigation for phenomenological research is indeed intentionality in its apriori, we may conclude, according to Heidegger, that the so-called logical comportment of thinking or objective theoretical knowing represents only a particular and narrow sphere within the domain of intentionality, and that the range of functions assigned to logic in no way exhausts the full sweep of intentionality. (HCT, 78)

Intentionality in its apriori status understood as a whole of *intentio* and *intentum* embraces all kinds of acts and correlates and is by no means exhausted by the "logical comportment of thinking or objective theoretical knowing." The latter is a subset of intentionality. Intentionality is the whole of which they are parts, in which they find their foundation.

Phenomenology is not a theory of knowledge in which intentionality is the principle that explains how something immanent can reach out to the transcendent world of objects. Rather, phenomenology seeks the true source of these traditional philosophical concepts in an investigation of intentionality itself. Intentionality, then, is the principle that explains the concepts 'immanent' and 'transcendent.' It shows that these concepts do not refer to two ontologically isolated spheres, that they are not as mutually exclusive and as foundational as often believed. By presupposing a distinction between two ontological isolated spheres, referred to by the terms 'immanent' and 'transcendent,' from the outset we are left with unsurpassable and severely counterintuitive epistemological problems. Phenomenology reveals that the aim is not to bridge this gap but to provide these distinctions with the necessary foundation that can account for them. Interpreted along the lines of *intentio* and *intentum* the terms 'immanence' and 'transcendence' are provided with such a foundation. The guiding principle for this enterprise is always to see the right relation between wholes and parts, *abstracta* and *concreta*, and never to force an *abstractum* into being a *concretum*. That is what laying a foundation is all about — not constructing but disclosing.

Having specified the field of subject matter, Heidegger goes on to discuss "what mode of treatment corresponds to this field" (HCT, 78). He begins by recalling the investigations of categorial intuition and the new sense of the apriori.

The characterization of the apriori as well as the specification of categorial intuition have already shown that this mode of treatment is a simple originary apprehension and not a kind of experimental substructing in which I construct hypotheses in the field of the categorial. (HCT, 78)

Given that apriori is "a *title for being*" (HCT, 74), it follows that the apriori is not a construction but in fact enjoys an objective status. Since it is also "a feature of the being of entities and not of the entities themselves" (HCT, 75), the apriori is not given to sense-perception but is rather a correlate to a categorial act. Obviously, the mode of treatment corresponding to such a field of non-sensory and ideal objects must necessarily reflect this fundamental phenomenological discovery. Thus, Heidegger claims,

> the full content of the apriori of intentionality can be apprehended in simple commensuration with the matter itself. Such a directly seeing apprehension is traditionally called *description. Phenomenology's mode of treatment is descriptive.* (HCT, 75)

We are often told that phenomenology is a descriptive enterprise without also being told what, specifically, 'descriptive' means in this context. In an everyday and vague sense description simply means reporting on what is perceived without adding or withholding any information. If this were all phenomenology means by descriptive, then it would be a rather trivial and unsophisticated endeavor. However, that is not the case. As we may recall, phenomenology underscores that description is not simply a matter of indiscriminately reporting what is perceived. Indeed, phenomenology cautions that such reporting may not in fact be unprejudiced, but may harbor certain metaphysical presuppositions which phenomenology is designed to overcome. Description, according to phenomenology, refers not to any passive report of what takes place, but to a very specific activity. "To be more exact," Heidegger claims, "description is an *accentuating articulation [Gliedern] of what is itself intuited*" (HCT, 75).[2] Description demands a specific kind of participation in both the subjective and objective domains. The former must provide an accentuating articulation, a structuring, but not in some creative sense. What is to be structured is "what is itself intuited" (HCT, 75). Thus, although there is a structuring on the part of the subjective perspective, it is not a free-floating construction. This structuring is a founded activity.

Heidegger uses the term 'accentuating' (*heraushebende*) to characterize the kind of structuring involved in description. Recall that the very same term surfaced in Heidegger's treatment of categorial intuition and that the latter was referred to as an act of accentuating.[3] Thus, description, the mode of treatment corresponding to the field of investigation for phenomenology, is

---

[2] Kisiel's translation of '*Gliedern*' as '*articulation*' is probably motivated by the necessity of distancing Heidegger's phenomenology from idealism. That motivation is also operative in our approach to Heidegger and, indeed, in Heidegger's own approach. Nevertheless, Heidegger chooses to use the term '*Gliedern*' in this context, and it is a matter of fact that this term is more accurately translated by 'structuring,' 'organizing,' or 'classifying.' Hence, this term seems to indicate a more active participation on the part of the subject than what is captured by 'articulation.' Does Heidegger thereby disturb the balance between the subjective and the objective domain? Or contention is that he does not. Rather, he underscores this balance by emphasizing that both domains partake in the descriptive enterprise.

[3] Cf. HCT, 64.

categorial intuition, specifically ideation, for as he says, the "discerning of the apriori is called *ideation*" (HCT, 95). Heidegger goes on to further qualify description by claiming that "accentuating articulation is *analysis*" and hence that "*the description is analytical*" (HCT, 95). Heidegger tends to use 'analysis' to refer to any endeavor attempting to articulate essences, and he concludes that "*Phenomenology is the analytic description of intentionality in its apriori*" (HCT, 79).

3. PURE CONSCIOUSNESS

Heidegger argues that a fundamental problem is left unaddressed in the early development of phenomenological research.

This problem is the basic phenomenological question of the sense of being, a question which an ontology can never pose but already constantly presupposes and thus uses in some sort of answer, grounded or otherwise. (HCT, 91)

The aim of early phenomenology was, Heidegger claims, a relatively circumscribed one. It focused on "the intentional comportments which are essentially theoretical in character" (HCT, 91), and did not attempt "to mark off and bring out the whole [phenomenological] field itself in a basic way" (HCT, 91). Although intentionality was investigated in the two directions of *intentio* and *intentum*, "these two essential structural moments of the basic constitution of intentionality were as such not yet brought to full clarity" (HCT, 91). In other words, one had yet to thematize the *concretum* for these moments and, in the end, to disclose the absolute *concretum*.

This situation changed during the first decade after the publication of Husserl's LI, as phenomenologists started articulating the thematic field of phenomenology. Heidegger's articulation of this field begins by investigating how "the fundamental and explicit elaboration of the thematic field of phenomenology [was] carried out by Husserl" (HCT, 94). He continues, "phenomenology was characterized as the analytic description of intentionality in its apriori. Can intentionality in its apriori be singled out as an independent region, as the possible field of a science?" (HCT, 94-5). The key-word in this passage is "independent region." Can intentionality in its apriori be given as a whole, as an independent region of being? And, we might add, if it can, how is it given? Heidegger's point of departure is what he refers to as Husserl's aim to discover a new scientific domain.

This new region is called the region of *pure lived experiences*, of *pure consciousness with its pure correlates*, the region of the *pure ego*. This region is a new domain of objects and — as Husserl puts it — a region of being which is in principle special, the specifically phenomenological region. (HCT, 96)

In what follows we shall see how Heidegger interprets Husserl's approach to this region. "What is to be seen and traced," he says, "is how the 'new scientific domain' of phenomenology arises from what is given in the natural attitude" (HCT, 95). Heidegger's primary basis for this investigation of how human beings are given in the natural attitude is Husserl's *Ideas I*. According to Husserl, he says, we are given as "real object[s] like others in the natural world" (*Ideas I*, 64). Since "human beings ... occur *realiter* in the world, among them I myself" and "I perform acts (*cogitationes*)" (HCT, 96), it follows that these acts belongs to the same natural reality. And, Heidegger continues, "the totality of such a continuity of lived experiences in the human ... subject can be called an *individual stream of lived experiences*. The experiences are themselves 'real occurrences in the world'" (HCT, 96). Thus, in the natural attitude human being is given as an object among objects, as a real occurrence among real occurrences. In the natural attitude, as described by phenomenology, the focus is on the objects of acts. For something to be given, it must appear, and appearances are objective correlates. In this natural attitude, then, human being is necessarily given as an object.

So far we have distinguished between real and ideal objects as correlates to transcendent perception. However, although real and ideal objects represent an exhaustive division of correlates, transcendent perception does not represent the only field of appearance for such objects. The natural attitude includes another field of appearance, immanence. The difference between these two fields concerns the origin of their objects, that is, the sphere of being to which they belong. Although correlates, objects of transcendent perception are not really contained in this perception the way immanent objects are. The latter belong to the same sphere of being as the acts to which they are given. These objects are given as we direct ourselves towards our own experiential continuity; they are correlates of reflection. "In such acts of reflection we find something objective which itself has the character of acts, of lived experiences, of modes of consciousness of something" (HCT, 96). In reflection, Heidegger claims, "we ourselves are directed toward acts" (HCT, 96).

The peculiar feature of reflection is ... that the object of the reflection, acts, belongs to the same sphere of being as the contemplation of the object ... The object, the contemplated, and the contemplation are *really* [*reell*] included in one another. (HCT, 96)

Immanence is this "unity of the same reality" (HCT, 96), this "inclusion of the apprehended object in the apprehension itself" (HCT, 96). Thus, what distinguishes transcendence and immanence is not that the former harbors real objects and the latter ideal. Real and ideal objects are to be found both in the transcendent sphere and in the immanent sphere. What distinguishes these two spheres is rather the way they harbor their objects. While immanence has "the sense of the real togetherness of the reflected and the reflection" (HCT, 97),[4] transcendent perceptions do not exhibit that kind of unity with their objective correlates.

Thus, the sphere of immanence or lived experience has an essentially different relation to its object than does transcendent perception. Whereas the latter exists "apart from any and all {properly} essential unity with the thing" (HCT, 97),[5] the former does not. "A lived experience can 'only be joined with lived experiences into a whole whose total essences comprises the particular essences of these experiences and is founded on them'" (HCT, 97).[6] The stream of experience can make up a whole only as based on lived experiences; its wholeness must be grounded on the latter. There can be no wholeness of consciousness apart from this. If this whole is to form a unity in the sense of a continuity of experience, it follows that it "is determined purely by the particular essences of the lived experiences" (HCT, 97).[7] It is the parts that make up a whole, and if a whole is to form a unity, its parts must by their very essence render that possible. That is, they must be non-independent parts, i.e., moments. If the parts of the stream of experience were independent parts, pieces, there would be no unity in the sense of continuity of experience. Indeed, there would be no experience. The very fact that immanence constitutes unity implies a certain exclusiveness on its part.

This wholeness of the stream of experience as a self-contained totality excludes every thing, that is, every real object, beginning with the entire material world. Over against the region of lived experience, the material world is other, alien. (HCT, 97)

However, this exclusiveness must not be confused with detachability in the sense that consciousness is a private world detached from the real world. That is not the case. The stream of consciousness is essentially conjoined with the real world, and it is so conjoined in a twofold manner. On the one hand, "consciousness is always a consciousness in a man or animal. It makes up the psychophysical unity of an *animal* which occurs as a given real object"

---

[4] Here Heidegger quotes the following passage from Husserl: "Consciousness and its object {reflection and act as object of reflection} form an individual unity produced purely through lived experiences." *Ideas I*, 79; Heidegger's insertion.

[5] Heidegger quotes this passage from Husserl, *Ideas I*, 80; Heidegger's insertion.

[6] The quote inside this passage is from *Ideas I*, 80.

[7] Again Heidegger utilizes the insights of Husserl's theory of wholes and parts in order to approach the nature of consciousness. He says: "The unity of a whole is after all only one by way of the particular essence of its parts" (HCT, 97).

(HCT, 97). Thus, consciousness is not something detached from the real world, it is essentially tied to it by being a part of animal unity. But, on the other hand, consciousness is also tied to the real world in another way, and this connection is a result of its separation from it or, more precisely, of the distinction between immanence and transcendence.

[T]his separation into two spheres of being is remarkable precisely because the sphere of immanence, the sphere of lived experience, establishes the possibility within which the transcendent world ... can become objective at all. (HCT, 98)

In other words, consciousness is tied to the transcendent world by constituting it. Given this twofold relation between consciousness and the real world, can we still uphold the exclusiveness of consciousness described above? We have shown that this is not a matter of detachability, but have we not gone too far in that regard? Is there still room for such an exclusiveness on the part of consciousness? Heidegger asks:

How can it still be said that consciousness has its 'own essence,' an essence particular to it? That it is a self-contained continuity? How is the drawing out and highlighting of consciousness as an independent region of lived experiences, as an independent region of being, still at all possible? (HCT, 98)

The problem we are facing at this point is maintaining the exclusiveness of consciousness without detaching it from the world. We must uphold a balance in the sense that consciousness must not be reduced either to worldlessness or to world. In the latter case, consciousness would no longer be an independent region of lived experiences. Thus, it would not be a whole and, by the same token, not a unity. The continuity of experience could no longer be accounted for, and the immanent sphere could no longer be regarded as "the possibility within which the transcendent world ... can become objective at all" (HCT, 98). In the former case, objectivity would be equally disturbed. If consciousness is considered a world for itself, essentially detached from the real world, it would follow that the principle of intentionality no longer obtains. Phenomenology would thus have done away with consciousness and also with objectivity. Hence, it is paramount for phenomenology to interpret the exclusiveness of consciousness without disturbing the balance between worldlessness and world. This is Heidegger's aim when he inquires into the essence of consciousness. He starts this endeavor with the following statement:

[W]e have seen that the region of lived experience is specified by the character of intentionality. Because of their intentionality, the transcendent world is in a sense there in the lived experiences. (HCT, 98)

Thus, Heidegger emphasizes phenomenological orthodoxy — the principle of intentionality precludes any treatment of consciousness as a detached, cabinet-like entity. But he goes on to qualify this position. Drawing on Husserl, he distinguishes between directing-itself-towards and apprehension. He says: "just because the transcendent world ... is objective, this is no reason to assume that this is necessarily apprehended" (HCT, 98). Everyday life offers a vast range of acts in which the correlate is not an object in the sense of an apprehended object. There is nothing about the principle of intentionality that suggests that objects must be thematically apprehended. Indeed, most of the objects of everyday activity are not thematized, rather we live directly in them, so to speak.

In order to avoid narrowing down the concept of intentionality, it must be seen that apprehension is not identical with directing-itself-toward. Apprehension is only a very particular and not necessarily even a predominant mode of intending entities. (HCT, 98–9)

If we approach reflection from this angle it follows that, when we are directed upon a specific experience like the perception of a tree in reflection, we are "thematically focused upon the perception and not upon the perceived" (HCT, 99). Reflection is disclosive, not constructive. It cannot install into the act on which it reflects something that was not there in the first place. Thus, since the original act of perceiving the tree was not an apprehension, reflection cannot become thematically aware of the tree when focusing upon this act. If this were the only way consciousness is given, then it seems as if detachability is an accurate description of the nature of this entity. But that is not the case.

I can of course make the perception itself the theme such that the perceived ... is itself co-apprehended, but in such a way I do not *live directly* in the perception, say, of the chair, but rather *live thematically* in the apprehension of the perceptual act and of what is perceived in it" (HCT, 99).

This way of considering the act and its object differs from the notion of reflection outlined above. The difference rests in a change of attitude. In the natural attitude reflection is not carried out in accordance to the phenomenological principle of intentionality. Instead it simply goes along with the concrete perception. The notion of reflection in which the perceived is co-apprehended has abandoned this natural attitude in favor of a phenomenological attitude in which intentionality is the guiding principle. What characterizes this approach, Heidegger claims, is that "I to some extent do 'not go along with' the concrete perception" (HCT, 99).

I do not really live in the perception of the chair but in the attitude of the immanent reflective apprehension of perceiving the chair, not in the thesis of the material world but in the thematic positing of the act apprehending the perception and of its object as it is there in the act. (HCT, 99)

Thus, a phenomenological analysis of acts differs from ordinary reflection in that it does not follow the thematic sense of the act, and this, Heidegger claims, "is called *epoché*, refraining" (HCT, 99). By refraining in this manner, one makes the act itself the theme rather than going along with it. By virtue of this approach one is able to co-apprehend the object of the act.

This implies that the perceived is not directly presumed as such, but in the how of its being. This modification, in which the entity is now regarded to the extent that it is an object of intentionality, is called *bracketing*. (HCT, 99)

Through this approach consciousness is given in a way that precludes detachability.

What we have outlined here in fact echoes Husserl's description of what characterizes phenomenological analysis. There are two ways in which to approach acts of consciousness. One can approach them as immanent psychic events, i.e., as objects, and in this case one does not find the object of this act. An object does not have an object, only acts do. Hence, as soon as one turn an act into an object one loses its original object, that is, one creates an immanence free of transcendence. However, if one investigates consciousness in accordance to the principle of intentionality, one does not approach acts as objects but the objects of these acts.[8] And in that case the situation is entirely different. The sphere now disclosed is not one free of transcendence. Instead, it is one that essentially embraces immanence and transcendence.

Through bracketing the focus shifts from objects to the objectivity or being of objects. But it is not some kind of systematic doubt in which the existence of the world is fundamentally questioned.

This bracketing of the entity takes nothing away from the entity itself, nor does it purport to assume that the entity is not. This reversal of perspective has rather the sense of making the being of the entity present. The phenomenological suspension of the transcendent thesis has but the sole function of making the entity present in regard to its being. (HCT, 99)

Heidegger refers to this reversal of perspective as the first stage in a twofold process called phenomenological reduction. What characterizes this stage,

[8] Recall Heidegger's quotation of Husserl: "*It is not in the reflection upon judgments nor even upon fulfillments of judgments but rather in these fulfillments themselves that we find the true source of the concepts State of Affairs and Being* (in the copulative sense). Not in these *acts as objects*, but in *the objects of these acts*, do we have the abstractive basis which enables us to realize the concepts in question." (HCT, 59/LI, VI, #44)

i.e., the transcendental reduction, is that one still has the same concrete experiential continuity. Although the perspective is reversed it is still one's own stream of consciousness. But, Heidegger notes, "now I do not have it in such a way that I am engrossed in the world, following the natural direction of acts themselves. Now I have acts themselves present in their full structure" (HCT, 99).

The second step in the phenomenological reduction is the eidetic reduction. The target of this reduction is precisely what survived the first reduction, that is, the singularity of our one field of experience.

The acts and their objects now are not studied as concrete individuations of my concrete being, as this stream of experience. Rather, this unity of the stream of experience is now regarded ideatively. (HCT, 99)

Through this reduction individuality is suspended and what is left is the structure of perception or of any other kind of directedness as such, "regardless whether this ... perceiving is mine, regardless whether it takes place in this moment either in this concrete constellation or in another" (HCT, 99). What is left after this double reduction is the *pure field of consciousness*, that is, a field that is no longer individual and concrete.

The basis for the phenomenological reduction is the region of lived experience and that determines the character of pure consciousness. As we remember, what distinguishes the objective correlates of transcendent perceptions from those of immanent perceptions is that the latter are included in the same sphere of being as immanent perception itself. With reference to Husserl, Heidegger claims that this "implies that the object of immanent perception is *absolutely given* [and hence] the stream of lived experience is therefore a region of being which constitutes a sphere of *absolute position*" (HCT, 99). In this context, "absolutely given" means that "the reflection upon acts gives entities whose existence cannot in principle be denied" (HCT, 99). Whereas it is possible for an object of transcendent perception not to be, an object of immanent perception must be. Immanence, i.e., the inclusion of the apprehended object in apprehension itself, represents a unity that does not allow the non-existence of the object. Without the entity there would be no inclusion and hence no immanence. Thus, Heidegger claims, "immanent perception ... gives entities whose existence cannot in principle be denied" (HCT, 99). And, he concludes,

we now see that the sphere of pure consciousness obtained by way of transcendental and eidetic reduction is distinguished by the character of being *absolutely given*. Pure consciousness is thus for Husserl the sphere of absolute being. (HCT, 101)

The phenomenological reduction underscores in a systematic manner a fundamental phenomenological tenet, the distinction between the psychological sphere and the subjective perspective. The former is disclosed through ordinary reflection, the latter is disclosed as reflection is carried out in accordance with the phenomenological principle of intentionality. In the latter case, the subjective perspective, one has secured a ground into which one can inquire without the risk of falling back into psychologism or any of the other reductive strategies phenomenology is designed to overcome.

4. THE BEING OF CONSCIOUSNESS

Having delineated Husserl's phenomenological reduction and his introduction of pure consciousness as a sphere of absolute being, Heidegger sets out to present an immanent critique of phenomenological research. The target of this discussion is the nature of pure consciousness. Heidegger begins by asking whether "this elaboration of the thematic field of phenomenology, the field of intentionality, raise[s] the question of the *being of this region, of the being of consciousness?*" (HCT, 102). According to Heidegger, it does not. Phenomenology has yet to develop a proper apriorism, that is, it has yet to unfold the theory of wholes and parts in its full range. What has been achieved so far has not arrived at the "methodological ground enabling us to raise this *question of the sense of being*, which must precede any phenomenological deliberation" (HCT, 102). For this reason, Heidegger claims, the position delineated above is phenomenologically inadequate. The determinations of being given to pure consciousness do not live up to the full meaning of the phenomenological maxim. Rather they testify to an unstable course with regard to the fundamental principles of phenomenological inquiry.

> Consciousness is plainly identified as a region of absolute being. It is moreover that region from which all other entities (reality, the transcendent) are set off. In addition, this particular distinction is specified as the *most radical distinction in being* which can and must be made within the system of categories. (HCT, 102)

According to Heidegger, then, the determinations of being which Husserl gives to the region of pure consciousness have their origin in positing rather than in description. They do not arise from a regard for the subject matter itself and thus they are not a product of an inquiry guided by the theory of wholes and parts. For this reason, the determinations are not necessarily wrong, but they do not take us to intentionality in its apriori status as a whole.

There are four determinations of being given to pure consciousness.

Heidegger sets out to discuss all four in detail, asking whether they are "determinations of being which are drawn from the consciousness and from the very entity intended by this term?" (HCT, 103). The first determination discussed is the notion of consciousness as an immanent being. Immanence, Heidegger notes, is "not a determination of the entity in itself with regard to its being" (HCT, 103). It is rather a relation between reflection and reflected object that distinguishes itself from transcendent perception and its objects by belonging to the same sphere of being.

> This relation is characterized as a *real in-one-another*, but nothing is actually said about the being of this being-in-one-another, about the "immanent reality" [*Reellität*], about the entity for the whole. (HCT, 103)

Thus, according Heidegger, what is determined by the term immanence is not being but a relation between entities. That is, it stops short of determining the being of consciousness.

The second determination discussed by Heidegger is the notion of consciousness as absolute being in the sense of absolute givenness. The weakness of this determination is the same as the previous one in that it "implies a determination of the region of lived experiences with reference to its being apprehended" (HCT, 104). The focus is not the entity in itself; "what does become thematic is the entity insofar as it is a possible object of reflection" (HCT, 104).

The third determination also concerns consciousness as an absolute being but now 'absolute' is taken in a different sense. This sense concerns constitution.

> Consciousness, immanent and absolutely given being, is that in which every other possible entity is constituted, in which it truly 'is' what it is. Constituting being is absolute. All other being, as reality, is only in relation to consciousness, that is, relative to it. (HCT, 105)

Thus, consciousness is that which constitutes and for that reason is not itself constituted. Or, more accurately, it is constituted but not by another consciousness. Consciousness is a kind of being that constitutes itself and "in constituting itself, itself constitutes every possible reality" (HCT, 105).

> Absolute being accordingly means not being dependent upon another specifically in regard to constitution; it is the first, that which must already be there in order that what is presumed can be at all. Consciousness is the earlier, the apriori in Descartes's and Kant's sense. (HCT, 105)[9]

---

[9] Hence, this notion of consciousness as absolute in the sense of constituting brings us back to the notion of apriori discussed in the first section. The question still remains: consciousness is apriori in the sense that it constitutes objectivity, but in what sense is it prior

The problem with this characterization of consciousness as absolute is that it still does not address the entity itself in its being. According to Heidegger, it rather "sets the region of consciousness within the order of constitution and assigns to it in this order a formal role of being *earlier* than anything objective" (HCT, 105–6; our emphasis). At this point Heidegger sees the danger of an idealistic reading of phenomenology as a result of an inconclusive and phenomenologically inadequate determination of the being of pure consciousness. In short, if consciousness's formal role of being *earlier* is interpreted in terms of being *temporally prior to* the world, this will entail a worldless consciousness.

The last of the four determinations discussed by Heidegger is the notion of consciousness as pure being. This, Heidegger claims, is "even less than the other three a characterization of the being of the intentional, that is, of the entity which is defined by the structure of intentionality" (HCT, 106). Heidegger targets the eidetic reduction and its outcome. The fundamental weakness of this approach is the attempted detachment of consciousness from its concrete individuation in a living being. "[C]onsciousness is called pure to the extent that every reality and realization in it is disregarded. This being is pure because it is defined as *ideal*, that is, *not real* being" (HCT, 106). This suggests, Heidegger claims, that the determination concerns not "the being of the entity which has the structure intentionality, but ... the being of the structure itself as intrinsically detached" (HCT, 106). Heidegger's point is that these determinations of consciousness represent a violation of the phenomenological maxim.

The elaboration of pure consciousness as the thematic field of phenomenology is *not derived phenomenologically by going back to the matters themselves* but by going back to a traditional idea of philosophy. (HCT, 107)

Heidegger here accuses Husserl of falling back into an essentially Cartesian notion of philosophy, thus abandoning the fundamental discoveries of his own endeavor.

However, having underscored that Husserl's determinations are not originary determinations of being, Heidegger makes a statement that can be

to objectivity? In this passage Heidegger seems to give Husserl less credit on the topic of the apriori than he did when he developed his own understanding of this concept. Recall our discussion of Heidegger's analysis of the phenomenological sense of the apriori and compare it to the passage above. On the one hand, Heidegger credits Husserl with the introduction of the original sense of the apriori on which his own project is grounded. On the other hand, he suggests that Husserl interprets consciousness as apriori in the tradition of Descartes and Kant, which is exactly the tradition Heidegger claims had abandoned the original sense of the apriori. In other words, Husserl violated fundamental phenomenological principles or, at best, did not realize the full scope of his own discoveries. The latter view characterizes Heidegger's approach to Husserl on several fundamental phenomenological issues.

taken to indicate that he knows that this was not Husserl's intention at this stage of his analysis.

> If these determinations are not originary determinations of being, then on the positive side it must be said that they only determine the region as region but not the being of consciousness itself, of intentional comportments as such; they are concerned solely with the being of the region consciousness, the being of the field within which consciousness can be considered. (HCT, 108)

This is a very interesting statement in that Heidegger admits that Husserl's aim at this point is not to provide originary determinations of being. These determinations are, he says, "concerned solely with the being of the region of consciousness" (HCT, 108), and thus do not intend to address the more fundamental question of being itself. The interesting question, however, is whether Heidegger thinks of this inquiry as a step in the right direction towards the question of being or whether he in fact thinks it blocks a proper approach to this question. Heidegger seems to hold the latter view, and it is especially the eidetic reduction that is the target of his criticism. As he sees it, the eidetic reduction violates fundamental phenomenological principles and as such it disturbs the unfolding of the theory of wholes and parts in its full range. In short, it disturbs the self-understanding of phenomenology.

With reference to his claim concerning the aim of Husserl's determinations, Heidegger notes that such a "consideration is in fact possible" (HCT, 108). One can inquire into essences without also focusing upon the mode of being of the objects in question. A mathematician, for instance, "can provide a certain definition of the objects of mathematics without ever necessarily posing the question of the mode of being of mathematical objects" HCT, 108).

> Precisely the same way, it can at first be granted with some justification that here the region of phenomenology can simply be circumscribed by these four aspects without thereby necessarily inquiring into the being of that which belongs in this region. (HCT, 108)

Heidegger does not take issue with the fact that this is possible, that is, that one in fact can circumscribe the region of phenomenology without also inquiring into the being of consciousness. Thus, he says, "the final critical position cannot be based upon this initial critical consideration" (HCT, 108). What must be investigated is whether "in the whole of this elaboration of consciousness ... being is explored within it" (HCT, 109).

Heidegger starts this investigation by focusing upon the methodological task of the phenomenological reduction, which is "to arrive at the pure consciousness starting from the factual consciousness given in the natural attitude" (HCT, 109). This is to be accomplished by systematically disregarding the reality of consciousness and any particular individuation. Let us consider Heidegger's appraisal of the first stage in the phenomenological reduction, the transcendental reduction: "We start from the real consciousness in the factually existing human being, but this takes place only in order finally to disregard it and to dismiss the reality of consciousness as such" (HCT, 109). This, Heidegger concludes, "is in principle inappropriate for determining the being of consciousness positively" (HCT, 109). That is, "the sense of the reduction involves precisely giving up the ground upon which alone the question of the being of the intentional could be based" (HCT, 109). The systematic bracketing in which one does "not go along with" the concrete perception in the sense of following its thematic theme but rather makes the act itself the theme is evidently considered an inappropriate method for addressing the question of the being of consciousness. However, this is a view that seems to be somewhat in conflict with the outcome of Heidegger's analysis of categorial intuition outlined in the previous chapter. The dismissal of reality that takes place in the reduction is not a matter of giving up the ground it dismisses. On the contrary, the movement from the natural attitude to the phenomenological attitude is guided by the principle of intentionality. Thus, it is not a movement in which a new sphere is constructed at the cost of the old one. Admittedly, such a movement leaves reality in favor of ideality, but, as we may recall, phenomenology makes specific demands on such acts. Acts through which a non-real or ideal objectivity is disclosed are categorial acts, and these acts are founded. Founded acts cannot detach themselves from founding acts, nor can the correlates of founded acts detach themselves from the correlates of founding acts. Thus, the sense of the reduction does not involve giving up the ground from which it springs. That is effectively precluded by the phenomenological notion of categorial intuition. Indeed, phenomenological orthodoxy prescribes the opposite — the very fact that these acts are founded guarantees that the ground is essentially included and thus secured. Thus, Heidegger's interpretation of the reduction seems to disregard fundamental tenets of phenomenology. This also characterizes his interpretation of the reduction's systematic disregard of any particular individuation of consciousness.

The second stage of the phenomenological reduction is eidetic reduction. An act of ideation discloses generality (constitutes essences) and thus has to disregard individuality.

It disregards the fact that the acts are mine or those of any other individual human being and regards them only in their *what*. It regards the what, the structure of the acts, but as a result does not thematize their *way to be*, their being an act as such. (HCT, 109)

This is an accurate interpretation of ideation. But, according to Heidegger, this occasions a detachment from particular individuation that in fact blocks any phenomenological access to the being of consciousness.

> [I]n the consideration and elaboration of pure consciousness, merely the *what-content* is brought to the fore, without any inquiry into the being of the acts in the sense of their existence. Not only is this question not raised in the reductions, the transcendental as well as the eidetic; it *gets lost precisely through them*. (HCT, 110)

It is in this point that the controversy resides. According to Heidegger, the phenomenological reduction blocks a proper approach to being. Not only is the question not raised; it also gets lost because ideation seeks generality and thus has to disregard individuality.

> [T]his conception of ideation as disregard of real individuation lives in the belief that the what of any entity is to be defined by disregarding its existence. But if there were an entity *whose what is precisely to be and nothing but to be*, then this ideative regard of such an entity would be the most fundamental of misunderstandings. (HCT, 110)

What Heidegger has in mind is the fact that the being who constitutes essences cannot itself have a *what* in the ordinary sense of this term. It does not follow, however, that one cannot disclose generality of this being. Evidently Heidegger accepts the latter. How else could he refer to this being as an entity "*whose what* [i.e., essence] *is precisely to be and nothing but to be?*" (HCT, 110; our insertion).[10] But the generality pertaining to the constituting being does not have its origin in its being constituted by another consciousness. Thus, the *what* of this being does not spring out of the being of another consciousness, but out of its own being.

As Heidegger sees it, this discovery is exactly what is missed by the emphasis on ideation. He maintains that ideation in regard to this being represents a fundamental misunderstanding and concludes that it will "become apparent that this misunderstanding is prevalent in phenomenology, and dominates it in turn because of the dominance of the tradition" (HCT, 110). We argue that this conclusion is mistaken. Heidegger seems once again to disregard the fact that ideation is a founded act. Admittedly, it differs from other categorial acts by not co-intending the founding objectivity, but it is nevertheless a founded act. This point is emphasized by Heidegger in his treatment of categorial intuition. While acts of synthesis disclose state of affairs or relations within the things themselves, acts of ideation disclose

---

[10] Also bear in mind that the aim of the published part of BT is an inquiry into the essence of Dasein. Although this essence is existence, it refers to a structure that everyone that is Dasein shares.

generalities. But since ideation is a founded act, this generality is not something detached from the founding objectivity, even if it does not cointend this objectivity. This is precisely the strength of the phenomenological concept of ideation. Thus, Husserl's eidetic reduction does not introduce a structure that is intrinsically detached from the being of the entity which has this structure even if this being is not cointended.

Heidegger is surely correct in maintaining that the question of being is not yet raised in the reductions, but he is mistaken in his claim that it gets lost through the reductions. The ground upon which the being of the intentional could be based is essentially included and thus secured in the reductions. Moreover, it is secured in a way that renders an inquiry into this being possible without falling back into psychologism.

Heidegger's claim that Husserl's determinations "are attributed to [consciousness] insofar as this consciousness is placed in a certain perspective" (HCT, 108), and thus are not determinations of the being of the entity itself, is not necessarily wrong. What is wrong is the suggestion that Husserl, through these determinations, actually attempted, unsuccessfully, to provide an originary determination of being. These determinations are not meant as the final characterization of the being of pure consciousness. Heidegger neglects to mention that Husserl does address the being of pure consciousness in his analysis of time, and that Husserl describes its being through temporal metaphors. According to Husserl, the ground must first be secured in a way that allows for a phenomenological inquiry into the being of consciousness. That is, it must be subjected to the fundamental principle of phenomenology: intentionality. Only then can one approach the being of this entity without the risk of reintroducing the reductive strategies phenomenology is designed to overcome. Having secured the ground, Husserl does provide a temporal characterization of the being of pure consciousness. Indeed, Heidegger's characterization of the being of Dasein in the second division of BT bears strong resemblance to Husserl's own description.

In order to argue in favor of this interpretation we must proceed step by step. Let us first consider how Heidegger's critique of Husserl's phenomenological reduction in fact hides a deeper agreement between the two philosophers. This agreement consists in regarding apriorism as the unfolding of the theory of wholes and parts in its full range. Heidegger never explicitly admits to this, but a close reading of his presentation of the problem exhibits quite unambiguously that this is a fact. We shall see that Heidegger's analysis and critique of Husserl's phenomenological reduction must be considered as having more of a rhetorical nature than one is often led to believe.

5. A PRIORI AND *CONCRETUM*

In our first chapter we called attention to the intrinsic relation between the theory of wholes and parts and transcendental phenomenology by pointing out that this theory harbors a notion of consciousness as the only absolute concretion. We also pointed out the presence of Husserl's theory of wholes and parts in Heidegger's *Daseinsanalytik*. Finally, we indicated that this presence was motivated by the importance of this theory for the peculiar approach to the *Seinsfrage* in BT.

The task of BT is "to work out the question of *Being* and to do so concretely" (BT, 19). However, the concrete working out of the question of Being must be preceded by an analysis of human being. We must, as Heidegger puts it, "make a being — the inquirer — perspicuous in his own Being" (BT, 27). But one may ask why it is necessary for Heidegger to make this detour. Why not proceed directly to Being itself? The reason for this procedure is to be found in the treatment of categorial intuition. The concept of categorial intuition underscores the objective status of Being, that is, it leads directly to Being itself as something other than human being. Thus, the concept of categorial intuition renders possible a direct approach to Being by emphasizing its objective status. In so doing it also makes Being a correlate and hence one is inevitably confronted with human being. In other words, the concept of categorial intuition furnishes us with an access to Being which in turn throws us back to the subjective perspective. It is the direct approach to Being itself thematized through the concept of categorial intuition that discloses the necessity of preceding the question of Being with an analysis of human being. In short, the importance of Husserl's concept of categorial intuition for Heidegger's *Seinsfrage* consists in showing that Being has objective status but that it also cannot be disengaged from human being.

This insight, however, presupposes the theory of wholes and parts since the objective status of Being is secured by showing that the non-sensory and ideal are moments of the objective correlates of straightforward perception. By taking over this insight Heidegger borrows much more than Husserl's concept of categorial intuition. He also takes over the formal structure operative in this discovery and thus places the theory of wholes and parts at the very foundation of his own approach to the *Seinsfrage*. For this reason it is hardly surprising that the terminology of this theory surfaces in Heidegger's *Daseinsanalytik*.

Heidegger refers to the analysis of human being as a "concrete disclosure of Dasein" (BT, 358) which will seek a "concrete understanding of the basic constitution of Dasein" (BT, 446). Thus, a concrete analysis of Being must be preceded by a concrete analysis of Dasein. In the first division of BT,

Heidegger begins this concrete analysis of Dasein with an analysis of Being-in-the-world as the basic state of Dasein. As we may recall, Heidegger makes a claim about this expression that testifies to the presence of Husserl's theory of wholes and parts.

> The compound expression 'Being-in-the-world' indicates the very way we have coined it, that it stands for a *unitary* phenomenon. This primary datum must be seen as a whole. But while Being-in-the-world cannot be broken up into contents which may be pieced together [*zusammenstückbare Bestände*], this does not prevent it from having several constitutive moments in its structure [*konstitutiver Strukturmomente*]. (BT, 78; translation altered)

The presence of the terminology of Husserl's theory of wholes and parts in this section is undeniable. Dasein, qua Being-in-the-world, is a unitary phenomenon which must be understood as a whole. This whole can consist of parts, but not separable pieces. This whole is not a product of parts in the sense that the parts precedes the whole. On the contrary, the whole is a primary datum composed of non-independent parts, i.e., moments.

A comparison between this quote and a statement made about ten pages earlier in BT reveals that the theory of wholes and parts, the interpretation of Dasein as Being-in-the-world, and the phenomenological sense of the apriori are intrinsically interrelated. "In the interpretation of Dasein this structure [Being-in-the-world] is something '*apriori*;' it is not pieced together, but is primordially and constantly a whole" (BT, 65). According to Heidegger, then, the apriori is a primordial whole, and a primordial whole is something that can only consist of a certain kind of parts, *moments*. It follows that the nature of the apriori, its prior-character, must be interpreted along the lines of a whole's priority over its non-independent parts. Just as the whole is prior to its moments in the sense that the latter depend on it for their appearance, so the apriori is prior to appearances. According to this analogy, the apriori is not prior in the sense that it appears as temporally prior to or before appearances. A whole does not appear independently of its parts. It appears along with the parts.

Is this just an analogy? Does the apriori merely have a structure similar to that of a whole, or does Heidegger in fact claim that the apriori *is* a whole? The above quotes seems to marshal evidence in favor of the latter possibility. In what follows, we further substantiate this claim by exposing the intrinsic relation between Heidegger's notion of the phenomenological sense of the apriori and what Husserl refers to as absolute *concretum*.

First let us investigate whether any kind of a whole is apriori or whether this term must be reserved for a specific kind of whole. Consider the following passage:

The question of Being aims therefore at ascertaining the *a priori* conditions not only for the possibility of the sciences which examine entities as entities of such and such type, and, in so doing, already operate with an understanding of Being, but also for the possibility of those ontologies themselves which are prior to the ontical sciences and which provide their foundations. (BT, 31)

According to Heidegger, then, the term apriori refers not to any kind of wholes, but to those that are conditions of possibility. Thus, we can exclude as apriori those wholes that do not enjoy such a status. Heidegger also excludes the apriori conditions captured through the development of regional ontologies, that is, "the apriori conditions for the sciences which examine entities as entities of such and such type" (BT, 31). Analysis of these conditions is not Heidegger's aim. Heidegger's project is more closely related to that of Aristotle in the *Metaphysics* in the sense that he seeks to develop a science, not of Being qua quantity, motion, or anything else, but of Being qua Being. Thus, Heidegger seeks to develop an ontology of the "ontologies that are prior to the ontical sciences and which provide their foundations" (BT, 31), that is, a fundamental ontology.

This hierarchy of ontical sciences, ontologies which provide their foundations, and the apriori conditions for the possibility of these ontologies seems to follow the same logic as does Husserl's transcendental turn. In LI Husserl distinguishes between '*abstractum*' and '*concretum*' and between 'absolute *concretum*' and 'relative *concretum*.' We may recall that, for Husserl, *abstractum* means the same thing as moment and a *concretum* is that of which an *abstractum* is a part. However, only absolute *concreta* — those *concreta* that are abstract in no direction — are wholes. The fundamental distinction for this hierarchy of *abstracta* and *concreta* is between independence and non-independence. This distinction is also at work in Heidegger's classification of different levels of ontologies. Ontical sciences are dependent upon regional ontologies because the latter provide the foundation for the former. Regional ontologies, in turn, are dependent upon a higher level ontology made possible by the question of Being which aims at ascertaining the apriori conditions for the regional ontologies. This higher level ontology is a *concretum* for the regional ontologies, and the regional ontologies are *concreta* for the ontical sciences. But while the regional ontologies are concrete in one direction, they are abstract in another and thus not absolute *concreta*, that is, they are not wholes. According to this hierarchy, then, only the apriori dimension revealed by the question of Being qualifies as an absolute *concretum*.

Heidegger's notion of the apriori clearly refers to those wholes that are abstract in no direction, that is, to absolute *concreta*. But where are such wholes located? According to Husserl, there is only one absolute *concretum*: pure consciousness. Absolute or pure consciousness is essentially independent in that "it need[s] [no] worldly being for its existence" (*Ideas I*, 116). This echoes a passage in LI where Husserl, while discussing the nature of independence and non-independence, claims that no object is independent in the sense that it can be torn from the unity of consciousness. Objects are not independent and non-independent in themselves but only in so far as they *appear* one way or the other.

To what extent can we claim that Heidegger makes a similar move? We have concluded that his notion of apriori refers to an absolute *concretum*, but we have yet to determine where this whole is located. In what follows, we attempt to provide a textual basis for the claim that Dasein is structurally related to Husserl's notion of pure consciousness because both refer to subjectivity, that is, to that to which appearances appear. In this sense they are both absolute *concreta* in relation to reality.

Let us begin this inquiry by discussing two passages in Heidegger that at first glance seem to falsify such a thesis. In BT Heidegger makes the following statement about the nature of the apriori: "This term [*a priori*] does not mean anything like previously belonging to a subject which is proximally still worldless" (BT, 146). In 1943 he makes another, similar observation: "Any attempt ... to rethink *Being and Time* is thwarted as long as one is satisfied with the observation that, in this study, the term 'being there' [Dasein] is used in place of 'consciousness.'"[11] We shall see, however, that neither of these quotes are inconsistent with our claim about the structural isomorphism between Dasein and pure consciousness. The first quote is perfectly compatible with an earlier reference on which we based our claim about such an isomorphism. What Heidegger maintains is that the apriori is not something that belongs to a worldless subject. This is fully consistent with the claim that "in the interpretation of Dasein this structure [Being-in-the-world] is something *'apriori'*" (BT, 65). It is Being-in-the-world that is apriori, not worldlessness.

The second quote seems, however, to pose a more difficult problem for our thesis. Here Heidegger unambiguously asserts a fundamental incompatibility between the terms 'Dasein' and 'consciousness.' But in what sense does Heidegger use the term consciousness in this context? In BT Heidegger often uses the term 'consciousness' in order to refer to certain ways of thinking about consciousness from which he seeks to distance himself. According to

---

[11] Heidegger, "The Way Back Into the Ground of Metaphysics" in *Existentialism from Dostoevsky to Sartre*, edited by W.Kaufmann (New York: Meridian Books, 1957), 270–1. The reason we mention this passage is the fact that it is often quoted by scholars who seek to underscore the fundamental difference between Husserl and Heidegger. See for instance Dreyfus *Being-in-the-world*, 13.

Heidegger, what characterizes these positions is the interpretation of consciousness as a cabinet-like interiority[12] or as a thing-like entity.[13] In other words, Heidegger often uses the term 'consciousness' in order to refer to a non-intentional interpretation of consciousness.[14] In that sense, the term 'consciousness' is obviously not an adequate translation of Dasein. This is an argument in favor of our thesis.

Recall from our previous chapter how Heidegger takes issue with the tendency to consider consciousness without taking intentionality into account. This, he claims, "was the typical way of considering it before" (HCT, 59). Here Heidegger emphasizes the need to look towards consciousness in order to achieve an accurate appreciation of Husserl's notion of categorial intuition. This presupposes that one is investigating consciousness in accordance with the concept of intentionality. Given the importance of categorial intuition for Heidegger's project, it seems plausible that the term 'Dasein' is introduced in order to counter a non-intentional notion of consciousness. It seems equally plausible that it is the substitution of the latter for Dasein that thwarts the understanding of BT.[15] When Heidegger claims in BT that "the intentionality of 'consciousness' is *grounded* in the ecstatical temporality of Dasein" (BT, 414n), he may be taken to imply that Dasein is the *concretum* for the appearance of correlates. Remember that Heidegger characterizes the peculiar nature of the phenomenological concept of intentionality as one which emphasizes a focus not on acts as objects, but on the objects of acts.[16] Thus, for Heidegger, the term 'intentionality of consciousness' refers to the latter. Hence, his claim that this is grounded in Dasein does not seem to introduce anything radically incompatible with Husserl's transcendental phenomenology. Like Husserl's notion of absolute consciousness, the term 'Dasein' refers solely to the being we ourselves are, that is, to human being. What characterizes both entities is that they are wholes in relation to which reality is a moment.

Having underscored that Heidegger's references to the incompatibility of the terms 'Dasein' and 'consciousness' do not falsify the suggested isomorphism between Dasein and Husserl's notion of absolute consciousness, let us turn now to a closer description of the relation between the apriori and

[12] Cf. BT, 89.

[13] Cf. BT, 150.

[14] Heidegger often uses the term consciousness in order to refer to a worldless *res cogitans*, see BT, 75, 246, 251.

[15] However, one should remember that the passage in question came along almost 20 years after was BT written and that Heidegger at this point had gone through a lot of changes. It falls beyond our thesis to discuss the development of Heidegger's thinking from 1926 to 1943 but our point is that this quote does not necessarily indicate that every concept of consciousness is incompatible with the term Dasein in BT.

[16] Cf. HCT, 59, and Heidegger's reference to Husserl's LI, VI, #44.

subjectivity. In discussing the spatiality of Being-in-the-world, Heidegger makes some comments on Kant that also display his own notion of the apriori.

> He [Kant] merely wants to show that every orientation requires a 'subjective principle.' Here 'subjective' is meant to signify that this principle is *a priori*. Nevertheless, the *a priori* character of directedness with regard to right and left is based upon the 'subjective' *a priori* of Being-in-the-world, which has nothing to do with any determinate character restricted beforehand to a worldless subject. (BT, 144)

Let us focus not upon Heidegger's interpretation of Kant in this passage but rather upon his conception of the apriori. He claims that Kant's use of the term 'subjective' in 'subjective principle' is meant to signify that the principle is apriori, that is, that subjective means apriori. He agrees with this point but he still wants to distance himself from what he considers a fundamental weakness in Kant, namely the interpretation of the apriori as something belonging to a worldless subject.[17] The key phrase is to be found in the last sentence. Let us begin with the first part of this sentence which reads "the *apriori* character of directedness ... is based upon the 'subjective' *a priori* of Being-in-the-world" (BT, 144). Here Heidegger makes it clear that the apriori is something that arises out of the basic state of Dasein.[18] Thus, the apriori is subjective in the sense that it belongs to Dasein, but for the very same reason it "has nothing to do with any determinate character restricted beforehand to a worldless subject" (BT, 144). In other words, Being-in-the-world characterizes a new kind of subjectivity. It is still the origin of the apriori and has still apriority in relation to the world, but this kind of priority must not be understood along the lines of worldlessness but rather in terms of the whole's priority over its moments, i.e., as something that appears not before but rather with its moments. This view is reflected in a rhetorical question Heidegger asks himself in a lecture held after the publication of BT: "The world is only insofar as Dasein exists. But then is the world not something 'subjective?' In fact it is. Only one may not at this point reintroduce a common, subjectivistic concept of 'subject'" (MFL, 195). Thus, Dasein is a subject but not in the common subjectivistic concept of this term. According to Heidegger, the common notion of subjective is something worldless, something given prior to the appearance of the transcendent world. In this sense Dasein is not a subject. But Dasein nevertheless designates the subjective perspective in the phenomenological sense of this term. Dasein is in the world but is still something apriori. It is worldliness that characterizes

---

[17] In Chapter V we challenge this interpretation of Kant.

[18] Not only is the basic state of Dasein apriori, it is, Heidegger says, necessary apriori. "Being-in-the-world is a state of Dasein which is necessary *a priori*" (BT, 79).

Dasein and this worldliness is characterized by having a measure of primacy over the world. Dasein is given with the appearance of the world in the way that a whole is given with the appearance of its moments.

According to Heidegger, the topic of phenomenology is the interpretation of intentionality in its apriori. The vehicle of such an interpretation is the theory of wholes and parts. Apriorism is the unfolding of this theory in its full range. In Husserl the phenomenological reduction is a means to achieve this goal. While the first step of the reduction, the transcendental reduction, is designed to disclose an absolute *concretum*, the second step, the eidetic reduction, is designed to elicit an investigation of the nature or essence of this prior whole.

Bringing the apriori into view is a categorial act. Heidegger admits to this by using the term 'accentuating' (*heraushebende*) in order to refer to the description of intentionality in its apriori. For Heidegger, categorial intuition is an act of accentuation. Given the fact that this accentuating is done in accordance with the theory of wholes and parts, it follows that Heidegger is in fact carrying out a transcendental reduction. He has disclosed a prior whole that seems to be structurally related to what Husserl calls pure consciousness. This entity is constituting insofar as it is an absolute concretion. It is a whole which is abstract in no direction, and thus it is that entity upon which all other entities are dependent. It is itself prior and independent of all other entities, but not in the sense of appearing independently before objects. It is prior in the way a whole is prior to its parts.

The problem facing us has to do with the appearance of this entity. If it is apriori in the way a whole is prior to its parts, it follows that it must appear. If it appears, it must somehow appear to itself. Constituting being cannot be constituted by another consciousness. In other words, nothing less than the problem of self-consciousness is at stake at this level of phenomenological inquiry; what is the nature or essence of this constituting entity? Our essence is to constitute essences, and by doing so we constitute ourselves. Or, more accurately, we constitute, in constituting ourselves, every possible reality.

In what follows we elaborate on this self-constitution or self-appearance and we shall see that Heidegger seeks to give an eidetic description of this entity as he inquires into the essence of Dasein. His aim is to disclose a structure that every Dasein shares. We shall see, therefore, that Heidegger's approach requires both a transcendental and an eidetic reduction.

CHAPTER IV

EXISTENCE

Heidegger's emphasis on phenomenology as the analytic description of intentionality in its apriori determines the task of phenomenology as that of inquiring into the being of that entity which constitutes itself and, in so doing, also constitutes reality. In Heidegger's terminology this entity is known as Dasein, and what characterizes Dasein is existence.

Heidegger criticizes Husserl's approach to this entity, noting that it is one thing to determine its distinctive character, another to inquire into its being. A constituting entity cannot be fully determined by disclosing its essential properties in the same way that one determines constituted entities. Such an endeavor must necessarily fail because its focus is so set on the properties that it will not be able to capture the determining activity itself, i.e., what characterizes the constituting entity. A constituting entity cannot be determined, qua constituting, with reference to constituted properties.

We have argued that the fourfold determination of consciousness that Heidegger finds in Husserl's approach is not an accurate interpretation of Husserl's final determination of the being of consciousness. For Husserl, the reduction is a step towards the determination, but not the final one. The final determination of the being of the constituting entity takes place in the delineation of the temporal constitution of transcendental subjectivity. It is our contention that a similar step-by-step approach to subjectivity is at work in Heidegger's existential analytic. In this chapter we focus upon the first stages of this process and the *Leitmotif* will be Heidegger's determination of Dasein as existence. First we investigate the structure of Heidegger's approach to Dasein, and we argue that the phenomenological reduction is fully at work in Heidegger's analysis. Having underscored this point, we shall have a look at Heidegger's use of the concepts 'Dasein' and 'existence' and we show (i) that Dasein refers to human being; (ii) that existence is an essential determination of the being of Dasein; (iii) that existence thus refers to a kind of being that all things that are Dasein share insofar as they are Dasein; and (iv), that existence refers to Dasein alone. Hence, Heidegger undoubtedly brackets individuality in favor of generality in his approach to the being of the constituting entity.

After clarifying this point we investigate the being of this entity. Although Heidegger does not define Dasein as a substance with certain properties, he does call attention to certain aspects that constitute the being of Dasein. These aspects are introduced as existentials and they differ from properties or categories in that they are not to be understood as modifications of a substance. Existentials are structural moments and they are related to the being of Dasein the way moments are related to a whole. Hence, it follows that Dasein cannot be thought of as an entity whose being can be considered apart from these structural moments. Admittedly, the being of Dasein is something "more" than these existentials, but it is not thereby something other in the sense that it can appear independently of them. It is something "more" in the sense that it is not merely the sum of these existentials, it is the unity of them. A unity, however, cannot precede its parts. It can be ontologically prior to them, but it can still only appear with its moments.

The two major existentials are situatedness (*Befindlichkeit*) and understanding (*Verstehen*). These structural moments are united in the phenomenon of care (*Sorge*) which designates the being of Dasein. This phenomenon is the ground sought by Heidegger's existential analytic, and although he will offer a temporal reinterpretation of it, he does not transcend it. His analysis of temporality does not introduce a new phenomenon but rather is designated to provide the full meaning of care. In other words, in Heidegger, just as in Husserl, the final determination of the being of the constituting entity takes place in the temporal delineation of it.

1. PHENOMENOLOGICAL REDUCTION AND THE ANALYSIS OF DASEIN

Heidegger emphasizes the necessity of making "an entity — the inquirer — transparent in its own being" (BT, 27) in order to carry out the task of inquiring into Being. "This entity which each of us is himself and which includes inquiring as one of the possibilities of its Being, we shall denote by the term '*Dasein*'" (BT, 27). Hence, 'Dasein' refers to individual persons and not, as some interpreters have suggested, to institutions. J. Haugland is one well-known advocate of the latter position. He seeks to disassociate 'Dasein' from individual human being by claiming that it refers to social institutions.[1] Although he modifies this view somewhat in a later article[2] that reserves the term Dasein for human beings, he still argues against interpreting Dasein as an individual person and claims that Dasein is a "way of life" while individual

---

[1] J. Haugland, "Heidegger on Being a Person" *Noûs*, Vol. XVI, March 1982, 15-26.

[2] J. Haugland, "Dasein's Disclosedness," *The Southern Journal of Philosophy*, Supplement, Vol. XXVIII, 1989, 52-73.

human beings are instances of Dasein. C. Guignon similarly claims that Dasein is not equivalent to man or human being.[3] H. Dreyfus[4] acknowledges this line of interpretation as a "well-motivated and well-argued corrective to the almost universal misunderstanding of Dasein as an autonomous, individual subject" (Dreyfus, 14), though he admits that Haugland's interpretation "runs up against many passages that make it clear that for Heidegger Dasein designates exclusively ... individual persons" (Dreyfus, 14).[5]

Heidegger himself, however, is quite clear on this topic. Dasein is not an institution or a network of social norms within which the individual person is a more or less unresisting placeholder. Dasein is a person; a subject of action. Admittedly, in BT Heidegger for the most part avoids using the term 'subject' as a translation of Dasein, but he nevertheless emphasizes that it is subjectivity that is at the center of his attention. For instance, he claims that his analytic of Dasein in a Kantian language might be described as "a preliminary ontological analytic of the subjectivity of the subject" (BT, 45). If we go to his lectures from this period we will, however, see that Heidegger is considerably more at ease with introducing the concept of subjectivity into his existential analytic. For instance, in BP he says that

Being-true is unveiling, unveiling is a comportment of the ego, and therefore, it is said, being-true is something subjective. We reply, 'subjective' no doubt, but in the sense of the well-understood concept of the 'subject', as existing Dasein, the Dasein as Being-in-the-world. (BP, 216)

Likewise, in MFL Heidegger identifies Dasein with a concept of subjectivity

---

[3] C. Guignon, *Heidegger and the Problem of Knowledge* (Indianapolis: Hackett Publishing Company, 1983): "[T]he technical term 'Dasein' cannot be taken as shorthand for 'human being' as this term is generally used" (104).

[4] H. Dreyfus, *Being-in-the-world* (Cambridge: The MIT Press, 1991). Hereafter Dreyfus.

[5] Dreyfus' adherence to a non-individual approach to Heidegger arises out of a fear of distorting Heidegger's ideas by interpreting Dasein as a conscious subject. It will, however, be our contention that this fear is in conflict with the very phenomenological principles on which Heidegger bases his project. According to Dreyfus, the interpretation of Dasein as a conscious subject implies seeing it as a worldless entity — an "I" given prior to and independently of the world — and hence, one would in fact end up identifying Heidegger with the very position he criticizes. However, it does not at all follow from an intentional interpretation of consciousness that subjectivity is worldless. On the contrary, According to phenomenological orthodoxy, a conscious subject is essentially and exhaustively characterized by intentionality. That is, there is, according to this principle, no non-intentional residue of consciousness or subjectivity withholding from intentionality. Thus, there is no "inner" worldless subject prior to its involvement with the world. Rather, subjectivity comes into being with its engagement with the world. In what follows, we underscore this point by showing that a notion of self-consciousness coherent with phenomenological principles is a self-directedness that essentially involves the world.

that is not synonymous with "a common, subjectivistic concept of 'subject'" (MFL, 195). And in his last lecture in Marburg, *Einleitung in die Philosophie*,[6] Heidegger explicitly says that "Dasein is nothing other than what we have already called 'subject;' subject, that which relates to objects the way we have explained" (EP, 72).[7] However, although Heidegger makes clear that Dasein is a subject,[8] we shall see that he emphasizes that it is not thereby a worldless subject.

Heidegger maintains that the objective of his ontological analytic is to exhibit essential structures.

[T]here are certain structures which we shall exhibit — not just accidental structures, but essential ones which, in every kind of Being that factical Dasein may possess, persist as determinative for the character of its Being. (BT, 38)

This exhibition of essential structures takes its point of departure in what Heidegger refers to as average everydayness (*durchschnittlichen Alltäglichkeit*).[9] This is fully coherent with the phenomenological principle of presuppositionlessness, of staying away from constructions. Instead of starting out from a notion of subjectivity that is already on the level of philosophical reflection and thus making certain metaphysical presuppositions, Heidegger emphasizes the comportment of everyday life as the point of departure. One should not let the terms 'average' and 'everydayness' overshadow what Heidegger is in fact saying, though. Recall that Heidegger warns against, not looking to subjectivity or consciousness in order to ground what is non-sensory and ideal, but of doing so without taking intentionality into account. Thus, Heidegger does not reject consciousness as such as a starting point for an analysis of subjectivity. On the contrary, in maintaining

---

[6] GA, 27 (Frankfurt am Main: Vittorio Klostermann, 1996). Hereafter EP.

[7] EP, 72 (our translation). The original reads: "Das Dasein ist aber nichts anderes, als was wir bisher 'Subjekt' nannten, Subjekt, das zu Objekten in der besagten Beziehung steht."

[8] See T.R. Schatzki's article "Early Heidegger on Being, The Clearing, and Realism" in *Heidegger: A Critical Reader*, edited by H.L. Dreyfus & H. Hall (Oxford: Blackwell, 1992), 82-4, for a conclusive argument in favor of interpreting Dasein as an individual person or subject. F. Olafson makes a similar claim in *Heidegger and the Philosophy of Mind* (New Haven: Yale University Press, 1987). We quote: "We must now look at the kind of entity that is in the world in the special Heideggerian sense — namely the 'existing subject,' whose mode of being is the topic of *Being and Time*" (52). In a subsequent footnote he claims "That a *seiender Subjekt* is the equivalent of *Dasein* is made clear in GP, 308" (52n). We get back to this discussion in Chapter V, Self-Consciousness, last section.

[9] "[W]e have no right to resort to dogmatic constructions and to apply just any idea of being and actuality to this entity, no matter how 'self-evident' that idea may be; nor may any of the 'categories' which such an idea prescribes be forced upon Dasein without proper ontological considerations. We must rather choose such a way of access and such a kind of interpretation that this entity can show itself in itself and from itself. And this means that it is to be shown as it is *primarily and usually* — in its average *everydayness*" (BT, 37-8).

the necessity of taking intentionality into account, he underscores the importance of starting out from consciousness. Thus, Heidegger's notion of average everydayness is not an invitation to arbitrariness; rather it is a methodological way of securing intentionality as the point of departure for an analysis of the subjectivity of the subject.

Even though he takes everyday comportments as his point of departure, Heidegger admits that the essential structures he is seeking are not given on the surface of everydayness. They must be brought out. These ontological structures are hidden, so to speak, in the very comportments in which they are to be found. Heidegger distinguishes between being-ontological and actually developing an ontology. While the latter belongs to a specific philosophical attitude, the former is a way of being which characterizes Dasein:

> Dasein is an entity which does not just occur among other entities. Rather it is ontically distinguished by the fact that, in its very Being, that Being is an *issue* for it. ... *Understanding of Being is itself a definite characteristic of Dasein's Being.* Dasein is ontically distinctive in that it *is* ontological. (BT, 32)

Hence, although Dasein appears, it does not appear the same way as other things in the world. Dasein's appearance differs from that of other things by being characterized by directedness and, by the same token, by appearing as that to which appearances appear. Thus, not only beings, but the being of beings is an issue for Dasein; it is simultaneously ontical and ontological. However, Heidegger maintains,

> "Being-ontological" is not yet tantamount to "developing an ontology." So if we should reserve the term 'ontology' for that theoretical inquiry which is explicitly devoted to the meaning of entities, then what we have in mind in speaking of Dasein's "Being-ontological" is to be designated as something "pre-ontological." It does not signify simply "being-ontical," but rather "being in such a way that one has an understanding of Being." (BT, 32)

Heidegger's objective in BT is to develop an ontology, and the pre-ontological being of Dasein is to serve as a basis for this endeavor. Thus, Heidegger's ontological inquiry is the theoretical elaboration of the understanding of being that already is at work in everyday comportments. Every step made in this inquiry must receive a "pre-ontological confirmation" (BT, 227). Hence, Heidegger is in full agreement with the fundamental tenets of phenomenology. The disclosure of an essence is a founded act.

However, the disclosing of the essential structures of Dasein demands a very specific approach. Dasein's structures do not surrender themselves to every kind of inquiry. "Ontically, of course, Dasein is not only close to us — even that which is closest: we *are* it, each of us, we ourselves. In spite of this, or rather just for this reason, it is ontologically that which is farthest" (BT, 36). Dasein is ontologically farthest away from us in everydayness because everyday Dasein is directed at the world and the essential structures of our being are precisely what ground this directedness. In everyday life we are not directed towards our own directedness, we are directed towards what is other, towards the world.

> The kind of Being which belongs to Dasein is rather such that, in understanding its own Being, it has a tendency to do so in terms of that entity towards which it comports itself proximally and in a way which is essentially constant — in terms of the 'world.' (BT, 36)

Thus, in order to get to the essential structures and develop an ontology, Heidegger must emphasize the necessity of not going along with the comportments of everydayness or, in a Husserlian idiom, the comportments of the natural attitude. In other words, Heidegger, like Husserl before him, takes his point of departure in the natural attitude when he seeks to disclose the essential structures of subjectivity. And, like Husserl, he observes that before the essential structures of Dasein can be disclosed one has to perform a change in one's attitude towards everydayness.

Hence, not only is Heidegger attempting an eidetic reduction, but he also recognizes the necessity of carrying out something that strongly resembles Husserl's transcendental reduction beforehand. Admittedly, he uses neither the term 'eidetic reduction' nor the term 'transcendental reduction,' but there can be no doubt that when Heidegger claims that he seeks to exhibit essential structures of Dasein, he has ideation in mind. This follows from the fact that this disclosure is a founded act. Heidegger does not construct essential structures, he discloses them. The basis of this disclosure is everyday comportments or, one might say, straightforward perceptions. Furthermore, it follows from the claim that everyday comportments in fact hide the essential structures that one cannot entirely go along with these comportments. In other words, in order to disclose the essential structures of Dasein, one must first somehow distance oneself from the acts. Although everydayness is the foundation, one cannot go along with the thematic sense of everyday comportments. The philosopher makes everydayness itself the theme instead of following its thematic sense, and by so doing he is no longer in the everyday attitude. Indeed, this is exactly how Heidegger interprets Husserl's notion of transcendental reduction, of bracketing. We may recall that in his treatment he concluded that the aim of this bracketing is to lay the ground open for an investigation of being.

> This bracketing of the entity takes nothing away from the entity itself, nor does it purport to assume that the entity is not. This reversal of perspective has rather the

sense of making the being of the entity present. The phenomenological suspension of the transcendent thesis has but the sole function of making the entity present in regard to its being. (HCT, 99)

The phenomenological reduction is undoubtedly structurally present in Heidegger's approach to being. In fact, Heidegger acknowledges this influence in a lecture given shortly after the publication of BT.

For Husserl the phenomenological reduction ... is the method of leading phenomenological vision from the natural attitude of the human being whose life is involved in the world of things and persons back to the transcendental life of consciousness and its noetic-noematic experiences, in which objects are constituted as correlates of consciousness. For us phenomenological reduction means leading phenomenological vision back from the apprehension of a being, whatever may be the character of that apprehension, to the understanding of the being of this being ... (BP, 21)

There is nothing to indicate that the reduction Heidegger refers to as operative in his endeavor is radically different from Husserl's phenomenological reduction.[10] This concerns both his own comment on the reduction above, and the nature of his own investigation. Heidegger does suggest, however, that the reduction leads him to a more original insight than it led Husserl. While for Husserl the reduction brings the vision "back to the transcendental life of consciousness and its noetic-noematic experiences" (BP, 21), it brings Heidegger's vision back "to the understanding of the being of this being" (BP, 21). Heidegger continually accuses Husserl of dealing in the end only with an ideal realm in which an ideal ego relates to ideal objects. What he suggests here echoes what he argued in the treatment of the reduction in HCT. His interpretation does not admit the possibility that Husserl provides an originary determination of the being of pure consciousness. But, one could ask, why should the phenomenological reduction take Heidegger further than Husserl? How could it ever get Heidegger to an understanding of being if it was not on this track from the outset? We thus conclude that the phenomenological reduction is operative in Heidegger's approach to being in that it structures the analysis of Dasein.

2. DASEIN AS EXISTENCE

Heidegger's investigation of subjectivity begins with an emphasis on

---

[10] There is, however, one difference. Whereas in Husserl the phenomenological reduction requires a "leap" (*Sprung*) on the part of an inquiring subject Heidegger is more phenomenologically sound in that he offers a pre-ontological confirmation for the phenomenological reduction. We return to this point in Chapter VI, Constitution.

existence rather than essence. This allows for a fundamentally non-reductionist position according to which human beings are essentially in the world, but not in the way objects are in the world. The subject is both in the world and a subject.

At the beginning of BT we read the following definition of Dasein: "The 'essence' of Dasein lies in its existence" (BT, 67). This apparently contradictory use of two fundamental philosophical terms inaugurates Heidegger's radically non-objective interpretation of human being. 'Existence' is derived from the Latin word '*existentia*,' and in traditional usage it pertains to whether something actually is or not. Essence, on the other hand, concerns what a thing is, its what-ness. Given a thing, one can distinguish *what* it is, whether a car, a bike, a house, or a unicorn, for that matter. *Essentia* concerns what makes a thing be what it is. When interpreted according to this traditional understanding of the terms 'existence' and 'essence,' however, Heidegger's definition of Dasein is not very instructive at all. Since 'existence' has traditionally been understood in the sense of actual endurance, thus coinciding with the ordinary meaning of 'Dasein' (there-being), it seems as though his definition of Dasein proves to be nothing but a mere tautology. This is, however, not the case. When he claims that "the 'essence' of Dasein lies in its existence," Heidegger is not suggesting that the essence of Dasein is that it is actually there. What characterizes the being of man is not *existentia* but existence. In other words, Heidegger distinguishes the traditional concept of existence (*existentia*) from his own concept of existence. While *existentia* cannot be associated with Dasein,[11] existence designates a way of being which can be attributed to Dasein alone.[12] By reserving the term 'existence' for human being, Heidegger proposes a definition of being which exclusively belongs to human being.

Having clarified that the essence of Dasein is *not* subsistence or actual endurance, let us go on to determine what *is* meant by this definition of human being. We start by investigating the relation between Dasein and its essence. One way to interpret Heidegger's definition of Dasein is to consider existence a property of Dasein, i.e., as a way in which a substance (Dasein) can be modified. Dasein is then a substance modified by existence, much as a physical substance has temporal and spatial properties. This interpretation, however, is precisely what Heidegger rejects. By claiming that man has no *existentia*, he takes issue with our tendency to confuse Dasein's way of being with that of other things in the world. To seek a definition of human being by adding properties to an already given substance is, Heidegger claims,

---

[11] "[O]ntologically existentia is tantamount to being-present-at-hand, a kind of being which is essentially inappropriate to entities of Dasein's character" (BT, 67).

[12] "the term "existence," as a designation of being, will be allotted solely to Dasein" (BT, 67).

fundamentally mistaken. Human being is not a thing modified by a thinking faculty, soul, or spirit. Human being is not a thing at all; it is not a *res*.

Heidegger rejects Descartes not because of his turn towards subjectivity, but because this turn fails to discuss the being of the subject.

> Descartes, who carried through the turn to the subject that was already prepared for in different ways, not only does not pose the question of the being of the subject but even interprets the subject's being under the guidance of the concept of being and its pertinent categories as developed by ancient and medieval philosophy. (BP, 123–4)

Heidegger advocates a turn towards subjectivity, but this turn must be a radical one. It must inquire into the being of subjectivity instead of approaching it as a quasi-objective entity. The difference between subjects and objects is not a difference in properties, it is a difference in being. Dasein is an ongoing comp In order to characterize this difference in being, and thus to overcome the view of subjectivity as a substance, Heidegger refers to Dasein a process of self-directedness which is never completed. Dasein is an ongoing completion of itself which is never fully realized as long as it exists.

Things have an entirely different way of being. They are characterized by a fully realized completion. A chair, for instance, does not have the character of self-directedness. Rather, it is determined in its being once it is produced. At this point it is given in its completion, and it can effect no change by itself. With Dasein, however, it is quite different. Dasein is, Heidegger claims, unique among entities in that "in its being, it has a being relation to this being" (BT, 12). "These entities [Dasein], in their being, comport themselves towards their being. As entities with such being, they are delivered over to their own being" (BT, 67). Dasein, as opposed to an artefact, is not once and for all determined in its being. On the contrary, Dasein is constantly determining its being. What characterizes its being is that it is continually to be actualized. Dasein's existence must first and foremost be understood in terms of relating itself to its being. As Heidegger says, "Being is that which is an issue for every such entity" (BT, 67).

Heidegger's definition of Dasein as essentially self-comporting renders the tendency to see the self as an object or thing (substance) of any sort impossible. To be self-comporting is not a property of a substance in the way being a chair is a property of a substance. Dasein is, qua existence, never given as a whole the way a substance is given as whole. As essentially an ability-to-be (*Seinkönnen*), Dasein is characterized by a certain "lack of totality." According to Heidegger, "as long as Dasein exists, it must in each case ... not yet be something" (BT, 276). He adds, "in Dasein there is always something still outstanding, which, as an ability-to-be for Dasein itself, has not yet become 'actual'" (BT, 279). Thus, Dasein can never, as long as it exists, *be* something in the sense of a modified substance. Existence is a self-comportment to which Dasein is constantly handed over. Dasein relates to this being through the actualization of possibilities and, by the same token, through the annihilation of possibilities. Dasein is absorbed in its possibilities and it exists in as much as it actualizes one possibility and eliminates another. According to Heidegger, there is no human essence beneath or other than this self-comportment. Thus, the relation between Dasein and its essence is not a relation between a pre-given substance and a property. Dasein is simply given as self-directedness or self-comportment.

Heidegger emphasizes that the ways in which Dasein's being takes on a definite character are not the focus of his analysis.

[T]hey must be seen and understood *a priori* as grounded upon the state of Being which we have called "*Being-in-the-world.*" An interpretation of this constitutive state is needed if we are to set up our analytic of Dasein correctly. (BT, 78)

Dasein's relating to its own being is fundamentally a 'Being-in-the-world' and, Heidegger continues, this term "stands for a *unitary* phenomenon" (BT, 78). That is, Dasein is not, qua existence, a being which happens to be in the world. Nor is world the place in which Dasein relates to its own being. Being-in-the-world is a primary datum and this "primary datum must be seen as a whole" (BT, 78). The status of Being-in-the-world as a whole and the fact that this is also the basic state of Dasein precludes any attempt at distinguishing between Dasein and world as two different entities. Dasein is not merely the being which is in the world, Dasein is Being-in-the-world. This, however, does not render impossible an investigation of the different moments of the basic state of Dasein.

But while Being-in-the-world cannot be broken up into contents which may be pieced together, this does not prevent it from having several constitutive structural moments [*konstitutiver Strukturmomente*]. (BT, 78; translation altered)

From Being-in-the-world three aspects can be brought out for emphasis: world, the entity which has Being-in-the-world as the way in which it is, and being-in. However, although these aspects can be given separate emphasis, Heidegger underscores their non-independent character:

Emphasis upon any of these constitutive moments [*Verfassungsmomente*] signifies that the others are emphasized along with it; this means that in any such case the whole phenomenon gets seen. (BT, 79; translation altered)

In this chapter we intend to emphasize the phenomenon in question by focusing upon the third aspect, being-in (*In-Sein*). The primary reason for doing so is the fact that being-in is the key to an understanding of the being of Dasein and of what distinguishes Dasein from other beings. Heidegger himself acknowledges this: "*Being-in' is ... the formal existential expression for the Being of Dasein, which has Being-in-the-world as its essential state*" (BT, 80). In the next chapters we shall see how our interpretation of being-in leads to an understanding of world as an aspect of the basic state of Dasein. This interpretation will concern itself with Heidegger's notion of constitution. In that context we also have a look at the second structural moment of Being-in-the-world — the entity which has Being-in-the-world as the way in which it is.

Dasein has a different way of being in the world than other beings. Existence refers to a way of being in the world that cannot be understood along the lines of one object being contained in another, like water in a glass, or a chair in a room. According to Heidegger, there is "no such thing as the 'side-by-side-ness' of an entity called 'Dasein' with another entity called 'world'" (BT, 81). The being-in of Dasein is of a different nature; it is an *existential* being-in, instead of a *spatial* being in. The latter refers to a definite location-relationship between entities "whose kind of Being is not of the character of Dasein" (BT, 79). Dasein's existential being-in must not be interpreted in terms of a spatial "in-one-another-ness." Dasein is not in the world, but is, so to speak, "worlding." In a more familiar metaphysical idiom, one might say that Dasein's connection to the world is not that of being in it like any other entity, but rather that of constituting it.

At this point one may ask what it is about existence that makes world an essential part of Dasein's being. How can self-comportment include the world the way Heidegger suggests? It would take a long argument to answer this question properly, but a short answer would be that Dasein relates to its own being through constituting the world. In the remaining part of this chapter, we shall work out the first part of this answer systematically. This inquiry will focus on the existential structure of Dasein's self-comportment. In the subsequent chapters we establish that this self-comportment necessarily must include the world, and how this takes place.

So far we have seen that Dasein cannot, insofar as it is characterized by a lack of totality, be determined by distinctive categories or properties. Even if Dasein does not have an essence the way substances do, the term 'existence' refers to something that must be possessed by all things that count as Dasein. Existence is, after all, Dasein's essence. But how are we to characterize this essence further? We cannot utilize categories to define the structure of existence. Instead Heidegger uses 'existentials' to capture the general characteristics of Dasein.

Because Dasein's characters of Being are defined in terms of existentiality, we call them *"existentialia."* These are to be sharply distinguished from what we call *"categories"* — characteristics of Being for entities whose character is not that of Dasein. (BT, 70)

A nexus of existentials provides the formal definition of existence. These are equiprimordial structural moments of Dasein. The two major existentials are situatedness and understanding and in what follows we elucidate these structural moments in order to give a first account of the formal definition of Dasein.

3. SITUATEDNESS

Heidegger introduces the phenomenon of situatedness by pointing out that what "we indicate *ontologically* with the term 'situatedness' is *ontically* the most familiar and everyday sort of thing; our mood [*Stimmung*], our Being-attuned" (BT, 172). However, his concept of situatedness is much broader than the ordinary meaning of 'mood.' Firstly, what Heidegger has in mind is not a feeling, rather feelings have their ontological basis in situatedness. Secondly, situatedness designates a mode of being which Dasein can never escape.

With regard to the latter, in ordinary usage the term 'mood' is often related to specific experiences of one's own state of mind, such as being in particularly good spirits, in a bad mood, or in some other kind of somewhat conspicuous frame of mind. By the same token, this usage suggests that the normal everyday state of mind is characterized by a kind of balanced lack of mood. Admittedly, Heidegger's point of departure in the development of his notion of situatedness is our ordinary experience of mood, but he emphasizes that the "fact that moods can deteriorate [*verdorben werden*] and change over means simply that in every case Dasein always has some mood [*gestimmt ist*]" (BT, 173). Thus, Heidegger's notion of mood must be understood in relation to notions such as being-attuned and situatedness. The German term in question is '*Befindlichkeit.*'[13] This term translates "state" in the sense of "the state in which one may be found." Even though this would be understood

---

[13] We shall use the term 'situatedness' in translating the German term '*Befindlichkeit*'. We find that the translation of '*Befindlichkeit*' as 'state-of-mind' is very unfortunate. Other possible translations of this term are "affectedness," "disposition," and "where-you're-at-ness" suggested by H. Dreyfus in *Being-in-the-world*; "disposition," "being-disposed," and "disposedness," suggested by T. Kisiel in the Glossary of German Terms in his translation of HCT; and "already-having-found-itself-there-ness," suggested by W. Richardson in *Heidegger: Through Phenomenology to Thought*. Our choice of translation is suggested by C. Guignon in *Heidegger and the Problem of Knowledge*. These terms are all approximations of '*Befindlichkeit*,' but together they should indicate the meaning of this German term.

in terms of how one is feeling or doing in colloquial German, Heidegger's usage should be taken in a more literal sense. What he has in mind is not first and foremost how one feels or how one finds oneself, but the fact that one always already finds oneself in a state. In everyday life human being is always already in a situation; it is, at any time, *already-in* the world; it is already existing.

> In having a mood, Dasein is always disclosed moodwise as that entity to which it has been delivered over in its Being; and in this way it has been delivered over to the Being which, in existing, it has to be. (BT, 173)

In order to further characterize this being to which Dasein is "delivered over" Heidegger speaks about the "naked 'that it is and has to be'" (BT, 173). As existing, Dasein cannot escape the fact that it is always already existing. At any point in its existence, Dasein is confronted with its own being. At any point of existence one relates to its being there. Even when one's response is complete passivity or utter lack of interest, this can occur only on the basis of a being there, and hence, it bears witness to a confrontation with one's being.

However, this confrontation is for the most part not a thematic confrontation with our own being, if by that one means explicitly relating to being alive or thinking about one's life or inquiring into the meaning of life or something like that. Heidegger emphasizes that 'disclosed' does not here mean that Dasein is thematically aware of being delivered over to its being. On the contrary, for the most part Dasein does not follow up this "disclosure and allow itself to be brought before that which is disclosed" (BT, 173). Ontically, "Dasein for the most part evades the Being which is disclosed in the mood" (BT, 174). That does not mean that Dasein in fact escapes its character of situatedness, but merely that it is not focusing on it. Dasein is ontically directed towards what is other than itself, and in so doing aware of the fact that its everyday course of action is a response to its being there, and thus a confrontation with its own being. Even if Dasein, in an ontico-existentiell sense, does not focus upon its own being, ontologically this "focusing away" testifies to its being delivered over to its being.

> In an *ontologico*-existential sense, this means that even in that to which such a mood pays no attention, Dasein is unveiled in its Being-delivered-over to the "there." In evasion itself the "there" *is* something disclosed. (BT, 174)

Heidegger refers to this "being-delivered-over to" as thrownness (*Geworfenheit*).

> This characteristic of Dasein's Being — this 'that it is' ... we call it the "*thrownness*"

of this entity into its "there"; indeed, it is thrown in such a way that, as Being-in-the-world, it is the "there." The expression "thrownness" is meant to suggest the *facticity of its being delivered over*. (BT, 174)

The terms 'situatedness,' 'thrownness,' and 'facticity' are all used to refer to the same character of Dasein's being: its having been delivered over to the being which, in existing, it has to be.

Throughout his existential analytic, Heidegger emphasizes the difference between the ontico-existentiell level and the ontologico-existential level. Whereas the former is characterized by a focusing away, towards what is other, the latter is meant to account for this directedness. This project is descriptive, not ontically instructive. That is, the objective of the existential analytic is to account for everyday directedness, for existence, not to instruct it. The fact that Dasein cannot escape its situatedness should have no consequences for how we ought to live our lives. For instance, Heidegger points out that it is not an invitation to irrationalism. The phenomenon of situatedness should not lead us to think that we ought to give in to any kind of mood, and that rationality must go because we are simply slaves of our moods. In factical life, Heidegger insists, Dasein "can, should, and must, through knowledge and will, become master of its moods; in certain possible ways of existing, this may signify a priority of volition and cognition" (BT, 175). We must only remember not to ontologize this necessary mastering of moods, thereby "denying that ontologically mood is a primordial kind of Being for Dasein, in which Dasein is disclosed to itself *prior to* all cognition and volition, and *beyond* their range of disclosure" (BT, 175). In other words, mastering moods is not a matter of escaping situatedness, and therefore the phenomenon of situatedness does not suggest that we ought to give in to any mood.

Heidegger lists three essential characteristics of situatedness. The first essential characteristic of this phenomenon is that it "*disclose[s] Dasein in its thrownness, and — proximally and for the first part — in the manner of an evasive turning-away*" (BT, 175). Hence, technically speaking, there is a difference between the terms 'situatedness' and 'thrownness.' The former refers to the disclosedness of thrownness, and to the way it discloses itself. Likewise, there are some fine technical differences between the terms 'thrownness,' 'mood,' and 'facticity.' The concept of mood finds its true meaning in the notion of thrownness, and the latter "is meant to suggest the *facticity of its being delivered over*" (BT, 174). From this first essential characteristic of situatedness there follows another characteristic, which substantiates our initial claim that moods are not feelings. According to Heidegger, from the above discussion of situatedness it follows that it "is very remote from anything like coming across a psychical condition by the kind of apprehending which first turns round and then back" (BT, 175). "Indeed it is so far from this, that only because the 'there' has already been disclosed in situatedness can immanent reflection come across 'Experiences' at all" (BT, 175). In situatedness, facticity announces itself, but this does not take place in reflection. Rather, Heidegger argues, "a mood assails us. It comes neither from 'outside' nor from 'inside,' but arises out of Being-in-the-world" (BT, 176). It follows, then, that the *"mood has already disclosed, in every case, Being-in-the-world as a whole, and makes it possible first of all to direct oneself towards something"* (BT, 176). Thus, moods are not feelings or something that springs from the psychical realm; the notion of mood instead belongs to the existential constitution of Dasein and hence, it is the condition of possibility of feelings.

Having a mood is not related to the psychical in the first instance, and is not itself an inner condition which then reaches forth in an enigmatical way and puts its mark on things and persons. (BT, 176)

Besides the disclosing of thrownness and the disclosing of Being-in-the-world, there is a third essential characteristic of situatedness which concerns the submissive aspect of this phenomenon. According to Heidegger, this aspect contributes to a more accurate appreciation of the relation between Dasein and world. For Dasein to be in the world is not a matter of first being Dasein and then going on to discover the world. Dasein is not a being that is in the world, but a Being-in-the-world. At any point of its existence, Dasein is always-already in the world. Dasein is always-already thrown into the world, into a situation where things matter. Only because of this structural submission to the world, which is also at the same time a disclosure or a primary discovery of the world, can Dasein discover entities within-the-world.

Existentially, situatedness implies a disclosive submission to the world, out of which we can encounter something that matters to us. Indeed *from the ontological point of view* we must as a general principle leave the primary discovery of the world to 'bare mood.' (BT, 177)

This observation has certain consequences for an understanding of the theoretical attitude and of science. It is commonly argued that Heidegger rejects the theoretical attitude as a proper point of departure for an investigation of human being. However, this should not be taken to indicate that Heidegger looks down on the theoretical attitude or that he has low regard for it. After all, the project of existential analytic is itself extremely theoretical. Rather, Heidegger seeks to reinterpret the notion of theoretical attitude by reversing the hierarchy between everyday involvement with the world and theoretical inquiry.

There has been a tendency among philosophers to take their point of departure in the activity closest to themselves when discussing human being. Thus, theoretical attitude has often been considered the defining feature of this being, and the ideals of this activity such as disengagement, unaffectedness, and reflection have been exalted to the level of essential characteristics of subjectivity. From this follows a notion of the subject as a worldless and isolated thinking thing. Heidegger does not categorically reject approaching human being as a being capable of cognizance. Indeed, his own definition of Dasein as understanding seems to indicate a certain kinship between his conception and modern metaphysics. However, Heidegger is not merely postulating understanding as a definition of human being, but is inquiring into the being of understanding. His aim is to show that, ontologically speaking, what constitutes understanding is not disengaged reasoning and worldless reflection, but rather worldliness and absorption. On the one hand, Heidegger equates theoretical behavior, or at least a certain understanding of it, to a mere looking. Heidegger does not dispute that the theoretical attitude, as this is put into practice in the sciences, should aim at the greatest possible disengagement and unaffectedness in order to achieve objectivity. What he challenges is that this ontical ideal of theoretical behavior should lead us to an ontological conclusion about Dasein's nature. Thus, on the other hand he claims that "even the purest *theoria* has not left all moods behind it" (BT, 177). "Any cognitive determining has its existential-ontological Constitution in the situatedness of Being-in-the-world; but pointing this out is not to be confused with attempting to surrender science ontically to 'feeling'" (BT, 177). In other words, although cognitive determining has its ontological constitution in the situatedness of Being-in-the-world, this should not lead us to conclude ontically that science is, or should be, based on feelings. Conversely, the scientific ideal of disengagement and unaffectedness should not lead us to conclude ontologically that cognitive determining is essentially non-situated and worldless.

4. UNDERSTANDING

Equiprimordial with situatedness in constituting the being of Dasein there is another existential, namely understanding (*Verstehen*). Heidegger delineates the relation between these two existentials as follows:

Situatedness always has its understanding, even if it merely keeps it suppressed. Understanding always has its mood. If we interpret understanding as a fundamental *existentiale*, this indicates that this phenomenon is conceived as a basic mode of

Dasein's *being*. (BT, 182)

However, by interpreting understanding as a fundamental existential, Heidegger is not about to appoint one kind of cognizing as the basic mode of Dasein's being. He specifically distinguishes between existential understanding and understanding as one possible kind of cognizing. The latter is, like any kind cognizing, to be interpreted as an existential derivative of primary understanding.

> With the term 'understanding' we have in mind a fundamental *existentiale*, which is neither a definite *species of cognition* distinguished, let us say, from explaining and conceiving, nor any cognition at all in the sense of grasping something thematically. (BT, 385)

In what follows we discuss this claim by having a look at what distinguishes understanding as a fundamental existential from understanding as a definite species of cognition. We shall first see that it differs from the latter in that it designates a kind of self-understanding. Moreover, this self-understanding is "the condition of possibility for all kinds of comportments, not only practical but also cognitive" (BP, 276). Hence, it differs from ontical comportments by being the condition of their possibility. Secondly, we shall see that this self-understanding is not a thematic self-understanding. That is, primary understanding is not a matter of being thematically directed upon our own being in the sense of self-reflection or introspection. It does not, Heidegger claims, "first arise from an immanent self-perception" (BT, 184). Rather, Dasein understands itself through its involvement with the world.

In ordinary usage, the word understanding designates our ability to do something or to figure something out. It refers then to our competence in relation to entities other than ourselves. However, in its existential sense understanding designates a competence in relation to our own being.

> In understanding, as an *existentiale*, that which we have competence over is not a "what," but Being as existing. The kind of Being which Dasein has, as potentiality-for-Being, lies existentially in understanding. (BT, 183)

As we have already pointed out, the definition of Dasein as existence implies that Dasein is essentially relating to its own being. Thus, if understanding is one of the constitutive moments of the being of Dasein, it follows that primary understanding in fact is a self-directed understanding. This is substantiated by Heidegger when he claims that "To exist is essentially, even if not only, to understand" (BP, 276).[14]

Heidegger distinguishes between understanding qua comportment towards beings and primary understanding which is a kind of self-understanding. Between these two notions of understanding there is an ontological difference, but not an indifference. That is, these two notions of understanding are closely interrelated in a whole-part structure. On the one hand, primary understanding is self-directed understanding, and this is the condition of possibility for all kinds of comportments. In other words, primary understanding is a *concretum* for understanding in the sense of comportment towards beings. On the other hand, primary understanding is not something wholly other than comportment towards beings. As we indicated above, primary understanding is not a matter of being thematically directed upon our own being prior to our involvement with the world. Rather, Dasein understands itself *through* its involvement with the world. Thus, the relation between primary understanding and comportment towards beings is in accordance with the notion of apriorism developed on the basis of the theory of wholes and parts. Primary understanding is prior to, and a *concretum* for, comportment towards beings, but it does not appear temporally prior to and independent of this comportment. Rather, it appears with it as the for-the-sake-of-which of any ontical comportment.

This notion of apriorism is essential to Heidegger's existential analytic. The definition of Dasein as existence implies that Dasein is characterized by a specific kind of self-directedness, and that it has an understanding of its own being. However, Heidegger's aim is to develop a notion of the being we ourselves are that is both non-reductive and non-constructive. Thus, on the one hand, he must avoid likening Dasein to other entities in the world, and the notion of understanding takes care of that by pertaining solely to Dasein. On the other hand, he must also not construct a worldless entity, and again the notion of understanding plays a decisive role since Heidegger's concept of primary understanding essentially includes the world.

---

[14] What Heidegger has in mind with the phrase "not only" is obviously the fact that existence is also essentially situated. However, although the importance of facticity in Heidegger's existential analytic is indisputable, one must be careful not to overstate its importance and claim that facticity is the guiding principle for his analytic. Heidegger does claim that "existentiality is essentially determined by facticity" (BT, 236), but this is not an invitation to disturb the balance between the two existentials situatedness and understanding. The claim that existence is essentially understanding does at least suggest that understanding is as foundational as facticity. Moreover, Heidegger's presentation of understanding seems to indicate a certain emphasis on understanding. Understanding is terminologically more closely associated with existence than is situatedness; indeed, understanding is existence. Thus, Heidegger himself seems to stress the importance of understanding. However, it is our argument that he still upholds the fine equilibrium between these two existentials; they are structural moments and should be treated accordingly.

What characterizes Dasein's being is a potentiality-for-Being (*Seinkönnen*). As we recall, Dasein is, qua existence, never given once and for all, rather "in Dasein there is always something *still outstanding*, which, as a potentiality-for-Being for Dasein itself, has not yet become 'actual'" (BT, 279). According to Heidegger, this kind of being "lies existentially in understanding" (BT, 183). "If the term 'understanding' is taken in a way which is primordially existential, it means *to be projecting towards a potentiality-for-Being for the sake of which any Dasein exists*" (BT, 385). The term 'potentiality-for-Being' characterizes the peculiar nature of Dasein's being that distinguishes it from other entities in the world. As long as it exists Dasein is never fixed in its being once and for all but instead is always relating to this being by pressing forward into possibilities. However, Heidegger points out that this potentiality-for-Being "does not signify a free-floating potentiality-for-Being in the sense of the 'liberty of indifference' (*libertas indifferentiae*)" (BT, 183).

In every case Dasein, as essentially situated, has already got itself into definite possibilities ... [T]his means that Dasein is Being-possible which has been delivered over to itself — *thrown possibility* through and through. (BT, 183)

Thus, Dasein's being-possible is always limited by its thrownness. In order to achieve an accurate appreciation of the phenomenon of understanding one must, however, focus closely upon the nature of projection. According to Heidegger, understanding "always press forward into possibilities ... because the understanding has in itself the existential structure which we call '*projection*' ['*Entwurf*']" (BT, 184–5). Thus, we have the following composition: the essence of Dasein is existence, existence is understanding, understanding is self-understanding, and self-understanding is an incessant projection towards possibilities.

Since primary understanding has the existential structure of projection it follows that this self-understanding is not a projection back on itself. Pressing forward into possibilities is precisely projecting towards what one is not yet. Thus, primary understanding cannot be a matter of thematically grasping an already appearing self in the sense of introspection. This is due to the fact that prior to primary understanding there is no self; the self instead appears with the projection. For this reason the projective structure of primary understanding also cannot be interpreted as an activity of carrying out something already planned out.

Projecting has nothing to do with comporting oneself towards a plan that has been thought out, and in accordance with which Dasein arranges its Being. On the contrary, any Dasein has, as Dasein, already projected itself; and as long as it is, it is projecting. As long as it is, Dasein always has understood itself and always will understand itself in terms of possibilities. (BT, 185)

Projecting cannot be interpreted as a comportment done in accordance with a plan because the self, which is a necessary presupposition for working out a plan, is not given prior to the projection.[15] To summarize, then, the self-understanding of primary understanding is not an understanding that is occupied thematically with a self. Rather, this understanding constitutes a self. It is a structural moment in the constitution of the being we ourselves are, of Dasein.

As we have already pointed out, though, this primary understanding is not something fundamentally other than ontical comportment towards beings. We do not on the one hand have comportment towards beings and on the other hand acts directed towards a nuclear self. Rather, primary understanding and ontic comportment are intrinsically interrelated. The ontological meaning of ontic comportment is precisely primary understanding. This is, however, something that for the most part goes unnoticed in our everyday pressing forward into possibilities. As long as everything works properly we are not thematically aware of the for-the-sake-of-which of our activities but are instead object-oriented. It is only when our projection into possibilities runs into problems and things do not work appropriately that our ontical comportment announces itself as self-comportment. It is then that we first see that we ourselves are the for-the-sake-of-which of the activity.[16]

5. SEEING: UNDERSTANDING, INTERPRETATION, ASSERTION

Heidegger's investigation of understanding is also an investigation of seeing. The reason for this is that in "its projective character, understanding goes to make up existentially what we call Dasein's *sight* [*Sicht*]" (BT, 186). Heidegger distinguishes between different kinds of seeing, such as circumspection (*Umsicht*), which is the seeing of our everyday manipulation of things; considerateness (*Rücksicht*), which is the seeing guiding our relation to other human beings; and "that sight which is directed upon Being as such [*Sicht auf das Sein als Solches*], for the sake of which any Dasein is

---

[15] However, projection is not thereby mere behavior and thus Heidegger by no means advocates a kind of behaviorism. As we shall see in Chapter VI, Constitution, projection is not blind stimulus-response. It has its own kind of sigth, circumspection.

[16] This theme will be treated extensively in the chapters to follow. The fact that our everyday comportment towards beings does not focus upon the proper meaning of this comportment will be dealt with in Chapter V, Self-Consciousness. The way the proper meaning of ontic comportment announces itself in situations of breakdown will be thoroughly discussed in Chapters VI, VII, and VIII.

as it is" (BT, 186).

The sight which is related primarily and on the whole to existence we call *transparency* [*Durchsichtigkeit*]. We choose this term to designate "knowledge of the Self" ["*Selbsterkenntnis*"] in a sense which is well understood, so as to indicate that here it is not a matter of perceptually tracking down and inspecting a point called the Self [*Selbstpunktes*], but rather one of seizing upon the full disclosedness of Being-in-the-world *throughout all* the constitutive moments which are essential to it. (BT, 186-7)[17]

The notion of transparency underscores something we have already mentioned. The seeing directed upon being as such, our self-seeing, is not a continuous inspection of an "I-thing." This seeing is characterized by an openness towards the world, and hence, the intrinsic interrelation between primary understanding and ontical comportment follows. Just as primary understanding and ontical comportment cannot be construed as separate in the sense of being two different comportments, so too the notions of seeing that guide them cannot be construed as two isolated phenomena. The difference between circumspection and the sight which is directed upon being is not an ontical difference, it is an ontological difference. The former finds its meaning in the latter. The ontological meaning of circumspection is the transparency of our self-seeing. If the self-seeing were directed towards an inner ego-entity it would create an opaqueness that in fact would undermine the worldliness of Dasein.[18]

Heidegger emphasizes the necessity of providing a proper existential characterization of the concept of seeing. Firstly, he makes it clear that "'seeing' does not mean just perceiving with the bodily eyes" (BT, 187). Seeing is not merely a passive reception of impressions but is rather an activity. Secondly, seeing does not "mean [a] pure non-sensory awareness of something present-at-hand in its presence-at-hand" (BT, 187), either.

[17] A note on terminology: when Heidegger uses traditional philosophical terms he often adds phrases like "in a well-understood sense" in order to point out that he is concerned with the entities of traditional metaphysics, but he rejects the meaning ascribed to these entities. For instance, Heidegger refers on several occasions to Dasein as a subject, adding "in the well-understood sense of this term." That is, Dasein designates the entity traditionally referred to as the subject, but it does not thereby take over the meaning traditionally assigned to this entity. Dasein is not a worldless thing-like entity; *this* subject is a Being-in-the-world. Likewise, Heidegger uses the term '*Selbsterkenntnis*,' but emphasizes that it must be taken "in a sense which is well understood." In this context this means that it must not be understood as a matter of "inspecting a point called the Self." Self-directedness *is* a central topic in Heidegger's analytic, but one must remember that his objective is to provide this phenomenon with a phenomenal basis. In our next chapter we discuss Heidegger's notion of self-directedness in relation to notions of self-consciousness found in Kant and Sartre.

[18] We investigate this claim in more detail in our analysis of Sartre's notion of self-consciousness in the following chapter.

Heidegger's concept of seeing has a broader meaning. It designates an act that "lets entities which are accessible to it be encountered unconcealedly in themselves" (BT, 187).

It is our argument that this concept of seeing refers to the same phenomenon as the concept of sensuousness introduced in the preliminary part of HCT. Firstly, both refer to a sensuous receptivity. This receptivity is radically different from a traditional modern notion of sense perception for it is not a passive reception of discrete atomic impressions, but rather an activity. Moreover, this activity gives objectivity in its broadest sense. As Heidegger puts it in HCT:

Sensuousness is a formal phenomenological concept and refers to all material content as it is already given by the subject matter themselves ... *Sensuousness is therefore the title for the total constellation of entities which are given beforehand in their material content.* (HCT, 70)

Secondly, both seeing and sensuousness are understood as rehabilitating a notion of seeing present in Greek philosophy. In BT Heidegger makes the following claim:

[F]rom the beginning onwards the tradition of philosophy has been oriented primarily towards 'seeing' as a way of access to entities *and to Being*. To keep the connection with this tradition, we may formalize "sight" and "seeing" enough to obtain therewith a universal term for characterizing any access to entities or to Being, as access in general. (BT, 187)

Thus, according to Heidegger, the notion of seeing as access in general, as "a way of access to entities *and to Being*" is present already from the beginning of philosophy. In HCT Heidegger introduces his broad concept of sensuousness by pointing out that sense intuition is the way of access to being, and moreover, he likens this position to an Aristotelian one.

Everything categorial [being] ultimately rests upon sense intuition, no objective explication floats freely but is always an explication of something already given. The thesis that everything categorial ultimately rests upon sense intuition is but a restatement of the Aristotelian proposition: "The soul can presume nothing, apprehend nothing objective in its objectivity, if nothing at all has been shown to it beforehand." (HCT, 69)[19]

In other words, Heidegger introduces both in BT and in HCT a notion of seeing or sense intuition as access in general which relates back to a Greek, specifically an Aristotelian, notion of sense intuition.

A third similarity between seeing and sensuousness is that both are

---

[19] In quotation marks, Heidegger's own translation of Aristotle's *De Anima*, 431a16f.

understood as something which grounds cognitive activity. In BT Heidegger argues that since seeing is to be understood as access in general, and also has its existential foundation in understanding it follows that understanding is the condition of possibility of access in general. By this, he claims, "we have deprived pure intuition [*Anschauen*] of its priority, which corresponds noetically to the priority of the present-at-hand in traditional ontology" (BT, 187). What he has in mind is that cognition or pure thinking is no longer seen as the primordial way of relating to the world.

> 'Intuition' and 'thinking' are both derivatives of understanding, and already rather remote ones. Even the phenomenological 'intuition of essences' ['*Wesensschau*'] is grounded in existential understanding. (BT, 187)[20]

This view is also present in the discussion of sensuousness in HCT. By rejecting the traditional way of interpreting sensuousness as the passive reception of atomic impressions, Heidegger criticizes not only modern empiricism but also addresses those rationalist positions which emphasize the priority of unfounded cognitive acts.

Compared to the discussion of sensuousness carried out in HCT, the presentation of the concept of seeing in BT is very brief, and it is hard to see what other interpretation could be given of this notion as it stands. The fact that there is such a striking similarity between the notion of seeing discussed in BT and the notion of sensuousness developed in the preliminary part of HCT (a lecture Heidegger gave only one year before he finished BT) seems to justify such an approach. Even if they were not completely compatible (though we would argue that they are), the latter can at least legitimately serve as a vehicle for understanding what is meant be 'seeing' in BT.

Heidegger not only distinguishes between primary understanding and comportment towards beings, but he also distinguishes between different

---

[20] It is very interesting that Heidegger here seems to equate intuition and thinking. As we have seen, Husserl's notion of categorial intuition plays a fundamental role in Heidegger's existential analytic. His development of the notion of sensuousness is precisely a result of his analysis of the founding/founded relationship between sense intuition and categorial intuition. When Heidegger suggests in this quote that his notion of understanding goes beyond the phenomenological intuition of essences, he is in fact simply repeating the insight he gained through an investigation of Husserl's notion of categorial intuition. An intuition of an essence (eidetic intuition) is a categorial intuition and hence, it is a founded act. It is founded upon sense intuition. Indeed, in order to make his case and emphasize the priority of a founding sensuousness over cognition, Heidegger quotes the following passage from Husserl's LI: "The idea of a 'pure intellect' could only be conceived '*before* an elementary analysis of knowledge in the irrevocable evidence of its composition'" (HCT, 69/LI, #60). Thus, when Heidegger equates intuition and thinking and claims that both are derivatives of understanding, he is by no means confronting Husserl. Rather, he is introducing a fundamental Husserlian insight: that categorial intuition is founded upon sense intuition.

kinds of comportments. This is also done in accordance with the theory of wholes and parts where different kinds of comportment stand in an *abstractum-concretum* relationship to one another. We shall briefly discuss the notion of understanding as interpretation and the notion of assertion as a derivative mode of interpretation. Interpretation and assertion are intrinsically interrelated as the former is a *concretum* for the latter.

According to Heidegger, interpretation is "the working-out of possibilities projected in understanding" (BT, 189). Understanding is thus a *concretum* for interpretation, but the latter is not therefore something other than understanding. On the contrary, "in interpretation, understanding does not become something different. It becomes itself" (BT, 188). Heidegger distinguishes between understanding and interpretation by claiming that when circumspection (i.e., the seeing of our everyday manipulation of things[21]) discovers "the 'world' which has already been understood comes to be interpreted" (BT, 189). Interpretation is what takes place in ontical comportment, and understanding is the ontological meaning of this activity. Thus, interpretation is not a theoretical activity, it is a matter of literally *taking something as something*.

In dealing with what is environmentally ready-to-hand by interpreting it circumspectively, we 'see' it *as* a table, a door, a carriage, or a bridge; but what we have thus interpreted [*Ausgelegte*] need not necessarily be also taken apart [*auseinander zu legen*] by making an assertion which definitely characterizes it. Any mere pre-predicative seeing of the ready-to-hand is, in itself, something which already understands and interprets. (BT, 189)

The distinction between understanding and interpretation will be discussed in detail in our treatment of disclosedness and discoveredness. We shall see that while understanding discloses the world, interpretation discovers things in the world. The former is a condition of possibility of the latter in the sense that for something to be discovered *as* something, the world must always already be disclosed. However, this disclosure is not something that takes place temporally ahead of circumspective interpretation; it takes place *with* it as that within which something can be discovered.

In this section the objective is merely to point out the formal distinction between understanding, interpretation, and assertion. Thus far we have seen that both understanding and interpretation are matters of seeing, but while understanding refers to a seeing which is directed upon being as such, interpretation is a seeing of something *as* something. The former is ontological, the latter is ontical. In the above quote Heidegger also introduces the

---

[21] Although this will not be given a thorough treatment until Chapter VI, Constitution, we shall be using some of the terminology of the structure of Dasein's worldliness (constitution) in order to shed light on the phenomenon of interpretation.

third phenomenon, assertion, and he distinguishes it from both understanding and interpretation. While interpretation refers to any pre-predicative seeing of ready-to-hand entities, assertion designates acts that are traditionally referred to as judgments. While interpretation "is carried out primordially not in a theoretical statement but in action" (BT, 200), an assertion takes place in a theoretical statement.

We emphasize two aspects of Heidegger's discussion of assertion. Firstly, we shall see that assertion is a derivative mode of interpretation, and, secondly, we shall see that assertion is not therefore the primary locus of truth. As we recall from our investigation of the preliminary part of HCT, Heidegger believes that the universality of evidence represents a radicalization of the scholastic definition of truth. This radicalization arises from the fact that evidence is no longer restricted to the realm of assertions, predications, and judgments, but is "*a universal function, first, of all acts which give their objects, and then, of all acts*" (HCT, 51). As a result, Heidegger argues that "[p]henomenology thus breaks with the restriction of the concept of truth to relational acts, to judgments" (HCT, 55).

While truth is traditionally linked to the relational acts of judgment, the term 'being' is readily attributed to the correlate of non-relational, single-rayed acts, as a specification of the object, of the subject matter itself. But just as truth must undergo a 'widening,' so too must 'being,' a widening not only from the subject matter but from the state of affairs — being and being-such-and-such. (HCT, 55)

This widening of truth takes us into the realm of "that which *makes* knowledge *true*" (HCT, 53). In BT this notion of truth is called *aletheia*, which is a matter of "taking entities out of their hiddenness and letting them be seen in their unhiddenness (their uncoveredness)" (BT, 262).[22]

Heidegger distinguishes between articulation (*gliedern*) and making a judgment. While a judgment is carried out in a theoretical statement, articulation takes place in understanding and interpretation, which is a pre-predicative activity.

That which has been articulated as such in interpretation and sketched out beforehand in the understanding in general as something articulable, is the meaning. In so far as assertion ('judgment') is grounded on understanding and presents us with a derivative form in which an interpretation has been carried out, it *too* 'has' a meaning. Yet this meaning cannot be defined as something which occurs 'in' a judgment along with the judging itself. (BT, 195)

Thus, we see that while interpretation articulates, this articulation is based

[22] It is not our intention at this time to analyze Heidegger's discussion of truth in § 44 of BT, but we do contend that this discussion is to a large extent a repetition of the analysis carried out in HCT. The difference is for the most part merely terminological.

upon understanding in general which is a prior sketching out of something as articulable. An assertion is secondary to interpretation in that it is a "pointing-out" (*Aufzeigen*) of something that has already been interpreted.[23] "The pointing-out which assertion does is performed on the basis of what has already been disclosed in understanding or discovered circumspectively" (BT, 199). While the interpretive taking of something *as* something is presented as the "existential-hermeneutical '*as*,'" Heidegger refers to the '*as*' of assertion as an "apophantical '*as*.'" Heidegger recognizes that the notion of the apophantical 'as' as abstract to the existential-hermeneutical 'as' is extremely important to his own project. That allows him to free the concept of truth from its restriction to judgments and thus to develop a notion of truth as *aletheia*, as letting entities be seen in their unhiddenness. This project is, however, entirely dependent upon the notion of the universality of evidence discussed by Heidegger in HCT, and it is therefore our contention that the phenomenon of *aletheia* is strongly related to what is normally termed constitution in more traditional phenomenological language.[24]

6. BEING-THERE: DISCOURSE AND FALLING

Dasein is a "there-being" and the existential structure of this being-there is thrown projection. However, there is a third structural moment of existence in addition to the existentials situatedness and understanding. This existential is the "there" constituted by these two other existentials, and it is intrinsically related to articulation.

Although what distinguishes assertion from interpretation and understanding is that it is a predicative pointing-out, this must not lead us to any conclusions concerning the nature of language. It is not assertion that is the foundation of language. Rather, "*the existential-ontological foundation of language is discourse [Rede]*" (BT, 203). Moreover, "*discourse is existentially equiprimordial with situatedness and understanding*" (BT, 203). In other words, discourse designates a third structural moment of

---

[23] The fact that assertion is secondary to interpretation and understanding has an implication for the project of existential analytic in that the assertions of this project too are a pointing-out of something already understood. That means that the ontological structure of Dasein's being (which Heidegger seeks to point out in BT) somehow announces itself in our circumspective dealing with the world. This implies a problem of phenomenological evidence. Is there a phenomenal basis for claiming that we see our seeing and that we also see that this seeing primarily is a sight which is directed upon being as such? It is one thing to claim that we see things in the world, but another to argue that we see the seeing itself. Heidegger takes this problem extremely seriously, and we shall see how he deals with it in our discussion of pre-ontological confirmation.

[24] This will be discussed more systematically in Chapter VI, Constitution.

Dasein's being; it is an existential. This existential articulates intelligibility, and therefore, Heidegger claims, "it underlies both interpretation and assertion" (BT 204). Hence, while interpretation is a *concretum* for assertion, it is an *abstractum* to discourse. But interpretation is, as we mentioned above, an *abstractum* to understanding. Does it then follow that interpretation is abstract in relation to two different *concreta*? It is indeed correct to say that interpretation is abstract to both discourse and understanding, but these two are not all that different.

Although discourse is an existential in its own right and thus is equiprimordial with understanding and situatedness, it nevertheless seems less fundamental than the other existentials. Heidegger suggests as much with the claim that the "fundamental *existentialia* which constitute the Being of the 'there' ... are situatedness and understanding" (BT, 203). While understanding and situatedness, even as structural moments, are not defined in terms of each other, discourse is an amalgamation of these two fundamental existentials. Discourse is the articulation of disclosedness whose structure is that of being simultaneously *delivered over* and *pressing forward into possibilities*. It is what thrown projection amounts to.

Although it gets expressed in language, discourse is not reducible to language. On the contrary, discourse is an existential foundation of language. There are several ways in which discourse gets expressed in language; assertion is one way, vocal utterance more broadly defined is another, and *hearing* and *keeping silent* are still others. What characterizes the expression of discourse (i.e., language) is not what we normally associate with language, but a certain "about-ness" (intentionality).

Talking is talk about something. That which the discourse is *about* [das *Worüber* der Rede] does not necessarily or even for the most part serve as the theme for an assertion in which one gives something a definite character. Even a command is given about something; a wish is about something. And so is intercession. (BT, 204-5)

Thus, for Heidegger language is a technical term and it designates any kind of expressing discourse, which amounts to any articulation of intelligibility. Just as this can take place with vocal utterances in general, and assertions in particular, so too can it take place in both hearing and keeping silent.[25]

[25] Heidegger carries out an elaborate analysis of the status of hearing and keeping silent as articulations of intelligibility. We have seen that the key issue in this regard is the "about-ness" (intentionality) of the activity. With reference to hearing Heidegger points out that "what we 'first' hear is never noises or complexes of sounds, but the creaking wagon, the motor-cycle. We hear the column on the march, the north wind, the woodpecker tapping, the fire crackling" (BT, 207). Thus, hearing is every bit as object oriented as other ways of relating to the world, and Heidegger points out that "it requires a very artificial and complicated frame of mind to 'hear' a 'pure noise'" (BT, 207). Concerning the activity of keeping silent Heidegger points out

Heidegger is very critical of the philosophy of language throughout his career. In BT, for instance, he claims that "philosophical research will have to dispense with the 'philosophy of language' if it is to inquire into 'the things themselves'" (BT, 209-10).[26] Although Heidegger never offers a systematic treatment or critique of philosophy of language, several passages in his writings suggest that he accuses this philosophy for taking a reductive approach to language.

Attempts to grasp the 'essence of language' have always taken their orientation from one or another [moment constitutive for discourse]; and the clues to their conceptions of language have been the ideas of 'expression,' of 'symbolic form,' of communication as 'assertion,' of the 'making-known' of experience, of the 'patterning' of life. (BT, 206)

For Heidegger it is imperative to approach language as a phenomenon intrinsically rooted in Dasein's existence, and not as a self-contained and self-sufficient linguistic system. This, however, is not necessarily inconsistent with some philosophies of language, and several scholars have emphasized a certain affinity between Heidegger and the later Wittgenstein.[27]

that "the person who keeps silent ... can develop an understanding" (BT, 208). By developing an understanding, the person who keeps silent articulates intelligibility, and hence, it follows that silence can perfectly well be in the mode of discoursing. However, it should be noted that Heidegger makes it clear that keeping silent not necessarily is in the mode of discourse. The keeping silent Heidegger has in mind is not just a matter of not speaking, it is a matter of "having something to say." Heidegger refers to this kind of keeping silent as *reticence*.

[26] This negative opinion surfaces in some shape or form throughout Heidegger's career. A couple of examples: in *What is Called Thinking?*, translated by J.G. Gray and F. Wieck (New York: Harper & Row Publishers, 1968), Heidegger talks about shaking the foundation of the philosophy of language (see 200); and in *The Question Concerning Technology and Other Essays*, translated by W. Lowitt (New York: Harper & Row Publishers, 1977), Heidegger identifies philosophy of language with the theoretical, objectifying languages (see 175-6).

[27] Already in 1931 Wittgenstein discussed the issue of what constitutes, and what makes possible, an understanding of language. In his notebooks he writes: "Perhaps what is inexpressible (what I find mysterious and am not able to express) is the background against which whatever I could express has its meaning," *Culture and Value*, translated by P. Winch (Oxford: Blackwell, 1980), 16. In *Philosophical Investigations*, translated by G.E.M. Anscombe (Oxford: Basil Blackwell, 1958), this mysterious and inexpressible "background" gets expressed as a "form of life." In section 19, Wittgenstein says that "to imagine a language means to imagine a form of life." This sentence exemplifies at the very least a dominant theme of PI, namely the theme that concepts such as meaning, rule-following, and language itself cannot be adequately treated apart from the context of our everyday practices. We are not about to claim that this is entirely compatible with Heidegger's position, but one can at least argue that there are certain parallels between their positions. Several scholars have discussed this affinity, see for example C. Taylor "Lichtung or Lebensform: Parallels Between Wittgenstein and Heidegger," *Theoria*, 1, 1989, 9-21; S. Mulhall *On Being in The World, Wittgenstein and Heidegger On Seeing Aspects* (London and New York: Routledge, 1990);

Heidegger's discussion of language is a discussion of existence, and language expresses the "there" of Dasein. Discourse is the articulation of intelligibility, it gets expressed in language, and this language encompasses more than vocal utterances. What essentially characterizes language is a certain "about-ness," and language thus includes hearing and keeping silent as well as assertions and other speech acts. Heidegger distinguishes between two major ways of expressing the "there" of Dasein; one is directed towards what is other than itself, and one is directed back upon itself. As characterized by intentionality, language is normally directed at what is other, but Heidegger calls attention to certain experiences we have of the "there" disclosing its own structure that is absolutely imperative to his project.

Our discussion of the structural moments of Dasein has thus far not been descriptive in the strict sense. It has rather been a formal presentation of Dasein's existential make-up which has yet to receive a phenomenal basis. One could therefore argue that Heidegger not only starts in the wrong place but also violates his own principles, but this is not the case. In Division One of BT Heidegger only undertakes a preparatory fundamental analysis of Dasein, and the objective of this analysis is to present a preliminary account of the structure of existence. What is preliminary about this account is that he does not present the phenomenal basis grounding this analysis, and hence, he is not presenting the full meaning of Dasein's existence. That will be the topic of Division Two.

As we pointed out above, Heidegger distinguishes between two ways in which discourse expresses itself, and he refers to the normal, everyday expression of the 'there' as *falling* (*Verfallen*). The everyday being of the 'there' is characterized by falling because of its absorption in the world. Heidegger emphasizes, however, that "this term does not express any negative evaluation, but is used to signify that Dasein is proximally and for the most part *being-amidst* [*Sein-bei*] the 'world' of its concern" (BT, 220).[28] The phenomenon of "fallenness" refers to a mode of being in which "Dasein has, in the first instance, fallen away [*abgefallen*] from itself as an authentic potentiality for Being its Self, and has fallen into the 'world'" (BT, 220). Thus, while the 'there' of Dasein for the most part reflects a concern with what is other than itself — with the world — the 'there' expressed through Heidegger's endeavor is of another order. It turns its focus back upon

and C. Guignon "Philosophy After Wittgenstein and Heidegger," *Philosophy and Phenomenological Research*, Vol. 1, June 1990, 649–672. See also M. Murray "A Note on Wittgenstein and Heidegger," *The Philosophical Review* 83, 1971, 501–3. On a more general treatment of Heidegger's relation to philosophy of language see W.D. Owens "Heidegger and the Philosophy of Language," *Auslegung*, Vol. VIV, No.1, 1987, 49–66.

[28] Instead of the unfortunate translation of '*Sein bei*' as being-alongside in the original translation of BT, we shall use a translation suggested by Dreyfus: being-amidst.

existence itself. However, the relation between these two attitudes must not be conceived as one in which fallenness is something less genuine than the seeing that focuses back on itself.

> Not-Being-its-self [*Das Nicht-es-selbst-sein*] functions as a *positive* possibility of that entity which, in its essential concern, is absorbed in a world. This kind of *not-Being* has to be conceived as that kind of Being which is closest to Dasein and in which Dasein maintains itself for the most part. (BT, 220)

Thus, as Heidegger continues, "we must [not] take the fallenness of Dasein as a 'fall' from a purer and higher 'primal status'" (BT, 220).

By claiming that everyday Dasein is in the mode of falling just after he has presented an outline of the essential structural moments of Dasein's existence, Heidegger makes it quite clear that his analysis is *not* in the everyday attitude. First, by claiming that everydayness is characterized by falling he has turned it into an object of investigation. Second, he is presenting the structure of existence from which everydayness has fallen away. This substantiates our claim concerning the role of the phenomenological reduction in Heidegger's existential analysis. In order to disclose the essential structures of existence, Heidegger distances himself from the everyday attitude by turning it into an object of investigation. This approach embraces the two constituting elements of a phenomenological reduction: eidetic and transcendental reduction.

Heidegger carries out an elaborate analysis of the everyday being of the 'there,' and he identifies certain modes of being that characterize it: *idle talk* (*Gerede*), curiosity (*Neugier*), and ambiguity (*Zweideutigkeit*). The term 'idle talk' refers to an everyday expression of discourse, that is, a fallen discourse. This phenomenon is characterized by an absorption in the world and therefore by an intrinsic blindness to the structure of its own being, hence, the term 'idle talk.' But though idle talk seems to suggest something negative, Heidegger emphasizes that it is not used "in a disparaging signification ... [rather] it signifies a positive phenomenon which constitutes the kind of Being of everyday Dasein's understanding and interpreting" (BT, 211). The term 'curiosity' refers to an everyday pressing into possibilities — an everyday projection — which does not reflect the essential situatedness of understanding. This phenomenon designates a continuous distraction by new possibilities and it "reveals a new kind of Being of everyday Dasein — a kind in which Dasein is constantly uprooting itself" (BT, 217). Curiosity, like idle talk, also designates a positive phenomenon in the sense that it constitutes Dasein's everyday mode of being. Ambiguity refers to a third phenomenon constituting everydayness, and this term designates a fallen situatedness.

Ambiguity not only affects the way we avail ourselves of what is accessible for use and enjoyment, and the way we manage it; ambiguity has already established itself in the understanding as a potentiality-for-Being, and in the way Dasein projects itself and presents itself with possibilities. (BT, 217)

By the term 'ambiguity' Heidegger emphasizes that our understanding not only is thrown and situated, but that it is situated within an already established framework of average intelligibility. Dasein is always already absorbed in the world, it is always already in the mode of "not-being-its-self." This entails an ambiguity in the sense that an essential structural moment of Dasein's existence, that is, of Dasein's self-directedness, implies that Dasein for the most part is always already in the mode of "not-being-its-self."

While the structural moments situatedness, understanding, and discourse make up the constitution of Dasein's being, these structures appear in its everyday kind of being as ambiguity, curiosity, and idle talk, respectively. Whereas the former represent an ontological definition of Dasein's being, the latter designate the ontical and inauthentic mode of this being. In addition, there is a third mode of being — an authentic mode — which serves as a pre-ontological justification for moving from the ontical to the ontological level.[29]

7. CARE

As we recall, Heidegger emphasizes that the existential structures of Dasein are parts of a whole. Moreover, as structural moments, they are non-independent parts of this whole.

These existential characteristics are not pieces [*Stücke*] belonging to something composite, one of which might sometimes be missing; but there is woven together in them a primordial context which makes up that totality of the structural whole which we are seeking. (BT, 235-6)

Although presented somewhat independently of each other, these structural moments are intrinsically interrelated. They are all aspects of the same structural whole, and Heidegger underscores this essential interdependence by showing how each aspect includes the others.

According to Heidegger, the notion of "understanding as self-projective Being towards its ownmost potentiality-for-Being" (BT, 236) means ontologically that "in each case Dasein is already *ahead* of itself [*ihm selbst ... vorweg*] in its Being" (BT, 236). Thus, the structure of understanding is ontologically designated as "*Being-ahead-of-itself.*" But, he points out, this

---

[29] This mode of being, and its role in Heidegger's analytic, will be discussed in detail in Chapters VI, VII, and VIII.

"does not signify anything like an isolated tendency in a worldless 'subject,' but characterizes Being-in-the-world" (BT, 236). The notion of being-ahead-of-itself implies that Dasein "has been delivered over to itself — that it has in each case already been thrown *into a world*" (BT, 236). Thus, Heidegger concludes, "'Being-ahead-of-itself' means, if we grasp it more fully, *ahead-of-itself-in-already-being-in-a-world*'" (BT, 236). However, "Dasein's factical existing is not only generally and without further differentiation a thrown potentiality-for-Being-in-the-world" (BT, 236). That is, Dasein is not merely 'ahead of its being already there,' it is also 'there,' "absorbed in the world of its concern" (BT, 237). According to Heidegger, the structure 'ahead-of-itself-Being-already-in-a-world' essentially includes one's being-amidst and absorbed in the world. Based on this delineation of the ontological meaning of the structural moments of existence, Heidegger presents the following hyphenated formal definition of Dasein:

[T]he being of Dasein means ahead-of-itself-being-already-in-(the-world) as being-amidst (entities encountered in-the-world). This Being fills in the signification of the term '*care*' [*Sorge*]. (BT, 237).[30]

Thus, care is the "formal existential totality of Dasein's ontological structural whole" (BT, 237).

Although somewhat bizarre, this definition does indeed capture the essential interdependency among structural moments and between moments and the whole. The hyphens bring out the intrinsic relation between situatedness and understanding, which in turn means being-amidst the world. This tripartite structure finds its wholeness and unity in care. Care is not something other than the existentials, and yet it is not the sum of these structural moments either; care embraces the *unity* of them. Care is the whole, the final *concretum* for the structural moments constituting existence, and hence, it is something *apriori*, in the phenomenological sense of this term.

Care, as a primordial structural totality, lies 'before' ['*vor*'] every factical 'attitude' and 'situation' of Dasein, and it does so existentially *a priori*; this means that it always lies in them. (BT, 238)

The existentially apriori status of care does not imply that it can appear

---

[30] Heidegger quickly points out that the term 'care' "is used in a purely ontologico-existential manner" (BT, 237). "[Care] is to be taken as an ontological structural concept. It has nothing to do with 'tribulation,' 'melancholy,' or the 'cares of life,' though ontically one can come across these in every Dasein. These — like their opposites, 'gaiety' and 'freedom from care' — are ontically possible because Dasein, when understood *ontologically*, is care" (BT, 84).

temporally prior to and independently of the existentials, rather it appears *with* these structural moments as their unity. Care is "ontologically 'earlier' than the [existentials]" (BT, 238), not ontically earlier. For this reason Heidegger emphasizes that care "cannot stand for some special attitude towards the Self" (BT, 237). That is, care is not a directedness towards the self that comes in addition to the existential structures. Care is an ontological concept and it is the condition of possibility for any kind of directedness, whether practical or theoretical intentionality. Heidegger emphasizes that the phenomenon of care "by no means expresses a priority of the 'practical' attitude over the theoretical" (BT, 238). Rather, "'theory' and 'practice' are possibilities of Being for an entity whose Being must be defined as 'care'" (BT, 238).

Heidegger distinguishes between an ontical interpretation and an existential-ontological interpretation of Dasein. Although the latter needs a pre-ontological confirmation, and thus is connected to the former, it is not "merely an ontical generalization which is theoretical in character" (BT, 243).

The 'generalization' is rather one that is *ontological and a priori*. What it has in view is not a set of ontical properties which constantly keep emerging, but a state of Being which is already underlying in every case, and which first makes it possible for this entity to be addressed ontically as "*cura*" [care]. (BT, 244)

In phenomenology, generality is constituted through ideation. Essences can be constituted in the objective realm as well as in the subjective, but in the case of the latter, only after a transcendental reduction. The generalization Heidegger has carried out here is referred to as apriori which, in his earlier use of this term, embraces wholes or absolute *concreta*. According to Husserl, there is only one absolute *concretum*; pure or transcendental consciousness. In Heidegger a similar entity — a structural whole — is disclosed through the interpretation of Dasein as care.

The transcendental 'generality' of the phenomenon of care and of all fundamental *existentialia* is ... broad enough to present a basis on which *every* interpretation of Dasein which is ontical and belongs to a world-view must move. (BT, 244)

Heidegger would argue that he has in fact transcended Husserl because care refers to the being of this entity, that is, to "a state of Being which is already underlying in every case." At this point in the analysis, this might be an accurate description. But we shall see later that the full meaning of the being of this entity is not reached before the existentials are redefined in temporal distinctions that strongly resemble Husserl's temporal determinations of transcendental subjectivity. We return to that topic in the final chapter.

The purpose of this chapter has been to investigate Heidegger's notion of

Dasein and his definition of Dasein as existence. Firstly, we have seen that (i) Dasein refers to human being, (ii) existence is an essential determination of the being of Dasein, (iii) existence thus refers to a kind of being that everybody that is Dasein share insofar as they are Dasein, and (iv), existence refers to Dasein only. Hence, Heidegger undoubtedly brackets individuality in favor of generality in his approach to this entity we ourselves are. That is, he is carrying out an eidetic investigation of Dasein. Secondly, this investigation is one which aims at the essential structures, not of constituted objects, but of constitution as such. It is therefore preceded by something which bears a strong resemblance to a Husserlian notion of a transcendental reduction. This reduction turns the focus back on the being of that entity to which appearances appear.

Although Heidegger does not define Dasein as a substance with certain properties, he does call attention to certain aspects that constitute the being of Dasein. These aspects are introduced as existentials and they differ from properties or categories in that they are not to be understood as modifications of a substance. Existentials are structural moments and they are related to the being of Dasein the way moments are related to a whole. It follows, then, that Dasein cannot be thought of as an entity whose being can be considered apart from these structural moments. Admittedly, the being of Dasein is something "more" than these existentials, but it is not thereby something other in the sense that it can appear independently of them. It is something "more" because it is not merely the sum of these existentials but is the unity of them. However, a unity cannot precede its parts. It can be ontologically prior to them, but it can still only appear with its moments.

The existentials situatedness (facticity), understanding (existentiality), and discourse (falling) are united in the phenomenon of care (*Sorge*) which designates the being of Dasein. This phenomenon is the ground sought by Heidegger's existential analytic, and although he will offer a temporal reinterpretation of it, he does not transcend it. His analysis of temporality does not introduce a new phenomenon but rather provides the full meaning of care. In other words, in Heidegger, just as in Husserl, the final determination of the being of the constituting entity takes place in the temporal delineation of it.

CHAPTER V

SELF-CONSCIOUSNESS

The basic state of Dasein is Being-in-the-world, and the essence of this being is existence. In the previous chapter we investigated the formal structure of existence, and we have seen that it is constituted by three structural moments which find their unity in the phenomenon of care. Hence, the meaning of existence is care.

At this point the following question surfaces: what is it about existence that makes world an essential part of Dasein's being? Our initial response was that Dasein relates to its own being through constituting the world, but we shall now discuss this issue in more detail. In this chapter we focus on the subjective aspect of this question and show that self-comportment or primary understanding necessarily includes the world. In the next chapter we shall have a look at the objective aspect and see how world necessarily presupposes primary understanding.

Existence designates a kind of self-directedness which is not an inward self-reflection. Dasein understands itself not through introspection, but through its involvement with the world. It is our argument that this position introduces a phenomenological notion of self-consciousness. In order to clarify this position we relate it to Sartre's discussion of the status of the ego in *The Transcendence of the Ego*[1] and to Kant's discussion of the original synthetic unity of apperception in the first Critique. For the most part, then, this chapter will not deal directly with Heidegger but with Sartre and Kant. But the position we are discussing is intrinsically Heideggerian, and we use Sartre and Kant in order to elucidate it.

Although TE is a response to issues in Husserlian phenomenology, Sartre makes occasional comments about Kant which reveal an intrinsic relationship between Kantian philosophy and phenomenology. The core of this relationship concerns the nature of self-consciousness or transcendental apperception. About this we propose three theses. First, the tension within phenomenology discussed by Sartre about whether consciousness contains an ego or whether it is simply a spontaneity transcending towards objects echoes a

[1] J.P. Sartre, *The Transcendence of the Ego, An Existentialist Theory of Consciousness*, translated by F. Williams and R. Kirkpatrick (New York: Hill and Wang, 1960). Hereafter referred to as TE.

similar tension in Kant. Second, Sartre's rejection of the primacy of the actual reflection 'I think' in favor of a prior unity (TE, 36) is in fact a point already made by Kant in his distinction between the synthetic and analytic unity of apperception. In claiming that "the synthetic unity of apperception is [the] highest point" (Kant, B134n), Kant in effect states that the reflection 'I think' through which "I represent to myself the analytic unity" (Kant, B134n) presupposes a prior unity, namely the synthetic unity of apperception. Third, Kant's identification of the synthetic unity of apperception with "understanding itself" (Kant, B134n) testifies to a notion of pure or original apperception that bears strong resemblance to what Sartre calls non-positional awareness. The claim that apperception is a non-positional awareness of the activity of thinking would entail that self-consciousness is consciousness not of *a* self, but of *it*self.

It will be our argument that this introduces a kind of egology which is compatible with Heidegger's determination of Dasein as existence. Existence refers to a notion of self-directedness which is not a directedness towards, or consciousness of, a self appearing prior to the world. The self is not given as an object of consciousness but is given *with* our consciousness of objects. This chapter will investigate Dasein's existence with an emphasis on its self-constitution. The next chapter will show, in turn, how self-constitution is intrinsically related to constitution of the world in a way that does not allow for a detached, worldless subject.

1. PHENOMENOLOGY AND SELF-CONSCIOUSNESS

As Okrent points out in *Heidegger's Pragmatism*, in spite of the fact that Heidegger tries to break with the traditional way of defining human being, his definition of Dasein seems, at least at first glance, traditional in two ways. First, he claims, Dasein is "defined by mentioning a trait which all things that count as Dasein must possess insofar as they are Dasein, and which no being that is not Dasein possesses" (Okrent, 18). Thus, Heidegger seems to suggest that Dasein is an entity which is modified by a certain essential feature. Second, the feature used to define Dasein "appears to be just the one that has traditionally been taken to be distinctive to human beings ... since Descartes: self-awareness, or self-consciousness" (Okrent, 18). Whereas Okrent rejects both claims as inappropriate accounts of Heidegger's project, we show that the latter is not off target. We counter his claim that "self-comportment is *not* self-awareness" (Okrent, 18) by arguing that existence or self-comportment in fact designates a phenomenological notion of self-consciousness.

Regarding the former, we agree with Okrent, and we have already shown why it is inappropriate to see self-comportment as a feature or property at all.

Admittedly, existence refers to something every being that is to count as Dasein must possess, but this essence must not be understood in terms of a property. Dasein is not a substance whose essence is a necessary property that makes it distinctive. Rather, Dasein's essence consists in it being. "The 'essence' of this entity lies in its 'to be' [*zu-sein*]" (BT, 67).

However, the second claim that Heidegger's concept of self-comportment seems to resemble the feature traditionally used to define human being, namely self-consciousness, is not as easy to address, for this phenomenon brings us to the very heart of Heidegger's philosophy. A first reply to this observation could be the following: yes, Heidegger's concept of existence does refer to a kind of self-consciousness but — and this is pivotal — to a phenomenological notion of self-consciousness. Existence refers to a notion of self-directedness which is not a directedness towards, or consciousness of, a self appearing prior to the world. The self is not given as an object of consciousness, rather it is given *with* our consciousness of objects. In the following, we delineate this position in more detail and we begin by having a look at Heidegger's determination of existence as understanding.

According to Heidegger, Dasein's self-comportment, its existence, is "essentially, even if not only, to understand" (BT, 182). Hence, an essential characteristic of Dasein is that it relates to itself by way of understanding. Traditionally the term 'understanding' has been used to refer to a certain range of cognitive abilities that result in knowledge. However, if we are to take the right approach to Heidegger's account of understanding, it is essential that we do not think of understanding as primarily a cognitive phenomenon.

With the term "understanding" we have in mind a fundamental existentiale, which is neither a definite species of cognition distinguished, let us say, from explaining and conceiving, nor any cognition at all in the sense of grasping something thematically. (BT, 385)

On the basis of Heidegger's conception of understanding as a fundamental existentiale of Dasein we can delineate three distinctive features of his use of the term 'understanding.' First, understanding belongs to Dasein, and only those beings that are characterized as being Dasein can understand. Second, Dasein always understands. Understanding is not an activity among others that Dasein might engage in on occasion. Rather, understanding is essential to Dasein in the sense that there could be no Dasein without understanding. Third, what Dasein primarily understands is itself, that is, its own being. Although Dasein understands a variety of things, Heidegger nevertheless grants priority to Dasein as self-understanding.

Points one and two have in fact already been dealt with in the previous section. They follow from the following premises: (i) existence is an essential characteristic of Dasein, and pertains to Dasein alone, and (ii) existence is understanding. In the rest of this section we focus solely on point three. Given the fact that Dasein "always understands itself in terms of its existence" (BT, 33), it is necessary to elucidate what this understanding is all about. In what manner does Dasein understand itself?

What is of importance for Heidegger is the fact that the self-comportment that takes place by way of understanding should not be thought of as some kind of inner cognitive process, i.e., as introspection. If that were the case, Heidegger would find himself back in the very philosophy of immanence he is rejecting. Heidegger does maintain that

Dasein is such that in every case it has understood (or alternatively, not understood) that it is to be thus or thus. As such understanding it 'knows' what it is capable of — that is, what its ability-to-be is capable of. (BT, 184)

But he also claims that "[t]his 'knowing' does not first arise from an immanent self-perception, but belongs to the being of the 'there,' which is essentially understanding" (BT, 184). Thus, Dasein's understanding of its being is not a product of inward self-reflection. On the contrary, Dasein takes a stand with regard to itself through its involvement with things and people. Dasein's existence, its self-comportment, is not some inner thought or experience; it is the way Dasein acts.

In everyday terms we understand ourselves and our existence by way of the activities we pursue and the things we take care of. (BP, 159) ... To exist then means, among other things, relating to ourselves by being with beings. (BP, 157)

The understanding of ourselves, then, takes shape not so much in introspection as in action.

In German we say that someone can *vorstehen* something — literally, stand in front of or ahead of it, that is, stand at its head, administer, manage, preside over it. This is equivalent to saying that he *versteht sich darauf*, understands in the sense of being skilled or expert at it. The meaning of the term "understanding"... is intended to go back to this usage in ordinary language. (BP, 276)

This understanding is more fundamental than the distinction between theoretical and practical intentionality. "It is," Heidegger claims, "the condition of possibility for all kinds of comportment, not only practical but also cognitive" (BP, 276). Hence, it follows that for Heidegger our self-understanding is something that expresses itself in all our actions. Understanding is not in our minds, but in Dasein. Furthermore, this implies that the self no longer appears as a worldless subject which subsequently has to get hooked up with a world. On the contrary, given the fact that Dasein takes a stand on itself through its involvement with the world, the self becomes a self only through the total context of the world.

We have now established the following about Heidegger's concept of Dasein: (1) the essence of Dasein is existence; (2) qua existence, Dasein is essentially relating to its own being;[2] (3) to exist is primarily to understand,[3] and what Dasein understands is essentially itself; and (4), self-understanding is not a product of inward self-reflection.[4] Dasein understands itself through its involvement with things and people, not by means of introspection.[5] Let us keep these four points in mind while we pursue a line of reasoning which may seem to be a digression in relation to the main topic of our discussion. Although we leave Heidegger for a while to examine Sartre and Kant we shall see that there is a strong thematic continuity between the above discussion and the theme we emphasize in Sartre and Kant. In fact, we move on to the latter for a while in order to determine Heidegger's position more accurately.

In the short introductory note to TE (which we quote in its entirety) Sartre makes the following claim:

For most philosophers the ego is an "inhabitant" of consciousness. Some affirm its formal presence at the heart of *Erlebnisse*, as an empty principle of unification. Others — psychologists for the most part — claim to discover its material presence, as the center of desires and acts, in each moment of our psychic life. We should like to show here that the ego is neither formally nor materially *in* consciousness: it is outside, *in the world*. It is a being of the world, like the ego of another. (TE, 31)

In this passage Sartre distinguishes his view from that of Kant on the one hand and from that of psychologism[6] on the other. This is a typical strategy for a phenomenologist. But Sartre makes an additional move by claiming that the ego is not in the consciousness but rather is in the world. This comment is not only directed at Kant and psychologism but also at Husserl.

The target of Sartre's criticism in TE is not Kant but the notion of a transcendental ego as an inhabitant of consciousness. The tendency to interpret the unity of the self as though it were a thing-like entity remains within the framework of a Cartesian egology. It is not entirely clear whether

---

[2] "These entities [Dasein], in their being, comport themselves towards their being. As entities with such being, they are delivered over to their own being"(BT, 67).

[3] "To exist is essentially ... to understand"(BP, 276).

[4] It does not, Heidegger claims, "first arise from an immanent self-perception"(BT, 184).

[5] "In everyday terms we understand ourselves ... by way of the activities we pursue and the things we take care of"(BT, 157). "To exist means ... relating to ourselves by being with beings"(BT, 159).

[6] By 'psychologism' we mean the view according to which the ego has a material presence in each moment of psychical life. We are well aware of the fact that this differs from other notions of psychologism like, for instance, the view of J.S. Mill.

or not Sartre includes Kant in this group, but one might take the above passage as textual evidence suggesting that he believed Kant advocated a view of the ego as some kind of a formal inhabitant of consciousness. However, there are other passages in Sartre that would suggest that this is in fact a view that he ascribes to the post-Kantians and that he held that Kant himself did not make such a claim.[7] Husserl, on the other hand, is accused of introducing classical egology into phenomenology and thereby of reintroducing the very problems the phenomenology set out to dissolve.

Sartre introduces TE by commenting upon different interpretations of what Kant refers to as the principle of the necessary unity of apperception.

It must be conceded to Kant that "the I Think *must be able* to accompany all our representations." But need we then conclude that an *I in fact* inhabits all our states of consciousness and actually effects the supreme synthesis of our experience. This inference would appear to distort the Kantian view. (TE, 32)

Sartre points to a tendency in contemporary philosophy to make the condition "*must be able* to accompany" into a reality and thereby claiming that an *I* inhabits all conscious states. This, he claims, represents a fundamental misunderstanding of Kant. He also calls attention to a residual ambiguity in Kant's position. He formulates this in a question that in fact sums up the task of this inquiry: "is the *I* that we encounter in our consciousness made possible by the synthetic unity of our representations, or is it the *I* which in fact unites the representations to each other?" (TE, 34). This passage testifies to the fact that Sartre was aware of the fundamental problem in the realm of self-consciousness, i.e., whether primacy should be attributed to the synthetic unity or the analytic unity of apperception. The former emphasizes the primacy of spontaneity, with the consequent danger that it is not obvious how to account for identity. The latter leaves us with an indisputable identical self at the basis of synthesis, but this entity might turn out to be so substantial that it in fact blocks the view of consciousness, thus destroying what it is supposed to ground.

In what follows we shall see that the latter — the conception of an ego as inhabiting or resting behind consciousness and thus given prior to each consciousness-of — is attributed to Husserl, whereas Sartre himself is an advocate of the former. Kant is not so much identified with either position as he is used as a point of reference. Our argument shall be that the position ascribed to Husserl is excessively egological and that the position Sartre ends up defending is excessively non-egological. Both positions undermine

---

[7] To consider the transcendental I as an inhabitant, even a formal inhabitant, seems to be on the verge of making it into a reality. Sartre specifically says that this is "to take a point of view radically different from Kant"(TE, 33).

phenomenology, the former by representing the death of consciousness, the latter by taking on its object. We argue that a nuanced interpretation of Kant will disclose the kind of moderate egology that Sartre set out to define and also that this position in fact is held by Husserl.

After having set forth his problem, Sartre turns to Husserl. Like all phenomenologists, Sartre distances himself from the interpretations of the 'I think' offered by Neo-Kantians. He sees phenomenology as the proper method by which to approach this problem. Sartre claims that Husserl, unlike Kant, reaches a transcendental consciousness through the *epoché* that is "no longer a set of logical conditions" (TE, 35).

It is a real consciousness accessible to each of us as soon as the "reduction" is performed. And it is indeed this transcendental consciousness which constitutes our empirical consciousness, our consciousness "in the world," our consciousness with its psychic and psychophysical *me*. (TE, 35-6)

Sartre thus accepts the existence of a constituting consciousness, and notes that the psychic and psycho-physical me is a transcendent object that must fall before the *epoché*. But he asks, "is not this psychic and psycho-physical *me* enough? Need one double it with a transcendental *I*, a structure of absolute consciousness?" (TE, 36). In response to this question Sartre presents a fourfold thesis in which the distinction between the transcendental field and the transcendental *I* is paramount. He suggests that (i) the transcendental field is impersonal; (ii) the *I* is an aspect of the *me*; (iii) the "*I think* can accompany our representations because it appears on a foundation of unity which it did not help to create; rather, this prior unity makes the *I Think* possible" (TE, 36); and (iv), personality is not a necessary accompaniment of consciousness. The third thesis is especially interesting for what we are to discuss. We argue that it is compatible with Kant's view on the topic in that it testifies to the primacy of the synthetic unity of apperception.

2. SARTRE'S CRITIQUE OF HUSSERL

Husserl's view on the topic of the transcendental ego developed through different stages. In his earliest phenomenological work, LI, Husserl maintains a position that is compatible with Sartre's. He claims that although he can find an empirical self, reflection cannot lead him to a transcendental ego, i.e., a stable ego to which things appear. However, later in his career Husserl argues in favor of a transcendental *I*, a pure ego, i.e., a point-like center of experience. Sartre interprets this as a radical change; a move from rejection to affirmation of a transcendental ego.[8]

> After having determined (in *Logische Untersuchungen*) that the *me* is a synthetic and transcendent production of consciousness, he reverted in [the *Ideas*] to the classic position of a transcendental *I*. This *I* would be, so to speak, behind each consciousness, a necessary structure of consciousness whose rays (*Ichstrahlen*) would light upon each phenomenon presenting itself in the field of attention. (TE, 37)

Thus, as Sartre sees it, by the introduction of a transcendental *I*, Husserl has fallen back into classical egology.

According to Sartre, such a move introduces a superfluous entity into phenomenology. the existence of a transcendental *I* was introduced in order to secure the unity of consciousness, but Sartre claims that phenomenology needs no such appeal because consciousness is defined by intentionality. He puts it, somewhat cryptically, "[b]y intentionality consciousness transcends itself. It unifies itself by escaping from itself" (TE, 38). The notion of intentionality is a fundamental tenet of phenomenology and it emphasizes that there is no consciousness apart from consciousness-of; consciousness *is* simply a relational directedness. Thus, consciousness is not a thing-like entity that by means of intentionality transcends its own confines and thus directs itself towards the world. Intentionality is not something that belongs to consciousness like a property. It is not something consciousness has or needs. Intentionality is what consciousness is.

This view of consciousness is the guiding principle in Sartre's treatment of classical egology. Consciousness is not a substance, but a directedness-towards. For this reason the unity of consciousness cannot be treated as if consciousness were a unity in itself, apart from this directedness. If one investigates consciousness according to the doctrine of intentionality, one does not approach its acts as objects but the objects of its acts.[9] Therefore

---

[8] Sartre's TE is mainly a critique of Husserl. Although it is our contention that this critique fails, the objective of this interpretation is not so much to discuss the accuracy of Sartre's interpretation of Husserl as it is to indicate a relationship between Kant and Sartre and thus to delineate a position on the topic of transcendental apperception. In order to give an account of Sartre's position, we will, of course, have to go through his critique of Husserl but we will confine our own comments to some concluding remarks in this chapter. In our last chapter, Temporality, we indicate that Sartre's critique of Husserl fails because the position developed by Sartre is already held by Husserl.

[9] In LI Husserl puts it like this: "*It is not in the reflection upon judgments nor even upon fulfillments of judgments but rather in these fulfillments themselves that we find the true source of the concepts* [in question] ... Not in these *acts as objects*, but in *the objects of these acts*, do we have the abstractive basis which enables us to realize the concepts in question" (LI, VI, #44). From this Heidegger concludes: "The category 'being,' 'and,' 'or,' 'this,' 'one,' 'several,' 'then' are nothing like consciousness, but are correlates of certain acts. ... I find the categorial of identity not in the reflection upon consciousness and the subject as a process of ideating comportment, but in the reference to what is intended in this comportment as such"

Sartre claims that "[t]he unity of a thousand active consciousnesses by which I have added, do add, and shall add two and two to make four, is the transcendent object 'two and two make four'" (TE, 38). And he goes on to say that "[w]ithout the permanence of this eternal truth a real unity would be impossible to conceive, and there would be irreducible operations as often as there were operative consciousnesses" (TE, 38). Sartre's point is that those who believe that a state of affairs such as "two and two make four" is actually a content of our own representation need to "appeal to a transcendental and subjective principle of unification" (TE, 38). But, according to an intentional interpretation of consciousness, a state of affairs is nothing *in* consciousness; it is an objective correlate of consciousness. Therefore, Sartre claims that Husserl does not need a subjective principle of unification. "The object is transcendent to the consciousnesses which grasp it, and it is in the object that the unity of the consciousness is found" (TE, 38). Thus, Sartre concludes,

the phenomenological conception of consciousness renders the unifying and individualizing role of the *I* totally useless. It is consciousness, on the contrary, which makes possible the unity and the personality of my *I*. (TE, 40)

According to Sartre, the transcendental *I* is not merely useless, it will destroy consciousness.[10]

Given the phenomenological notion of consciousness as intentional it follows that consciousness can only be aware of itself "*in so far as it is consciousness of a transcendent object*" (TE, 40). This consciousness of consciousness, he adds, "is not *positional*, which is to say that consciousness is not for itself its own object" (TE, 41). And Sartre goes on to ask,

is there room for an *I* in such a consciousness? The reply is clear: evidently not. Indeed, such an *I* is not the object (since by hypothesis the *I* is inner); nor is it an *I of consciousness*, since it is something for consciousness. It is not a translucent quality of consciousness, but would be in some way an inhabitant. (TE, 41)

It is Sartre's argument that if one were to insert an *I*, one would destroy consciousness. A central distinction in this regard is the one between the *opacity* of objects and the *translucency* of consciousness. What is distinctive for consciousness is that it is a directedness-towards, a movement which finds its target as it hits against the opacity of objects. However, if these objects are other than consciousness, it follows that consciousness must be translucent to itself. If not, consciousness could not be intentional. If opacity were inserted into consciousness, consciousness would be a non-starter, so to speak; it would be locked up within itself. Through such a move, Sartre (HCT, 59).

---

[10] Sartre says, "the transcendental *I* is the death of consciousness" (TE, 40).

claims, "one congeals consciousness, one darkens it" (TE, 41). "Consciousness is then no longer a spontaneity; it bears within itself the germ of opaqueness" (TE, 41–2).[11]

Sartre seems to direct much of his criticism of Husserl's notion of a transcendental ego against *Ideas I* and CM. Sartre accepts the notion of a unity of consciousness within duration as it is described by Husserl in his investigation of temporality, but notes that Husserl "never had a recourse to the synthetic power of the *I*" (TE, 39). Sartre acknowledges that Husserl's notion of absolute consciousness differs from a Cartesian *Cogito* in being a non-substantial absolute. But this, Sartre claims, changes in Husserl's later works. Although Husserl "preserved intact this conception of consciousness unifying itself in time" (TE, 39), he introduces a certain monadological direction that endangers the phenomenological notion of consciousness.

As a response to what he considers to be Husserl's position, i.e., the view that the *I* is an inhabitant of consciousness uniting representations to one another, Sartre claims that the *I* we encounter in consciousness is, in fact, made possible by the synthetic unity of our representations. Through this discussion of the status of the ego in phenomenology, Sartre has thus revealed an intrinsic relationship between phenomenology and Kantian philosophy.

3. KANT ON THE ORIGINAL SYNTHETIC UNITY OF APPERCEPTION

Kant introduces section 16 of the Transcendental Deduction[12] with the following claim:

It must be possible for the 'I think' to accompany all my representations; for otherwise something would be represented in me which could not be thought at all, and that is equivalent to saying that the representation would be impossible, or at least would be nothing to me. (Kant, B131–2)

Kant thus precludes the possibility of having a representation without also being able to be aware of oneself having it. Such a representation would be impossible or, if I had such a representation, it would simply be nothing to me.[13] Being able to be aware means the reflective awareness manifested in

---

[11] Thus, Sartre concludes: "All the results of phenomenology begin to crumble if the *I* is not ... a relative existent: that is to say, an object *for* consciousness" (TE, 42).

[12] If not otherwise indicated Transcendental Deduction means the B-Deduction.

[13] This passage exhibits a certain ambiguity with regard to the degree of impossibility of having a representation without the possibility of the 'I think' accompanying it. Is such a representation impossible or is it possible in the mode of being nothing to me? It falls beyond our intent to discuss this in any further detail but we are inclined to settle for the impossibility

the representation 'I think.' By claiming that it must be possible to accompany all my representations with 'I think,' Kant makes a claim to the effect that consciousness presupposes self-consciousness. But the problem of how self-consciousness is to be interpreted remains. One possible interpretation is to treat it as, indeed, a consciousness of a kind of a self. That would amount to the claim that the consciousness of a self, i.e., the reflection 'I think,' is a necessary condition of experience. This would seem to imply the notion of a transcendental *I* given prior to any consciousness-of, i.e., an inhabitant of consciousness, a pre-given source of identity residing within consciousness uniting the representations to one another. However, even apart from the fact that Kant claims that the 'I think' must, not accompany my representations, but *be able to* accompany my representations, the treatment of pure apperception as a consciousness of a self is an approach which is not in keeping with other central tenets in Kant. If original apperception is considered consciousness of a self, the self is turned into an object of consciousness and thus Kant's (presumably exhaustive) distinction of objects into phenomena and noumena is violated. This self could not be the phenomenal self, because this would imply a confusion of the conditioning self with the conditioned self. It could not be the noumenal self, either, because we have knowledge of it. Hence, if apperception is consciousness of a self, this self has to be a third kind of self, neither phenomenal nor noumenal.

Interpreting the subject of apperception as an object of consciousness would also lead to an infinite regress in the sense that it would imply that one could experience the condition of possibility of experience. For this reason, Allison[14] points out that although there is nothing highly problematic in Kant's claim that we can be aware of ourselves as thinking, nor in his notion of this awareness as a consciousness of spontaneity, this self-awareness should not be interpreted as an experience. Hence, in Allison's view, although apperception is a consciousness of spontaneity, consciousness does not thereby become its own object, i.e., as something to be experienced. In what follows, we accept this view. Our task will be to relate it to the position delineated by Sartre in TE.

In his treatment of Kant in TE, Sartre evades these questions concerning apperception by referring to it as a formal principle. Sartre speaks of Kant's notion of transcendental consciousness as "a set of logical conditions" (TE, 35) and "a formal structure of consciousness" (TE, 54). Although there is some evidence to support this view in Kant, these claims are certainly at

of such a representation and thus consider the "being nothing to me" a different way of stating the impossibility.

[14] H. Allison, *Kant's Transcendental Idealism* (New Haven and London: Yale University Press, 1983).

variance with other passages where Kant claims that "apperception is something real" (Kant, B419). Allison argues that "this is a point on which the ontologically oriented interpreters of Kant rightly insist" (Allison, 273).

Although Sartre was evidently unaware of it, we claim that his approach to Kant's notion of apperception shows that Kant and Sartre have in common a view of self-consciousness that acknowledges the fact that there is a real self-awareness, but that this self-awareness is a matter of consciousness being aware, not of *a* self, but of *it*self. Self-awareness does not mean that consciousness is set over against itself as its own object. Rather, consciousness is aware of itself in a non-reflexive manner, and it is so only in so far as it is consciousness of objects. In order to marshall evidence in favor of this claim, we show that Kant and Sartre share an emphasis on the primacy of a prior unity over the representation of the 'I think.' Moreover, we argue for the kinship between Kant's and Sartre's prior unity, the synthetic unity of apperception and non-positional awareness, respectively.

We have already quoted Kant's formulation of the principle of the necessary unity of apperception. In what follows, we contend that, according to Kant, the representation 'I think' is not itself the original apperception, but, as Sartre puts it, "can accompany our representations because it appears on a foundation of unity which it did not help to create; rather this prior unity makes the *I think* possible" (TE, 36).

The first indication in favor of this claim comes immediately after the formulation of the principle in the following passage.

[T]his representation [I think] is an act of *spontaneity*, that is, it cannot be regarded as belonging to sensibility. I call it *pure apperception* to distinguish it from empirical apperception, or, again, *original apperception*, because it is that self-consciousness which, while generating the representation '*I think*'... (Kant, B132)

At first sight this passage seems to add up to the claim that spontaneity is generated. Kant first claims that the 'I think' is an act of spontaneity and then goes on to refer to the representation 'I think' as generated. One way to resolve this apparent self-contradiction is to look more closely at the first sentence. Although Kant's claim that the 'I think' is an act of spontaneity reads in English as an identification between the 'I think' and the act itself, this identification is not so obvious in German. One indication in favor of this should be the awkwardness of referring to a representation as an act. But we can make an even stronger case by pointing to a linguistic matter. The German term in question is *'Actus.'* This term not only refers to the act in itself; it can also refer to the effect of the act. If we understand 'act' in the latter sense, the 'I think' is an act of spontaneity in the sense of being the outcome of this act. From this it follows that spontaneity is the pure apperception or original apperception that generates the representations 'I think.' On this interpretation one would in fact be able to argue that Kant, like Sartre, holds that the 'I think' is an effect of something "prior."[15]

Let us now attempt to marshal further textual evidence in favor of this interpretation and of the further point that Kant interprets this "prior" as a unity and as synthetic. We take as our point of departure the following passage:

> This principle of the necessary unity of apperception is itself, indeed, an identical, and therefore analytic, proposition; nevertheless it reveals the necessity of a synthesis of the manifold given in intuition, without which the thoroughgoing identity of self-consciousness cannot be thought. (Kant, B135)

What Kant claims here is, firstly, that the principle of the necessary unity of apperception is analytic. Even if this claim is not entirely self-evident, we shall not dispute it.[16] Our interest is the second part of the passage, the part claiming that the analytic proposition reveals (*erklärt*) the necessity of a synthesis. According to Kant, the analytic unity of apperception is the concept of *I* as an identical self. However, this *I* does not occur prior to our synthesizing activity.

> Only in so far ... as I can unite a manifold of given representations in *one consciousness*, is it possible for me to represent to myself the *identity of the consciousness in [i.e., throughout] these representations*. (Kant, B133)

Sartre's claim that consciousness can be aware of itself only in so far as it is consciousness of an object seems to be a phenomenological version of this statement. Kant concludes this passage as follows: "In other words, the *analytic unity* of apperception is possible only under the presupposition of a certain *synthetic* unity" (Kant, B133).[17] Thus, it would seem that Kant and

---

[15] This certainly goes against an interpretation of Kant according to which the "pure" 'I think' is a ground and the empirical 'I think' is an effect. There are several advocates of this position, for instance D. Henrich, *Identität und Objektivität, Eine Untersuchung über Kants transzendentale Deduktion* (Heidelberg: Carl Winter Universitäts-Verlag, 1976), and O. Höffe, *Immanuel Kant*, translated by M. Farrier (Albany: State University of New York Press, 1994). However, we do not intend to engage in a discussion with the advocates of this position at this time — that falls beyond the scope of this thesis. Our intent is merely to underscore the affinity between Kant and phenomenology on the notion of self-consciousness. But the reader should be aware of the fact that by so doing we are disagreeing with some Kant-scholars.

[16] We are, however, convinced that Kant is right about this claim, but its justification goes beyond the scope of the present investigation. For a thorough analysis, see Allison, 137–40.

[17] Recall that Sartre asks "is the *I* that we encounter in our consciousness made possible by the synthetic unity of our representations, or is it the *I* which in fact unites the representations to each other?" (TE, 34). And a couple of pages later he answers "the *I think* can accompany our representations because it appears on a foundation of unity which it did

Sartre both believe that the analytic unity of apperception — the concept of *I* as an identical self — presupposes a prior unity and that this prior unity is a synthetic unity. Let us now look into this apparent kinship more thoroughly. Our claim is that Sartre's notion of non-positional awareness is quite similar to Kant's notion of transcendental apperception as we have interpreted it above.

4. TRANSCENDENTAL APPERCEPTION AND NON-POSITIONAL AWARENESS

Having shown that Kant and Sartre share an emphasis on the primacy of a prior unity over the representation 'I think,' we shall now indicate the kinship between Kant's concept of transcendental apperception and Sartre's concept of non-positional awareness.

Sartre's position is non-egological. He agrees with Kant's principle of the necessary unity of apperception but, he claims, one should not thereby conclude that "an *I in fact* inhabits all our states of consciousness and actually effects the supreme synthesis of our experience" (TE, 32). Sartre underscores the "must-be-able-to-accompany"-character of the 'I think' in order to preclude the claim that there is an *I* inhabiting all our conscious states. Although the 'I think' can be attached to representations by self-reflective consciousness, this *I* is not an entity given ahead of synthesis.

Before inquiring further into Sartre's position, let us investigate certain claims made by Kant in section 16 of his Transcendental Deduction, The Original Synthetic Unity of Apperception. We have already established that "the *analytic* unity of apperception is possible only under the presupposition of a certain *synthetic* unity" (Kant, B133). This precludes any attempt at considering the identical self as given prior to our synthesizing activity. Moreover, it shows that the identical self simply appears in a way fundamentally different from the way objects appear. It is not given as an object of consciousness, rather it is given *with* our consciousness of objects. Hence, it is essentially not capable of being any kind of an inhabitant.

Thus far, we have not said much about this primary unity. Let us take as a point of departure the last two sentences of the footnote on B134. We begin with the first sentence.

The synthetic unity of apperception is therefore that highest point, to which we must ascribe all employment of the understanding, even the whole of logic, and conformably therewith, transcendental philosophy.

not help to create; rather, this prior unity makes the *I Think* possible" (TE, 36).

Here Kant emphasizes the primacy of the synthetic unity of apperception noting that it is the summit of understanding. It would seem to follow that it would also be the summit of transcendental philosophy. In the last sentence Kant brings the topic to a very interesting conclusion. He says, "[i]ndeed this faculty of apperception [the synthetic unity of apperception] is the understanding itself." Hence, the highest point of all employment of understanding is understanding itself.

Kant does not provide us with much to go on here, but by claiming that pure or original apperception is the understanding itself he seems to indicate something to the effect that understanding is non-reflectively aware of itself. On this interpretation, the reflection 'I think' is an effect of consciousness's prior non-reflective awareness of itself qua thinking. Early in section 16 of the Transcendental Deduction Kant makes a similar claim.

[T]his representation [I think] is an act of *spontaneity*, that is, it cannot be regarded as belonging to sensibility. I call it *pure apperception* to distinguish it from empirical apperception, or, again, *original apperception*, because it is that self-consciousness which, while generating the representation '*I think*'... (Kant, B132)

We have already made use of this quote in order to argue in favor of the fact that the representation 'I think' is not itself pure apperception but is an effect of pure apperception. But Kant makes an additional claim in this passage. On a close reading, we discover that the third word of the second sentence (the 'it') refers, not to 'this representation' in the beginning of the first sentence — that would imply that the 'I think' generated itself — but to 'spontaneity.' Thus, according to Kant, spontaneity is pure or original apperception. Hence, there are at least two places in the *Deduction* where Kant refers to pure apperception as spontaneity or understanding. As is well known, for Kant, the former defines the latter.

Kant takes as his point of departure the necessary possibility that the 'I think' may accompany all of my representations. However, what he says is not that it is necessary to reflect on one's thoughts, but that it necessarily must be possible to do so. This principle of the necessary unity of apperception is, he claims, analytic. But it "nevertheless reveals the necessity of a synthesis" (Kant, B135). This synthetic unity of apperception is the understanding itself. This is the capacity by virtue of which we are able to add an 'I think' to our thoughts. For that very reason, this capacity, this pure apperception, must somehow be aware of itself as thinking but in a way that does not include an 'I think.' On this interpretation, pure apperception seems to imply a notion of self-consciousness as an unreflected consciousness, not of *a* self (that would be a contradiction in terms; adding a self, an 'I think,' is exactly what makes consciousness reflective), but of *it*self as a synthesizing activity. This brings us very close to Sartre's concept of non-positional awareness.

As we have already pointed out, for Sartre "consciousness is aware of itself *in so far as it is consciousness of transcendent objects*" (TE, 40), and "this consciousness of consciousness ... is not positional, which is to say that consciousness is not for itself its own object" (TE, 40-1). If consciousness is a directedness towards objects, it follows that consciousness is not directed at itself. That would imply the possibility of looking in opposite directions at the same time, i.e., thinking the objective correlate and the intending consciousness at once. Consciousness is, qua intentional, by its very nature geared towards what is other than itself. If it were in the same moment directed at itself, it would not be intentional and hence it would immediately set into an isolated interiority.

We often comment upon the things we do by saying that we were not really conscious of what we were doing. What this means is that we were not conscious of ourselves as we were doing it. We were definitely conscious of what we were doing, but not self-reflectively. When we are conscious of transcendent objects we are conscious of them, not of our own consciousness of them. This does not mean that consciousness is unaware of itself; what it means is that consciousness is not conscious of itself.[18] When directed towards objects consciousness is not at the same time its own object. If that were the case, consciousness would lose its translucent character and hence it would be locked inside of itself. However, the fact that one can always look back on one's acts and say "I was reading the book" or "I was running after the streetcar" (to use Sartre's examples) suggests a certain kind of awareness by consciousness of itself. Sartre's point is that such acts do not reveal a pre-given identical self, an *I* inhabiting this consciousness of the book or the streetcar. These acts constitute the *I*.

According to phenomenological orthodoxy, an act cannot be directed at itself qua act. Acts are essentially directed towards what is other. One act can definitely be directed at another act, but in this case the latter is an object of the former, that is, it is not the acting act but act qua object. This is what motivates Sartre's remarks on the distinction between the reflecting consciousness and the reflected consciousness.

[M]y reflecting consciousness does not take itself for an object when I effect the

---

[18] In order to resolve the apparent contradiction in claiming that consciousness is not consciousness of itself but still not unaware of itself we introduce a distinction between consciousness of and being aware of. While the term 'being aware of' embraces both positional and non-positional awareness, 'consciousness of' refers exclusively to positional awareness. Thus, our above statement simply means that although consciousness is not positionally aware of itself it does not follow that it is unaware of itself.

Cogito. What it affirms concerns the reflected consciousness. Insofar as my reflecting consciousness is consciousness of itself, it is *non-positional*. (TE, 44–5)

Thus, Sartre, like Kant, considers the conscious reflection 'I think' to be an effect; it is an object of an act. Sartre adds that when effecting the 'I think,' I do not apprehend the non-positional awareness, I apprehend the effect, not the "effector." "Thus, the consciousness which says *I Think* is precisely not the consciousness which thinks. Or rather, it is not *its own* thought which it posits by this thetic act" (TE, 45). For this reason Sartre can claim that "All reflecting consciousness is, indeed, in itself unreflected" (TE, 45). Sartre concludes this line of reasoning by claiming that

the *I* never appears except on the occasion of a reflective act. In this case, the complex structure of consciousness is as follows: there is an unreflected act of reflection, without an *I*, which is directed on a reflected consciousness. The latter becomes the object of the reflecting consciousness without ceasing to affirm its own object (a chair, a mathematical truth, etc.). At the same time, a new object appears ... This transcendent object of the reflective act is the *I*. (TE, 53)

However, Sartre does not want to base his claim on theoretical considerations only. He sees the necessity of calling attention to concrete experience. He acknowledges the fact that doing so might easily betray the issue. "One must evidently revert to a concrete experience, which may seem impossible, since by definition such an experience is reflective, that is to say, supplied with an *I*" (TE, 46). But Sartre defends the legitimacy of this approach by pointing out that "every unreflected consciousness, being non-thetic consciousness of itself, leaves a non-thetic memory that one can consult" (TE, 46). Thus, the above theoretical considerations do not entail the impossibility of relating to reflecting consciousness qua reflecting, that is, to the unreflected consciousness involved in the consciousness-of objects (whether that be the *I* or other objects). But this can only be done in memory.

Sartre's first example concerns how he was "just now" absorbed in his reading. If he reconstitutes the complete moment of this act, the circumstances of the reading, his attitude, the lines read, there is, Sartre claims, "no doubt about the result" (TE, 46).

[W]hile I was reading, there was consciousness *of* the book, *of* the heroes of the novel, but the *I* was not inhabiting this consciousness. It was only consciousness of the object and non-positional consciousness of itself. (TE, 46–7)

And he continues, "I can now make these a-thetically apprehended results the object of a thesis and declare: there was no *I* in the unreflected consciousness" (TE, 47). Other examples considered by Sartre are acts like running after the streetcar, looking at the time, and contemplating a portrait. In these acts, he concludes "there is no *I*" (TE, 49). "There is consciousness *of-the-streetcar-having-to-be-overtaken*, etc., and non-positional consciousness of consciousness" (TE, 49). Sartre sums up his analysis by maintaining that given the fact that "all the non-reflective memories of unreflected consciousness show me a consciousness *without a me*" (TE, 48), and that "theoretical considerations ... have constrained us to recognize that the *I* cannot be a part of the internal structure of *Erlebnisse*" (TE, 48), we must simply conclude that "there is no *I* on the unreflected level" (TE, 48).

At this point it seems plausible to claim that there is a kinship between Kant's concept of pure apprehension and Sartre's notion of non-positional awareness.[19] Both terms refer to a kind of awareness that can effect the conscious reflection 'I think' and that therefore cannot itself contain an *I*. The act of thinking, i.e., reflecting consciousness, cannot become its own object. On this generating level there is nevertheless a consciousness, not of *a* self, but of *it*self. This level of apperception is a non-positional awareness of the activity of thinking.

5. HEIDEGGER AND EGOLOGY

Having established that the tension within phenomenology about the status of the ego echoes a similar tension in Kant, we may now engage in a broader investigation. We have shown that Sartre's rejection of the primacy of the actual reflection 'I think' in favor of a prior unity is in fact anticipated by Kant in his distinction between the synthetic and analytic unity of apperception. We have also seen that Kant's identification of the synthetic unity of apperception with understanding itself reveals a notion of pure or original apperception that bears strong resemblance to what Sartre calls non-positional awareness. Now the task is to burrow deeper, into the very structure and being of this pure apperception.

It is our contention that Heidegger's investigation of Dasein qua existence is just such an inquiry, and that his formal definition of Dasein is a step

---

[19] It is highly unlikely that Sartre himself was aware of this aspect of Kant's thinking. His comments on Kant suggests an interpretation emphasizing the primacy of the analytic unity of apperception. He rightfully acknowledges the fact that Kant does not turn this condition into a reality but he fails to see that Kant nevertheless refers to apperception as something real. He says: "For Kant, transcendental consciousness is nothing but a set of conditions which are necessary for the existence of an empirical consciousness" (TE, 33). Sartre seems to adhere to the view that Kant's emphasis on the primacy of the analytic unity commits him to an inconclusive position on the topic of apperception. Kant is right in pointing out that 'I think' must be able to accompany all my representations, and he is sound in not turning this into a reality, but this is but half the story. The rest of the story must necessarily address the nature of this kind of consciousness, and this is what Sartre takes on himself to provide.

towards the determination of the structure and being of the notion of pure apperception outlined above. Instead of returning immediately to Heidegger, however, let us first make some remarks that substantiate our initial claim about Sartre's critique of Husserl. This will function as a transition into Heidegger's further elaborations on Dasein.

We have indicated that Sartre's critique of Husserl fails because the position developed by Sartre is to a large extent already held by Husserl. Or to put it differently, Husserl would have agreed with Sartre's critique of the notion of the ego as an inhabitant of consciousness because that is an inversion and distortion of his own position. Husserl did not place the ego in the world, but the world in the ego, so to speak.

In the conclusion of TE, Sartre offers the following remark about the achievement of his treatise.

The conception of the ego which we propose seems to us to effect the liberation of the Transcendental Field, and at the same time its purification. The Transcendental Field, purified of all egological structure, recovers its primary transparency. (TE, 93)

The distinction between the Transcendental Field and the ego is very interesting in that it seems strongly related to Kant's distinction between the synthetic and the analytic unity of apperception. The former is the condition of possibility of the latter. But Sartre claims that the latter is thereby construed as a transcendent object that should fall under the *epoché*, which confuses the analytic unity of apperception with the empirical ego, i.e., the experiencing subject with the experienced subject.[20] This failure on Sartre's part leads to an interpretation of Husserl that does not capture the egology Husserl advocates, but that instead forces Husserl back into a Cartesian position.

Even if Husserl's terminology in CM is excessively Cartesian, Sartre's interpretation fails to grasp the true nature of his notion of a transcendental ego. Admittedly, Husserl refers to it as an 'I pole' which is always the same. This might lead one to think in terms of a thing-like entity. But the concept of an 'I pole' is the concept of an identical self, i.e., the analytic unity of apperception. If we take a closer look at the structure of Husserl's ego, we will find that it is a temporal unity which is never given apart from its constituting activity.[21]

A recurring problem for transcendental philosophy is that the enterprise

[20] It is our argument that Sartre is led astray by not being sufficiently sensitive to certain features of the principle of the necessary unity of apperception. He fails to see the correct distinction between the synthetic and analytic unity of apperception and therefore ends up presenting an excessively formalist interpretation of Kant and an excessively egological interpretation of Husserl.

[21] We shall go into this in more detail in Chapter IX, Temporality.

of describing conditions of possibilities has to make use of ordinary language, and language is geared to the realm of what is conditioned. Thus, the very terminology of transcendental philosophy can mislead one to think that it is violating its own basic principles. For instance, although Husserl's concept of a transcendental ego suggests a thing-like entity the *structure* of this pure ego does not have the identity of an object. Temporality, not spatiality, is the lifestyle of the ego. The transcendental ego has a horizon-structure and is spread out in time. Husserl does refer to this self as a fixed point, but its continuity must be talked about in temporal, rather than spatial, metaphors. This ego does not appear prior to the constituting activity, rather it appears as appearance itself, as that within which things can appear. It is simply what Sartre calls the Transcendental Field.

It is our argument that this theme inaugurates a new kind of egology. Though Sartre claims that he has purified the transcendental field of all egological structure, it is not egology as such that has been removed, but a certain kind of egology; a certain notion of the ego. What has been removed is what is often referred to as a Cartesian ego, i.e., the notion of an "I" inhabiting consciousness. But consciousness itself has survived. This consciousness is a transcendental consciousness, a prior unity that refers exclusively to the being we ourselves are. What is new is neither the priority nor the unity; what is new is that the priority is not one that appears independently of the world. Thus, the notion of a worldless ego appearing to itself independently of the world has been replaced by the notion of a worldly ego. In other words, it is our contention that what Sartre calls the Transcendental Field is consistent with what Kant refers to as the Synthetic Unity of Apperception and that this position designates a new kind of egology. One can legitimately refer to this position as egology because it accounts for the identity of the self which the traditional ego was supposed to take care of — without falling prey to the same problems. It is our contention that this is also the kind of egology Heidegger advocates.

One problem with relating Heidegger to the position delineated above is the fact that it involves certain metaphysical entities from which, it is commonly argued, Heidegger radically distances himself. Terms like consciousness, ego, and subject — to which the prefix 'transcendental' is often added — are typically used as labels for metaphysical positions that Heidegger seeks to overcome.

In the course of ... history certain distinctive domains of Being have come into view and have served as the primary guides for subsequent problematics: the *ego cogito* of Descartes, the subject, the "I," reason, spirit, person. But all these remained uninterrogated as to their Being and its structure, in accordance with the thorough-going way in which the question of Being has been neglected. (BT, 44)

In BT, the term 'ego' is used only to refer to a Cartesian worldless ego.[22] Likewise the terms 'subject,' 'consciousness' and 'I' are terminologically linked to the oblivion of the question of Being.

One of our first tasks will be to prove that if we posit an "I" or subject as that which is proximally given, we shall completely miss the phenomenal content [*Bestand*] of Dasein. *Ontologically*, every idea of a 'subject' — unless refined by a previous ontological determination of its basic character — still posits the *subjectum* along with it, no matter how vigorous one's ontical protestations against the 'soul substance' or the 'reification of consciousness.' (BT, 72)

Note that Heidegger does not forbid the use of the term 'subject' if it is "refined by a previous ontological determination of its character" (BT, 72). He makes the same allowance in a lecture in which he seems to refer to a concept of subjectivity that is not synonymous with "a common, subjectivistic concept of 'subject'" (MFL, 195). Moreover, he maintains that the world is something subjective, insofar as it is constituted by Dasein (MFL, 195). Hence, it is not unreasonable to assume that Dasein in fact refers to an ontologically refined subject.

All these terms ['subject,' 'soul,' 'consciousness,' 'spirit,' 'person'] refer to definite phenomenal domains which can be 'given form' ["*ausformbare*"]: but they are never used without a notable failure to see the need for inquiring about the Being of the entities thus designated. (BT, 77)

As we have repeatedly pointed out, Heidegger's phenomenology is a reaction against a specific notion of subjectivity, i.e., the Cartesian conception of the subject as essentially a worldless *res cogitans*. But Heidegger does not eliminate the subjective perspective, he recognizes that such a move would reduce human being to an object in a mechanistic physical universe. He does not see the modern shift in emphasis away from *res cogitans* to *res extensa* — with the result that subjectivity is virtually ignored as a significant area of investigation in its own rights — as any more tenable than the traditional emphasis on a mental reality. Thus, Heidegger seeks to get beyond the entire dichotomy and aims at rehabilitating the subjective perspective without restoring the *res cogitans*.

We have shown that what characterizes this refined subjectivity is existence, i.e., a certain kind of self-directedness. In order to provide a more accurate interpretation of this phenomenon, we relate it to the notion of self-consciousness delineated above. Admittedly, Heidegger himself never uses the term 'self-consciousness' [*Selbstbewusstsein*] in BT. The term appears

---

[22] See BT, 44, 71, 123, 254.

only in quotations from Yorck and Hegel.[23] Nor does Heidegger use the term apperception, though it also appears in quotations from Kant.[24] However, in a footnote Heidegger refers to KPM for an analysis of transcendental apperception.[25] We cannot consider Heidegger's interpretation of Kant in all its nuances here. The point of our discussions of Kant and Sartre was merely to map out a position to which we believe Heidegger, given his determination of Dasein as existence, is committed. Since there is a line of influence going from Kant to Heidegger — and also one going from Heidegger and Kant to Sartre — we consider this a justifiable approach to Heidegger. In this way we will also be able to show that nothing less than the quintessential philosophical question (at least since Descartes) constitutes the center of Heidegger's attention: the self-appearance of the ego. His propensity for neologisms notwithstanding, Heidegger's originality as a philosopher surfaces not primarily in his choice of topic but in the way in which he endeavors to handle it in a phenomenologically sound manner.

In what follows, we argue that Heidegger's determination of Dasein as existence not only is in accordance with the notion of self-consciousness developed above, but also that Heidegger in fact is committed to such a position. We readily admit that this is a radical departure from much of what is commonly said about Heidegger, and that it also can be argued to be contrary to Heidegger's self-interpretation. But it is our contention that if one sets aside what Heidegger himself says about his relation to the tradition, and instead examines the philosophical investigations he carries out, it becomes clear that our reading is not such an inaccurate description of Heidegger after all.

Recall the fourfold thesis we developed on the basis of Heidegger's determination of Dasein as existence. According to the first and the second statement, the essence of the being we ourselves are is self-directedness but, according to the third and the fourth, Dasein is directed towards itself, not as an object, but by being directed towards other things in the world. At first glance this seems highly compatible with Sartre's claim that consciousness can be aware of itself "*in so far as it is consciousness of a transcendent object*" (TE, 40). Admittedly, Sartre uses the term 'consciousness' and Heidegger 'Dasein,' but since both terms refer to the entity that we ourselves are, and whose essential characteristic is to be directed towards itself by being directed towards objects, it is hard to see any decisive differences between these terms.

[23] See BT, 453, 485.
[24] See BT, 366-7.
[25] *Op.cit.* This note replaces the following note in the earlier editions: "The first division of the second part of this treatise will bring the concrete phenomenologico-critical analysis of transcendental apperception and its ontological signification".

It is commonly argued that the term 'consciousness' carries with it the presupposition that cognition is the primary way of interacting with the world. The term 'Dasein,' on the other hand, is considered an attempt to abandon the traditional focus upon knowing as cognition (*knowing that*) and to emphasize *knowing how* as that which is essentially distinctive of human being. However, this interpretation identifies existence (the essence of Dasein) with practical intentionality which simply is not in keeping with the text. Heidegger specifically says that he is not more interested in practical intentionality than in theoretical intentionality.[26] His attention is directed upon a more primordial level in that he attempts to investigate the grounds of the intentionality of consciousness.[27]

The existential nature of man is the reason why man can represent beings as such, and why he can be conscious of them. All consciousness presupposes ... existence as the *essentia* of man.[28]

It seems highly likely that Heidegger here uses the term 'consciousness' to refer to any kind of intentionality, theoretical or practical. It is equally obvious that Dasein is neither theoretical nor practical, but more than either alone or the sum of both: all consciousness-of, whether theoretical or practical, presupposes the essence Dasein. The latter is a condition of possibility for the former. Given that the essence of Dasein is self-directedness, it follows, according to Heidegger, that all consciousness presupposes self-directedness, or, since consciousness is nothing but directedness, that all

---

[26] See for instance BT, 238: "[T]his phenomenon [care] by no means expresses a priority of the 'practical' attitude over the theoretical. When we ascertain something present-at-hand by merely beholding it, this activity has the character of care just as much as does a 'political action' or taking a rest and enjoying oneself. 'Theory' and 'practice' are possibilities of Being for an entity whose Being must be defined as care." This passage contradicts Okrent's claim that "for Heidegger, intentionality is always practical rather than cognitive and ... the primary form of intending is doing something for a purpose rather than being conscious of something," (Okrent, 10). Okrent also makes a peculiar and somewhat misguided distinction between intending qua doing something for a purpose and intending qua being conscious of something, which seems to identify being conscious of something with theoretical intentionality. Intentionality is an exhaustive definition of consciousness, and to be conscious of something means simply to be directed towards something, whether practically or theoretically. Thus, the correct distinction would be between practical and theoretical intentionality, which, of course, can be phrased as the distinction between a practical "being conscious of something," and a theoretical "being conscious of something."

[27] Recall the note on BT, 498: "The intentionality of 'consciousness' is grounded in the ecstatical temporality of Dasein." See also BP, 59: "The task is now to pursue [the] structure of Dasein's comportments ... and to ask how this structure of intentionality itself looks, but above all *how it is grounded in the basic constitution of Dasein.*"

[28] Heidegger, "The Way Back Into the Ground of Metaphysics" in *Existentialism from Dostoevsky to Sartre*, edited by W. Kaufmann (New York: Meridian Books, 1957), 272.

consciousness presupposes self-consciousness. Thus, Dasein is not synonymous with consciousness, if by this term one means merely practical consciousness, theoretical consciousness, or both. Dasein is the condition of possibility for both, and it is so by virtue of the fact that existence, self-directedness or self-consciousness, is its essence. Hence, Dasein is not merely consciousness, it is self-consciousness.

Now let us also add some remarks regarding the claim that the term 'consciousness' carries with it an emphasis on theoretical activity (*knowing that*) as the primary way of interacting with the world. Husserl is often accused of understanding consciousness in this manner, and his early writings are indeed focused upon cognition. But Føllesdal has pointed out that Husserl is perfectly open to the idea that practical activity is an equally primordial way of being directed towards the world.

[A]fter he came back to Freiburg in 1916 ... Husserl clearly became more and more aware that our practical activity is an important part of our relation to the world ... There is, according to Husserl, 'an infinite chain of goals, aims, and tasks' that our actions and their products relate to.[29]

It is clear then that transcendental or absolute consciousness can be reduced neither to practical nor to theoretical consciousness. It embraces both in the sense that it is "*the only absolute concretion*" (CM, 84). Practical and theoretical consciousness both belong to the natural attitude; neither then can be synonymous with an entity that is revealed by bracketing that attitude.

Let us now examine in more detail our equation between Dasein's existence and the phenomenological notion of self-consciousness. In a letter to Husserl written while he was working on BT Heidegger says "[t]he constituting subject is not nothing, hence, it is something and has being ... The inquiry into the mode of being of the constituting subject is not to be evaded."[30] It is quite reasonable to assume that Heidegger's analysis of Dasein is precisely such an "inquiry into the mode of being of the constituting subject." It is equally reasonable to maintain that the formal definition of Dasein — care — refers to the mode of being of this constituting subjectivity. This constituting subject is an ideal subject — in the phenomenological sense of ideal. Towards the end of Division One, in section 44, Heidegger says

with the question of the Being of truth and the necessity of presupposing it, just as

---

[29] D. Føllesdal, "Husserl and Heidegger on the Role of Actions in the Constitution of the World," in *Essays in Honour of Jaakko Hintikka*, edited by E. Saarinen (Dordrecht: Reidel, 1979), 371-2. Føllesdal specifically refers to three Fichte lectures that Husserl gave in November 1917 and repeated twice in 1918.

[30] Appendix to E. Husserl, *Phänomenologische Psychologie* (The Hague: Nijhoff, 1962), 601.

with the question of the essence of knowledge, an 'ideal' subject has generally been posited. The motive for this ... lies in the requirement that philosophy should have the '*a priori*' as its theme, rather than 'empirical facts' as such. (BT, 272)

And he continues, "[t]here is some justification for this requirement, though it still needs to be grounded ontologically" (BT, 272). At this point we know which notions of ideality and aprioricity are acceptable to Heidegger, and which are not. The notion of an ideal subject appearing prior to and independently of the world belongs to the latter group. This notion does not capture the apriori character of constituting subjectivity. As a response to his own claim about the justification of the requirement that philosophy should have the apriori as its theme, Heidegger asks the following rhetorical questions.

Yet is this requirement satisfied by positing an 'ideal subject'? Is not such a subject a *fanciful idealization*? With such a conception have we not missed precisely the *a priori* character of that merely 'factual' subject, Dasein? (BT, 272)

Of course we have! But this results not from the ideation that has taken place but from the *fanciful* manner in which it was carried out, that is, in a way that is phenomenologically unsound. A fanciful idealization is one that posits rather than discloses, i.e., one that forgets that ideation is a founded act. Such an approach leads to a notion of the being of constituting subjectivity that has no foundation in the phenomena.

The ideas of a 'pure "I"' and of a 'consciousness in general' are so far from including the *a priori* character of 'actual' subjectivity that the ontological characters of Dasein's facticity and its state of Being are either passed over or not seen at all. (BT, 272)

The "pure 'I'" and "consciousness in general" are products of a fanciful idealization. Such idealizations cannot capture the apriori character of Dasein because they posit entities that are worldless. As we know, for Heidegger the apriori character of Dasein is not that of appearing prior to and independently of the world. Rather, Dasein is prior to the world the way a whole is prior to its parts. Thus, Heidegger continues,

[r]ejection of a 'consciousness in general' does not signify that the *a priori* is negated, any more than the positing of an idealized subject guarantees that Dasein has an *a priori* character grounded upon fact. (BT, 272)

Heidegger is not here campaigning against an ideal subject, but against positing one. 'Positing' is almost a technical term in Heidegger. It refers to an approach that is phenomenologically unsound because it does not take into account fundamental tenets such as the theory of wholes and parts, the notion of categorial intuition, and the new sense of the apriori. The distinction and relation between founded and founding acts is especially violated in the act of positing.

The disclosure of an apriori character grounded upon fact exhibits an entity whose being cannot be separated from the world. Its being is essentially different from that of objects, but it is not thereby indifferent to the world. Dasein is different from the world insofar as it relates to its own being, but it is essentially tied to it because this relating can only be carried out in relation to the world. Dasein — qua existence and care — refers to the being or appearance of constituting subjectivity. It appears to itself, but not as an object, and not independently of the appearance of the world. Thus, it is not its own object but is nevertheless aware of itself, i.e., of its very essence. Hence, this must be a matter of non-positional awareness. In other words, it is only possible to reflect back on our acts and say "I did this" or "I did that," i.e., to reflectively add an "I" to our acts,[31] on the basis of a prior unity. This prior unity is Being-in-the-world whose formal existential expression is "being-in." It accounts for identity without positing an identical self inhabiting consciousness — identity can only appear in relation to the world. It is our contention that this position is extremely close to the Kantian-Sartrean position outlined above.

At the beginning of this chapter we asked what it is about existence that makes world an essential part of Dasein's being. So far the task has been to work out the first part of this question by laying bare the nature of Dasein's self-comportment. In order to do so, we have taken as a point of departure a notion of self-consciousness to be found in the intersection between Sartre and Kant. According to this position consciousness is aware not of *a* self as an object, but of *it*self in so far as it is directed towards what is other. The self is not given as an object of consciousness, rather it is given with our consciousness of objects.

It is our contention that Heidegger's determination of Dasein as existence embraces the same notion of self-consciousness. We have shown that Dasein refers solely to human being whose essence — existence — is self-directedness; that existence is not a directedness towards an object (it refers neither to theoretical nor practical intentionality), thus, it cannot refer to a kind of self-awareness where consciousness is aware of itself as an object; that

---

[31] The strength of Heidegger's approach is that even what causes the 'I think' or reflection to occur is also given in intuition, in the breakdown of everyday activities. Even conscious reflection has its origin in the world and not in an isolated subject. Thus, Heidegger has a preontological confirmation for a transcendental reduction. On this point Heidegger might prove more phenomenologically sound than Husserl. We develop this point more thoroughly in the following chapter.

existence has Being-in-the-world as its essential state, Being-in-the-world is a prior unity; and that the identical self can only appear on the basis of this prior unity. This leaves us with an identical self which cannot appear prior to the world. It does not follow from the fact that one can add an "I" to one's acts that an "I" inhabits consciousness. Reflection is only possible on the basis of a prior unity of non-positional awareness. Thus, as in Kant, the analytic unity of apperception presupposes the synthetic unity.

Having indicated the structural relationship between Heidegger's concept of Dasein and the notion of self-consciousness delineated above, we must now go on to investigate the intrinsic relation between self-constitution and the constitution of the world. Although Dasein does not appear prior to the world in an independent sense, it is still prior to the world in that it constitutes it.

CHAPTER VI

CONSTITUTION

The term 'existence' refers both to constitution and self-constitution; these are two aspects of Dasein's essence. Whereas the previous chapter focused on existence qua self-constitution, this chapter will deal with constitution. We shall see that there is an intrinsic relation between these two themes.

Towards the end of Chapter II, Categorial Intuition, we introduced a phenomenological concept of constitution. What characterizes this notion of constitution is that it is non-creative. "*'Constituting'* does not mean producing in the sense of making and fabricating; it means *letting the entity be seen in its objectivity*" (HCT, 71). Since constituting is a matter of "letting the entity be seen in its objectivity," it follows that objectivity is constituted. Dasein is the entity in which this constitution has its origin.

As Heidegger points out, the phenomenological notion of constitution is non-creative in the sense that it does not refer to any kind of fabrication on the part of the subject. The act of letting the entity be seen in its objectivity is a categorial act and, as we remember, categorial acts are founded acts. Although these acts introduce a surplus of meaning that cannot be borne by the founding objectivity, their correlates are nevertheless phenomena. That is, they are not constructed by the subject; they are disclosed. "Founded acts," Heidegger claims, "*disclose* the simply given objects *anew*" (HCT, 62).

This notion of constitution is tied to the essence of Dasein, and to the phenomenological notion of the apriori discussed in the previous chapters. We have seen that the notion of apriori goes through a transformation as it enters the phenomenological universe. Like any other phenomenological concept, it is subordinated the theory of wholes and parts. We have also seen that the essential state of Dasein, Being-in-the-world, is referred to as apriori because "it is not pieced together, but is primordially and constantly a whole" (BT, 65). The apriori character of Dasein takes place as a priority in relation to the world which satisfies the fundamental tenets of phenomenology: Dasein is prior to the world the way a whole is prior to its moments. Hence, it follows that Dasein must appear and, subsequently, that it must appear to itself. This brings us to the determination of Dasein as existence. We have seen that Dasein does not appear to itself independently of the world. On the contrary, Dasein takes a stand on itself by directing itself towards what is other, towards the world. Through this directedness Dasein constitutes the world in the sense that it lets entities appear in their objectivity, but this constitution is essentially non-constructive.

In construction or fabrication the fabricat*or* must appear prior to and independently of what is fabricated. Since the goal and completeness of fabrication is something that lies outside the agent — in the work that is to be produced — it follows that the craftsman can and must appear independently of the product. Interpreting the constitution of the world this way testifies to a theistic influence, creative constitution is simply a secularization of Genesis. As we know, the priority that conditions a creative notion of constitution does not characterize Dasein's relation to the world. Since Dasein does not appear independently of and temporally prior to the world, it follows that letting entities be seen in their objectivity must be a non-creative activity.

The objective of this chapter is to delineate Heidegger's notion of constitution, and we will introduce this discussion by redeeming the results of some of our previous investigations. We take our point of departure in the notion of constitution indicated in our treatment of categorial intuition. The following sections will show how the notion of worldliness (*Weltlichkeit*) developed in BT is in keeping with this notion. While the first sections will delineate Heidegger's analysis of the structure of the world — and also investigate Heidegger's pre-ontological confirmation of the possibility of doing so — the last section will discuss the concepts of discoveredness (*Entdecktheit*) and disclosedness (*Erschlossenheit*) in relation to constitution. It will be our contention that these concepts are intrinsically related to the notions of straightforward perception and categorial intuition.

1. BEING AND CONSTITUTION

Although Heidegger delineates a phenomenological concept of constitution in HCT, he does not use the term 'constitution' in order to technically refer to this "letting the entity be seen in its objectivity" in his writings after this lecture. In BT 'constitution' is used in several different senses. One way in which it is frequently used is to indicate that different phenomena make up the structure of another phenomenon.[1] In this form it refers, not to an act, but to structures making up a whole. Another usage indicates the opposite, i.e.,

---

[1] "The fundamental *existentialia* ... constitute [*konstituieren*] the Being of the 'here'..." (BT, 203). See also BT 194, 226.

that one phenomenon consists of different structural entities.[2] A third usage adds a slight nuance to the second. The difference is only that 'constitution' appears as a noun, but it still refers to a structural make-up of a whole. Hence, the term 'constitution' is typically used in order to refer either to the fact that several structural moments make up a whole or that a whole is made up of different moments. If it is ever used technically in BT it is in this sense. Thus, in BT 'constitution' is not used in order to refer to an *act* of constitution. For this we shall see that a new term is introduced, namely 'disclosedness' (*Erschlossenheit*). However, this term is not merely an arbitrary translation of 'constitution.' On the contrary, it brings out the full meaning of this phenomenon. It introduces, we argue, a more faithful delineation of the insights discussed in HCT, and hence, it underscores the continuity between the concepts of categorial intuition and ontological difference.

Having clarified this terminological issue, let us now take our point of departure in the above quotation of Heidegger's notion of constitution. We may recall that Heidegger distinguishes between real objectivity and ideal objectivity. While the former refers to real objects, that is, to entities with coordinates in space and/or time, the latter refers to those that possess neither spatial nor temporal properties. Both are objects in the sense that they are given as correlates of acts, but ideal objectivity cannot be grasped by ordinary sense-perception; they are correlates of categorial acts. Like Husserl, Heidegger ascertains that the non-real character of these objects does not imply their non-objectivity. Although they are neither real things nor real parts of given things, they are nevertheless correlates of acts of objectification. Moreover, not only can the terms 'real' and 'objective' not be used interchangeably, because objectivity includes both real and ideal objectivity, but Heidegger also indicates that the latter possesses a measure of primacy over the former. Recall the following claim from HCT:

[B]y way of understanding what is present in categorial intuition, we can come to see that the objectivity of an entity is really not exhausted by this narrow definition of reality, that objectivity in its broadest sense is much richer than the reality of a thing, and what is more, that the reality of a thing is comprehensible in its structure only on the basis of the full objectivity of the simply experienced entity. (HCT, 66)

What Heidegger suggests here is that not only does real objectivity not exhaust the definition of objectivity in its broadest sense, it is also comprehensible only on the basis of a full objectivity. *Real objectivity can only be grasped within the framework of ideal objectivity.* This theme will surface in Heidegger's discussion of worldliness as the distinction between a

---

[2] "Being-in-the-world ... [has] several constitutive moments in its structure" (BT, 78; translation altered). See also BT 41, 97.

particular piece of equipment (*Zeug*), and the referential whole (*Verweisungsganzheit*) within which a piece of equipment can be the equipment that it is. We shall see that this referential whole is essentially Dasein-dependent; it comes into being with Dasein.

We may recall that Husserl's concept of categorial intuition is of paramount importance for Heidegger's philosophical endeavor. At this point, we are prepared to appreciate more fully Heidegger's fascination with this concept and the role it plays in his attempted reappropriation of the *Seinsfrage*. Heidegger himself says that the "difference between sensuous and categorial intuitions ... revealed to me its importance for the determination of the 'manifold meaning of Being'" (MWP, 78). And that is exactly what it does. It allows Heidegger to discuss different meanings or "levels" of being without falling back into the reductive strategies of realism or idealism, and in this way to honor Aristotle's assertion that being is said in many ways.

The concept of categorial intuition renders possible a distinction between being and beings without relinquishing their objective status. Of course, being and beings differ in their objectivity in that the former is ideal and the latter is real, but neither is a construction. This is particularly important in regard to ideality, but subsequently also in regard to real objectivity. Traditionally, the distinction and difference between reality and ideality has been understood along the lines of independence, that is, that they can appear independently of each other. This can either mean that ideality appears prior to and independently of real objects, or vice versa. While the former typically has been understood to the point where ideality is seen as somehow causing the existence of real objects, the latter has surfaced as empiricist theories of how ideas occur through inductive generalization based on the prior appearance of real objectivity. The strength of the concept of categorial intuition is precisely that the distinction and difference between being and beings does not imply their indifference, i.e., that they can appear independently of one another. Since the correlates of sensuous acts — real objects — make up the founding objectivity of categorial acts, it follows that the priority of ideal objectivity over real objects is of a kind that presupposes the appearance of the latter. As we have already suggested, the priority of ideal objectivity over real objects is tantamount to the priority of a whole over its moments.

While the correlates of sensuous acts are beings, the correlate of a categorial act is being. The latter is apriori in relation to the former but the former makes up the founding objectivity for the latter. On this basis we can formulate four claims concerning the relation between being and beings. These four claims have their basis in the delineation of categorial intuition — and thus constitution — in the preliminary part of HCT: (1) being appears, but not independently of beings; it appears with the appearance of beings, (2) being appears as appearance itself, i.e., as the horizon within which beings can appear, thus, (3) being is a condition of possibility for the appearance of beings, and (4), the way in which being has priority over beings is analogous to the way in which a whole is prior to its moments. Heidegger's concept of disclosedness or disclosure embraces this fourfold determination of the relation between being and beings, and it underscores that ontological difference is not an ontological indifference. In other words, the concept of ontological difference does not imply a two-world theory, i.e., a world of the real and a world of the ideal. Rather the real and the ideal are amalgamated in what *is* and beyond that there is nothing. In a lecture delivered after the publication of BT, Heidegger emphasizes this in a discussion of the 'there is' (*es gibt*).

Perhaps there *is* no other being beyond what has been enumerated, but perhaps, as in the German idiom for 'there is' *es gibt* [literally, it gives], still something else *is given*. Even more. In the end something is given which *must* be given if we are to be able to make beings accessible to us as beings and comport ourselves toward them, something which, to be sure, is not but which must be given if we are to experience and understand any beings at all. (BP, 10)

We shall see that this presence of the categorial or ideal objectivity is what Heidegger refers to as disclosure in BT. However, in HCT the terms 'disclosedness' and 'discoveredness' are still not used as unambiguously as technical terms typically are, and as they in fact are used in BT.[3] Nor are they used consistently in order to refer to specific phenomena. This fluidity makes it possible to trace the development of these concepts, and we shall see that the term 'disclosedness' bears a strong resemblance to a key-term in Husserl's phenomenology, namely 'appresentation' (*Appräsentation*).

We have seen that, according to Heidegger, the presence of a thing — a being — implies the co-presence of ideal objectivity. In his investigation of categorial intuition, Heidegger emphasized the significance of this double presence and the importance of understanding their relationship. As we know, the relation between something being presented (*präsentiert*) in straightforward intuition and the presencing (*Gegenwärtigung*) of categorial intuition reflects the theory of wholes and parts. When we see, say, a red car not only is the red and the car presented to us, but also the car's *being* red is present. This is a relation within the thing itself; a state of affairs. There is, founded upon straightforward intuition, a second act — categorial intuition — which focuses upon a moment that belongs to the whole. This moment is the *presencing* of the objective correlate of straightforward intuition.

The notion of presencing developed by Heidegger in his interpretation of

---

[3] See the Editors Epilogue, HCT, 322.

categorial intuition is a distinction that is also found in Husserl. About a decade after the publication of LI this distinction occurs in *Ideen II*.[4] Husserl distinguishes between primary presence (*Urpräsenz*) and appresence (*Appräsenz*).[5] While the former refers to the objective correlate of straightforward perception, i.e., of sense-perception, the latter refers to a further presence which is founded upon the former, in the sense that it is a co-presence, but which nevertheless represents the horizon within which the former takes place. According to Husserl, "that which is primarily experienced, the primarily presented [*urpräsentierbare*] being is not all of being, and also not all of being that can be experienced [*nicht alles erfahrbare Sein*]" (*Ideen II*, 163).[6] Thus, being encompasses more than real objectivity, more than the objective correlates of sense-perception. It also includes something whose "givenness presupposes primary presence [*Urpräsenzen*] but which is itself not given in primary presence" (*Ideen II*, 16).[7] This is the context or horizon which is appresented, while real objectivity is given in straightforward intuition. In *Experience and Judgment*,[8] Husserl likewise refers to "indeterminate generalities" which are prescribed by the "apperceptive horizon of perception" (EJ, 96-7). In *Ideen II* he emphasizes that primary presence (*Urpräsenz*) of an object does not refer to "primary presence of all its characteristics" (*Ideen II*, 162).[9] Primary presence is what is given in sense perception, and sense perception is perspectival. We only see an aspect of an object, we never see all sides. But, when we see an object, we nevertheless grasp its having characteristics on its as yet unseen sides. Thus, primary presence is a founding presence in the sense that it refers to or appresents the unseen sides. In so doing, it also appresents categories. In *Formal and Transcendental Logic*,[10] Husserl refers to "categorial formations" that "make their appearance apperceptionally" (FTL, Appendix 2, section c).

---

[4] *Ideen zu einer reinen Phänomenologie und phänomenologische Philosophie. Zweites Buch: Phänomenologische Untersuchungen zur Konstitution*, edited by M. Biemel, Husserliana Band IV (The Hague: Martinus Nijhoff, 1952).

[5] Cf. *Ideen II*, 162-3.

[6] Our translation, the original reads: "... dass das im ursprünglichen Sinne Erfahrbare, das urpräsentierbare Sein nicht alles Sein ist, auch nicht alles erfahrbare Sein."

[7] Our translation, the original reads: "... Gegebenheit derart haben, dass sie Urpräsenzen voraussetzen, während sie selbst in Urpräsenz nicht zu geben sind."

[8] Husserl, *Experience and Judgment*, translated by J. S. Churchill and K. Ameriks (Evanston: Northwestern University Press, 1973). *Erfahrung und Urteil* (Hamburg: Claassen, 1954). Hereafter EJ.

[9] Our translation, the original reads: "... Urpräsenz aller seiner inneren oder eigenschaftlichen Bestimmungen."

[10] Husserl, *Formal and Transcendental Logic*, translated by D. Cairns (The Hague: Nijhoff, 1969). *Formale und transzendentale Logik* (The Hague: Martinus Nijhoff, 1974). Hereafter FTL.

We shall not elaborate any further on Husserl's notion of appresentation, but we may conclude that there is a continuity between the notion of categorial intuition in LI — as this is interpreted by Heidegger in HCT— and the distinction between primary presence and appresence presented by Husserl in *Ideen II*, a manuscript read by Heidegger before he held the lecture HCT. Thus, it is hardly surprising that the development in Heidegger's thinking from categorial intuition to disclosedness should include the concept of appresence.

It is our contention that Heidegger's distinction between discoveredness and disclosedness closely resembles Husserl's distinction between primary presence (*Urpräsenz*) and appresence (*Appräsenz*). Both sets of distinctions echo the distinction between straightforward and categorial intuition, and their founding/founded relationship as this is developed in LI. In response to this thesis, one might argue that, despite all resemblance, Heidegger nevertheless differs from Husserl in that he reverses the priority of disclosedness over discoveredness. Heidegger grants primacy to disclosedness (appresence), while Husserl emphasizes primary presence (discoveredness). However, the primacy assigned by both obeys the theory of wholes and parts. Neither Husserl nor Heidegger ever suggest that primary presence and appresence can appear independently of each other. Thus, the primacy assigned cannot mean that one appears prior to another in an independent sense of this term. But one could still argue that they disagree over primacy in a way that is compatible with the theory of wholes and parts. That would imply, however, that Husserl maintained that primary presence is a *concretum* for appresence while Heidegger contended the opposite, i.e., that disclosedness is a *concretum* for discoveredness. There are definitely indications in favor of the latter, but a look at Husserl may help us to reach a more accurate understanding of Heidegger on this topic. In the case of Husserl, the reciprocal relation between primary presence and appresence is somewhat overshadowed by the fact that neither is an absolute *concretum*. For Husserl, there is only one absolute *concretum* and that is transcendental subjectivity.[11] Thus, it is probably more in keeping with Husserl's position to desist from ranking primary presence and appresence and instead to refer to them as *abstracta*, i.e., as moments of transcendental subjectivity.

However, when it comes to Heidegger it seems more obvious that disclosedness has primacy over discoveredness, but, as we will see in the sections to follow, although discoveredness presupposes disclosedness, the latter only appears with the former. At this point it may be helpful to add a nuance to our previous claims about the relation between full and ideal objectivity. Towards the end of our treatment of categorial intuition we saw

---

[11] Cf. CM, 84.

that objectivity was not exhausted by real objectivity, but that objectivity in its broadest sense is much richer than the reality of a thing. And we further observed that, according to Heidegger,[12] the latter is only comprehensible on the basis of full objectivity. From this we concluded that real objectivity can only be grasped within the framework of ideal objectivity, thus suggesting that the latter is identical with full objectivity. It is correct that real objectivity only can be grasped within the framework of ideal objectivity, but ideal objectivity is not thereby identical with full objectivity. Full objectivity embraces *both* real and ideal objectivity, that is, the latter are both *abstracta* to full objectivity. It is full objectivity that has primacy and this *concretum* comes into being with Dasein. We shall see (in the last section) that the same argument also applies to the relation between discoveredness and disclosedness.

Before we go on to substantiate this claim on the basis of Heidegger's analysis in BT, let us first provide some textual evidence in favor of our above claim concerning the kinship between terms 'appresentation' and 'disclosedness.' Since 'appresentation' does not occur in BT, we shall have to look at HCT. In this lecture Heidegger makes use of the terms 'discoveredness' and 'disclosedness.' But he also uses the term 'appresentation' and does so in contexts where one later will find the term 'disclosedness.' In the discussion of the disclosure of the world as meaningfulness Heidegger makes use of 'appresentation' in a way that is highly interesting. Let us follow his investigation from the following claim: "*Meaningfulness is first of all a mode of presence* in virtue of which every entity in the world is discovered" (HCT, 210). Heidegger reject certain theories of meaning as mistaken in that they begin with verbal sounds and then go on to explain how these are endowed with meaning. "Sounds do not acquire meaning; rather, it is the other way around: meanings are expressed in sounds" (HCT, 210). And, he continues, "meanings are to be understood on the basis of meaningfulness, and this in turn means only on the basis of Being-in-the-world" (HCT, 210).[13] In order to understand meaningfulness this way one must, Heidegger claims, "return to a more original phenomenon of Being-in-the-world, which we call understanding" (HCT, 210). He adds that it is "Being-in-the-world as understanding" that "*appresents* the world" (HCT, 210; our emphasis). Thus, 'appresentation' obviously refers to the disclosedness of the world, but it does so in a way that underscores the founded character of the latter. Heideg-

---

[12] The passage on which we were resting our claim is also quoted above in this section.

[13] This is in full keeping with Heidegger's view in BT: "Meaning is an existentiale of Dasein, not a property attaching to entities, lying 'behind' them, or floating somewhere as an 'intermediate domain'" (BT, 193).

ger puts it even clearer later on in HCT: "Discoveredness is constitutive of in-being. All concern is as such discovery and interpretation, inasmuch as it *appresents* its disclosed environing world, the work-world ..."(HCT, 274). The strength of this claim is that it enables us to see the balance between discoveredness and disclosedness indicated above. The assertion "discoveredness is constitutive of in-being" (HCT, 274) seems at first sight to be in conflict with Heidegger's later claim that "Dasein is its own disclosedness" (BT, 171). However, this is not the case. Instead it emphasizes the fact that disclosedness, although it has measure of primacy in relation to discoveredness, does not occur independently of the latter. The founding/founded relationship between sensible and categorial intuition is still at work in the relationship between discoveredness and disclosedness, and thus it is correct to maintain that discoveredness appresents its disclosed world.

In what follows, we first investigate Heidegger's notions of equipment and worldliness in order to see how these themes are actually laid out. In the last section we perform the opposite movement and return to the phenomena of discoveredness and disclosedness thus discussing these on the basis of worldliness and equipment.

2. EQUIPMENT

As already mentioned, the analysis of Dasein takes its point of departure in what Heidegger refers to as average everydayness (*durchschnittlichen Alltäglichkeit*). Instead of beginning with a notion of subjectivity that is already on a level of philosophical reflection, Heidegger emphasizes the necessity of taking the comportments of everyday life as the point of departure.

At the outset of our analysis it is particularly important that Dasein should not be interpreted with the differentiated character of some definite way of existing, but that it should be uncovered in the undifferentiated character which it has primarily and usually.... We call this everyday undifferentiated character of Dasein "averageness." (BT, 69)

Although Heidegger's favorite example of our everyday dealing with the world is that of ordinary involvement in a workshop, everydayness refers to any situation in which one does something in order to achieve something else. Thus, directedness (towards what is other) is an essential characteristic of the situations from which Heidegger's analysis takes its point of departure.

It is commonly argued[14] that Heidegger distinguishes himself from Husserl by advocating the priority of practical intentionality over theoretical intentionality. However, this claim is ambiguous. First, it is correct that Heidegger takes his point of departure in a practical everyday dealing with the world. "The kind of dealing which is closest to us is ... not a bare perceptual cognition, but rather that kind of concern which manipulates things and puts them to use" (BT, 95). However, Heidegger does not restrict the notion of everydayness to a narrow notion of the 'practical.' Everydayness includes any situation in which one does something in order to achieve something else. And it is possible to imagine situations of that kind that would not normally be referred to as practical. Secondly, as we have already indicated above, it is not obvious that Husserl maintains the primacy of theoretical intentionality over practical intentionality. On the contrary, there is evidence in favor of the view that Husserl in fact agrees with Heidegger's emphasis on practical activity. Thirdly, practical and theoretical intentionality are aspects of intentionality in its apriori, and the latter is what is the primary focus for both Heidegger and Husserl.

When describing the nature of the entities of which we make use in our everyday dealing with the world Heidegger refrains from using the term 'thing.' This term is already charged with certain metaphysical presuppositions that betray the descriptive and non-constructive character of the point of departure. According to Heidegger, "in addressing these entities as 'Things' (*res*), we have tacitly anticipated their ontological character" (BT, 96). The entities of everyday activities are not experienced as mere things, i.e., as objects of "bare perceptual cognition;" they are experienced by way of

---

[14] For instance, Okrent argues in *Heidegger's Pragmatism* (10) in favor of a structural analogy between Husserl and Heidegger with the one difference that Husserl is a mentalist and Heidegger emphasizes priority of practical intentionality over theoretical. Okrent is right about the structural analogy between Husserl and Heidegger, but the elements he mentions in order to establish a difference between them are not correct. Firstly, the presentation of Husserl as a mentalist is fundamentally mistaken. Husserl's concept of intentionality is a rejection of mentalism. Indeed, the major target of Husserl's early phenomenology, the one that in fact triggered off the development of phenomenology, is psychologism. Moreover, it is this project that lies at the ground of Heidegger's fundamental ontology, and it is here the basis for the structural analogy is to be found. Secondly, Heidegger specifically says that his position does *not* "express a priority of the 'practical' attitude over the theoretical" (BT, 238). H. Dreyfus criticizes Okrent on this point by claiming that "reduction of Heidegger's work to a practical variation of Husserl's" (*Being-in-the-world*, 345n) trivializes Heidegger. But Dreyfus refers to this approach as a trivializing reduction because Husserl upholds a generally Cartesian notion of a detached, worldless subject. In our last chapter we shall see that this is simply not correct. Heidegger's concept of Dasein and Husserl's notion of subjectivity have the same temporal constitution. Thus, if Husserl's subject is detached and worldless, so is Dasein.

a concern that puts them to use. Heidegger claims that this concern's use "has its own knowledge" (BT, 95). Thus, he settles for the term 'equipment' (*Zeug*). This term is more in keeping with what goes on in everydayness. If the act-side is characterized as putting something to use in order to achieve something else, it follows that the correlate appears as a tool or a piece of equipment. According to Heidegger, "in our dealings we come across equipment for writing, sewing, working, transportation, measurement" (BT, 97). Thus, entities in the world are primarily experienced as tools or equipment. However, 'equipment' is a technical term and refers to more than we usually associate with it; it encompasses everything of which we make use in order to achieve something. A piece of equipment is "essentially 'something in order to...' [*etwas um-zu...*]" (BT, 97). To be a knife is to be a piece of equipment we use in order to cut, and likewise, to be a personal computer is to be a piece of equipment we use in order to write, among other things. However, it is perfectly imaginable that the sun and the wind and other entities less typically referred to as equipment can be used in order to achieve something else, and thus fall within the set of equipment.

A piece of equipment is exhaustively defined by its functionality. It is the latter that makes it what it is. Thus, functionality is not something that is added on to a primary given entity. Rather, "the functionality that goes with a chair, blackboard, window is exactly that which makes the thing what it is" (BP, 164). To be a piece of equipment is to be something that appears in relation to bringing about certain goals, to achieve something. Thus, equipment always appears within a certain context and, moreover, the latter has primacy over the former. "Taken strictly, there 'is' no such thing as *an* equipment. To the Being of any equipment there always belongs a totality of equipment, in which it can be this equipment that it is" (BT, 97). In other words, there is no such thing as an isolated piece of equipment. Every piece of equipment is a placeholder in a totality of equipment (*Zeug-Ganzheit*). This equipmental totality makes up a referential whole (*Verweisungsganzheit*) in which one piece of equipment always refers to another.

In the 'in-order-to' as a structure there lies an *assignment* or *reference* of something to something ... Equipment — in accordance with its equipmentality— always is *in terms of* [*aus*] its belonging to other equipment: ink-stand, pen, ink, paper, blotting pad, table, lamp, furniture, windows, doors, room. (BT, 97)

According to Heidegger, "these 'Things' never show themselves proximally as they are for themselves, so as to add up to a sum of *realia* and fill up a room" (BT, 97–8). If a piece of equipment is what it is only in regard to a broader context of equipment, the latter must somehow be prior to the former.

What we encounter closest to us (though not as something taken as a theme) is the room; and we encounter it not as something 'between four walls' in a geometrical spatial sense, but as equipment for residing. Out of this the 'arrangement' emerges, and it is in this that any 'individual' piece of equipment shows itself. *Before* it does so, a totality of equipment has already been discovered. (BT, 98; translation altered)

The relation between equipment and the totality of equipment is thus presented in a way that testifies to the presence of the theory of wholes and parts, or at least in a way that commits Heidegger to compliance with the tenets of this theory. The fact that a piece of equipment cannot appear independently of the whole to which it belongs does not suggest that the whole can appear independently of the equipment. It appears before the equipment but also only with the latter.

A piece of equipment is determined by its referential character. Its essence or "whatness" is constituted by its function (its in-order-to) which in turn is determined by its place in a context of use.

Equipment can genuinely show itself only in dealings cut to its own measure (hammering with a hammer, for example); but in such dealings an entity of this kind is not *grasped* thematically as an occurring Thing, nor is the equipment-structure known as such in the using. (BT, 98)

Thus, when a piece of equipment appears as it is, in a context of use, it appears in a non-thematic way. Since the act to which it appears is "not a bare perceptual cognition [but] has its own kind of knowledge" (BT, 95), it follows that the correlate cannot appear as an object of perceptual cognition. "[T]he less we stare at the hammer-Thing, and the more we seize hold of it and use it, the more primordial does our relationship to it become, and the more unveiledly is it encountered as that which it is — as equipment" (BT, 98). It is the use itself that encounters the essence of a piece of equipment.

The hammering itself uncovers the specific 'manipulability' ["*Handlichkeit*"] of the hammer. The kind of Being which equipment possesses — in which it manifests itself in its own right — we call *readiness-to-hand* [*Zuhandenheit*]. (BT, 98)

Heidegger emphasizes that the ready-to-hand character of a hammer does not surrender itself to "pure perception." This characteristic of a piece of equipment consists in its having a certain significance. And this, in turn, consists in its pertinence for achieving certain goals. But, Heidegger claims, the functionality of a piece of equipment is not to be understood in terms of a property of a thing.

[T]he 'hammering' of the hammer are not properties of entities. Indeed, they are not properties at all, if the ontological structure designated by the term 'property' is that of some definite character which it is possible for Things to possess [*einer möglichen Bestimmtheit von Dingen*]. Anything ready-to-hand is, at worst, appropriate for some purposes and inappropriate for others. (BT, 114)

According to Heidegger, properties are what characterize entities considered independently of the significance attached to them through use. Knowledge of properties is secondary to knowing the essence of a given entity. For instance, before a hammer can be a thing with this or that shape and color, made of this or that material, etc., it must already be a hammer. Admittedly, we can run into an object which we do not recognize. But in that case it is highly unlikely that shape, material, size, and color will enlighten us in regard to the what-ness of the unknown object. The question "what is it?" can in fact be replaced by "what is it used for?". If one does not already know what a hammer is, then one must proceed from the first to the second question and answer that "this is a device used in order to drive in nails," etc.

Given the fact that entities are primordially individuated as "something-in-order-to..." within a context of use, it follows that it is not the separation of a given entity from the significance it has due to its place in this context that takes us back to the entity as it is in itself. It is not as though we are first introduced to a plain object with certain properties, and then go on to affix a specific significance to it. On the contrary, a hammer is primarily ready-to-hand and only subsequently accessible as an object with properties. While the latter are given as correlates of perceptual cognition, this is not the case with the former.

No matter how sharply we just *look* [*Nur-noch-hinsehen*] at the 'outward appearance' ["*Aussehen*"] of Things in whatever form this takes, we cannot discover anything ready-to-hand. (BT, 98)

Thus, since "the ready-to-hand is not grasped theoretically at all" (BT, 99), it follows that the use of equipment is not something that is guided by a theoretical awareness. But this activity is not thereby a blind one. It has its own kind of sight and this sight Heidegger refers to as circumspection [*Umsicht*]. Circumspection is an atheoretical sense of direction that accompanies and guides practical activity. But, Heidegger cautions, "'practical' behavior is not 'atheoretical' in the sense of 'sightlessness'" (BT, 99).

The way it differs from theoretical behavior does not lie simply in the fact that in theoretical behavior one observes, while in practical behavior one *acts* [*gehandelt wird*], and that action must employ theoretical cognition if it is not to remain blind; for the fact that observation is a kind of concern is just as primordial as the fact that action has *its own* kind of sight. (BT, 99)

According to Heidegger, if we look at our everyday activities — intellectual as well as practical — we will find that our attention for the most part "passes through" the equipment we employ in order to achieve our goals. To the extent that we relate to what we are doing at all it is normally those purposes towards which we aim that capture our attention.

> The peculiarity of what is proximally ready-to-hand is that, in its readiness-to-hand it must, as it where, withdraw [*zurückzuziehen*] in order to be ready-to-hand quite authentically. That with which our everyday dealings proximally dwell is not the tools themselves. On the contrary, that with which we concern ourselves primarily is the work — that which is to be produced at the time. (BT, 99)

Hence, it follows then, that in our primordial understanding of a given piece of equipment, the tool itself is invisible, so to speak; it withdraws in its availability. "In the indifferent imperturbability of our customary commerce with them [equipment], they become accessible precisely with regard to their unobtrusive presence" (BP, 309). However, this invisibility does not imply the necessity of breaking out of the context of use in order to grasp the essence of a piece of equipment. Withdrawal is a mode of being in which equipment presents itself as it is in itself.

Heidegger's concept of circumspection has been highly disputed among scholars. However, many of these discussions rest on premises that are in conflict with fundamental phenomenological tenets. One way the problem is presented is as follows: given the fact that we spend most of our life in a state of everyday dealing with the world while a relatively small part of it is spent in a state of deliberate, thematic awareness, which state should be emphasized philosophically? Does our everyday use cover up a tacit mental state awareness which, although unconscious, nevertheless underlies our employment of equipment, or can our alleged awareness in fact be reduced to mere behavior? Although Heidegger advocates the primacy of practical activity over theoretical contemplation he is not thereby promoting behaviorism at the cost of mentalism. In fact, his position does not relate at all to this debate. He would reject both positions. The reductive strategies of such approaches are exactly what phenomenologists repudiate.

A related, more frequently discussed problem, is the relation between theory (knowing that) and practical activity (knowing how) in Heidegger. Heidegger himself is, of course, quite clear on this issue. He rejects the view that "action must employ theoretical cognition if it is not to remain blind" (BT, 99). In other words, action is not mere behavior, but the sight of everyday activity is not thereby to be understood in terms of theoretical contemplation. Once again, one must be careful not to associate Heidegger with philosophical problems alien to his project. Heidegger's notion of everyday activity — of doing something in order to achieve something else — bears strong resemblance to the Aristotelian notion of *poiesis*. As we shall see, this activity has its own sight, not because it harbors a tacit theoretical contemplation, but because the world in which it takes place is already disclosed through *praxis* (another Aristotelian term important for Heidegger). Thus, with the concept of circumspection Heidegger is not taking a stand with regard to contemporary discussions concerning the primacy of knowing that and knowing how. As we shall see, in Heidegger this distinction is essentially tied to the distinction between *praxis* and *poiesis*.[15]

We have shown that a piece of equipment is always what it is within a totality of equipment. Thus, in order for equipment to appear the latter must also appear. According to Heidegger, "[b]*efore* [any 'individual' item of equipment shows itself] a totality of equipment has already been discovered" (BT, 98). In this passage the notion of "before" surfaces once again. Heidegger still holds that the "before" in the context of the relation between the individual piece of equipment and the totality of equipment is of the same nature as the "before" of the whole in relation to its moments. In order to understand a piece of equipment, he holds that we must already have in sight the equipmental totality to which it belongs. This sight is circumspection.

The view in which the equipmental nexus stands at first, completely unobtrusive and unthought, is the view and sight of practical *circumspection* [*praktische Umsicht*], of our practical everyday orientation. "Unthought" means that it is not thematically apprehended for deliberate thinking about things; instead, in circumspection, we find our bearings in regard to them. (BP, 163)

Thus, what makes the activity of everydayness possible is not deliberation, but circumspection. In everydayness we do not normally thematically confront what we are about to do and how to do it; we simply do it. Everydayness exhibits a broad range of situations that are not normally accompanied by deliberate thematic awareness. Just consider something as common as entering or leaving a room. Although we know how to open doors we rarely reflect upon doing it.

When we enter ... through the door, we do not apprehend the seats, and the same holds for the doorknob. Nevertheless, they are there in this peculiar way; we go by them circumspectly, avoid them circumspectly ... and the like. (BP, 163)

Circumspection refers to a "practical everyday orientation" (BP, 163), a familiarity by virtue of which we are able to respond to the demands of the situation. However, before we elaborate any further on this issue (which we will do in sections five and six) we should first consider Heidegger's pre-

---

[15] This will be treated more thoroughly in Chapter VII, Self.

ontological confirmation of turning everydayness into an object of inquiry as he has done above.

3. PRE-ONTOLOGICAL CONFIRMATION

Heidegger emphasizes the necessity of starting out from everydayness in order to avoid constructions. However, by so doing one necessarily turns everydayness into an object, and hence, one is no more in an everyday attitude. The investigation of everydayness cannot itself be in the everyday attitude. How can Heidegger account for such a move without violating his own tenets? Is the subject who initiates such a move itself a construction, or is Heidegger able to provide a pre-ontological confirmation for this transition? In what follows, we argue that Heidegger succeeds in giving this change of attitude a phenomenal foundation.

On several occasions we have suggested that Heidegger carries out something that highly resembles Husserl's notion of a transcendental reduction before he can proceed to exhibit the essential structures of Dasein. Heidegger takes his point of departure in everydayness, but admits nevertheless that everyday comportments hide these structures. Thus, one has to perform a change in one's attitude towards everydayness if these structures are to be disclosed. One has to make everyday comportments the theme instead of following their thematic sense. But at that point one is no longer in an everyday attitude. However, the question remains: what justifies the decision not to follow the theme of everyday comportments? This move must itself receive a pre-ontological confirmation if it is not to violate basic principles of phenomenology. At this point there might be a difference between Husserl and Heidegger in that the latter provides evidence in favor of the reduction while the former refers to it as a leap on the part of the inquiring subject. Phenomenologically speaking, Heidegger's position is superior in that he does not require an appeal to a capacity a subject can hold independently of the world.

Heidegger addresses this issue under the title "How the Worldly Character of the Environment Announces itself in Entities Within-the-world" (BT, 102). He introduces the problematic with the following questions:

Do we not have a pre-phenomenological glimpse of this phenomenon [the worldly character of equipment]? Do we not always have such a glimpse of it, without having to take it as a theme for ontological Interpretation? Has Dasein itself, in the range of its concernful absorption of in equipment ready-to-hand, a possibility of Being in which the worldliness of those entities within-the-world with which it is concerned is, in a certain way, lit up for it, *along with* those entities themselves? (BT, 102)

And, Heidegger continues,

[i]f such possibilities of Being for Dasein can be exhibited within its concernful dealings, then the way lies open for studying the phenomenon which is thus lit up ... and to interrogate it as to those structures which show themselves therein. (BT, 102)

Heidegger brings to the fore three modes of being in which the worldliness of equipment is lit up in everydayness. These are conspicuousness (*Auffälligkeit*), obtrusiveness (*Aufdringlichkeit*), and obstinacy (*Aufsässigkeit*). They all refer to situations where normal everyday activity runs into a breakdown. Conspicuousness refers to those situations where a piece of equipment appears as un-ready-to hand. It simply does not work the way it normally does. A hammer can break, a fuse can blow, or one can run out of gas on the way to work. Situations such as these are normal in the sense that we all experience them, but they are still less normal than their counterparts: hammers work more often than they break. However, in situations such as these the in-order-to character of a piece of equipment forces itself upon us in the sense that we suddenly find ourselves incapable of achieving a certain purpose. We suddenly realize that the hammer is a means we use in order to achieve a certain end. The entity loses its ready-to-hand character, and thus also retreats from its withdrawal. It stands out, so to speak, in its uselessness and displays the nature of equipment. While the in-order-to never announces itself, but rather withdraws in its usefulness, a breakdown exhibits the in-order-to character of equipment by featuring un-readiness-to-hand where readiness-to-hand is usually found.

[T]his implies that what cannot be used just lies there; it shows itself as an equipmental Thing which looks so and so, and which, in its readiness-to-hand as looking that way, has constantly been present-at-hand [*Vorhanden*] too. (BT, 103)

A present-at-hand entity is an entity considered in isolation from its in-order-to, i.e., as a mere thing which appears with such and such properties. However, Heidegger continues, this is not a permanent transformation.

Pure presence-at-hand announces itself in such equipment, but only to withdraw to the readiness-to-hand of something with which one concerns oneself — that is to say, of the sort of thing we find when we put it back into repair. (BT, 103)

Malfunction on the part of a piece of equipment is not the only situation that offers a pre-ontological glimpse of worldliness. Another example is what Heidegger refers to as obtrusiveness.

In our concernful dealings, however, we not only come up against unusable things *within* what is ready-to-hand already: we also find things which are missing — which not only are not 'handy' ["*handlich*"] but are not 'to hand' ["*zur Hand*"] at all. (BT, 103)

Again we find ourselves in a situation where we are unable to do something in order to achieve a certain goal. This time the piece of equipment obstructs our dealings by not appearing at all, and thus it reveals its character of in-order-to. "[T]o miss something in this way amounts to coming across something un-ready-to-hand. When we notice what is un-ready-to-hand, that which is ready-to-hand enters the mode of *obtrusiveness*" (BT, 103). A third example emphasized by Heidegger is what he refers to as obstinacy:

[T]he in-ready-to-hand can be encountered not only in the sense of that which is unusable or simply missing, but as something un-ready-to-hand which is *not* missing at all and *not* unusable, but which 'stands in the way' of our concern. (BT, 103)

Obstinacy occurs in situations in which a piece of equipment is neither broken nor missing, but nevertheless appears in a way that "stands in the way of our concern." This can happen in situations where a given piece of equipment, say, a hammer, exhibits obstinacy by being somehow inappropriate for the work we are about to carry out, thus disturbing the ordinary context of use. It forces us to attend deliberately to the in-order-to while we in fact are using the tool for a certain task. "With this obstinacy the presence-at-hand of the ready-to-hand makes itself known in a new way as the Being of that which still lies before us and calls for our attending to it" (BT, 103–4). All these examples have in common that the transparency of everyday dealing with the world disappears. Accordingly, equipment withdraws from its readiness-to-hand and "stands out" as an un-ready-to-hand entity with specific properties. At this point Heidegger asks: "Now that we have suggested ... that the ready-to-hand is thus encountered under modifications in which its presence-at-hand is revealed, how far does this clarify the *phenomenon of the world*?" (BT, 104). He answers:

Even in analyzing these modifications we have not gone beyond the Being of what is within-the-world, and we have not come closer to the world-phenomenon than before. But though we have not as yet grasped it, we have brought ourselves to a point where we can bring it into view. (BT, 104)

Thus, conspicuousness, obtrusiveness, and obstinacy are situations from which the investigation of the world-phenomenon can begin. Something pre-ontological is revealed. What is non-thematically understood in everyday dealing with the world is brought to the forefront as this dealing is disturbed.

In conspicuousness, obtrusiveness, and obstinacy, that which is ready-to-hand loses its readiness-to-hand in a certain way ... It does not vanish simply, but takes its farewell, as it were, in the conspicuousness of the unusable. Readiness-to-hand still shows itself, and it is precisely here that the worldly character of the ready-to-hand shows itself. (BT, 104)

In our everyday dealings with equipment, readiness-to-hand is necessarily understood, but not in a thematic way, and thus not in a way that can provide a foundation for an investigation of its ontological structure. It is only when we experience a breakdown in the ordinary use that this sphere is lit up. In ordinary use the assignments of an in-order-to to a towards-this are not observed, "they are rather 'there' when we concernfully submit ourselves to them" (BT, 105). This, however, changes radically in the case of breakdown. According to Heidegger, "*when an assignment has been disturbed* — when something is unusable for some purpose — then the assignment becomes explicit" (BT, 105). Likewise, when a specific piece of equipment is missing, as when an umbrella is unlocatable just as one is about to walk out in the pouring rain, we then become aware of this entity whose presence "has been so obvious that [you] have never taken any notice of it" (BT, 105).

[T]his makes a *break* in those referential contexts which circumspection discovers. Our circumspection comes up against emptiness, and now sees for the first time *what* the missing article was ready-to-hand *with*, and *what* it was ready-to-hand *for*. (BT, 105)

Heidegger emphasizes that this is not yet crucial to the explicit development of an ontological structure. So far this is nothing but a pre-ontological confirmation of the possibility of undertaking such an endeavor. What is lit up in these situations is something that is inaccessible to circumspection in the sense that it is not something ready-to-hand. Neither is it something present-at-hand. The latter is ontologically secondary to the former. What is lit up is the environment (*die Umwelt*), the "there" within which something can appear ready-to-hand. "It is itself inaccessible for circumspection, so far as circumspection is always directed towards entities; but in each case it has already been disclosed [*erschlossen*] for circumspection" (BT, 105). A key-term in this passage is 'disclosed.' This term, Heidegger asserts, is a technical term and signifies "to lay open." He adds: "'to disclose' never means anything like 'to obtain directly by inference'" (BT, 105). To disclose is not a matter of carrying out an inference where the ready-to-hand are premises from which one infers the notion of environment. The latter is not a construction, rather it is a condition of possibility for the appearance of equipment.

The environment or world is more than the ready-to-hand in the sense that it cannot be reduced to the latter. This, Heidegger argues, is obvious if one consults the situation in which the world is lit up.

> That the world does not 'consist' of the ready-to-hand shows itself in the fact ... that whenever the world is lit up ... the ready-to-hand becomes deprived of its worldliness. (BT, 106)

Hence, the world is never encountered along with equipment ready-to-hand. Equipment is encountered as circumspection is absorbed in the referential totalities, and as soon as the latter is lit up equipment loses its readiness-to-hand. Thus, Heidegger concludes, "[i]f it is to be possible for the ready-to-hand not to emerge from its inconspicuousness, the world *must not announce itself*" (BT, 106). According to Heidegger, if the world can be lit up or announce itself in this manner, it follows that the world has "already been disclosed beforehand whenever what is ready-to-hand within-the-world is accessible for circumspective concern" (BT, 106). It also follows that the world-phenomenon is given a pre-ontological confirmation, and thus the philosopher is free to investigate its ontological structure without falling prey to charges of construction. "The world is ... something 'wherein' Dasein as an entity already *was*, and if in any manner it explicitly comes away from anything, it can never do more than come back into the world" (BT, 106–7). It is our contention that Heidegger by this has given the transcendental reduction a pre-ontological foundation. The incentive to carry out such a reduction, by not going along with the thematic sense of everyday comportments, is itself given in intuition. It is not merely a leap on the part of an isolable subject who, by a sheer act of will, can effect a disengagement from the world. Rather, it is given as a phenomenon.

4. REFERENCE

Before we discuss Heidegger's ontological interpretation of the world, let us first have a brief look at an additional attempt at providing phenomenal support for this endeavor. This time the issue is not that of anchoring the transcendental reduction in the world but rather of anchoring ontological structures.

> In our provisional Interpretation of that structure of Being which belongs to the ready-to-hand (to 'equipment'), the phenomenon of reference or assignment became visible; but we merely gave an indication of it, and in so sketchy a form that we at once stressed the necessity of uncovering it with regard to its ontological origin. (BT, 107)

Since it also became plain that "assignments and referential totalities could in some sense become constitutive for worldliness itself" (BT, 107), the necessity of providing an ontological interpretation of these phenomena is obvious.

So far the world has been "lit up only in and for certain definite ways in which we concern ourselves environmentally" (BT, 107), that is, in conspicuousness, obtrusiveness, and obstinacy. In these situations the referential character of equipment announces itself, but only "*with* the readiness-to-hand of that concern" (BT, 107). It is, however, imperative also to grasp "the phenomenon of *reference* or *assignment* itself more precisely" (BT, 107),[16] and not merely as something that shows up with certain entities. Heidegger considers a certain kind of equipment which ontically has the character of referring, that is, entities "whose specific character as equipment consists in *showing* or *indicating*" (BT, 108), namely signs. The sign has a special status in that it leads ontically to the ontological structure of worldliness.

A sign is something ontically ready-to-hand which functions both as this definite equipment and as something indicative of [was ... anzeigt] the ontological structure of readiness-to-hand, of referential totalities, and of worldliness. (BT, 114)

According to Heidegger, the sign lends itself to a phenomenological inquiry into the nature of reference since reference *appears* with it in a way which differs from the way it appears with other tools. While a piece of equipment generally "hides" its references as long as it functions normally, signs are a kind of equipment whose normal function is precisely that of calling attention to the nexus of references that constitutes readiness-to-hand. A sign has a foot in two worlds, so to speak. On the one hand, it is a piece of equipment used in order to indicate, and thus it is itself a placeholder in a network of references. On the other hand, it does not point ahead to other tools the way ordinary equipment do; rather it raises the whole equipment-context into our circumspection, thus allowing us to see that equipment appears within a network of references. In this sense "the sign-structure itself provides an ontological clue for 'characterizing' any entity whatsoever" (BT, 108).

In his treatment of equipment Heidegger maintains that entities are primordially individuated as something-in-order-to within a use context.

---

[16] Whereas Dreyfus claims that the discussion of signs is merely one of two ways in which the phenomenon world is revealed, Heidegger's text suggests otherwise. Dreyfus maintains that the discussion of signs reveals a way in which we can become aware of the relational whole of significance that makes up the world without appealing to some type of disturbance (Dreyfus, 100). Heidegger, however, indicates that the discussion of signs represents a step further towards the determination of worldliness. While disturbance and breakdown reveals reference in relation to the readiness-to-hand of that specific concern, the discussion of signs treats a broader issue in that it attempts to investigate reference itself more precisely.

Hence, it is not the separation of a given entity from the significance it has due to its place in this context that takes us back to the entity as it is in itself. On the contrary, a hammer is primarily ready-to-hand and only subsequently accessible as an object with properties. Heidegger thus makes a claim to the effect that referentiality is ontologically primordial with regard to individual pieces of equipment. This can be summarized as follows: (1) things are primordially encountered as equipment, (2) a piece of equipment is essentially something in-order-to, thus, (3) there is no such thing as a single piece of equipment, every piece of equipment is a placeholder in a totality of equipment, and (4), this equipmental totality makes up a referential whole where one piece of equipment always refers to another. It follows that, according to Heidegger, referentiality is somehow prior to the appearance of equipment. Of course, it does not appear independently of equipment, but it nevertheless has a measure of primacy over the latter. However, this claim has yet to receive phenomenal support. We have seen that when the world is lit up through disturbance referentiality is revealed, but it is important to investigate the way reference itself appears.

The sign taken up by Heidegger is the "adjustable red arrow [that] motor cars are sometimes fitted up with" (BT, 108) — an indicator in a more modern idiom. This sign is not only ready-to-hand for the driver, but also for the drivers of nearby vehicles, and for everybody around him in the traffic. While the driver uses it in order to indicate his planned route, others use it in order to give way, or to stop, or to do whatever else that would be appropriate in a given circumstance.

This sign is ready-to-hand within-the-world in the whole equipment-context of vehicles and traffic regulations. It is equipment for indicating, and as equipment, it is constituted by reference or assignment. It has the character of the "in-order-to," its own definite serviceability; it is for indicating. (BT, 109)

Understanding a sign is not a matter of looking at it, but rather of looking away from it; towards what it indicates. It is, Heidegger claims, "*not authentically 'grasped'* [*"erfasst"*] *if we just stare at it and identify it as an indicator-Thing which occurs*" (BT, 109). A sign is not merely "a Thing which stands to another Thing in the relationship of indicating" (BT, 109). "[I]t is rather *an item of equipment which explicitly raises a totality of equipment into our circumspection so that together with it the worldly character of the ready-to-hand announces itself*" (BT, 109). The " adjustable red arrow" that indicates the direction of a car brings into view the whole equipment-context of vehicles and traffic regulations, within which the individual pieces of equipment appear. It does not point ahead to another piece of equipment, but rather to an entire environment of interwoven references.

However, if it is the case that a totality of equipment has priority over the individual piece of equipment, then it follows that we are not first theoretically acquainted with an undifferentiated set of bare objects present-at-hand, and then go on to attach meanings to these by establishing references. Obviously, a sign cannot be a sign before it has been established as a sign, nor does a completely unknown object appear to us as "something-in-order-to." At first sight, this seems to challenge the priority Heidegger grants to readiness-to-hand over presence-at-hand. Heidegger makes it clear that he is aware of this and says "[b]ut, one will protest, *that which* gets taken as a sign must first have become accessible in itself and apprehended *before* the sign gets established" (BT, 112).

Certainly it must in any case be such that in some way we can come across it. The question simply remains as to *how* entities are discovered in this previous encountering, whether as mere Things which occur, or rather as equipment which has not been understood — as something ready-to-hand with which we have hitherto not known 'how to begin,' and which has accordingly kept itself veiled from the purview of circumspection. (BT, 112)

If that which is taken as a sign has first become accessible as a mere present-at-hand thing, it follows that referentiality is something added to it on an ontical level, i.e., that referentiality is an ontical characteristic of readiness-to-hand. However, since referentiality does not have its nucleus, so to speak, in the individual entity, but rather resides in an environment of interwoven references, it follows that reference cannot be an ontical characteristic of equipment. The investigation of reference has shown that it is not something a piece of equipment can possess independently of or prior to a referential totality. Rather the latter is a presupposition for readiness-to-hand.

[W]hen the equipmental characters of the ready-to-hand are still circumspectively undiscovered, they are not to be Interpreted as bare Thinghood presented for an apprehension of what is just present-at-hand and no more. (BT, 112)

Thus, even if the ready-to-hand is undiscovered, we have no right to postulate an entity to which reference is added at the time of its being discovered. As we shall see, according to Heidegger, before an entity is discovered it is already disclosed. Thus, the basis for readiness-to-hand is not a mere present-at-hand thing to which different properties are added. The basis for ready-to-hand equipment is the referential totality.

In his treatment of equipment Heidegger already indicated that referentiality appears and that it does so prior to any individual piece of equipment. His discussion of signs attempts to grasp the phenomenon of reference itself more precisely thus "providing phenomenal support for our characterization of references or assignments" (BT, 113). At this point the characterization of references can be summarized as follows: "Reference is not an ontical characteristic of something ready-to-hand ... it is rather that by which readiness-to-hand itself is constituted" (BT, 114). Now the task is to investigate the sense in which "reference [is] 'presupposed' ontologically in the ready-to-hand" and also how it is "at the same time constitutive for worldliness in general" (BT, 114).

5. WORLD

Heidegger defines world as a structural moment in the basic state of Dasein. He is well aware of the fact that this notion of world is not in keeping with the general use of this term. Indeed, he maintains that there are at least three other ways in which this term is used. 'World,' Heidegger argues, can either be used as an ontical concept signifying "the totality of those entities which can be present-at-hand within the world" (BT, 93), or it can be used ontologically in regard to present-at-hand entities, thus signifying the being of these entities. However, 'world' can also be used in another ontical sense, and thus with another ontological counterpart. According to the latter sense, world is not meant as a collection of "these entities which Dasein essentially is not and which can be encountered within the world, but rather as that *'wherein'* a factical Dasein as such can be said to 'live'" (BT, 93). 'World' in this sense can refer to "the 'public' we-world, or one's 'own' closest (domestic) environment" (BT, 93). While the first two uses of 'world' represent a view from which Heidegger seeks to distance himself, the third notion refers to Heidegger's own understanding and use of the term 'world.' "We shall," he maintains, "reserve the expression 'world' as a term for our third signification" (BT, 93). To this ontical concept of world there is a corresponding ontological understanding of 'world.' In this sense "'world' designates the ontologico-existential concept of *worldliness* [*Weltlichkeit*]" (BT, 93).

Worldliness itself may have as its modes whatever structural wholes any special 'world' must have at the time; but it embraces in itself the *a priori* character of worldliness in general. (BT, 93)

Thus, when Heidegger uses the term 'world,' he is not referring to something like a totality of objects or our physical environment. He distinguishes this conventional understanding of world from a phenomenological sense according to which world is not primarily approached as a collection of objects facing us, but in terms of that wherein the being-in of Dasein takes place. For

Heidegger, world is primarily that wherein ready-to-hand equipment are encountered in everyday dealings. And the investigation of the worldliness of the world seeks to account for the way in which things are encountered in everydayness by uncovering the general structure of the world as that within which something can appear as ready-to-hand. Heidegger starts out his investigation with a claim that in fact summarizes the notion of worldliness suggested up to this point in the analysis.

In anything ready-to-hand the world is always 'there.' Whenever we encounter anything, the world has already been previously discovered, though not thematically ... The world is that in terms of which the ready-to-hand is ready-to-hand. (BT, 114)

However, it is not enough merely to postulate that "the world is that in terms of which the ready-to-hand is ready-to-hand" without also accounting for how this takes place.

Our analysis hitherto has shown that what we encounter within-the-world has, in its very Being, been freed for our concernful circumspection ... [But] what does this previous freeing amount to, and how is this to be understood as an ontologically distinctive feature of the world? (BT, 114)

In short, what notion of world can account for the way in which ready-to-hand equipment appears in everydayness?

We have already seen that those entities with which Dasein is involved in its everyday life are defined in terms of applicability. A piece of equipment is essentially something in-order-to and it is so within a broader context of equipment. This equipmental totality makes up a referential whole (*Verweisungsganzheit*) where one piece of equipment always refers to another. Thus, it is not things but references that have the primary function within the structure of world. Indeed, the world is itself a referential totality. This referentiality is, in turn, essentially Dasein-dependent, it comes into being with Dasein.

Heidegger thus suggests that reference is that by which readiness-to-hand is constituted. But we have yet to see what reference means and how it is constitutive for worldliness in general. Heidegger takes as his point of departure references such as serviceability-for and usability.

The "towards-which" [*das Wozu*] of a serviceability and the "for-which" [*das Wofür*] of a usability prescribed the ways in which such a reference or assignment can become concrete. (BT, 114)

But, again he warns against interpreting the different kinds of definite references as properties, that is, as "some definite character which it is possible for Things to possess" (BT, 114–5). There are at least two reasons why 'reference' cannot be interpreted as a kind of a property an entity can possess. Firstly, reference is not a definite character in the sense that it conclusively determines the nature of something in isolation from the environment. According to Heidegger, "anything ready-to-hand is, at the worst, appropriate for some purposes and inappropriate for others" (BT, 115). Just as presence-at-hand presupposes readiness-to-hand, so too are properties secondary to and dependent upon appropriateness and inappropriateness. Secondly, since there are no equipment independently of reference, one cannot interpret reference as something possessed by each piece of equipment individually. On the contrary, reference constitutes readiness-to-hand.

Serviceability ... as a constitutive state of equipment (and serviceability is a reference), is not an appropriateness of some entity; it is rather the condition ... which makes it possible for the character of such an entity to be defined by its appropriateness. (BT, 115)

But, Heidegger continues, "what, then, is 'reference' or 'assignment' to mean?" (BT, 115). He answers that it has "in itself the character of *having been assigned or referred*" (BT, 115). When discussing the ready-to-hand character of equipment, we saw that the in-order-to was established within a context of everyday purposive activity. Indeed, the very term 'in-order-to' signifies that equipment is goal-directed. A given entity cannot be what it is, i.e., something-in-order-to, unless it has a certain involvement (*Bewandtnis*).[17] "*With* any such entity [i.e. ready-to-hand] there is an involvement which it has *in* something. The character of Being which belongs to the ready-to-hand is just an *involvement*" (BT, 115). Thus, with any piece of equipment there is an involvement (in purposive activity) by which it is, as Heidegger puts it, freed (*freigegeben*). Whereas hammers make sense by referring to nails, this referentiality comes into being with the activity of hammering. And this activity, in turn, makes sense because it serves a purpose. Thus, any piece of equipment exhibits, qua something in-order-to, a 'towards-which' (*Wozu*) in its usability: the work to be produced. Such an involvement in purposiveness is constitutive for the referentiality by which the equipmental context comes into being.

[W]ith this *thing*, for instance, which is ready-to-hand, and which we accordingly call a "hammer," there is an involvement in hammering; with hammering, there is an involvement in making something fast; with making something fast, there is an involvement in protection against bad weather; and this protection "is" for the sake of providing shelter for Dasein - that is to say, for the sake of a possibility of Dasein's

---

[17] While in BT '*Bewandtnis*' is translated 'involvement,' it is translated as 'functionality' in BP. In the following we will use both translations.

being. (BT, 116)

Thus, just as an individual piece of equipment cannot appear apart from an equipmental context, so the equipmental context cannot appear apart from purposive activity. Both are *abstracta* in relation to the totality of involvements (*Bewandtniszusammenhang*), and the latter is thus "'earlier' than any single item of equipment" (BT, 116). "Whenever something ready-to-hand has involvement with it, *what* involvement this is, has in each case been outlined in advance in terms of the totality of such involvements" (BT, 116). But the totality of equipment is itself not an absolute *concretum*; although concrete in one direction, it is abstract in another.

[T]he totality of involvements itself goes back ultimately to a "towards-which" in which there is *no* further involvement: this "towards-which" is not an entity with the kind of Being that belongs to what is ready-to-hand; it is rather an entity whose Being is defined as Being-in-the-world, and to whose state of Being, worldliness itself belongs. (BT, 116)

Thus, what structures the entire framework of means and ends is an end that is not itself a means to anything else. This "towards-which" distinguishes itself from any other "towards-which" in a twofold manner. Firstly, it refers, not to ready-to-hand equipment, but to the being that is defined as Being-in-the-world, and, secondly, it is a final or primary "towards-which" (*primäre Wozu*). "The primary 'towards-which' is a 'for-the-sake-of-which' [*ein Worum-willen*] [and] the 'for-the-sake-of' always pertains to the being of Dasein, for which, in its being, that very being is essentially an *issue*" (BT, 116–7). At this point we recognize the formal determination of Dasein as self-understanding. Remember the last two points of the fourfold presentation of Dasein's essence in the previous chapter: (3) to exist is primarily to understand; what Dasein understands is essentially itself, and (4), self-understanding is not a product of inward self-reflection, simply because Dasein understands itself through its involvement with things and people, not by means of introspection. We are now in a position to see more clearly this formal definition of Dasein. Insofar as Dasein understands itself, it understands itself as a "for-the-sake-of-which," i.e., as an end to be accomplished or completed. And Dasein's being "for-the-sake-of-which" constitutes a referential totality of significance within which things can be encountered as ready-to-hand.

The 'for-the-sake-of-which' signifies an 'in-order-to'; this in turn a 'towards-this'; the latter an 'in-which' of letting something be involved; and that in turn a with-which of an involvement. These relationships are bound up with one another as a primordial totality; they are what they are as this signifying in which Dasein gives itself beforehand its 'Being-in-the-world as something to be understood. The relational totality of this signifying we call 'significance.' This is what makes up the structure of the world. (BT, 120)

According to Heidegger, then, just as Dasein's self-understanding cannot take place independently of the world, neither can the general structure of the world within which something can appear as ready-to-hand appear independently of Dasein. They are amalgamated in the phenomenon of Being-in-the-world.

6. DISCLOSEDNESS AND DISCOVEREDNESS

Before a piece of equipment can be discovered — can appear — in actual use, the referential totality to which it belongs must already have been unveiled beforehand. The latter is *apriori* in relation to the former in the sense that it is a *concretum* for readiness-to-hand. However, this *concretum* is not an absolute *concretum*, it is abstract from another point of view. The absolute *concretum* is an entity which itself is not a means to something else. This entity is Dasein whose basic state is Being-in-the-world.

The central issue in BT concerns the 'nature' of Dasein. So far we have encountered different determinations of this entity that we ourselves are. We have seen that the essence of Dasein is existence, that Dasein is understanding, and that this understanding essentially is a self-directed understanding. We have also indicated that Dasein relates to itself by Being-in the world — that it understands itself through its involvement with things and people — and that this being-in differs from the way other entities are in the world. Dasein is not a thing in the world, but rather a Being-in-the-world that is not a thing. All of these determinations of Dasein are intrinsically interrelated.

In what follows we introduce yet another determination of Dasein and we shall see that this is also compatible with those already introduced. According to Heidegger, "Dasein is its own disclosedness" (BT, 171). However, in order to reach a full appreciation of Heidegger's position on this issue, this determination of Dasein must always be seen in relation to another phenomenon, referred to by the term 'discoveredness.' In brief, his position is this: while equipment, or entities in the world, are discovered, the referential totality within which these appear, i.e., the world, is disclosed. In a more schematic manner we can put it like this: (1) discoveredness presupposes disclosedness; (2) entities in the world, equipment, are discovered; world is disclosed. Thus, discoveredness is directed towards equipment, disclosedness is directed towards world; (3) disclosedness is prior to discoveredness the way a whole is prior to its moments. Thus, there is no disclosedness independently of discoveredness; (4) Dasein is the phenomenon that brings about this primordial disclosure. Let us now return to the texts in order to substantiate this fourfold determination of the phenomena of discoveredness and disclosedness.

Firstly, whenever a piece of equipment is discovered the referential totality of significance that makes up the world must be disclosed in advance. In HCT Heidegger puts it like this:

> It is ... out of this totality [a referential contexture] that, for example, the individual piece of furniture in a room appears. My encounter with the room is not such that I first take in one thing after another and put together a manifold of things in order then to see a room. Rather, I primarily see a referential totality ... from which the individual piece of furniture and what is in the room stand out. (HCT, 187)

In BP he says something similar:

> World is that which is already previously unveiled and from which we can return to the beings with which we have to do and among which we dwell ... We always already understand world in holding ourselves in a contexture of functionality. (BP, 165)

As we have already emphasized, for Heidegger 'world' refers to the referential totality or contexture of functionality. Another term used is 'environment' (*Umwelt*). Now what is the relation between these passages and the terms 'discoveredness' and 'disclosedness?' While the former refers to our circumspective encountering of ready-to-hand equipment, the latter designates our encountering of the world or the environment.

> [The environment] is itself inaccessible to circumspection, so far as circumspection is always directed towards entities; but in each case it has already been disclosed for circumspection. 'Disclose' and 'disclosedness' will be used as technical terms in the passages that follow, and shall signify 'to lay open' and 'the character of having been laid open.' (BT, 105)

Thus, as we emphasized under (2), discoveredness is directed towards equipment, disclosedness is directed towards world. The former presupposes the latter. However, although disclosedness has a measure of primacy over discoveredness, it does not thereby follow that disclosedness can appear independently from discoveredness.

A key-term introduced by Heidegger in this regard is *'Bewendenlassen'* which is translated "letting-something-be-involved." "Ontically, 'letting something be involved' signifies that within our factical cöncern we let something ready-to-hand *be* so-and-so *as* it is already and *in order that* it be such" (BT, 117). When in actual encounter we use a hammer *as* a hammer and a nail *as* a nail, we let something be *what* it is. However, this ontical "letting-something-be-involved" is not merely an ontical phenomenon. "The way we take this ontical sense of 'letting-be' ('*sein lassens*')," Heidegger maintains, "*is, in principle, ontological*" (BT, 117; our emphasis). There is thus a mutual interdependence between the ontical and ontological notion of letting-something-be-involved. A piece of equipment cannot be involved only ontically or ontologically. It is always involved both ontically and ontologically.

About the ontological sense of being involved Heidegger says the following:

This '*a priori*' letting-something-be-involved is the condition for the possibility of encountering anything ready-to-hand, so that Dasein, in its ontical dealings with the entity thus encountered, can thereby let it be involved in the ontical sense. (BT, 117)

While ontically letting-something-be-involved is a matter of encountering an entity as something-in-order-to, thus freeing it for a totality of involvements, the ontologically letting-something-be-involved refers to the "freeing of *everything* ready-to-hand as ready-to-hand" (BT, 117). In other words, the latter is a matter of disclosing the totality of involvements within which an entity appears as ready-to-hand. Heidegger puts it like this: "In letting entities be involved so that they are freed for a totality of involvements, one must have disclosed already that for which [*woraufhin*] they have been freed" (BT, 118). Heidegger stresses the importance of emphasizing that ready-to-hand equipment is always already a part of a referential totality in order to distinguish his position from an empiricist notion of synthesis or constitution where the process is understood as a creative putting together of discrete atomic impression. We may recall that Heidegger distanced himself from this notion in his treatment of categorial intuition by referring to it as "the old mythology of an intellect which glues and rigs together the world's matter with its own forms" (HCT, 70). Therefore it is important for Heidegger to maintain the following:

To the extent that any *entity* shows itself to concern — that is, to the extent that it is discovered in its Being — it is already something ready-to-hand environmentally; it just is not 'proximally' a 'world-stuff' that is merely present-at-hand. (BT, 118)

Thus, there is no discoveredness apart from disclosedness. However, concerning the opposite, whether disclosedness can take place independently of discoveredness Heidegger's choice of terms and general approach exhibits a certain ambiguity. From his claim that the referential totality must be "disclosed already" or "previously unveiled," one might get the impression that this is something that takes place temporarily prior to the discovering of equipment. Likewise, the passage "I primarily see a referential totality ... from which the individual piece of furniture ... stands out" (HCT, 187), seems to indicate that one first sees the totality and then the entities. Of course, in one sense this is correct given the fact that the totality is prior to the entity, but it must not be construed as suggesting that disclosedness is seen as an event that can take place independently of discoveredness. There are two reasons why this would be incorrect. Firstly, Heidegger refers to the disclosedness of a referential totality as an "'*a priori*' letting-something-be-involved" (BT, 117). As we may recall from Heidegger's discussion of apriorism, the apriori possesses primacy not in the manner of appearing independently of that of which it is prior to, but in the way a whole is prior to its moments. For this reason disclosedness, qua apriori, can only appear with discoveredness. "[The *a priori*] does not mean anything ... belonging to a subject which is proximally still worldless" (BT, 146). This passage leads to our second reason. According to Heidegger, 'discoveredness' is to be reserved "as a term for a possibility of Being which every entity *without* the character of Dasein may possess" (BT, 146). Disclosedness, on the other hand, refers to the being of Dasein.[18] In this context he refers to the apriori letting-something-be-involved as "a *perfect* tense apriori which characterizes the kind of Being belonging to Dasein itself" (BT, 117). Thus, if disclosedness could appear prior to and independently of discoveredness, it would follow that Dasein can appear independently of intraworldly entities — which is exactly what Heidegger's determination of Dasein as existence precludes. Dasein takes a stand on itself, i.e., exists, through its involvement with things and people, not by means of introspection.

Having marshalled evidence in favor of our fourfold determination of the relation between discoveredness and disclosedness, we are now in a position to develop our argument concerning the relation between the phenomena discoveredness and disclosedness, and straightforward perception and categorial intuition. Straightforward perception and discoveredness have in common that they are directed towards entities in the world, towards beings. Although it has been argued that there is a fundamental difference between the two in that discoveredness refers to a circumspective encountering of ready-to-hand equipment while straightforward perception designate cognition, there seems to be no structural difference between these phenomena. Although the early Husserl has a propensity towards emphasizing theoretical activity as the primary way of interacting with the world, he is later more open to the idea that practical activity is an equally primordial way of being directed towards entities in the world — and that this is compatible with the

---

[18] cf. "Dasein is its own disclosedness" (BT, 171).

fundamental tenets of phenomenology. The interesting fact is that both Husserl and Heidegger emphasize that no entity can be encountered unless something else, which cannot be encountered the same way entities are encountered, is also encountered along with it. This other is the context, or the world, or the being of beings. The latter is appresented or disclosed. Thus, disclosedness resembles categorial intuition in being directed towards that within which beings appear, i.e., the world or being. This theme is to be found in both Husserl and Heidegger, and it arises out of early Husserl's elaborations on categorial intuition.

The objective of this chapter has been to delineate Heidegger's notion of constitution. We argued that this is in keeping with the notion of constitution suggested by Heidegger in his treatment of categorial intuition, and thus that the concepts of discoveredness and disclosedness are intrinsically related to the concepts of straightforward perception and categorial intuition. At this point in our investigation we have shown how this theme surfaces in Heidegger's analysis of equipment and worldliness. We have also indicated a line of influence going from Husserl to Heidegger. Both take their point of departure in Husserl's distinction between straightforward perception and categorial intuition. While in Husserl this surfaces as the distinction between primary presence and appresence, it appears in Heidegger as the distinction between discoveredness and disclosedness.

Some scholars might object that this is a rather rough and ready blending of Husserl and Heidegger. But it is my contention that if one carefully investigates the transition (especially the terminological transition) from the preliminary part of HCT to BT, one will find that there is a thematic continuity from early Husserl's notions of straightforward and categorial intuition, to the concepts of primary presence and appresence (the latter used by both Husserl and Heidegger), and finally to Heidegger's concepts of discoveredness and disclosedness.

Our investigation of constitution in this chapter is intrinsically related to the discussion of existence in the previous chapter. We remember that existence is a kind of self-directedness which does not take place as introspection. Dasein understands itself through its involvement with the world, not through inward self-reflection. However, Dasein nevertheless has a measure of primacy over the world in the sense that world is something which appears to Dasein. But this primacy must not be understood as Dasein's ability to appear independently of the world, as if Dasein were the world's creator. Constitution is not creation. And it is precisely not so because Dasein does not appear independently of the world the way the craftsman appears independently of what is fabricated. The world is a structural aspect of Dasein and hence, it cannot be a product of Dasein: there is simply no Dasein without the world.

Dasein, whose basic state is Being-in-the-world, is the only absolute *concretum*. Both the world and the self are aspects of this whole. While this chapter has been dedicated to investigate the relation between Dasein and world, the next chapter will focus upon the relation between Dasein and the self.

CHAPTER VII

SELF

The third structural moment of the basic state of Dasein is the entity which has Being-in-the-world as the way in which it is. This entity is the being we ourselves are. In-being and world never appear independently of the entity typically referred to as the self or the "I," and, by the same token, the self does not appear independently of the world. Moreover, it is not the identical self that possesses primacy over the world, it is Being-in-the-world that holds this priority and it does so over the world and the self.

Recall our previous discussion of Kant's distinction between synthetic and analytic unity of apperception and our emphasis upon the primacy of the former over the latter. We have already indicated the presence of a similar structure in Heidegger. In this chapter we lay the ground for a more thorough investigation of this kinship. It is our contention that Kantian distinctions such as synthetic and analytic unity of apperception, their interrelation, and differentiation from the empirical ego have their parallels in Heidegger. The relevant distinctions in Heidegger are the basic state of Dasein, Being-in-the-world, the structural moment referred to as the entity which has Being-in-the-world as the way in which it is, and the notion of the "One" (*das Man*).

In what follows, we keep in mind the perspective developed in our analysis of Kant's notion of the synthetic unity of apperception, but we shall refrain from any further discussions of Kant. The guiding thread in this chapter will be certain concepts from Aristotle. In order to single out these concepts and indicate their importance for the fundamental ontological project, we shall, however, not proceed directly to Aristotle but rather take our point of departure in Arendt's discussion of the human condition.[1] The

---

[1] Arendt, *The Human Condition* (Chicago & London: The University of Chicago Press, 1958). Hereafter referred to as HC. We do not attempt to undertake a full presentation of Arendt's thinking in HC, nor do we intend to carry out a broad discussion of the philosophical relation between Arendt and Heidegger. For such endeavors see for instance M. Canovan, *Hannah Arendt, A Reinterpretation of Her Political Thought* (Cambridge and New York: Cambridge University Press, 1992), and D.R. Villa, *Arendt and Heidegger, The Fate of the Political* (Princeton: Princeton University Press, 1996). The presentation of Arendt's discussion of the concepts of *poiesis* and *praxis* is meant to serve merely as a way in to Heidegger. As we see it, such an approach to Heidegger is justified by the fact that Arendt

reason for this detour is that while Aristotle's influence upon Heidegger's fundamental ontological project remains hidden in most of Heidegger's own writings, Arendt shows convincingly where Aristotelian themes are prominent in his work. Thus, the inquiry into Arendt will set the stage, so to speak, for a more thorough investigation of Aristotelian themes in Heidegger's fundamental ontology.

The two central concepts in this regard are *poiesis* and *praxis*. We shall see that an investigation of these concepts will elucidate several fundamental distinctions in Heidegger's thinking such as that between disclosedness and discoveredness, and between authenticity and inauthenticity, and it will also serve to introduce our discussion of the temporal constitution of Being-in-the-world. An analysis of *poiesis* and *praxis* will show why the nexus of means and ends of discoveredness presupposes an end that is not itself a means. While concrete in one respect, discoveredness is abstract in another. Or, conversely, disclosedness (*praxis*) is a *concretum* for discoveredness (*poiesis*). This, in turn, will enable us to reach a more accurate appreciation of the distinction between authenticity and inauthenticity. For Heidegger this is a technical distinction which in fact encompasses the fundamental tenets of his existential analytic. Getting this distinction right is thus paramount for understanding the notion of subjectivity developed in BT.

Having investigated the relation of the concepts of *poiesis* and *praxis* to Heidegger's existential analytic, we will be in a position to discuss the notion of self which Heidegger advocates in BT. We shall first discuss this in relation to themes such as being-with and the One, in order to lay the ground for a further investigation of this theme that will take place in the last two chapters.

1. ARENDT ON THE HUMAN CONDITION

A fundamental tenet of Arendt's discussion of the human condition is that human beings do not have an essence the way other things do. We have, she claims, simply no right to assume that man "has a nature or essence in the same sense as other things" (HC, 10). Moreover, even if we had something like an essence, it would not be possible for us to determine it.

> It is highly unlikely that we, who can know, determine, and define the natural essences of all things surrounding us, which we are not, should ever be able to do the same for ourselves — this would be like jumping over our own shadows. (HC, 10)

was greatly inspired by Heidegger's teachings on Aristotle. We are, however, perfectly aware of the fact that Arendt develops these themes in her own direction and that she was highly critical of some aspects of Heidegger's thinking. Thus, we are not about to suggest that Arendt's thinking is merely a transcript of Heidegger's.

For Arendt, as for Heidegger, the essence of man is its existence, and existence unfolds itself in active life. The objective of HC is to investigate this active life, and she analyzes it as consisting of three distinguishable aspects: labor, work, and action. To each of these aspects there are certain corresponding conditions and spheres. Life is the condition corresponding to the activity of labor; worldliness is the condition corresponding to the activity of work, and plurality is the condition corresponding to action. While the first two activities take place in the private sphere, the third takes place in the public domain. Each activity is autonomous in the sense that it has a different task. Labor is an activity directed towards sustaining human life, work is directed towards fabrication, and action is directed towards the disclosure of the agent and the world of meaning in speech and action.

Although Arendt sees all three activities as essential to human life, she explicitly states that it is action that distinguishes human being from other beings. "A life without speech and without action ... has ceased to be a human life" (HC, 176). Arendt defines action through freedom and plurality. By the term 'freedom,' she refers to the capacity that human beings have of doing something new. To act and to exercise freedom are basically the same thing in the sense that one cannot engage in one without the other.

Action is the only aspect of the *vita activa* through which freedom can be exercised. Labor and work, on the other hand, fall within the realm of necessity. These activities are simply active responses to the necessities of life such as the satisfaction of material needs and the like. They are means to achieve certain ends and thus remain under the spell of these ends in the sense that the value and completeness of these activities lies in something that falls outside the activities themselves. Thus, according to Arendt, labor and work are not free, but rather "in order to's" dictated by different needs that manifest themselves within the private sphere. They can be carried out privately in the sense that these "in order to's" do not necessarily involve other human beings. At this point, Arendt calls attention to a profound difference between labor/work and action. While labor and work tie human being to life and things, respectively, action ties us to other human beings by virtue of being conditioned by plurality. Plurality is the condition of action in the sense that action presupposes a sphere which features the simultaneous presence of *equality* and *distinction*.

Human plurality, the basic condition of both action and speech, has the twofold character of equality and distinction. If men were not equal, they could neither understand each other and those who came before them nor plan for the future and foresee the needs of those who will come after them. If men were not distinct, each human being distinguished from any other who is, was, or will ever be, they would need neither speech nor action to make themselves understood. (HC, 175-6)

In order to act, we must be in a space within which we can be simultaneously equal and distinct, that is, we must be with other human beings. It follows that only within a public space with fellow "essence-less" beings can a human being be truly human and disclose "who" s/he is. "In acting and speaking, men show who they are, reveal actively their unique personal identities and thus make their appearance in the human world" (HC, 179). For Arendt, then, human beings exist, i.e., take a stand on themselves, through action, not fabrication. In this way they simultaneously disclose the "who" of their own being and the public sphere, that is, the common world.

A central concept in Arendt's thinking is the concept of the *polis*. However, she is not referring to any specific *polis* such as, say, Athens 400 BC. When Arendt employs the term *polis*, she is first and foremost referring to the public space of appearance which reveals who we are as individuals.

The *Polis*, properly speaking, is not the city-state in its physical location; it is the organization of the people as it arises out of acting and speaking together, and its true space lies between people living together for this purpose, no matter where they happen to be ... It is the space of appearance in the widest sense of the word, namely, the space where I appear to others as others appear to me, where men exist not merely like other living or inanimate things but make their appearance explicitly. (HC, 198)

The *polis* is the space of appearance where human beings appear to one another and within which the "who" or the essence of the agent is disclosed. According to Arendt, this space of appearance or common world differs from nature in that it is of human origin. "The public realm, the space within the world which men need in order to appear at all, is ... more specifically 'the work of man' than is the work of his hands or the labor of his body" (HC, 208). However, although the public realm is the work of man, it is not *made*, it is disclosed. It comes into being through action, not fabrication, and, as we shall see, it is a condition of possibility of the latter.

In her discussion of instrumentality, Arendt demonstrates lucidly the dependence of work upon action by showing that the means/ends categories of work — the network of "in order to's" — is not a self-contained system. Utility cannot justify the category of means and ends, i.e., utility itself. Thus, in order to be meaningful, the whole system of means and ends presupposes an end that is not itself an "in order to" but a "for the sake of which." Therefore, Arendt claims,

[t]he perplexity inherent in all consistent utilitarianism ... can be diagnosed theoretically as an innate incapacity to understand the distinction between utility and meaningfulness, which we express linguistically by distinguishing between "in order to" and "for the sake of." (HC, 154)

Thus, meaning is not a product of use itself — of utility — but of the subjectivity of use. For this reason a consistent utilitarianism is doomed.

The perplexity of utilitarianism is that it gets caught in an unending chain of means and ends without ever arriving at some principle which could justify the category of means and end, that is, of utility itself. The "in order to" has become the content of the "for the sake of;" in other words, utility established as meaning generates meaninglessness. (HC, 154)

The categories of means and ends constitute the peculiar way we relate to things in the world (through work). Things are used as means to achieve certain ends, and these ends are what guide and justify the choice of means. But as soon as an end is reached, it turns into a means to some other end, and so the chain of means and end continues. In other words, within the sphere of utility there is simply no way to end the chain of means and ends and prevent all ends from becoming means to other ends. For this reason (as we have already pointed out) the categories of means and end cannot account for the use of use, or the value of utility, that is, for the network of the "in order to's" as such.

Without an end in itself, not only is there no way to end the chain of means and ends, there is also nothing to guide the choice of means and, hence, there is no chain of means and ends. At this point, Arendt claims, we have reached total meaninglessness. The attempt to locate meaning as a product of utility is an impossible task, because "meaning itself can appear only as an end, as an 'end in itself'" (HC, 154), and such an end is not to be found in the world of instrumentality. An end found in this world has a temporary status, and such an end, once it is attained "ceases to be an end and loses its capacity to guide and justify the choice of means, to organize and produce them" (HC, 154). Thus, although utilitarianism is a consistent description of the way we relate to things, as a theory of the world as a whole it leads to sheer meaninglessness, for it is impossible to locate the origination of meaning in a utilitarian world.

The only way out of the dilemma of meaninglessness in all strictly utilitarian philosophy is to turn away from the objective world of use things and fall back upon the subjectivity of use itself. (HC, 155)

Arendt's critique of utilitarianism has an unmistakable Kantian flavor to it; utilitarianism's failure is due to an inherent transcendental realism.

Only in a strictly anthropocentric world, where the user, that is, man himself, becomes the ultimate end which puts a stop to the unending chain of means and ends, can utility as such acquire the dignity of meaningfulness. (HC, 155)

According to Arendt, this anthropocentric utilitarianism has found its greatest expression in Kant, but at the cost of "degrad[ing] nature and world into mere means, robbing both of their independent dignity" (HC, 155).[2] She therefore rejects the Kantian approach and instead follows the path of the Greek (Aristotelian) tradition — a move which, in fact, is the trademark of the phenomenological movement.

When Arendt speaks of falling back upon the subjectivity of use, this must be interpreted in light of the hierarchy of the *vita activa*. According to this concept, the term 'subjectivity of use' refers to two levels in the hierarchy: 'use' refers to the activity of work, 'subjectivity' refers to action in the sense that subjectivity unfolds itself on the level of action. Thus, the term 'subjectivity of use' does not refer to use itself, but to the subjective aspect of use. This aspect is what provides the chain of means and ends with an "end in itself." In this way, Arendt provides an end that cannot be turned into a means because the definition of action is simply that which has no fulfillment outside of itself.

According to Arendt, then, the value of utility appears in the public realm.

> [V]alue consists solely in the esteem of the public realm where the things appear as commodities, and it is neither labor, nor work, nor capital, nor profit, nor material, which bestows ... value upon an object, but only and exclusively the public realm where it appears to be esteemed, demanded, or neglected. (HC, 164)

As we have already pointed out, this public realm is disclosed through action. It is the categories of action — equality and distinction — that make up the texture of the world.

> The space of appearance comes into being wherever men are together in the manner of speech and action, and therefore predates and precedes all formal constitution of the public realm ... and the various forms in which the public realm can be organized. (HC, 199)

Hence, Arendt claims that meaning can only appear as an end in itself, and an end in itself is only to be found on the level of action, i.e., of human existence.[3]

To summarize, then, we have seen that Arendt adheres to a line of reasoning that, roughly, can be summarized in the following manner: (1) the "essence" of man is his existence, (2) existence unfolds itself in active life,

---

[2] We do not entirely agree with this interpretation of Kant, but it falls beyond our intent to inquire into it in the present study.

[3] This echoes a claim Heidegger makes in BT: "Meaning is an existentiale of Dasein, not a property attaching to entities, lying 'behind' them, or floating somewhere as an 'intermediate domain'" (BT, 193).

and specifically as the activity that has its fulfillment within itself, (3) action unfolds itself in the public sphere (the world) — and the public sphere (the world) is disclosed through action. It is our argument that this line of reasoning characterizes Heidegger's existential analytic as well. It allows both thinkers to emphasize the worldliness of human being without thereby reducing the world to a private phenomenon (or human being to a thing in the world). On the one hand, the world of appearances has a human origin without thereby being a private world — because it is not a product of privacy — and on the other hand, the world is that within which the "who" of human being is revealed.

2. POESIS

Arendt's distinction between work and action draws heavily on Aristotle's distinction between *poiesis* and *praxis*. According to Aristotle, *poiesis* is an activity of fabrication whose goal and completeness lies in the work that is to be produced. Thus, *poiesis* reaches its fulfillment in something that lies outside the agent. *Praxis*, on the other hand, has no fulfillment outside itself. The goal of *praxis* is not a product that lies outside the activity, it is the quality of the action itself. It is not merely a means to an end, it is its own end — it is itself the "for the sake of which." In Arendt, this distinction is reflected in her distinction between activities that fall within the domain of necessity (labor/work) and acts that are free (action). The former corresponding to *poiesis* — in being merely a means to an end — and the latter to *praxis* — in being its own end.

Let us now focus upon the presence of these terms in Heidegger's fundamental ontology. It is our contention that the basic concepts of Heidegger's phenomenology such as presence-at-hand and Dasein are closely related to the Aristotelian concepts of *poiesis* and *praxis*.[4] By the same token, those phenomena constituting the latter concepts can also be found in Heidegger's existential analytic. However, this is not to say that the former are merely translations of the latter. Heidegger does not indiscriminately take over Aristotelian concepts. As they enter into his existential analytic, they go through a certain transformation. What interests Heidegger is not the indi-

---

[4] In "Being and Time: A 'Translation' of the *Nicomachean Ethics*?" in *Reading Heidegger From the Start*, Essays in His Earliest Thought, edited by T. Kisiel and J.v.Buren, (Albany: State University of New York Press, 1994) F. Volpi makes a slightly different claim in that he maintains a correspondence between readiness-to-hand, presence-at-hand, and Dasein and the Aristotelian determinations of *poiesis, theoria,* and *praxis* (201). However, we shall see that our presentation of this correspondence is more in keeping with the text. The latter position is also held by J. Taminiaux in "*Praxis* and *Poiesis* in Fundamental Ontology,"145-6.

vidual appearances of these phenomena, i.e., this particular fabrication or that particular action, what he emphasizes is the ontological aspect of these determinations according to which there is an intrinsic relation between fabrication and action, between *poiesis* and *praxis*. However, a close reading of Aristotle's *Metaphysics*[5] and *Nicomachean Ethics*[6] shows that such an interpretation is in keeping with Aristotle's own understanding of the relation between *poiesis* and *praxis*.[7]

In what follows, we investigate this Heideggerian appropriation of Aristotle.[8] We are not, however, about to undertake a full investigation of Heidegger's interpretation of Aristotle, nor will we attempt a conclusive disclosure of the latter's influence on the former.[9] Our objective is to reach a more accurate understanding of a theme already discussed in some detail - the distinction between discoveredness and disclosedness. As we have indicated, this is a distinction that is fundamental to Heidegger's ontology.

[5] *Metaphysics*, translated by W.D. Ross, in *The Complete Works of Aristotle*, The Revised Oxford Translation, edited by J. Barnes (New Jersey: Princeton University Press, 1984).

[6] *Nicomachean Ethics*, translated by W.D. Ross, revised by J.O. Urmson, in *The Complete Works of Aristotle*, The Revised Oxford Translation, edited by J. Barnes (New Jersey: Princeton University Press, 1984). Hereafter referred to as NE.

[7] See F. Volpi in "Being and Time: A 'Translation' of the *Nicomachean Ethics*?" 195-213. "[I]f one were to read the differentiation between *poiesis* and *praxis* in Book Zeta of the *Nicomachean Ethics* in conjunction with *Metaphysics*, Theta 6, one would clearly recognize that an ontic differentiation is not at issue, that is, a differentiation with reference to individual actualizations of action, where there are *poiesis* on the one hand and *praxis* on the other. Rather this differentiation has an ontological character; it distinguishes two different ways of being that do not ontically stand out from one another"(202).

[8] An important Heideggerian text in this regard is *Phenomenological Interpretations with Respect to Aristotle: Indication of the Hermeneutical Situation*, translated by M. Baur, in *Man and World* 25, 355-393, 1992. This is a translation of the introduction written in 1922 to a projected book on Aristotle, *Phänomenologische Interpretation zu Aristoteles (Anzeige der hermeneutischen Situation)*. Hereafter referred to as PIA. We base our investigation on this text. Another important text is Heidegger's discussion of Aristotle in the introductory part of the lecture *Platon: Sophistes*, GA 19 (Frankfurt am Main: Vittorio Klostermann, 1992). There are also several other texts from Heidegger's Marburg-period and early Freiburg-period that discuss Aristotle and which thus reveal the importance of Aristotle for Heidegger's endeavor.

[9] For such endeavors see J. Taminiaux, "*Poiesis* and *Praxis* in Fundamental Ontology," *Research in Phenomenology*, 17, 1987, 137-169; "The reappropriation of the Nicomachean Ethics: *Poiesis* and *Praxis* in the articulation of Fundamental Ontology," in J. Taminiaux, *Heidegger and the Project of Fundamental Ontology*, translated by M. Gendre, (Albany: State University of New York Press, 1991), 111-137; R. Bernasconi, "The Fate of the Distinction Between *Praxis* and *Poiesis*," *Heidegger Studies* 2, 1986, 111-139; and F. Volpi, "Being and Time: A "Translation" of the *Nichomachean Ethics*?" See also articles written by T. Kisiel, W. Brogan, and R. Makkreel.

While discoveredness designates the appearance of things in the world, disclosedness refers to the prior disclosure of the world within which things appear. In the previous chapter, we discussed the intrinsic relation between this distinction and Husserl's distinction between straightforward perception and categorial intuition and also his distinction between primary presence and appresence. However, while we have called attention to the non-creative world-constituting character of disclosedness, we have yet to investigate what kind of act it is. We know that it designates the being of Dasein and that it is a condition of possibility for discovering things as they are, but we have not shown what it is about this act that justifies this primacy. In the following sections, we discuss this kinship between Heidegger's concept of disclosedness and Aristotle's concept of *praxis*, along with the relation between their concepts of discoveredness and *poiesis*. We also demonstrate that Heidegger's distinction between disclosedness and discoveredness is an ontologized version of Aristotle's distinction between *praxis* and *poiesis*. This will enable us to reach a more accurate appreciation of that kind of act to which disclosedness refers, and thus we will be in a position to underscore further our previous claim concerning disclosedness as a *concretum* for discoveredness. This, in turn, will enable us to understand another essential distinction in Heidegger's existential analytic, namely the one between authenticity and inauthenticity.

The remainder of this section will focus upon the relation between Heidegger's concept of discoveredness and Aristotle's notion of *poiesis* and also on the distinction between presence-at-hand and ready-to-hand. Let us take as our point of departure the following lengthy passage in which Heidegger discusses what being means for Aristotle in general.

The object-field which provides the primordial sense of Being is the object-field of those objects which are produced and used in dealings. Thus, the That-with-respect-to-which towards which the primordial experience of Being is directed is not the Being-field of *things* as of a kind of object which is grasped in a *theoretical* and fact-like manner, but rather the world which is encountered in the dealings which produce, perform, and make use of. That which is finished in the movement of the dealings of production (*poiesis*) ... is that which is. (PIA, 375)

Several claims are made in this passage which are both thematically and terminologically compatible with the view Heidegger presents in BT, sections 15 to 18. Firstly, Heidegger claims that the "object-field which provides the primordial sense of Being is the objects-field of those objects which are produced and *used* in dealings" (PIA, 375). Compare this with the following passage in BT.

The being of those beings which we encounter as closest to us can be exhibited phenomenologically if we take as our clue our everyday Being-in-the-world, which we also call our *"dealings" in* the world and *with* entities within-the-world. (BT, 95)

Thus, in PIA, as well as in BT, the primordial sense of being is encountered in use, in productive dealings with entities in the world, in the "dealings which produce, perform, and make use of" (PIA, 375). Secondly, in PIA Heidegger emphasizes that this primordial sense of being does not refer to "the Being-field of *things* as of a kind of object which is grasped in a *theoretical* and fact-like manner" (PIA, 375). Once again, let us compare this to a statement in BT: "The kind of being that is closest to us is ... not a bare perceptual cognition, but rather that kind of concern which manipulates things and puts them to use" (BT, 95). Hence, in PIA, as in BT, primordial being does not refer to the objects of theoretical contemplation. "Such entities are not ... objects for knowing the 'world' theoretically; they are simply what gets used, what gets produced, and so forth" (BT, 95). Let us now move on to the third claim: "that which is finished in the movement of the dealings of production (*poiesis*) ... is that which is" (PIA, 375). In other words, in PIA Heidegger refers to everyday dealing in the world as *poiesis*, and this activity is described in a way that fully anticipates the descriptions of everyday activity in BT. Crucial to Heidegger's fundamental ontology is the deconstruction of the privileged status given to the concept of being as presence-at-hand in the tradition of metaphysics. Central to this endeavor is his emphasis on the foundational character of *poiesis* for Greek ontology. In PIA, he asks the following question: "What does Being mean for Aristotle in general; how is it accessible, graspable and determinable?" (PIA, 375). And he answers: "Being means *Being-produced* and, as something produced, it means something which is significant relative to some tendency of dealings; it means Being-available" (PIA, 375). In BP, Heidegger shows how these themes "which were fixed for the first time in Greek ontology ... later faded out and became formalized, that is, became part of the tradition and are now handled like well-worn coins" (BP, 108). Heidegger's point is that being present-at-hand in fact means being-produced, and he underscores this by discussing the origin of *essentia* and *existentia*. It is, however, not our intent to give a full account of this genealogy, nor do we intend to discuss the legitimacy of this interpretation. Our objective is merely to indicate the presence and importance of the concept of *poiesis* in Heidegger's thinking.

According to Heidegger, modern terms like 'reality' and 'actuality' have their origin in the scholastic concept of *actualitas* which, in turn,

refers back to an *acting* on the part of some indefinite subject or, if we start from our own terminology, that the extant [*das Vorhandende*] is somehow referred by its sense to something for which, as it were, it *comes to be before the hand*, at hand, to be handled. (BP, 101)

For this reason Heidegger refers, in PIA, to that "which is finished in the movement of the dealings of production (*poiesis*)" (PIA, 375) as "that which has arrived at its Being-present-at-hand [*Vorhandensein*]" (PIA, 375). Thus, the occurrence of the term 'present-at-hand' at this point, where one later will find the term 'ready-to-hand,' does not testify to a radical change in Heidegger's position. On the contrary, it shows that Heidegger's term 'ready-to-hand' is not taken out of the blue but is in fact a retrieval of the full meaning of the term 'presence-at-hand'. While presence-at-hand is later used to refer to a notion of being which is oblivious to the productive behavior of an indefinite subject, thus designating being as something disengaged from production, the original meaning of presence-at-hand is captured by the term 'ready-to-hand.'

In BT, Heidegger distinguishes between '*existentia*' and 'existence' by claiming that while the former refers to "a kind of Being which is essentially inappropriate to entities of Dasein's character" (BT, 67), the latter "as a designation of Being, will be allotted solely to Dasein" (BT, 67). In order to avoid misunderstanding, he decides to use the expression 'presence-at-hand' for the term '*existentia*.' Thus, the primary distinction in Heidegger's existential analytic is the one between presence-at-hand and existence. The fundamental difference between these concepts of being is, however, not also an indifference. On the contrary, these kinds of being are intrinsically tied together. The original meaning of presence-at-hand is readiness-to-hand and the latter can only be understood in relation to a creative and productive Dasein, that is, to existence. Thus, existence is a *concretum* for presence-at-hand.

3. INAUTHENTICITY

Poiesis refers to a creative and productive activity, and thus it is an activity more concerned with presence-at-hand entities than with entities of Dasein's character. Since this activity defines everydayness, it follows that everyday Dasein is not aware of itself in the sense that it focuses upon the apriori character of its own existential make-up. In everydayness, Dasein is oblivious to its ownmost being, or, as Heidegger puts it, everyday Dasein is *inauthentic*.

The concept of inauthenticity is essentially linked to the concept of authenticity; it designates an understanding of being which is not authentic. Although the distinction between inauthentic and authentic understanding is often considered the ultimate Heideggerian distinction, its presence in phenomenology precedes Heidegger's existential analytic. For instance, in a lecture on the consciousness of internal time from 1905 Husserl makes the following claim:

Since experiencing is split by the opposition between "proper" ["*eigentlich*"] and "nonproper" ["*uneigentlich*"], and since experience proper [*eigentliche Erfahrung*], which is intuitive and ultimately adequate experience, supplies the standard of valuation for experience, a phenomenology of experience "proper" ["*eigentlichen*" *Erfahrung*] is especially needed.[10]

Throughout his analysis of time consciousness Husserl distinguishes between authentic (*eigentlich*) and inauthentic (*uneigentlich*) understanding. What characterizes the former is an understanding that has its basis in adequate experience; what characterizes the latter is that such a foundation is missing. For Husserl, one of the most intriguing problems is how inauthentic thinking can arise. This problem is essentially related to the distinction between empty intentions and fulfillments, and to different kinds of fulfillments. Some fulfillments are inauthentic in the sense that they do not really exemplify their objects.[11] We shall not here engage in an in-depth analysis of Husserl's discussion of authentic and inauthentic givenness. Our objective is merely to point out that this distinction is present already in Husserl's earliest phenomenological work, and that it designates the difference between adequate and inadequate experience.

Husserl's discussion of this distinction is present throughout his carrier, and the most rigorous treatment of it is carried out much later in *Formal and Transcendental Logic*. However, Husserl did not himself come up with this essential distinction. In his *Philosophie der Arithmetik* from 1891 he credits Brentano for the introduction of it.

---

[10] E. Husserl, *On the Phenomenology of the Consciousness of Internal Time (1893-1917)*, translated by J.B. Brough (Dordrecht, Boston, London: Kluwer Academic Publishers, 1991), 9. Brough's translation of '*eigentlich*' and '*uneigentlich*' as 'proper' and 'nonproper,' instead of the more traditional 'authentic' and 'inauthentic,' helps to emphasize that the terms in question are not to be given a moral meaning. In both Husserl and Heidegger, the terms '*eigentlich*' and '*uneigentlich*' refer to a kind of understanding, which in turn has its basis in intuition. Although Brough's translation is in many ways preferable, we will nevertheless stick to the traditional translation of '*eigentlich*' and '*uneigentlich*.'

[11] One of Husserl's earliest discussions of this topic takes place in "Authentic and Inauthentic Givenness" (LI VI, #20). Here he distinguishes between hearing the name of a certain geographic area, imagining a map of this area, actually being presented with a map of it, and being presented to the area itself. According to Husserl, while the presence of the imagined map still leaves the act empty, the actual presence of the map involves a kind of fulfillment of the act. However, a map of a country does not really present this country; seeing a map of England is not equivalent to being there. Hence, the presentation of the map is an inauthentic fulfillment of an act.

The difference between "authentic" ["*eigentlichen*"] and "inauthentic" ["*uneigentlichen*"] or "symbolic" representations is given the most vigorous treatment by Fr. Brentano in his University-lectures. I thank him for the profound understanding of the utmost significance of inauthentic representations for our psychological lives. As far as I can see, if it had not been for him, no one would fully grasp this.[12]

Hence, Husserl makes clear that, at least for him, Brentano is the true source of the distinction between authenticity and inauthenticity. It is not unreasonable to assume that Heidegger's distinction has the same source. He was obviously not introduced to it through Brentano's lectures, but he was very familiar with the works by the early Husserl in which this distinction was originally introduced in relation to phenomenology. He was also familiar with the pre-phenomenological work in which Husserl credits Brentano for having introduced it, and, as we know, he *was* very influenced by Brentano's writings. Another reason for assuming this influence on Heidegger's thinking is the fact that the distinction between authenticity and inauthenticity has the same meaning in Heidegger's existential analytic as it does in Husserl's phenomenology. It still concerns the difference between the natural attitude's non-proper understanding of a phenomenon, and the proper understanding sought in the phenomenological attitude.

In what follows, we discuss Heidegger's concept of inauthenticity and we argue that it refers to an ignorance of the theory of wholes and parts to which everyday Dasein is destined. However, there is nothing negative or ungenuine about this inauthentic self-understanding. Indeed, Heidegger refers to it as a phenomenon that belongs to Dasein's positive constitution. In PIA, for instance, Heidegger maintains that this "is not a bad quality which surfaces from time to time, a quality which could be cultivated away in the more progressive and happier times of human culture" (PIA, 364). Likewise, in BP he says,

[t]his inauthentic self-understanding of the Dasein's by no means signifies an ungenuine self-understanding. On the contrary, this everyday having of self within our factical, existent, passionate merging into things can surely be genuine, whereas all extravagant grubbing about one's soul can be in the highest degree counterfeit or even pathologically eccentric. The Dasein's inauthentic understanding of itself via things is neither ungenuine nor illusory, as though what is understood by it is not the self but something else, and the self only allegedly. (BP, 160)

[12] E. Husserl, *Philosophie der Arithmetik*, Husserliana XII (Den Haag: Martinus Nijhoff, 1970), 193n. Our translation, the original reads: "Auf den Unterschied zwischen 'eigentlichen' und 'uneigentlichen' oder 'symbolischen' Vorstellungen hat Fr. Brentano in seinen Universitätsvorlesungen von jeher den grössten Nachdruck gelegt. Ihm verdanke ich das tiefere Verständnis der eminenten Bedeutung des uneigentlichen Vorstellens für unser ganzes psychisches Leben, welche vor ihm, soweit ich sehen kann, niemand voll erfasst hatte."

However, if one develops an ontology on this inauthentic self-understanding, then it becomes ungenuine. One then falls prey to the misinterpretation of the theory of wholes and parts that Heidegger would claim characterizes traditional metaphysics. We may recall that he distinguishes between the ontical, the ontological, and the pre-ontological, and that he emphasizes that the development of an ontology must always have a pre-ontological confirmation. However, if instead one settles for "ontical confirmation," one ends up making the category mistake of construing what is structured as that which structures, of forcing an *abstractum* to be a *concretum*. This can either be done by positing the appearance of an ego-entity prior to and independently of the world, a Cartesian *cogito*, or by going to the other extreme and positing the priority of world over subjectivity, thus reducing the latter to the former. In both cases a structural moment, an *abstractum*, either the entity which in each case has Being-in-the-world as the way in which it is or the world is construed as prior to the *concretum* Being-in-the-world. This is exactly what Heidegger criticizes in traditional metaphysics.

Given that everydayness is defined by *poiesis* and that *poiesis* is geared towards present-at-hand entities, it follows that insofar Dasein sees itself in the everyday attitude, it sees itself in the mode of being present-at-hand. It appears to itself as something belonging to the realm of presence-at-hand, as a thing-like entity. In other words, in this attitude Dasein fails to grasp itself as Being-in-the-world. Instead, it understands itself in the mode of being of entities abstract to this whole which defines its ownmost being. In this sense, everydayness remains ignorant to the theory of wholes and parts. However, although everyday activity hides the true nature of existence, it necessarily must do so. It is a blindness that stems from the fact that existence is a condition of possibility for everydayness. This does not imply that *poiesis* is blind. On the contrary, it is the peculiar seeing of the activity of production that brings about this blindness. Remember our previous discussion of the nature of circumspection. What guides everyday activity is practical circumspection, an openness to the environment by which Dasein is absorbed in the world in a way that enables it to manipulate equipment and, by the same token, renders impossible an understanding of Dasein's ownmost being in the everyday attitude.

Let us now return to a theme already discussed but which is still very central to our task, the theme of self-consciousness. In BP, Heidegger introduces the notion of everyday self-understanding with some remarks about the status of the ego that echo the problems discussed in relation to Kant and Sartre.

If intentionality means *self-direction-toward*, then it is obviously the ego that is directed. But then what about this ego? Is it a point or a center or, as is also said in phenomenology, a pole that radiates ego-acts? The decisive question arises once again: *What mode of being does this ego-pole "have"*? (BP, 158)

Emphasizing a fundamental phenomenological tenet, Heidegger concludes that we cannot simply infer from "the formal concept of intentionality ... an ego as bearer of this act," but instead "ask phenomenologically in what way its ego, its self, is given to the Dasein itself" (BP, 158). "*In what way is the Dasein, in existing, itself*, its own, or by strict literalness 'ownly' or authentic?" (BP, 158). Although we immediately recognize this topic from our earlier treatment of self-consciousness, what is intriguing in this passage is the fact that Heidegger relates it to the concept of authenticity and, by the same token, to inauthenticity.

According to Heidegger, three elements belong to intentionality: the self-directing-towards, the understanding of the being of that being to which it is directed, and "*the associated unveiling of the self* which is comporting itself here" (BP, 158). Thus, as Heidegger sees it, "the co-disclosure of the self belongs to intentionality" (BP, 158). But, again, the question remains:

In what way is the self given? Not — as might be thought in adherence to Kant — in such a way that an "I think" accompanies all representations and goes along with the acts directed at extant beings, which thus would be a reflective act directed at the first act. (BP, 158)

Heidegger points out that although it is formally unassailable to speak of the ego as "consciousness of something that is at the same time consciousness of *itself*" (BP, 158) this phrase does not tell us anything about "how this being shows itself to itself in its factual existence" (BP, 159).

Heidegger emphasizes the necessity of approaching this question in a manner that does not take over preconceived notions of the ego. He emphasizes that Dasein, qua existence, is there for itself, but he does not take that to mean that Dasein thereby "expressly directs itself to itself in the manner of its own peculiar turning around and turning back" (BP, 159). The latter, he says, is what phenomenology refers to as inner perception and that is not what characterizes being there for itself.

The self is there for Dasein itself without reflection and without inner perception, *before* all reflection. Reflection, in the sense of turning back, is only a mode of self-*apprehension*, but not the mode of primary self-disclosure. (BP, 159)

Curiously enough, though, Heidegger goes on to refer to primary self-disclosure as a kind of reflection. However, he emphasizes that this is not to be understood in the sense of "the ego bent around backward and staring at itself" (BP, 159). Primary self-disclosure is a reflection which must be conceived in the optical sense of the term 'reflection,' that is, in the sense of reflecting from something. Thus, to reflect is to "radiate back from there, to show itself in a reflection from something" (BP, 159). This notion of reflection is very intriguing in the sense that it situates reflection in the world, or, more accurately, within the realm of intentionality. It can make sense of the claim that a certain unveiling of the self belongs to intentionality. This, in turn, brings us back to our initial claim concerning everyday activity. Everydayness, we pointed out, refers to an attitude in which Dasein understands itself as belonging to the realm of being of those entities with which it is concerned, that is, it sees itself in the mode of being present-at-hand. Dasein, Heidegger emphasizes, "never finds itself otherwise than in the things themselves" (BP, 159).

The Dasein does not need a special kind of observation, nor does it need to conduct a sort of espionage on the ego in order to have itself; rather, as the Dasein gives itself over immediately and passionately to the world itself, *its own self is reflected to it from things*. (BP, 159; our emphasis)

There is a kinship between this notion of reflection and the notion of non-positional awareness developed in our discussion of Kant and Sartre. Heidegger's contribution is that he furnishes this position with a pre-ontological confirmation. However, before we elaborate further on this theme, let us make some additional remarks concerning the givenness of the ego in everyday activity.

There are two aspects of the self-reflection of everydayness that are here relevant. It is (i) inauthentic and (ii) authenticity is a modification of inauthenticity. Let us begin with the former. As we have already indicated above, everyday self-understanding is inauthentic.

We understand ourselves in an everyday way or, as we can formulate it terminologically, *not authentically* in the strict sense of the word ... but inauthentically, our self indeed but as we are *not our own*, as we have lost our self in things and humans while we exist in the everyday. "Not authentically" means: not as we at bottom are *able* to be own to ourselves. (BP, 160)

Now, in what sense have we lost our selves? Does this mean that we have lost our selves in the sense that we have lost something we previously had, that is, in the way we occasionally lose things? Not exactly. If that were the case we would have to assume that we were authentic before we got hooked up with the world. In turn, this implies a kind of Being-for-ourself as prior to Being-in-the-world which is simply the reinstatement of the worldless ego. That is definitely not what Heidegger means by losing our self.

The Dasein understands itself first by way of these [intraworldly] beings: it is at first unveiled to itself in its inauthentic selfhood. We have already said that inauthentic existence does not mean an apparent existence or an ungenuine existence. What is more, inauthenticity belongs to the essential nature of factical Dasein. *Authenticity is only a modification but not a total obliteration of inauthenticity.* (BP, 171; our emphasis)

Nevertheless, the very term 'to lose something' still suggests something to this effect. One cannot really lose something one never had. Heidegger is aware of this point. "[Dasein] *is* in such a way that it is in a certain way *its own*, and only on that account can it *lose* itself" (BP, 170). The three essential concepts in this context are the concepts of mineness, inauthenticity, and authenticity. In order to clarify the reciprocal relations among these concepts, let us relate them to another threefold, the concepts of ontical, ontological, and pre-ontological. This will help us to see what Heidegger means by saying that we "have lost our self in things and humans while we exist in the everyday" (BP, 160). Obviously, the concepts of ontical and inauthentic go together; they designate the everyday attitude of Dasein. Factual or ontical Dasein is inauthentic. This attitude, the *poietic* attitude that defines everydayness, hides the true nature of Dasein's existence. It follows that Dasein is characterized by mineness. As Heidegger puts it, "this being that we ourselves are and that exists for the sake of its own self is, as this being, *in each case mine*" (BP, 160). However, he continues,

[t]he Dasein is not only, like every being in general, identical with itself in a formal-ontological sense — every thing is identical with itself — and it is also not merely, in distinction from a natural thing, conscious of this selfsameness. (BP, 160)

Here, Heidegger points out that mineness and the ontological level are compatible, that is, mineness is an ontological concept. We have thus established the compatibility of the ontical and inauthenticity, and of the ontological and mineness. Heidegger emphasizes, however, that fundamental ontology is not a matter of leaping from ontical concepts to ontological concepts. It is the level of pre-ontological experience that justifies the development of Heidegger's ontology. Authenticity is a modification of inauthenticity in the sense that the former refers to marginal experiences in which existence announces itself and thus justifies the transition from the ontical to the ontological. These experiences offer a glimpse of the basic state of Dasein, of Being-in-the-world, as a whole which is essential for Heidegger's endeavor of developing a fundamental ontology.

In summary, to have lost our selves in the world is not a matter of losing something the way we lose things. Inauthentic self-understanding is indeed an understanding of our selves. We still have our selves, we are still in a state of mineness. Moreover, it is also not a matter of losing an authentic self-understanding acquired prior to our involvement with the world. Loss of self is a way in which the phenomenon of mineness appears in everyday activity. This activity is pre-reflective. While dealing with things in the world we do not also at the same time see ourselves as the for-the-sake-of-which of our dealings. We are not, to use a Sartrean locution, *positionally*[13] aware of our self in everydayness. We do not see ourselves as an entity that differs from all other non-human entities in having our own being as an issue. However, mineness is still at work, although in a discrete and non-positional manner. This becomes evident as inauthenticity is modified in authentic self-understanding.

We shall not elaborate any further on this topic now but conclude that the *poietic* attitude of everydayness is inauthentic in the sense that Dasein understands itself as belonging to the realm of present-at-hand entities. Later we shall see that when this self-understanding is modified in authenticity, we are provided with an insight that is not given in everydayness: that we are non-positionally aware of ourselves in everyday activity. However, let us first have a closer look at this "self" of everydayness.

4. THE ONE (*DAS MAN*)

Heidegger discusses the appearance of inauthentic self-understanding that characterizes everydayness by inquiring into the "who" of everyday Dasein. There are two major themes present in this discussion: one that emphasizes the inauthenticity of *poietic* activity and one that introduces the important concept of *praxis*. The former finds its expression in the claim that the "who" of everyday Dasein is anybody and nobody in particular. It "is the '*nobody*' to whom every Dasein has already surrendered itself in Being-among-one-another [*Untereinandersein*]" (BT, 166). The latter is expressed in the statement that "the 'One' itself articulates the referential context of significance" (BT, 167). These themes are closely interrelated. However, in his discussion Heidegger goes back and forth between these themes without always notifying the reader.

In HCT, while opening his discussion of the "who" of Dasein, Heidegger recalls that the designation of Dasein as "the entity which I myself am at any given time" (HCT, 236) should not be looked upon as establishing the

---

[13] As we may recall, Sartre claims that given the phenomenological notion of consciousness as intentional it follows that consciousness can only be aware of itself "*in so far as it is consciousness of a transcendent object*" (TE, 40). This consciousness of consciousness is "not *positional*, which is to say that consciousness is not for itself its own object" (TE, 41).

primacy of a worldless ego. Although he has no problem using the term 'I,' he prefers to leave it as neutral as possible.

The word 'I' in the meaning in which we first immediately understand it in an average way, is thereby left undefined. The more open we leave this word, not relating it directly to a 'subject' and the like, the less burdened the term remains and the more opportunity we then have to fix it more rigorously by way of the phenomena themselves. (HCT, 237)

According to Heidegger, the attraction of substance-egology — a notion of the self as a thing-like entity — is partly the fact that the givenness of the I seems, ontically speaking, so obvious. But, as we have pointed out, Heidegger rejects an unjustified passage directly from the ontical to the ontological level; what is ontically obvious does not necessarily need to be the case ontologically. Moreover, what seems ontically obvious may not itself be as unambiguous as commonly thought.

Heidegger admits that the notion of Dasein as "an entity which is in each case I myself ... tells us *ontically* ... that in each case an 'I' — not Others — is this entity" (BT, 150).

The question of the "who" answers itself in terms of the "I" itself, the 'subject,' the 'Self.' The "who" is what maintains itself as something identical throughout changes in its Experiences and ways of behavior, and which relates itself to this changing multiplicity in so doing. (BT, 150)

However, if this is naïvely accepted as a basis for an ontological inquiry into the status of the subject or the self, one ends up understanding it "as something which is in each case already constantly present-at-hand" (BT, 150). This, Heidegger claims, leads to the notion of the *subjectum*, that is, to a notion of subjectivity as something that appears prior to and independently of the world and whose constitution of the latter is understood in terms of fabrication. This is simply a matter of ontologizing everyday *poietic* activity instead of inquiring into its nature. This is, roughly, what Heidegger accuses traditional metaphysics of doing. "Dasein is tacitly conceived in advance as something present-at-hand. This meaning of Being is always implicated in any case where the Being of Dasein has been left indefinite" (BT, 150). Heidegger's reply is that, instead of ontologizing *poietic* seeing, the philosopher must attempt to see or understand this seeing itself more accurately. One cannot simply accept our ontical self-understanding as a starting point for an ontological inquiry.

The assertion that it is I who in each Dasein is, is ontically obvious; but this must not mislead us into supposing that the route for an ontological interpretation of what is 'given' in this way has thus been unmistakably prescribed. Indeed it remains questionable whether even the mere ontical content of the above assertion does proper justice to the stock of phenomena belonging to everyday Dasein. (BT, 150)

However, if phenomenology represents an attempt to stay away from constructions, how can a phenomenologist not go along with something that is ontically obvious? How can something that is ontically obvious mislead us? "[I]s it not contrary to the rules of all sound method to approach a problematic without sticking to what is given in the area of our theme? And what is more indubitable than the givenness of the 'I'?" (BT, 151). In one sense the givenness of the "I" is indubitable but, Heidegger points out, the "kind of 'giving' we have here is the mere formal, reflective awareness of the 'I'" (BT, 151). This is not the way the "I" is given in everydayness. As we have pointed out on several occasions, everyday activity is pre-reflective. In *poetic* activity, Dasein does not have itself, so to speak; its focus is precisely not on itself but rather on entities whose character is not that of Dasein. Everyday Dasein is not directed at itself but away from itself. Therefore, Heidegger can say, "Dasein is in each case mine, and this is its constitution; but what if this should be the very reason why, proximally and for the most part, Dasein *is not itself*" (BT, 151). This is a very intriguing passage and, despite its seemingly contradictory nature, it says something essential about Heidegger's approach. It simply follows from Heidegger's concept of existence, i.e., that Dasein relates to itself by directing itself towards things in the world, that the constitution of mineness is the reason why Dasein is not itself. However, Heidegger quickly points out that the *not having itself* is not to be understood in terms of lacking mineness or not being Dasein: "[T]he 'not-I' is by no means tantamount to an entity which essentially lacks 'I-hood' ['*Ichheit*'], but is rather a definite kind of Being which the 'I' itself possesses, such as having lost itself [*Selbstverlorenheit*]" (BT, 152). If existential analytic really confines itself to what is given, it cannot start out from the formal givenness of the "I" despite its seemingly indubitable givenness. Instead, it has to investigate the ontical givenness of the self. The "who" of Dasein, Heidegger claims, "is not only a problem *ontologically*; even *ontically* it remains concealed" (BT, 152).

Heidegger admits that there is a sense in which the I is given, but the problem still remains: in what sense is it given? We must be careful not to accept as our starting point a position that already gives an answer to this question.

We have indeed not ... let it be noted, assumed a starting point for analysis such that we said: first I am alone in the world, or first only the 'I' is given without the world. With the rejection of this approach and the uncovering of Being-in-the-world, there can be no question of the isolation of the I, and therefore no talk of 'I am alone in the world'. Already the last formulation of the phenomenal finding in Dasein, 'I am alone in the world', would be essentially more appropriate than this: 'first a bare subject exists without a world'. But even this formulation of the starting point, 'first an I is given with my Being-in-the-world' is false. (HCT, 237-8)

Heidegger thus emphasizes that not only is the "I" not given without the world, but also that the interpretation of Dasein as Being-in-the-world precludes not only a bare worldless subject, but a subject alone in the world as well.

Yet even the positive interpretation of Dasein which we have so far given, already forbids us to start with the formal givenness of the "I," if our purpose is to answer of the "who" in a way which is phenomenally adequate: in clarifying Being-in-the-world we have shown that a bare subject without a world never 'is' proximally, nor is it ever given. And so in the end an isolated "I" without others is just as far as being proximally given. (BT, 152)

Our encountering of equipment is not something that is done in seclusion from other human beings. The world of fabrication also refers to other fabricat*ors*.

[A]long with the work, we encounter not only entities ready-to-hand but also entities with Dasein's kind of being — entities for which, in their concern, the product becomes ready-to-hand; and together with these we encounter the world in which wearers and users live, which is at the same time ours. Any work with which one concerns oneself is ready-to-hand not only in the domestic world of the workshop but also in the *public world*. (BT, 100)

This passage echoes Arendt's discussion of fabrication. Although the activity of work itself does not constitute the public sphere, this activity presupposes the activity that does take place in and constitutes the public world. In her discussion of instrumentality Arendt demonstrates the dependence of work upon action by showing that the means/ends categories of work presuppose action, and that activity essentially includes other people because the condition corresponding to this activity is plurality. Heidegger also emphasizes that when others are encountered in the work-world along with ready-to-hand equipment, these others are encountered within a world that is at one time theirs and mine.

The Others who are thus 'encountered' in a ready-to-hand, environmental context of equipment, are not somehow added on in thought to some Thing which is proximally just present-at-hand; such 'Things' are encountered from out of the world in which they are ready-to-hand for Others — a world which is always mine too in advance. (BT, 154)

At this point, we have reached a culminating point of our discussion in these sections, namely to investigate the relation between discoveredness and disclosedness. In the previous section, we underscored the kinship between the discoveredness and *poiesis*. Now we see that in Heidegger, as in Arendt, this activity takes place within the public world . In what follows, we shall see this more thoroughly developed in Heidegger as he introduces the concept of the One. As we pointed out above, Heidegger presents his argument in favor of the public character of the world in the course of developing his notion of the inauthentic self-understanding of everyday Dasein.

According to Heidegger, the term 'others' must not be seen as confirming a notion of an isolated subject, in the sense that this term refers to those whom oneself is not. On the contrary,

By 'Others' we do not mean everyone else but me - those over against whom the "I" stands out. They are rather those from whom, for the most part, one does *not* distinguish oneself — those among whom one is too. (BT, 154)

Heidegger maintains that the expression "those among whom one is too" does not refer to a being with others that has "the ontological character of Being-present-at-hand-along-'with' them within a world" (BT, 154). Instead, the 'with' must be understood existentially, as something that belongs to the structure of Dasein. "The world of Dasein is a *with-world*. Being-in is a *being-with* others. Their being in themselves within-the-world is *Dasein-with*" (BT, 155).[14] In maintaining being-with as an existential characteristic of Dasein, Heidegger rules out the possibility of understanding Being-in-the-world along the lines of an isolated subject being in a private world. Given the fact that Dasein, in its most primordial nature, is Dasein-with, it follows that "Being-alone is a deficient mode of Being-with" (BT, 157).

It seems obvious that Heidegger thus maintains that the world within which everyday activity takes place is the public world and that he rules out the notion of a private world, at least as something prior to and foundational for the public world. Thus, Heidegger seems to agree with Arendt's view that the everyday activity of work, or production, or *poiesis*, i.e., the world of means and ends, takes place within a public sphere. However, the question remains as to whether Heidegger actually claims that the former presupposes the latter. To answer that question we shall first have to investigate the outcome of Heidegger's discussion of the "who" of everyday Dasein.

When Heidegger asks "who it is that Dasein is in its everydayness" (BT, 149), he answers it "could be that the 'who' of everyday Dasein is *not* the 'I-myself'" (BT, 150). Having emphasized the ontological status of being-with,

---

[14] Heidegger designates our Being-with-Others as solicitude, not care or concern which designate our directedness towards objects. He also discusses the different modes of solicitude and refers to two extreme possibilities as leaping in for the other and leaping ahead of the other. However, it falls outside our scope to discuss this in any detail.

Heidegger has already suggested that everyday Dasein must be interpreted in terms of a certain publicness. When he claims that "Being with Others belongs to the Being of Dasein" (BT, 160) he means that "Being-with is an existential constituent of Being-in-the-world" (BT, 163). He further emphasizes this publicness when he goes on to refer to the "who" of everyday Dasein as the One.

According to Heidegger, "Being-with-one-another has the character of *distantiality* [*Abständigkeit*]" (BT, 164), and this character, in turn, "is such that Dasein, as everyday Being-with-one-another, stands in *subjection* [*Botmässigkeit*] to Others" (BT, 164). Now, what does he mean by claiming that everyday Dasein is not itself and that it is under the spell or subjection of others? To answer that question let us have a closer look at the term 'others'. Firstly, Heidegger uses this term technically. He specifically states that these others "are not definite Others" (BT, 164).

On the contrary, any Other can represent them. What is decisive is just that inconspicuous domination by others which has already been taken over unawares from Dasein as Being-with. (BT, 164)

Secondly, this concept of the others answers the question concerning the "who" of everyday Dasein. "The 'who' is not this one, not that one, not one-self [*man selbst*], not some people [*einige*], and not the sum of them all. The 'who' is the neuter, *the* 'One' [*das Man*]" (BT, 164; translation altered). The concept of the One must be understood in terms of conformity and normativity, that is, in terms of what one is supposed to do. That is why the term 'One' more fully captures Heidegger's intentions than the English translation the "they."

We take pleasure and enjoy ourselves as *One* [*man*] takes pleasure; we read, see, and judge about literature and art as *One* sees and judges; likewise we shrink back from the 'great mass' as *One* shrinks back; we find shocking what *One* finds shocking. The 'one,' which is nothing definite, and which all are, though not as a sum, prescribes the kind of being of everydayness. (BT, 164; translation altered)

However, the concept of the One does not refer to a negative phenomenon and therefore one which should be avoided. "The One," Heidegger claims, "is an existentiale; and as a primordial phenomenon, it belongs to Dasein's positive constitution" (BT, 167; translation altered). Since the One is an existential characteristic of Dasein, it follows that for everyday Dasein, any notion of escaping this phenomenon would be an instance of ungenuine inauthenticity. In BP, for instance, after having assured that there is nothing ungenuine about inauthentic self-understanding he goes on to claim that "all extravagant grubbing about one's soul can be in the highest degree counterfeit" (BP, 160). Likewise, in BT Heidegger refers to an "exaggerated 'self-dissection' tempting itself with all possibilities of explanation" (BT, 222) as alienated.

In *poietic* activity Dasein is directed, not at itself, but towards intraworldly entities. In order for Dasein to be directed towards these entities, the referential context of significance, i.e., the world within which they appear, must already have been disclosed. In other words, in order for Dasein to take a stand on itself by directing itself to intraworldly entities, that is, to exist, it must already have given itself over to the public world. This is precisely what Heidegger maintains in the following passage. "Dasein is for the sake of the 'one' in an everyday manner, and *the 'one' itself articulates the referential context of significance*" (BT, 222; our emphasis). Like Arendt, Heidegger thus claims that the everyday activity of work, or *poiesis*, takes place within a public sphere. Since it is the One that articulates the referential context of significance, the world within which things appear, it follows that Heidegger's view is in keeping with Arendt's, or vice versa, on this issue. The notion of the One as the "who" of everyday Dasein and the claim that it belongs to Dasein's positive constitution underscores the publicness of the world within which *poietic* attitude appears.

Heidegger's discussion of the One constitutes a significant part of his existential analytic but, alas, not an entirely unambiguous one. At first sight, the discussion of the One seems merely to represent an ontologization of colloquial notions of the banality of the crowd in which we are submerged and from which we have to escape if we are to retrieve our true selves. Admittedly, there are passages in Heidegger that substantiate such a reading. By using terms like 'falling,' 'inauthentic,' and 'having lost itself' in describing everydayness, Heidegger obviously invites such an interpretation, as does most certainly his reference to the "dictatorship of the One" (BT, 164). Moreover, in the analysis of the falling Heidegger uses terms like 'idle talk,' 'curiosity,' and 'ambiguity' in order to characterize the everyday Being of Dasein. Now if Heidegger is up to something other than criticizing the inauthenticity and banality of the public world, why does he make use of terms that are so charged? Undeniably, there are passages where Heidegger criticizes modern society and these terms surely reflect that critique. But this is not the essential outcome of the discussion of the One. As we have seen, the One does not designate a negative phenomenon that man has to evade in order to reach an understanding of its true self.

Authentic Being-one's-Self does not rest upon an exceptional condition of the subject, a condition that has been detached from the "One;" *it is rather an existentiell modification of the "One" - of the "One" as an essential existentiale*. (BT, 168; translation altered)

This relationship between authenticity and inauthenticity echoes a theme discussed several times and in relation to several distinctions in the previous chapters: that one phenomenon may account for another phenomenon but may still be founded upon the latter. We have seen this theme in relation to the distinctions between straightforward acts of perception and categorial intuition, between equipment and world, and thus between discoveredness and disclosedness. This notion of the relation between founding and founded acts permeates phenomenology; it is an instantiation of the phenomenological sense of the apriori which, in turn, reflects the theory of wholes and parts. Hence, it is our contention that Heidegger's distinction between authenticity and inauthenticity ultimately reflects this theory. In the remaining sections of this chapter, we discuss this claim in more detail.

5. *PRAXIS*

In the previous chapter, we discussed the distinction between equipment and world, and we established that the appearance of discoveredness, of everyday dealing with equipment, presupposes the appearance of disclosedness. Disclosedness belongs to the being of Dasein which is the "for-the-sake-of-which" that structures the means/ends chain of *poietic* activity. Thus, according to Heidegger, the latter presupposes an activity that is an end in itself. This distinction between fabrication and the kind of activity that is an end in itself, i.e., action, is probably emphasized more systematically by Arendt than by Heidegger. However, we have established that Heidegger refers to everyday dealings with equipment as *poiesis*, and we have also ascertained that the world in which this activity takes place is publicly constituted. Thus, in Heidegger, as in Arendt, fabrication presupposes an activity that is its own end. In Aristotle such activity is known as action (*praxis*).[15]

A central Aristotelian distinction which assists in distinguishing between *poiesis* and *praxis* is the one between potentiality (*dynamis*) and actuality (*energeia*). The relationship between the latter is different for *poiesis* and *praxis*. Let us first have a look at the former.

Where ... the result is something apart from the exercise, the actuality is in the thing that is being made, e.g., the act of building is in the thing that is being built and that of waving in the thing that is being woven, and similarly in all other cases, and in general the movement is in the thing that is being moved. (*Metaphysics*, 1050a 30-34)

In the case of fabrication, the actuality is in the thing being made and thus in something apart from the activity of making. In *praxis* this is entirely differ-

[15] Cf. *Metaphysics*, Book IX, 1048b 22: "that in which the end is present is an action."

ent in the sense that the end is included in the activity itself.

[W]hen there is no product apart from the actuality, the actuality is in the agents, e.g., the act of seeing is in the seeing subject and that of theorizing is in the theorizing subject and the life is in the soul. (*Metaphysics*, 1050a 35-50)

To see is also at the same time to have seen, likewise to understand is to have understood. Whereas what is built is different from the activity of building, there is simply no opposition or difference between the activity of understanding and having understood. In the case of the former, the actuality is external to potentiality in the sense that the actuality of the activity finds its completeness in something that falls outside of the activity, in what is fabricated. In the case of the latter, the actuality is not external to the potentiality. The activity of seeing finds its completeness in the seer, that is, the "actuality is in the agents" (*Metaphysics*, 1050a 35-50).

The fundamental difference between *poiesis* and *praxis* pertains to the goal of the activity. While *poiesis* is directed at what is other — at making something else — the goal of *praxis* concerns the agent itself. It is that of acting well. However, this difference between *poiesis* and *praxis* is not also an indifference. Although Aristotle emphasizes the difference between *poiesis* and *praxis*, there are passages that indicate an intrinsic relation between these activities. More specifically, in the following passage, Aristotle seems to suggest that the latter rules over the former:

Intellect itself, however, moves nothing, but only the intellect which aims at an end and is practical; for this rules the productive intellect as well, since every one who makes makes for an end, and that which is made is not an end in the unqualified sense (but only relative to something, i.e., of something) — only that which is *done* [*to prakton*] is that; for good action [*eupraxia*] is an end, and desire aims at this. (NE, 1139a 35-b 4)

Scholars seems to agree[16] that Aristotle thus indicates a hierarchical relationship between *poiesis* and *praxis* according to which the former is under the spell of the latter. On this reading, it seems quite obvious that Heidegger's distinction between that which is not an end in itself, but merely a means for something else (*das Wozu*) and that which is an end in itself, the "for-the-sake-of-which" (*Worum-willen*) is anticipated by Aristotle's distinction between *poiesis* and *praxis*. While the former is not an end in an unqualified sense, but only relative to something (*pros ti*), the latter is an end in itself (*hou heneka*). In Aristotle, as in Heidegger, the former is ruled by the latter or, in phenomenological idiom, the latter is the *concretum* of the former.

[16] Cf. R. Bernasconi, "Heidegger's Destruction of Phronesis," 137, and J. Taminiaux, *Heidegger and the Project of Fundamental Ontology*, 124.

This kinship between Heidegger and Aristotle is even more conspicuous, given the fact that we already know that Heidegger refers to Dasein's everyday dealing with the world, i.e., discoveredness, as *poiesis*. Could it be that the relation between discoveredness and disclosedness in Heidegger is a reappropriation of Aristotle's concepts of *poises* and *praxis*? Obviously, that is what we are about to suggest. The only problem with making such an argument is the fact that we do not have much textual evidence directly pointing out the affinity between the being of Dasein and *praxis*. In PIA, for instance, Heidegger specifically identifies the dealings of everyday Dasein with *poiesis*, but he never makes the similar unambiguous kind of claim with regard to *praxis*. However, he does use this term and he uses it in a context and with a meaning that suggests a kinship between Dasein's being and *praxis*.

In PIA, Heidegger carries out a close reading of Aristotle's NE, Book VI. In what follows, we inquire into this interpretation in order to shed light on the basic concepts of Heidegger's existential analytic. In this section, we establish that these concepts are presented by using Aristotelian terms and that Heidegger refers to the disclosure of being as *praxis*. Heidegger takes as his point of departure the discussion of the *dianoetic* excellences, but he points out that "the interpretation is conducted with a preliminary disregard for the specifically ethical problematic" (PIA, 377). Contrary to the more traditional view advocated by, for instance, Aquinas, according to which there are five excellences (*techne, episteme, phronesis, sophia, nous*), Heidegger goes on to claim that there are only two: *sophia* and *phronesis*.

Sophia (authentic, observing understanding) and *phronesis* (solicitous circumspection) are interpreted as the authentic ways of the actualizing of *nous*: of pure *beholding* as such. (PIA, 377)[17]

According to Heidegger, the "difference between the two basic ways of beholding [likewise] allows the two different regions of Being to become visible" (PIA, 377). In regard to *techne* and *episteme* — translated as "routine-directive-productive operating" and "observing-discussing-revealing determination" — Heidegger claims that these do not "give the being as uncovered [*unverhüllt*] but only give it such ... that what is intended puts itself in front of the being and thus deceives" (PIA, 377). Heidegger bases this claim on a passage in NE where Aristotle indicates that neither *episteme* nor *techne* are intellectual excellences.[18] Another way this can be put is to call attention to a distinction already made between real and ideal objects on

---

[17] For an interesting discussion of this interpretation see R. Bernasconi, "Heidegger's Destruction of Phronesis."

[18] Heidegger refers to NE, Book VI, 1141a 3.

the one hand and full objectivity on the other. In Aristotle, *episteme* designates knowledge of what is eternal and necessary. In other words, *episteme* is directed towards ideal objects. *Techne*, on the other hand, is a know-how adjusted to *poiesis*, i.e., it is directed towards real objects. As we may recall, according to Heidegger, neither of these defines full objectivity; on the contrary, they are both abstract in relation to full objectivity. Full objectivity embraces both real and ideal objectivity and it comes into being with Dasein. Thus, for Heidegger it follows that neither *techne* nor *episteme* are their own excellences; they are abstract in relation to the agent. *Phronesis*, on the other hand, is not concerned with manipulating real objects or with seeing ideal objects, *phronesis* is self-referential, it refers back to the agent. The aim of *phronesis* is nothing external to the activity, the aim of *phronesis* is good action (*eupraxia*). *Phronesis* designates a kind of understanding that is directed not at beings, whether real or ideal objects, but at the being of that to which beings appear, at the being of the agent. Hence, the terms '*phronesis*' and '*hou heneka*' are intrinsically related in that the latter is the principle of *praxis*. It is not unreasonable to assume that this distinction has found its way into Heidegger's existential analytic as the distinction between circumspection (*Umsicht*) and the "for-the-sake-of-which" (*Worum-willen*) - given the fact that the former is Heidegger's translation of *phronesis* in PIA. We support this argument by showing that Heidegger explicitly refers to *praxis* as the activity through which disclosedness takes place.

Heidegger introduced his interpretation of NE, Book VI, by claiming that this interpretation "makes the 'dianoetic virtues' understandable as ways of having at one's disposal the possibility of actualizing the genuine *truthful safe-keeping of Being*" (PIA, 377). About these virtues he later makes the following claim:

The "virtues" which are under discussion here are those ... corresponding to whose pure manner of being actualized the soul "most of all" gives the present being as unconcealed [*unverborgen*] in primordial truthful safe-keeping. (PIA, 377)

Recall Heidegger's discussion of the scholastic definition of truth as *veritas est adaequatio rei et intellectus* in relation to the phenomenological discovery of evidence as being at once regional and universal.[19] The regional character of evidence represents a concretization of the scholastic definition of truth that brings into view the double meaning of *adaequatio*. From this two concepts of truth can be obtained, one designating the being-identical of the intended and the intuited, and one designating the *intentio*. To these concepts of truth there corresponds different notions of being. To the first there corresponds a notion of being as being-real — i.e., that a judged state

---

[19] Discussed in Chapter II, section 6.

of affairs truly is. To the second there corresponds a notion of being that springs out of an interpretation of truth as a specific correlation of acts. However, Heidegger maintains, both notions of truth are incomplete. "Neither the one oriented toward the state of affairs nor the one oriented toward the act captures the original sense of truth" (HCT, 53). Both positions presuppose a more original sense of truth. Truth cannot be reduced to either *intentum* or *intentio*; it is the *concretum* of both. While the first two concepts of truth are based upon the concretization of the *adaequatio* that follows from the discovery of the regional character of evidence, Heidegger maintains that the universality of evidence represents a radicalization of the scholastic definition of truth. Given the fact that evidence is no longer restricted to the realm of assertions, predications, and judgments, but is a "*universal function, first, of all acts which give their objects, and then, of all acts*" (HCT, 52), it follows that "phenomenology breaks with the restriction of the concept of truth to relational acts, to judgments" (HCT, 55). Original truth is "what makes knowledge *true* [i.e., the true-making matter, the entity itself as intuited matter]" (HCT, 53). Original truth is being, and this notion of truth, Heidegger claims, goes back to early Greek philosophy.

Now let us go back to Heidegger's discussion of the dianoetic virtues and the way being is given as unconcealed in "primordial truthful safe-keeping." A central concept in this regard is the Greek concept of *aletheia*, of truth. Heidegger takes issue against those who sees Aristotle as the progenitor of the notion of truth as something which occurs in judgment.

In Aristotle, there is not a trace either of this concept of truth as "agreement" or of the common conception of logos as valid judgment or — least of all — of the "representation-theory." (PIA, 378)

Thus, original truth, *aletheia*, is not something that occurs in judgment; rather it is what makes agreement of thought with object possible. To locate original truth in the judgment is to force an *abstractum* into being a *concretum*. From this follows, Heidegger claims, "the epistemological freak-birth of so-called 'critical realism' — which is done in apologetics over against a misunderstood 'idealism'" (PIA, 378).

According to Heidegger, the sense of *alethes* is "Being-there [*da-sein*] as unconcealed, i.e., as Being-intended in itself" (PIA, 378).

[It] does not mean: "to seize hold of the truth;" it means rather to take the being which is intended, and which is intended as such, as uncovered in truthful safe-keeping. (PIA, 378)

It is our contention that there is a strong kinship between this notion of *aletheia* and the original notion of truth mentioned in Heidegger's discussion of the universal character of evidence. In both cases, truth is understood, not as the "agreement" of thought with object, but as the disclosure of being, i.e., as constitution. We underscore this by having a closer look at Heidegger's analysis in PIA.

According to Heidegger, *aisthesis* is the "providing of something objective as something uncovered" (PIA, 378). With reference to Aristotle,[20] he claims that perception is not true or false. Truth and falsity, he claims, is only possible when there occurs a synthesis. Is Heidegger by this contradicting the view he advocates three years later in HCT, according to which synthesis is present in straightforward sense-perception? Admittedly, Heidegger's use of 'synthesis' in this context is not a happy choice, but what he has in mind is consistent with the view he advocates in HCT. In this context, 'synthesis' refers, not to a moment of straightforward perception but to a "combination made in thought."[21] The condition of possibility of falsity, and thus also truth in the sense of correspondence between thought and object, is the prior appearance of *noetic* truth. *Noetic* truth refers to a founding sensuousness, a founding *aisthesis* already discussed in our previous discussion of categorial intuition.

Everything categorial ultimately rests upon sense intuition, no objective explication floats freely but is always an explication of something already given. The thesis that everything categorial ultimately rests upon sense intuition is but a restatement of the Aristotelian proposition: "The soul can presume nothing, apprehend nothing objective in its objectivity, if nothing at all has been shown to it beforehand." (HCT, 69)[22]

In this context, sense intuition refers to a broad concept of sensuousness. It embraces more than can be exhausted by the concept of sense data. It is, Heidegger claims, "*the title for the total constellation of entities which are given beforehand in their material content*" (HCT, 70). Sensuousness gives objectivity in its broadest sense, and, as we may recall, the latter is much richer than the reality of a thing. Full objectivity embraces both real and ideal objectivity, it is a *concretum* for both, and it has its origin in Dasein. This is what *noetic* truth refers to, to an original disclosure of being belonging to intentionality. "The term 'truth' is originally and properly attributed to intentionality, but this is done on the basis of its being composed of both the *intentio* and the *intentum*" (HCT, 55). Hence, the term 'truth' is originally attributed, not to the *intentio* or the *intentum*, but to intentionality in its apriori. This takes us beyond the realm of being-identical and beyond the acts of bringing-into-coincidence. It takes us into the realm of "that which

---

[20] Cf. *De Anima*, 427b 12.

[21] Again Heidegger refers to *De Anima* - this time to 430b - in order to clarify his view.

[22] In quotation marks is Heidegger's own translation of *De Anima*, 431a 16f.

makes knowledge *true*" (HCT, 53).

Intentionality now is nothing other than *the basic field* in which these objects are found. [As *intentio* and *intentum*, it is] the totality of comportments and the totality of entities in their being. (HCT, 53)

Thus, original truth refers to the appearance of the basic field in which objectivity is found. This field is the field of *noein*.

According to Heidegger, "*legein* gives the being in its own self" (PIA, 379), and "*logos, legein* is the way in which *noein* is actualized" (PIA, 379). Thus, *nous* has a measure of primacy over the former.

Noein has the basic character of beholding. *Nous* is beholding per se; that means it is that which in general makes possible, that which in general presents a That-with-respect-to-which for any oriented dealings whatsoever. (PIA, 380)

Nous, Heidegger claims, is like a light, it provides sight, "it provides a something; it provides a 'there'" (PIA, 380). As a sight and the "there" of our encountering of beings, *nous* is apriori — but in the phenomenological sense of this term. That is, it is prior to, but not independent of our dealings. The providing-sight, Heidegger maintains, appears "always such in a manner of concrete dealings with, in orienting, producing, handling, determining" (PIA, 380).

Insofar as *nous* gives sight to the dealings themselves, it can also be characterized as illumination-of-the-dealings, an illumination which, however, has the sense of the truthful safe-keeping of Being. (PIA, 380)

Hence, we are back to the notion of original truth as *aletheia*, as truthful safe-keeping of being. *Nous* is that to which appearances appear, hence it designates the clearing or disclosure within which beings can be encountered as what they are.

Nous is *aisthesis tis*, a beholding which in each case gives the appearance of the objects purely and simply ... just as a tool [*Werkzeug*] in the hand first comes to its authentic Being in *generating work* [*Werk-Zeugen*] - so too the *appearance* of the objects is within sight only through *nous* and "in" *nous*, as its That-with-respect-to-which; *it appears*. Insofar as an object-field as such stands within the task of becoming explicitly accessible (and that not simply in the sense of theoretical determining), the "from-whence" (*arche*) of the *legein* must be available in advance as that which is uncovered. (PIA, 380)

However, *nous* as the clearing or the "from-whence" is not something that appears temporally prior to or independent of appearances. It is prior to appearances in the sense that it is that to which appearances appear, that is, it is the very appearance of appearances, so to speak. Hence, it follows that it cannot itself appear independently of the latter. This activity is what Heidegger refers to as constituting in HCT and, as we remember, the latter is characterized as follows: "'Constituting' does not mean producing in the sense of making or fabricating; it means letting *the entity be seen in its objectivity*" (HCT, 71).

In what follows, we shall see that the activity of actualizing original truth, or truthful safe-keeping-of-Being shares this non-creative nature of constitution. First let us establish the way in which truthful safe-keeping is actualized. "[T]he concrete ways of actualizing this authentic truthful safe-keeping-of Being are *sophia* and *phronesis*" (PIA, 381). Although *phronesis* and *sophia* are both *noetic* activities, i.e., both ways in which truthful safe-keeping of being is fulfilled, it is the activity of *phronesis* that designates the movement of human being. *Sophia*, Heidegger suggests, is associated with a divine movement in that it "brings into truthful safe-keeping that being which is in such a way ... that [it] always and necessarily is what it is" (PIA, 381). By contrast, *phronesis*, or circumspection, brings into truthful safe-keeping "that being which *can be otherwise*" (PIA, 381).

Phronesis brings That-with-respect-to-which of the dealings of human life (and dealings with human life itself) and the "How" of these dealings in their own Being into truthful safe-keeping. (PIA, 381)

And Heidegger continues, "[t]hese dealings are *praxis*: the conducting [*Behandeln*] of one's own self in the How of dealings which are not productive, but are rather simply *actional* [*handelnd*]" PIA, 381).

We have established that *poietic* activity presupposes *praxis*. *Phronesis* is a *praxis* and, according to Heidegger, the former is precisely the sight of everyday *poietic* activity. Thus, it seems that the relation between discoveredness ("a possibility of Being which every entity *without* the character of Dasein may possess" (BT, 146)) and disclosedness (the being of Dasein) is a reappropriation of Aristotle's notion of the ontological relation between *poiesis* and *praxis*. However, this involves yet another equally fundamental and highly related distinction in Heidegger, namely the distinction between authenticity and inauthenticity.

In the introduction to this chapter, we maintained that our objective was to investigate the notion of self in BT and that we would lay the ground for a more thorough investigation of the kinship between Heidegger's analysis and Kant's distinction between synthetic and analytic unity of apperception. In Chapter V, in relation to Sartre's notion of non-positional awareness, we discussed Kant's emphasis on the primacy of the former over the latter and the claim that synthetic unity of apperception is the understanding itself. We indicated the presence of a similar structure in Heidegger. In this chapter, we have seen that what characterizes Dasein is not that it is a "point called the 'Self'" (BT, 187), but rather that it is a mineness that unfolds itself through our dealings with the world. This mineness appears as a non-positional self-awareness. In everydayness we are not directed at our own selves. On the contrary, the sight that guides everyday activity — *phronesis* — is an all-consuming directedness at, or openness for, the environment, the world. But since *phronesis* is also a *praxis*, it follows that this sight concerns the agent itself.

At this point, the following question surfaces: if Dasein is non-positional awareness of itself, how can it carry out an existential analytic, that is, how can it reach a positional awareness of this self? In everydayness Dasein does not focus upon the apriori character of its own existential make-up. Rather, the latter is a condition of possibility for the former. In everydayness Dasein is oblivious to its ownmost being — it is inauthentic. How can Heidegger account for the grasping of Dasein's ownmost being, its being as a whole — which is the pronounced aim of fundamental ontology — if this very being precludes such an endeavor. As we shall see, just as he provided the transcendental reduction with a pre-ontological confirmation, Heidegger once again calls attention to certain marginal experiences in which the full meaning of *phronesis* is given in intuition.

CHAPTER VIII

UNITY

Several concepts are used in Heidegger's description of the being of Dasein. Existence, understanding, disclosedness, mineness all pertain to this being we ourselves are. These terms can all be used, if not interchangeably, at least as complementary. The essence of Dasein is existence; existence is understanding; understanding is a kind of self-understanding through which the world is disclosed. Mineness is implicit in all of these concepts, as it also is in the concept of *phronesis*. In fact, Heidegger's phenomenological investigation of this concept seems to represent the basis for the development of his basic concepts. However, since *phronesis* refers to the guiding sight of everydayness, the question remains as to how this seeing itself can be seen, and indeed, how the full meaning of this phenomenon can be apprehended. This requires a two-step pre-ontological confirmation. Firstly, Heidegger must justify his arrival at the concept of care, and, secondly, given this ontological structure of Dasein, he must show how this phenomenon can be seen as a whole. This endeavor represents a transition from the preparatory fundamental analysis of Dasein carried out in Division One of BT to the primordial existential interpretation of this entity sought in Division Two — whose objective is to explain the wholeness and unity of care on the basis of temporality.

We shall see that this endeavor is permeated by the theory of wholes and parts. Heidegger defines the ontological characteristics of Dasein, i.e., the existentials, as structural moments. As we have seen, these are moments in the Husserlian sense of this term — they are non-independent parts. Thus, the ontological status of these structural moments depends upon the appearance of the absolute *concretum* to which they belong as non-independent parts. If Heidegger cannot provide a phenomenal basis for the appearance of Dasein as a whole, he has no right to refer to the existentials as structural moments. Indeed, he must evade the very concept of existentials, since 'structural moment' is exactly what defines this term. In that case Heidegger simply could not carry out an existential analytic.

One cannot utilize certain elements of Husserl's theory of wholes and parts and leave others out, at least not without adequate justification. For instance, once one makes use of the concept of moment — as Heidegger does when introducing his existentials — one must also introduce a whole, an absolute *concretum*. Moreover, one must be able to provide a phenomenal basis for this *concretum*. The theory of wholes and parts is not merely a logical or conceptual tool. It also sets forth phenomenal demands: if a moment is to appear, the whole of which it is a non-independent part must also appear. As already mentioned, Heidegger is fully aware of this. The importance of this theory is reflected in the very architecture of BT, and in the middle of the treatise Heidegger is obviously dealing with the problem of providing phenomenological justification for the givenness of an absolute *concretum*. In the first four sections of the last chapter of Division One, Heidegger carries out the first step of this endeavor, and in the first chapter of Division Two he carries out the second. In this chapter, we investigate this venture by first inquiring into how Heidegger justifies his arrival at the concept of care through his analysis of anxiety. In the subsequent section, we have a look at Heidegger's own discussion of the outcome of Division One and the aim of Division Two in his introduction to the latter. This will show how important the notion of Being-a-whole is for Heidegger's enterprise. In the subsequent sections, we investigate Heidegger's actual analysis of the possibility of Being-a-whole as this is carried out in his interpretation of death and anxiety. In the last two sections, we discuss how this theme founds the possibility for Dasein to grasp its ownmost being, that is, for Dasein to be authentic.

1. THE QUESTION OF PRIMORDIAL TOTALITY

In our initial discussion of Heidegger's formal definition of Dasein's being as care, we did not inquire into the phenomenal basis for the development of this definition. However, if Heidegger is to be true to his own tenets, such a basis must be provided in order to avoid ontological construction. Heidegger is quite aware of this requirement. In fact, his introduction of the phenomenon of care starts out with a discussion of the question concerning the primordial totality of Dasein's structural whole and the possible phenomenal basis for such an investigation. Heidegger opens this chapter with the following statement.

Being-in-the-world is a structure which is primordially and constantly *whole* [*eine ... ganze Struktur*]. In the preceding chapters (Division One, Chapters 2-5) this structure has been elucidated phenomenally as a whole, and also in its constitutive moments [*konstitutiven Momenten*], though always on this basis. (BT, 225; translation altered)

However, Heidegger maintains, since Dasein for the most part is inauthentic and thus oblivious to its ownmost being, the preliminary investigation is indeed preliminary. It has still to receive the necessary phenomenal foundation that justifies this interpretation. And, Heidegger asks, "[d]oes our present approach *via* the existential analytic provide us an avenue for arriving at this Being phenomenally?" (BT, 226). In what follows, Heidegger makes it clear that one cannot arrive at this being phenomenally by way of construction. A structural whole cannot be "reached by building it up out of elements" (BT, 226). This, he claims would require an architect's plan.

The Being of Dasein, upon which the structural whole as such is ontologically supported, becomes accessible to us when we look all the way *through* this whole *to a single* primordially unitary phenomenon which is already in this whole in such a way that it provides the ontological foundation for each structural moment [*Strukturmoment*] in its structural possibility. (BT, 226; translation altered)

Hence, the unity of a structural whole is not the sum of the parts of the whole, therefore we cannot get to it by adding together structural moments. What Heidegger is saying is that for something to be a moment there must be a whole to which it belongs, and since the whole is prior to its moments, it follows that the whole cannot be reached by gathering together the moments. This would imply that the moments could account for themselves and appear prior to the whole, i.e., that the existentials are in fact pieces rather than moments. However, this would be a contradiction in terms, since an existential by its very definition is a structural moment. Thus, the totality or the unity of the structural whole — the Being of Dasein — must become accessible to us, not as a sum, but as a "single primordially unitary phenomenon" which ontologically supports the structural whole.

This unitary phenomenon has a measure of primacy over the moments constituting the whole in the sense that it "provides the ontological foundation for each structural moment in its structural possibility" (BT, 226), but this does not imply that this unitary phenomenon appears prior to the whole in an independent sense. If this were the case, Heidegger would merely introduce an infinite regress. If the unitary phenomenon could appear independently of its structural moments, the latter would not be moments, and thus the former would not be a unitary phenomenon. Indeed, one would have to introduce yet another unitary phenomenon in order to account for any unity between these phenomena.

The unity of a totality is not that of being a heap of components. What makes something a unity is something more than a totality of components. Husserl's distinction between wholes and moments addresses this issue by showing that, on the one hand, moments are what they are only in relation to a whole and, on the other hand, that the whole is precisely the unification of the moments, and not some additional thing-like entity appearing alongside the moments. This is the source of the phenomenological sense of the apriori according to which it is "a feature of the being of the entities" (HCT, 75). Thus, the being of Dasein has an apriori status in relation to its structural moments, but it is not prior to these moments in the way that one entity can appear temporally prior to another. According to Heidegger, "[t]he question of Dasein's basic existential character is essentially different from that of the Being of something present-at-hand" (HCT, 75). But for this very reason it is difficult to grasp the apriori nature of Dasein. On the one hand, he claims,

[o]ur everyday environmental experiencing [*Erfahren*], which remains directed both ontically and ontologically towards entities within-the-world, is not the sort of thing which can present Dasein in an ontically primordial manner for ontological analysis. (HCT, 75)

In other words, Dasein does not appear to itself in everyday environmental experiencing as a "single primordially unitary phenomenon." On the other hand, "Dasein's being is not to be deduced from an idea of man" (HCT, 75). Thus, the problem remains as follows:

Does the Interpretation of Dasein which we have hitherto given permit us to infer what Dasein, *from its own standpoint*, demands as the only appropriate onticoontological way of access to itself?" (HCT, 75)

What Heidegger has to be able to call attention to is a situation in which Dasein is disclosed to its ownmost being. This is necessary if "the existential analytic of Dasein is to retain clarity in principle as to its function in fundamental ontology" (HCT, 75).

As we know, the problematic of fundamental ontology is the question of the meaning of being in general. But in order "to work out the question of the meaning of *Being* and to do so concretely" (BT, 19) we must "make a being — the inquirer — perspicuous in his own Being" (BT, 27). The latter is the objective of the existential analytic whose aim is to provide a "concrete understanding of the basic constitution of Dasein" (BT, 358). But if the latter is to retain clarity as to its function in relation to the project of fundamental ontology, it must do precisely so, i.e., reach a concrete understanding of this being we ourselves are. It must grasp this being in its concreteness, as a whole, and to do so it must be able to call attention to a situation in which it appears as a simple whole. But that, in turn, requires that one seeks "for one of the most *far-reaching* and *most primordial* possibilities of disclosure - one that lies in Dasein itself" (BT, 358).

The way of disclosure in which Dasein brings itself before itself must be such that in it Dasein becomes accessible as simplified in a certain manner. With what is thus disclosed, the structural totality of the Being we seek must then come to light in an elemental way. (BT, 226)

According to Heidegger, the situation or situatedness that satisfies "these methodological requirements is the phenomenon of *anxiety*" (BT, 227).

As one of Dasein's possibilities of Being, anxiety — together with Dasein itself is disclosed in it — provides the phenomenal basis for explicitly grasping Dasein's primordial totality of Being. Dasein reveals itself as *care*. (BT, 227)

However, even if the phenomenon of anxiety satisfies the methodological requirements concerning the disclosure of Dasein's being, one cannot simply proceed from the ontical appearance of anxiety to the ontological concept of care.

[T]he ontical approach with which we have tried to Interpret Dasein Ontologically as care, may appear far-fetched and theoretically contrived ... Accordingly our existential Interpretation of Dasein as care requires pre-ontological confirmation. (BT, 227)

To summarize, then, in order to grasp the whole which provides the ontological foundation for each structural moment in its structural possibility, one cannot simply add together these moments. That would imply that the latter could appear prior to and independently of the whole, a possibility which is barred by the very fact that the whole is the ontological foundation of these moments. Thus, Heidegger has to provide a way in which the primordially unitary phenomenon is given in its totality. For Heidegger the phenomenon of anxiety satisfies the methodological requirements through which the existential interpretation of Dasein as care can receive a phenomenal basis. But in order to provide a *bona fide* pre-ontological confirmation he cannot simply carry out a conceptual inference, he must also carry out an analysis of the phenomenon of anxiety.

2. ANXIETY

According to Heidegger, Dasein is capable of giving us ontical information about itself as an entity, of informing us of its ownmost being. The reason for this is that everydayness includes a range of marginal experiences in which ontological structures are given in intuition. There are three significant experiences on which the development of Heidegger's ontology is grounded. First, we have the breakdown of everyday activities in which the world announces itself as something that is essentially tied to the being of Dasein. This allows ontology to be ontology, that is, to inquire into the ontological meaning of everyday or ontical comportments. Hence, in the breakdown of everyday activities, the transcendental reduction is given in intuition. This lays the basis for a further inquiry whose aim is to exhibit essential structures of the being of Dasein, and it brings us to the second significant marginal experience, namely the phenomenon of anxiety. Through this experience the phenomenon of care announces itself, and thus the essential structures of Dasein also announce themselves, since the former provides the ontological foundation for the latter. The objective of this section is to inquire into the analysis of this experience. The third significant experience is Being-towards-death. This phenomenon provides a phenomenal basis for the possibility of grasping the being of Dasein as a whole. The phenomenon of death will be discussed in section four.

In order to provide a pre-ontological confirmation of the being of Dasein as care, Heidegger introduces a theme usually associated with existentialism in general and Kierkegaard in particular. There is no doubt that Heidegger's interpretation of anxiety is heavily influenced by Kierkegaard. Indeed, Heidegger credits Kierkegaard as "the man who has gone farthest in analyzing the phenomenon of anxiety" (BT, 235n). But the role this theme plays in Heidegger's existential analytic springs out of the general approach of this analytic. It is not so much anxiety itself that interests Heidegger as what this phenomenon discloses. It provides Heidegger with an experience in which the phenomenon of care is given in intuition.

Heidegger introduces his investigation of anxiety with the following question:

How is it that in anxiety Dasein gets brought before itself through its own Being, so that we can define phenomenologically the character of the entity disclosed in anxiety, and define it as such in its Being? (BT, 228)

In everydayness Dasein is oblivious to its ownmost being; it is inauthentic. Heidegger's refers to Dasein's absorption in the world, and thus in the One, as the *"fleeing* of Dasein in the face of itself — of itself as an authentic potentiality-for-Being-its-self" (BT, 229). This fleeing, he continues, "seems at least a suitable basis for the following investigation" (BT, 229). The fact that Dasein understands itself in everydayness as belonging to the realm of being of those entities with which it is concerned, that is, that it sees itself in the mode of being present-at-hand, constitutes the incentive for characterizing this possibility of being as a *fleeing* from its ownmost being. However, the term 'fleeing' does not imply a choice deliberately made by a subject, nor does it refer to a psychological disposition. In this context, 'fleeing' has a structural meaning, and thus it is not something Dasein can choose not to participate in. Throughout the analysis of inauthenticity Heidegger uses charged terms like 'falling' and 'fleeing.' These terms suggest something negative, something that should be avoided. However, this is not the case. These terms do not designate negative qualities that could perhaps be eliminated, rather they define everydayness in the sense that everyday Dasein is not aware of itself, i.e., does not focus upon the apriori character of its own being. But, one could ask, why refer to the everyday self-understanding as a turning away from one's ownmost being? Why cannot this self-understanding be the most proper understanding of our own being? However, the fact that the entity who is essentially characterized by understanding understands itself as belonging to the realm of the being of what it understands does seem to suggest the possibility of there being a more proper way in which to understand oneself. In other words, it seems that a more proper way of understanding this being would be to understand it as *that which understands*. Thus, it is everyday self-understanding itself that suggests a more proper way of understanding itself. This leads to the notion of everyday Dasein turning away from, or fleeing, its ownmost being, a move which in turn presupposes a something in the face of which it flees. "Only to the extent that Dasein has been brought before itself in an ontologically essential manner through whatever disclosedness belongs to it, *can* it flee *in the face of* that in the face of which it flees" (BT, 229). However, this is not to say that, ontically speaking, Dasein was originally authentic and then gradually was corrupted through socialization by fleeing from itself into the banality of the crowd. Heidegger is fully aware of the possibility of such a misinterpretation.

From an existentiell point of view; the authenticity of Being-one's-Self has of course been closed off and thrust aside in falling; but to be thus closed off is merely a *privation* of a disclosedness which manifests itself phenomenally in the fact that Dasein's fleeing is a fleeing *in the face of itself.* (BT, 229)

The "authentic potentiality-for-Being-its-Self" is not an ontical possibility. Thus, it is not that Dasein at one stage of its life appears as authentic and then suddenly or gradually turns inauthentic. Nor does Heidegger advocate the necessity of retrieving an authentic way of living in the world. Remember that there is nothing negative or ungenuine about inauthentic self-understanding. Indeed, Heidegger refers to it as a phenomenon that belongs to Dasein's positive constitution. Thus, any attempt to find a way back to an ontical and authentic way of Being-in-the-world is simply impossible, and thus in the highest degree ungenuine. Authenticity refers to the possibility of understanding the full meaning of Dasein's being — not to an ideal way of

Being-in-the-world.

According to Heidegger, the "authentic potentiality-for-Being-its-Self" is an ontological possibility.

[The] existentiell-ontical turning-away, by reason of its character as a disclosure, makes it phenomenally possible to grasp existential-ontologically that in the face of which Dasein flees ... Within the ontical 'away-from' which such turning away implies, that in the face of which Dasein flees can be understood and conceptualized by 'turning thither' in a way which is phenomenologically Interpretative. (BT, 229)

Thus, starting out from the phenomena of falling and turning away, Heidegger sees the possibility of "learning something ontologically about the Dasein disclosed in [those phenomena]" (BT, 229). Heidegger notices that in this approach one does not base the analysis on an artificial way in which Dasein understands itself. Rather, one takes one's point of departure in everydayness and seeks to explicate "what Dasein itself ontically discloses" (BT, 230). Hence, again we see how important it is for Heidegger to have a phenomenal basis for every step he makes in his existential analytic. This is what distinguishes his endeavor from that of Husserl's. Although Heidegger to a large extent adheres to a Husserlian line of reasoning, he seems better at providing the Husserlian themes with a phenomenal basis than is Husserl. In this way Heidegger's endeavor is more in keeping with the fundamental principle of phenomenological investigation expressed by the maxim "to the matters themselves." The phenomenological themes that guide Heidegger's investigation, the theory of wholes and parts, the concept of categorial intuition, and the phenomenological sense of the apriori, all emphasize the necessity of avoiding construction. These themes all underscore the founding/founded relation between philosophical concepts and sensuousness.

Heidegger introduces his investigation by distinguishing between fear and anxiety. This is necessary, since traditionally these phenomena have not been properly distinguished from one another. "[T]hat which is fear, gets designated as 'anxiety,' while that which has the character of anxiety, gets called 'fear'" (BT, 230). Heidegger is determined to approach the phenomenon of anxiety step by step in order to avoid blurring this distinction. He calls attention to an analysis of fear carried out previously in BT in relation to the presentation of the existential situatedness. In this analysis, Heidegger outlines three approaches from which the phenomenon of fear can be considered: "(1) that in face of which we fear, (2) fearing, and (3) that about which we fear" (BT, 179). That which we fear, Heidegger claims, is "in every case something which we encounter within-the-world and which may have either readiness-to-hand, presence-at-hand, or Dasein-with as its kind of Being" BT, 179). What we fear is an external entity threatening us. In fearing as such "what we have just characterized as threatening is freed and allowed to matter to us" (BT, 180). With regard to that about which we fear, Heidegger emphasizes that it is our own being: "*That which* fear fears *about* is that very entity which is afraid — Dasein. Only an entity for which in its Being this very Being is an issue, can be afraid" (BT, 180). The last sentence of this passage discloses Heidegger's notion of the ontological relation between fear and anxiety. Fear is directed at something external, at some definite entity within-the-world, but this fearing about one's own being is only possible, Heidegger points out, given the fact that Dasein is essentially characterized by existence. Thus, the concept of fear seems to suggest discretely the phenomenon of existence. However, in his treatment of anxiety Heidegger sees this phenomenon as fully disclosed.

According to Heidegger, while fear can make us turn away from or flee from a threatening entity within-the-world, the fleeing that characterizes everydayness is of a different kind. It is not "a fleeing that is founded upon a fear of entities within-the-world" (BT, 180).

Fleeing that is so grounded is still less a character of this turning-away, when what this turning-away does is precisely to *turn thither* towards entities within-the-world by absorbing itself in them. *The turning-away of falling is grounded rather in anxiety, which in turn is what first makes fear possible.* (BT, 180)

The notion of everyday Dasein as fleeing in the face of itself, of falling, must be seen in relation to the basic state of Dasein. "That in the face of which one has anxiety," Heidegger claims, "is not an entity within-the-world" (BT, 231), rather it is Being-in-the-world as such.

That in the face of which anxiety is anxious is nothing ready-to-hand within-the-world. But this "nothing ready-to-hand" ... is not totally nothing. The "nothing" of readiness-to-hand is grounded in the most primordial 'something' — in the *world*. Ontologically, however, the world belongs essentially to Dasein's Being as Being-in-the-world. So if the "nothing" — that is, the world as such —exhibits itself as that in the face of which one has anxiety, this means that *Being-in-the-world itself is that in the face of which anxiety is anxious.* (BT, 313-2)

Thus, anxiety discloses, not entities within-the-world, but world as world. Anxiety discloses disclosure itself.

Here the disclosure and the disclosed are existentially selfsame in such a way that in the latter the world has been disclosed as world, and Being-in has been disclosed as a potentiality-for-Being which is individualized, pure, and thrown. (BT, 233)

According to Heidegger, anxiety introduces an existential solipsism by individualizing Dasein. However, he cautiously adds that this is not to be understood as traditional solipsism. On the contrary, instead of "putting an isolated subject-Thing into the innocuous emptiness of a worldless occurring" (BT, 233), it brings Dasein "face to face with its world as world, and thus ... with itself as Being-in-the-world" (BT, 233). Being individualized is not a matter of being isolated.

[A]nxiety brings [Dasein] back from its absorption in the 'world.' Every familiarity collapses. Dasein has been individualized, but individualized *as* Being-in-the-world. Being-in enters into the existential 'mode' of the "not-at-home" [*Un-zuhause*]. (BT, 233)

Anxiety individualizes Dasein in the sense that it sees itself as Being-in-the-world, but by so doing Dasein is no longer absorbed or "at home" in the world. The "at-home-ness" or familiarity that characterizes everydayness, that is, the sight of everydayness, has itself become the "object" seen. It follows that this new sight is not itself characterized by "at-home-ness" or familiarity and, Heidegger adds, "nothing else is meant by our talk about 'uncanniness' [*"Unheimlichkeit"*]" (BT, 233).

According to Heidegger, "*from an existential-ontological point of view, the 'not-at-home' must be conceived as the more primordial phenomenon*" (BT, 234). The "not-at-home" and uncanniness represent the appearance of the basic state of Dasein, of the Being-in-the-world. In this sense it is necessarily the more primordial phenomenon. But it is not primordial in the sense that this is something we experience prior to our everyday engagement with the world, or have to experience in order to be able to put things to use. On the contrary, "uncanniness remains, factically, something for which we mostly have no existentiell understanding" (BT, 234). We are not given to ourselves in our ownmost being prior to our involvement with entities within-the-world. Remember that Heidegger specifically says that authenticity is a modification of inauthenticity. For the most part the primordial phenomenon "appears" in everydayness as something hidden.

The importance of the phenomenon of anxiety for Heidegger's existential analytic is its capacity to provide a phenomenal basis for inquiring into the being of Dasein. Anxiety is a specific kind of Being-in-the-world in which Being-in-the-world as such is disclosed.

[T]hat in the face of which we have anxiety is thrown Being-in-the-world; that which we have anxiety about is our potentiality-for-Being-in-the-world. Thus the entire phenomenon of anxiety shows Dasein as factically existing Being-in-the-world. The fundamental ontological characteristics of this entity are existentiality, facticity, and Being-fallen. (BT, 235)

Concerning these ontological characteristics, Heidegger specifically states that they must be conceived as a unity. Let us quote a passage already cited above in our treatment of the importance of the theory of wholes and parts for Heidegger's analytic.

These existential characteristics are not pieces [*Stücke*] belonging to something composite, one of which might sometimes be missing; but there is woven together in them a primordial context which makes up that totality of the structural whole we are seeking. (BT, 235-6)

This unity can be characterized as follows: ontologically speaking, being towards one's ownmost potentiality-for-Being — existentiality — implies that Dasein is a matter of Being-ahead-of oneself. "This structure of Being," Heidegger claims, "we shall denote as Dasein's '*Being-ahead-of-itself*'" (BT, 236). But, he continues, this "does not signify anything like an isolated tendency in a worldless 'subject,' but characterizes Being-in-the-world" (BT, 236).

To Being-in-the-world ... belongs the fact that it has been delivered over to itself - that it in each case already been thrown *into a world*. "Being-ahead-of-itself" means, if we grasp it more fully, "ahead-of-itself-in-already-being-in-a-world." (BT, 236)

Thus, existentiality structurally implies and is essentially determined by facticity. "Existing," Heidegger claims, "is always factical" (BT, 236), but he adds that "Dasein's factical existing is not only generally and without further differentiation a thrown potentiality-for-Being-in-the-world" (BT, 236).

[I]t is always also absorbed in the world of concern. Ahead-of-itself-Being-already-in-a-world essentially includes one's falling and one's *Being alongside* [*Sein beim*] those things ready-to-hand within-the-world with which one concerns oneself. (BT, 236-7)

At this point, Heidegger introduces the formal definition of Dasein's being as care.

The formally existential totality of Dasein's ontological structural whole must therefore be grasped in the following structure: the Being of Dasein means ahead-of-itself-Being-already-in-(the-world) as Being-alongside (entities encountered within-the-world). This Being fills in the signification of the term '*care*' [*Sorge*]. (BT, 237)

Thus, the unity is based on the fact that the fundamental ontological characteristics of Dasein — existentiality, facticity, and Being-fallen — are non-independent parts, that is, moments.

3. BEING-A-WHOLE

Having justified his arrival at the concept of care through an investigation of the concept of anxiety, Heidegger must now move on to the second step of his pre-ontological confirmation of the notion of Dasein's being as care. This introduces Division Two of BT whose objective is to show how this phenomenon can be seen as a whole, given this ontological structure of Dasein. This twofold pre-ontological confirmation is an attempt to account for the possibility of understanding understanding without resorting to construction. However, Heidegger focuses not only on an inquiry into the being of Dasein, but also at the same time on a justification of his method. This double endeavor is a responsibility Heidegger necessarily has to assume, like any philosopher attempting an inquiry into conditions of possibility. Since, as Heidegger puts it, "even the phenomenological 'intuition of essences' ['*Wesensschau*'] is grounded in existential understanding" (BT, 187), it follows that the latter must be possible if the intuition of essences — which is what Heidegger carries out when he inquires into the essential structures of Dasein[1] — is to be possible. Kant makes the same claim in his Transcendental Deduction.

> The synthetic unity of apperception is therefore that highest point, to which we must ascribe all employment of the understanding, even the whole of logic, and conformably therewith, transcendental philosophy. Indeed this faculty of apperception is the understanding itself. (B134)

The synthetic unity of apperception which Kant refers to as understanding plays the same role as that single primordially unitary phenomenon whose being is care and which serves for Heidegger as a justification of understanding as a whole.

Heidegger concludes his preparatory analysis of Dasein by claiming that in "Being-in-the-world, whose essential structures center in disclosedness, we have *found* the basic state of the entity we have taken as our theme. The totality of Being-in-the-world as a structural whole has revealed itself as care" (BT, 274). However, a question remains as to how we can "progress from the result we have obtained — that the Being of Dasein is care — to the question of the primordial unity of this structural whole?" (BT, 275). The concept of care defines the being of that being whose essence is its existence. Existence, in turn, means a continuous relating to its own being that can only be accounted for by existence itself. Dasein is not, like some

---

[1] Heidegger makes this point transparently clear in the following passage: "[T]here are certain structures which we shall exhibit — not just accidental structures, but essential ones which, in every kind of Being that factical Dasein may possess, persist as determinative for the character of its Being" (BT, 38).

manufactured tool, fixed in its being once and for all. On the contrary, Dasein is constantly "fixing" its being. Thus, Dasein is never given as a whole in the way a thing is given. As essentially an ability-to-be Dasein is characterized by a certain "lack of totality." According to Heidegger "as long as Dasein exists, it must in each case...not yet be something" (BT, 276). "[I]n Dasein there is always something still outstanding, which, as an ability-to-be for Dasein itself, has not yet become 'actual'" (BT, 279). Hence, it seems as if Dasein lacks a wholeness and thus a unity by its very essence. How can we, Heidegger asks, "progress from the result we have obtained in Division One — that the Being of Dasein is care — to the question of the primordial unity of this structural whole?" (BT, 275).

[H]ave we not at the very outset ... renounced the possibility of bringing Dasein into view as a whole? ... [I]f existence is definitive for Dasein's being and if its essence is constituted in part by potentiality-for-Being [*Seinkönnen*], then, as long as Dasein exists, it much in each case, as such a potentiality, *not yet be* something. (BT, 276)

Thus far, the analysis has not reached the level of primordiality. It has not yet grasped Dasein as a whole, not yet become fully concrete. Indeed, it seems to have precluded the entire possibility of bringing Dasein into view as a whole. Heidegger says, "[t]he possibility of this entity's Being-a-whole is manifestly inconsistent with the ontological meaning of care, and care is that which forms the totality of Dasein's structural whole" (BT, 279). This apparent inadequacy must be surmounted, if Heidegger's existential analytic is to avoid falling prey to a self-referential inconsistency. A fundamental tenet in Heidegger's phenomenology is that every step in the development of his fundamental ontology must receive a pre-ontological confirmation. The existential characteristics of Dasein are defined as structural moments, as non-independent parts. Hence, if these moments cannot be linked to the appearance of a *concretum*, an absolute *concretum*, or if they even preclude the appearance of such an entity, it follows that these characteristics have no ontological status. However, as should be evident from the above quotes, this is a problem — indeed a fundamental tension in all transcendental philosophy — of which Heidegger is fully aware. How can we ever grasp the condition of possibility of grasping, or understand the condition of possibility of understanding? One way to solve this problem is to attempt to carry out a purely conceptual or logical analysis, thus not committing oneself to the responsibility of providing a phenomenal basis for one's analysis. Another is to replace this inferential approach with an evidential approach. The latter method is what characterizes the approach of transcendental phenomenology.

In order to ensure the possibility of bringing the wholeness of Dasein into view, Heidegger investigates themes such as anxiety and death. These are essentially interrelated in the sense that they represent different steps towards the wholeness of Dasein. In Division One, he maintains that "the abandonment of Dasein to itself is shown with primordial concreteness in anxiety" (BT, 236). This claim is succeeded by the statement that "the constitution of Dasein, whose totality is now brought out explicitly as ahead-of-itself-in-Being-already-in ..., is primordially a whole" (BT, 236). Thus, the primordial concreteness displayed in anxiety seems to be related to the primordial wholeness of Dasein. At least, anxiety is the pre-ontological source, the mode of Being, that phenomenologically justifies the introduction of Heidegger's notion of Dasein as thrown understanding, i.e., as care.

In Division Two, this issue is more fully worked out in relation to death. The topic is no longer the mere potentiality-for-Being (*Seinkönnen*) but potentiality-for-Being-a-whole (*Ganzseinkönnen*). In order to ensure the wholeness of Dasein, Heidegger takes his point of departure in the structural moment of Dasein's being which seems to obstruct Dasein's Being-a-whole: the "ahead-of-itself." This structural moment suggests that, as long as Dasein is alive, there is necessarily something outstanding in its potentiality-for-Being and, by the same token, that if Dasein reaches wholeness that should imply that its being has been annihilated. It might seem that this structural moment suggests that Dasein's Being-a-whole can only be fulfilled by death and hence there is no such thing as Being-a-whole. Heidegger challenges this conclusion by emphasizing the nature of a moment. This leads to a phenomenological analysis of death whose objective is to account for the possibility of bringing the phenomenon of care into view as a whole and thus provide his existential analytic with a phenomenal basis. This, in turn, allows Heidegger to conclude his analytic by investigating the full meaning of Dasein's being. The first step of this process is to show that the phenomenon of death by no means precludes this possibility. The second step consists in what Heidegger refers to as an existentiell attestation of an authentic Being-towards-death through which Dasein is brought into view as a whole. The third step consists in investigating the full meaning of care. The first two steps will be treated in the remainder of this chapter. The third step will be the topic of our last chapter, Temporality.

At first sight, death seems to be beyond the reach of phenomenology. It seems to be something that, once it appears, represents the ultimate non-appearance of an inquirer. Moreover, it seems to be a phenomenon that precludes the possibility of Being-a-whole.

As long as Dasein is, there is in every case something still outstanding, which Dasein can and will be. But to that which is thus outstanding, the 'end' itself belongs. The 'end' of Being-in-the-world is death. (BT, 276–7)

However, this notion of death as an end of Being-in-the-world is not merely to be understood as the termination of life. According to Heidegger, death is not something that appears only when Dasein is dead. If that were the case, death would be out of reach of any kind of inquiry apart from one carried out by a psychic or a clairvoyant. Even if such an endeavor was possible the psychic would not really experience death; he would rather be communicating with the dead. This is not the point of a phenomenological inquiry into death. Nor is it an investigation of some kind of after-death experience.

Heidegger's phenomenological inquiry into the phenomenon of death suggests something far more radical which nevertheless has a phenomenal basis. It suggests that death is present while the agent is alive, that death is a way of being. According to Heidegger, death is something that has a certain presence throughout a human life, not in the sense that we experience the death of other people — because we do not actually experience their death — but in the sense that we stand always before our own death. This is a theme already emphasized in PIA. "Death is something that is imminent for factical life; it is something before which factical life stands as before something inevitable. Life is in such a way its death is always somehow there for it" (PIA, 365). In BT, this view is presented as follows: "Death is a way to be, which Dasein takes over as soon as it is" (BT, 289); "Death is a possibility-of-Being" (BT, 294). At first sight one might be tempted to reject this as simply an outrageous contradiction. Death is not a way of being; death is the ultimate non-being. Heidegger would not disagree with the obvious fact that when one is dead, one is not also at the same time alive. He does not claim that being dead is a way of being. Nor does he make suggestions concerning the possibility of life after death. His point is that death can be subjected to a phenomenological inquiry, because in one sense death is experienced while we are alive. Death is, he says, "*something that stands before us — something impending*" (BT, 294). Death is something to we are destined to relate, and hence it can be regarded the correlate of an act. This act is Being-towards-death.

4. DEATH

The objective of Heidegger's analysis of Being-towards-death is to provide a phenomenal basis for the possibility of bringing Dasein into view as a whole. As we have pointed out, Dasein's Being-a-whole is something that seems to be precluded by the very definition of Dasein's being as care. Due to the structural moment "ahead-of-itself," it follows that in Dasein there is always something still outstanding. When Dasein is in a way "that absolutely nothing more is still outstanding, then it has already for this reason become "no-longer-Being-there" [*Nicht-mehr-da-sein*]" (BT, 280).

Its Being is annihilated when what is still outstanding in its Being has been liquidated. As long as Dasein *is* an entity, it has never reached its 'wholeness.' But if it gains such 'wholeness,' this gain becomes the utter loss of Being-in-the-world. In such a case, it can never again be experienced *as an entity*. (BT, 280)

Heidegger maintains that we cannot "cross out the 'ahead-of-itself' as an essential moment in the structure of care" (BT, 280; translation altered). Instead, we must investigate what follows from this.

Has not the impossibility of getting the whole of Dasein into our grasp been inferred by an argument which is merely formal? Or have we not at bottom inadvertently posited that Dasein is something present-at-hand, ahead of which something that is not yet present-at-hand is constantly shoving itself? (BT, 280)

What Heidegger is calling attention to here is the question of whether Dasein's Being-a-whole is actually precluded by the structural moment "ahead-of-itself" or whether this is merely a result of a distorted interpretation of this phenomenon. "Have we, in our argument, taken 'Being-not-yet' an' the 'ahead' in a sense that is genuinely *existential*? Has our talk of the 'end' and 'totality' been phenomenally appropriate to Dasein?" (BT, 280). Do these phenomena really preclude the wholeness of Dasein, or do they just do so because they are understood in a way that is not "phenomenally appropriate to Dasein?". Obviously, what Heidegger is about to argue is that there is no opposition between the definition of Dasein's being as care and the possibility of bringing this being into the view as a whole. The key to this lies in a proper phenomenological investigation of death.

This question — both the existentiell question of whether a potentiality-for-Being-a-whole is possible, and the existential question of the state-of-Being of 'end' and 'totality' — is one in which there lurks the task of giving a positive analysis for some phenomena of existence which up till now have been left aside. In the center of these considerations we have the task of characterizing ontologically Dasein's Being-at-an-end and of achieving an existential conception of death. (BT, 280-1)

In what follows, we investigate Heidegger's analysis of that which is still outstanding, that is, his discussion of end and totality. This will enable us to reach an understanding of death, not as merely the finishing line of life, but as a Being-towards-death. Let us take our point of departure in the following passage: "In Dasein there is undeniably a constant 'lack of totality' which finds an end with death. This 'not-yet' 'belongs' to Dasein as long as it is; this is how things stand phenomenally" (BT, 286). Now, Heidegger continues, "is this to be Interpreted as *still outstanding*? With relation to what entities do we talk about that which is still outstanding?" (BT, 286). According to Heidegger, there are two ways of interpreting the "not-yet" — one in relation to entities that do not have the being of Dasein and one in relation to those beings that are Dasein. The former is inappropriate for entities having Dasein's character. In other words, the "not-yet" can be understood as still outstanding in the way a piece is missing from a jig-saw puzzle, or it can be understood as a moment of a whole whose character is that of "not-yet." In the former situation the being outstanding is understood as being missing, i.e., as "that which indeed 'belongs' to an entity, but is still missing" (BT, 286). Heidegger uses the example of a debt that has yet to be paid.

That which is still outstanding is not yet at one's disposal. When the 'debt' gets paid off, that which is still outstanding gets liquidated; this signifies that ... remainder comes successively along. By this procedure the "not-yet" gets filled up, as it were, until the sum that is owed is "all together." (BT, 286)

What characterizes this process is that "the 'lack-of-togetherness' gets 'paid off' by a cumulative piecing-together" (BT, 286). Thus, one way to interpret the still outstanding of the "not-yet" is as a "lack-of-togetherness" that can become the appropriate sum through a process of piecing-together. This notion of the "not-yet" belongs to entities other than Dasein.

Entities for which anything is still outstanding have the kind of Being of something ready-to-hand. The togetherness [*Das Zusammen*] is characterized as a "sum," and so is that lack-of-togetherness which is founded upon it. (BT, 286-7)

Remember Heidegger's distinction between wholes and parts in the lecture *Grundfrage der antiken Philosophie*.

The parts of a whole have a quite different way of being connected than do the parts of a sum. To differentiate: A sum and a whole both have the formal character of "togetherness." A "togetherness" consists of or covers parts. Kinds of "togetherness:" a) Sum, composite. Parts: Pieces; the adding together of pieces = sum. b) Whole, totum. The part-character corresponding to the whole is to be grasped as moment. (GA 22, 280; our translation)

Hence, we see that Heidegger distinguishes between the togetherness of sums and wholes. The former is the kind of togetherness where the totality, i.e., the sum, is reached through an adding together of pieces originally "not-yet" there. This kind of togetherness is a constructed togetherness and, according to Heidegger, one that does not pertain to the being of Dasein.

[T]his lack-of-togetherness which belongs to such a mode of togetherness — this being-missing as still-outstanding — cannot by any means define ontologically that "not-yet" which belongs to Dasein as its possible death. (BT, 287)

Dasein is a different kind of togetherness in that the "not-yet" does not refer to a missing piece but to a structural moment. Whereas entities within-the-world can jointly create a togetherness, a sum, by being pieced together, Dasein is a whole and as such is primordial with regard to its structural moments.

> The togetherness of an entity of the kind which Dasein is 'in running its course' until that 'course' has been completed, is not constituted by a 'continuing' piecing-on of entities which, somehow and somewhere, are ready-to-hand already in their own right. (BT, 287)

In the case of Dasein, its parts are non-independent parts, or moments. It follows that the "not-yet" does not refer to something missing, but is included in the being of Dasein. Any Dasein, Heidegger claims, "always exists in just such a manner that its 'not-yet' *belongs* to it" (BT, 287).

As an example of the possibility of having this relation to a "not-yet," Heidegger refers to the process of ripening of a fruit.

> When ... a fruit is unripe, it "goes towards" its ripeness. In this process of ripening, that which the fruit is not yet, is by no means pieced on as something not yet present-at-hand ... When we speak of the "not-yet" of the unripeness, we do not have in view something else which stands outside and which ... might be present-at-hand in it and with it ... The "not-yet" has already been included in the very Being of the fruit, not as something random characteristic, but as something constitutive. (BT, 288)

Thus, it makes sense, Heidegger argues, to claim that the phenomenon of "not-yet" can be included in a being rather than be construed as something missing. The "not-yet" does not necessarily have to be interpreted as a piece, it can also be interpreted as something constitutive for a being, as a structural moment. Just as the "not-yet" has already been included in the very being of the fruit, so is Dasein, as long as it is, "already its '"not-yet'" (BT, 288). Thus, Heidegger claims,

> [t]hat which makes up the 'lack of totality' in Dasein, the constant "ahead-of-itself," is neither something still outstanding in a summative togetherness, nor something which has not yet become accessible. It is a "not-yet which any Dasein, as the entity which it is, has to be (BT, 288).

This notion of the "not-yet" as something Dasein already is invites an interpretation of the ultimate "not-yet" — death — as something Dasein also already is. As Heidegger puts it: "just as Dasein *is* already its 'not-yet,' and is its 'not-yet' constantly as long as it is, it *is* already its end too" (BT, 289).

The "ending" which we have in view when we speak of death, does not signify

Dasein's Being-at-an-end [*Zu-Ende-Sein*], but a *Being-towards-the-end* [*Sein zum Ende*]. Death is a way to be, which Dasein takes over as soon as it is. (BT, 289)

At this point, Heidegger has shown how the "not-yet" of Dasein is not to be interpreted. But he has yet to provide a positive interpretation of the phenomenon of death. Heidegger is fully aware of this and maintains that in order to do so we must "take as our clue the basic state of Dasein at which we have already arrived - the phenomenon of care" (BT, 290).

An ontological interpretation of death is not directed towards a biological-ontical exploration of this phenomenon. While the latter approach is interested in the phenomenon and causes of death, understood as demise, Heidegger emphasizes that an ontological interpretation of death is concerned with how we are towards our death. Thus, he decides to reserve the term 'dying' "for that *way of Being* in which Dasein *is towards* its death" (BT, 291) and to use the term 'demise' for the biological notion of death. According to Heidegger, an existential interpretation of death takes precedence over a biological exploration of demise in the sense that the former is directed towards that pre-reflective understanding of death presupposed by our ontical approach to this phenomenon. This is, of course, not to say that an ontological interpretation is a more accurate ontical investigation of death, and thus can arrive at more proper results than medical and biological investigation of "demising." Heidegger is not about to replace the medical and biological sciences with an ontological investigation. On the contrary, he is trying to keep them separate and thus preclude the possibility of both ontical and ontological imperialism, so to speak. For the same reason Heidegger claims that an existential interpretation of death is the foundation for any ontical investigation of this phenomenon whether that be biographical, historiological, ethnological, psychological, or theological. But he is not thereby saying that an ontological interpretation of death can provide a more accurate psychological or historiological understanding of this phenomenon. What he is saying is that an ontological interpretation of death can provide a more accurate ontological interpretation of this phenomena, and that this pertains to the pre-reflective understanding of death presupposed by any ontical exploration of this phenomenon.

Heidegger begins his ontological investigation of death by noting that from his considerations of end and totality "there has emerged the necessity of Interpreting the phenomenon of death as Being-towards-the-end, and of doing so in terms of Dasein's basic state" (BT, 293). "Only so can it be made plain to what extent Being-a-whole, as constituted by Being-towards-the-end, is possible in Dasein itself in conformity with the structure of its Being" (BT, 293). Keeping in mind the definition of care as existence (ahead-of-itself), facticity (being-already-in), and falling (being-alongside), Heidegger must make plain how these structural moments reveal themselves in the phenomenon of death. This endeavor is in keeping with the general structure of his approach. First, he provides a preliminary sketch in which he makes plain how this takes place. Then he goes on to show how this is exhibitable in everydayness, although in an inauthentic manner. Finally, he proceeds to provide a full existential conception of death.

In the first stage of this process, Heidegger takes his point of departure in the above interpretation of the "not-yet" which concluded that this structural moment is not to be interpreted as something still outstanding. The "not-yet" must be understood as something which Dasein in every case is. Thus, existence reveals itself in the phenomenon of death in the sense that "it is a possibility-of-Being which Dasein itself has to take over in every case" (BT, 294).

With death, Dasein stands before itself in its ownmost potentiality-for-Being. This is a possibility in which the issue is nothing less than Dasein's Being-in-the-world. Its death is the possibility of no-longer being-able-to-be-there. (BT, 294)

Thus, with death, "Dasein has been *fully* assigned to its ownmost potentiality-for-Being" (BT, 294). In other words, Dasein faces its potentiality-for-Being in the uttermost way. Death, Heidegger claims, is non-relational, when Dasein "stands before itself in this way, all its relations to other Dasein has been undone" (BT, 294).

Death is the possibility for the absolute impossibility of Dasein. Thus death reveals itself as that possibility which is one's own ownmost, which is non-relational, and which is not to be outstripped [*unüberholbare*]. (BT, 294)

The existential possibility of death reveals that Dasein is disclosed to itself as "ahead-of-itself" and "this moment in the structure of care," Heidegger claims, "has its most primordial concretion in Being-towards-death" (BT, 294).

However, this ownmost possibility is something in which Dasein always-already finds itself. Not only does existence find its concretion in death, death is also given with the structural moment of facticity or thrownness. According to Heidegger, "if Dasein exists, it has already been *thrown* into this possibility" (BT, 295). Thus, since Dasein has been thrown into, or handed over to its death, it follows that death belongs to Being-in-the-world.

Thrownness into death reveals itself to Dasein in a more primordial and impressive manner in that situatedness we have called "anxiety." Anxiety in the face of death is anxiety 'in the face of' that potentiality-for-Being which is one's ownmost, non-relational, and not to be outstripped. (BT, 295)

Since the structural moments existence and facticity both find their primordial concretion in Being-towards-death, it seems reasonable to assume an equivalent relation between death and the third structural moment, "being-alongside." This moment finds its concretion in the everyday relation to death in which "Dasein covers up its ownmost Being-towards-death, fleeing *in the face* of it. In everydayness the structural moment "being-alongside" finds its concretion in falling which is a fleeing in the face of death. "In this falling Being-alongside, fleeing from uncanniness announces itself" (BT, 295–6).

On the basis of this analysis, Heidegger concludes that the structural moments of care reveal themselves in death.

Existence, facticity, and falling characterize Being-towards-the-end, and are therefore constitutive for the existential conception of death. *As regards its ontological possibility, dying is grounded in care.* (BT, 296)

However, this connection between the phenomenon of death and care is still nothing but a mere conceptual analysis. If it is the case that Being-towards-death belongs to the being of Dasein, "then it must also be exhibitable in everydayness, even if proximally in a way which is inauthentic" (BT, 296).

[I]f Being-towards-the-end should afford the existential possibility of an existentiell Being-a-whole for Dasein, then this would give phenomenal confirmation for the thesis that "care" is the ontological term for the totality of Dasein's structural whole. (BT, 296)

Having thus indicated the compatibility of the phenomenon of care and Being-a-whole in Being-towards-death, Heidegger must now provide a phenomenal basis for this possibility. Although he takes his point of departure in everydayness, which proximally and for the most part is fallen — thus covering up its ownmost Being-towards-death and thus not Being-a-whole — he will eventually call attention to an existentiell possibility of Being-a-whole. Again he will point to a marginal experience in which Being-towards-death is not covered up.

Since everydayness is under the spell of the One, Heidegger sets out to investigate how Being-towards-death is disclosed in the realm of publicness. According to this understanding, he claims, death is understood as something which arrives from somewhere at a certain point in one's life. It is "levelled off to an occurrence which reaches Dasein, to be sure, but belongs to nobody in particular" (BT, 297).

Death gets passed off as always something 'actual;' its character as a possibility gets concealed, and so are the two moments that belong to it — the fact that it is non-relational and that it is not to be outstripped. (BT, 297; translation altered)

But, Heidegger argues, even if the subject of everydayness "aggravates the *temptation* to cover up from oneself one's ownmost Being-towards-death" (BT, 297) in that "the One provides [*besorgt*] a *constant tranquillization about death*" (BT, 298), and even if "the One concerns itself with transforming this anxiety [in the face of death] into fear in the face of an oncoming event ... that *alienates* Dasein from its ownmost non-relational potentiality-for-Being" (BT, 298) this ownmost potentiality-for-Being is still an issue. Temptation, tranquillization, and alienation are characteristics of the everyday mode of Being-towards-death. Hence, Heidegger concludes, "in thus falling and fleeing *in the face of* death, Dasein's everydayness attests that the very One itself already has the definite character of Being-towards-death" (BT, 298-9). Put in a less dramatic fashion, even if Dasein in everydayness does not focus upon itself as a whole, as an end, this very activity discretely suggests that it is non-positionally aware of itself as a whole. Now the question remains as to how this claim can be provided with a full phenomenal foundation, so that Being-towards-death might appear in a non-covered up fashion. This would provide the ultimate pre-ontological confirmation of the interpretation of Dasein's being as care and allow the philosopher to go on to investigate the full meaning of this concept.

Before he begins an investigation of the possibility for an authentic understanding of Being-towards-death, Heidegger outlines the full existential conception of death. In everydayness, Heidegger maintains, "one *knows* about the certainty of death, and yet 'is' not authentically certain about one's own" (BT, 302).

The falling everydayness of Dasein is acquainted with death's certainty, and yet evades *Being*-certain. But in light of what it evades, this very evasion attests phenomenally that death must be conceived as one's ownmost possibility, non-relational, not to be outstripped, and — above all — *certain*. (BT, 302)

According to Heidegger, although everydayness is acquainted with the certainty of death "the One covers up what is peculiar in death's certainty — *that it is possible at any moment*" (BT, 302).

Along with the certainty of death goes the *indefiniteness* of its "when." Everyday Being-towards-death evades this indefiniteness by conferring definiteness upon it. (BT, 302)

According to the understanding of everydayness, death is something that will come along at a certain point but never immediately. But to the extent that the indefiniteness of death is covered up, so is the certainty. On the basis of this presentation and by means of a further elaboration of the everyday and inauthentic understanding of death, Heidegger develops a full existential conception of death.

The full existential-ontological conception of death may now be defined as follows: *death, as the end of Dasein, is Dasein's ownmost possibility — non-relational, certain and as such indefinite, not to be outstripped. Death is*, as *Dasein's* end, in the Being of this entity *towards* its end. (BT, 303)

Heidegger's lengthy interpretation of the phenomenon of death plays an important role in the argument of BT. In Division One, Heidegger presents a definition of Dasein's being without providing it with the necessary phenomenal basis. Admittedly, he justifies his introduction of the concept of care by introducing the phenomenon of anxiety, but he does not show how this phenomenon can be given as a whole, given this ontological structure of Dasein. The latter task is imperative for Heidegger's endeavor, since the ontological structures defining the being that are peculiar to the being we ourselves are, are introduced as moments. Without a whole, an absolute *concretum*, these structural moments do not have an ontological status. However, Heidegger cannot merely construct a whole. If moments appear it follows that that of which they are moments must also appear. Thus, Heidegger must account for the possibility of Dasein's Being-a-whole by providing a phenomenal basis for this claim. At this point, Heidegger has completed all but the final step of this attempt. He has justified his arrival at the phenomenon of care by providing a phenomenal basis through the discussion of anxiety; he has shown that there is no incompatibility between the concept of care and an understanding of this phenomenon as a whole; and he has pointed to the discrete presence of Being-a-whole in the everyday covering up of one's ownmost Being-towards-death. What remains is to provide a phenomenal basis for an authentic Being-towards-death.

5. DEATH AND POSSIBILITY

As a first step in providing a phenomenal justification for Dasein's understanding its ownmost possibility authentically, Heidegger inquires into whether "Dasein itself gives us any instructions for carrying it out" (BT, 304). On the basis of the existential conception of death, it has been established what "an authentic Being-towards-the-end should be able to comport itself towards" (BT, 304). It has also been established "how it is possible for an authentic Being-towards-death *not* to be" (BT, 304). These instructions must lead us to the authentic Being-towards-death.

Obviously, since an authentic Being-towards-death is what is going to justify our understanding of Dasein's being as a whole — a being that appears as disclosedness — it follows that this Being-towards-death cannot be a radically different way of Being-in-the-world. Authentic Being-towards-death is not a different kind of practical circumspection but rather a mode of being in which the full meaning of the latter is lit up. Being-towards-death is a being towards a possibility but it differs from a circumspective being towards a possibility in that its goal is not actualization. In everyday dealings with entities within-the-world, possibilities are constantly encountered — and constantly annihilated by being actualized. It is precisely the process of actualization that triggers the covering up of our ownmost Being-towards-death and thus the understanding of our ownmost being. Everyday dealing with the world can be characterized as an ongoing actualization of possibilities, a looking "*away* from the possible and [a] looking at that for which it is possible" (BT, 305). Circumspection is what guides this looking away towards the actualization of a possibility which withdraws in this process. Circumspection (*Umsicht/phronesis*) is the very annihilation of possibility which remains hidden in everyday activity.

Being-towards-death is a being towards a possibility whose goal is not to be actualized.

[D]eath as possible is not something possible which is ready-to-hand or present-at-hand, but a possibility of *Dasein's* Being. So to concern oneself with actualizing what is thus possible would have to signify "bringing about one's demise." But if this were done, Dasein would deprive itself of the very ground for an existing Being-towards-death. (BT, 305)

This is, however, not a matter of thinking about death and "pondering over when and how this possibility may perhaps be actualized" (BT, 305). We weaken the peculiar character of the possibility of death — the indefiniteness of its when — by thinking of it as something that is going to come along.

[I]f Being-towards-death has to disclose understandingly the possibility which we have characterized, and if it is to disclose it *as a possibility*, then in such Being-towards-death this possibility must not be weakened: it must be understood *as a possibility*. (BT, 306)

Being towards a possibility is usually referred to as expectancy, as awaitening, but this is still a waiting for an actualization and thus it draws the possible into the realm of the actual. Being-towards-death is a being towards a possibility in which death reveals itself as something possible and not as something that is to be actualized. Heidegger's technical term for this kind of being towards is 'anticipation' (*Vorlaufen*). Anticipation is a coming close to a possibility that does not tend towards actualization but rather to a coming closer as a possibility — and thus away from it as something actual. According to Heidegger, the *"closest closeness which one may have in Being towards death as a possibility, is as far as possible from anything actual"* (BT, 306-7). Anticipation designates this kind of being towards. It leaves the possible as possible. The more thoroughly it is grasped as a possibility "the more purely does the understanding penetrate into it *as the possibility of the impossibility of any existence at all"* (BT, 307).

Death, as possibility, gives Dasein nothing to be 'actualized,' nothing which Dasein, as actual, could itself *be*. It is the possibility of the impossibility of every way of comporting oneself towards anything, of every way of existing. (BT, 307)

Thus, Heidegger maintains, "Being-towards-death is the anticipation of a potentiality-for-Being of that entity whose kind of Being is anticipation itself" (BT, 307). Anticipation is the understanding of understanding itself, the disclosure of non-positional awareness, the disclosure of disclosure: "Anticipation turns out to be the possibility of understanding one's *ownmost* and uttermost potentiality-for-Being — that is to say, the possibility of *authentic existence*" (BT, 307). However, if it is the case that in anticipation Dasein discloses itself to itself in its ownmost being, it follows that anticipation must comply with certain standards which are set by the description of what an authentic Being-towards-death should be able to comport itself towards. Firstly, this means that "in anticipation any Dasein can have wrenched away from the One already" (BT, 307). Being towards one's ownmost potentiality-for-Being implies that Dasein is freed from the temptation, tranquillization, and alienation which characterizes our everyday dealings with the world. Thus, anticipation is not under the spell of the One. Secondly, it follows that anticipation establishes the non-relational character distinctive to the existential-ontological conception of death. "Anticipation allows Dasein to understand that potentiality-for-Being in which its ownmost Being is an issue, must be taken over by Dasein alone" (BT, 308). Thirdly, as opposed to inauthentic Being-towards-death, anticipation does not evade the fact that death is not to be outstripped, "instead, anticipation frees itself *for* accepting this" (BT, 308). Anticipation thus "discloses also all the possibilities which lie ahead of that possibility" (BT, 309). Hence, anticipation is an existentiell Being-a-whole for Dasein.

[A]nticipation includes the possibility of taking the whole of Dasein in advance [*Vorwegnehmens*] in an existentiell manner; that is to say, it includes the possibility of existing as a whole potentiality-for-Being. (BT, 309)

The existential conception of death also establishes the peculiar certainty of this ownmost, non-relational possibility, which is not to be outstripped. Hence, anticipation holds death for certain in a way that differs from holding something present-at-hand for certain. The latter presupposes that Dasein is already engaged in dealing with entities within-the-world and hence that Dasein is under the spell of the One and thus fallen.

Dasein must first have lost itself in the factual circumstances [*Sachverhalte*] ... if it is to obtain the pure objectivity — that is to say, the indifference — of apodictic evidence. (BT, 309)

The certainty of anticipation is primordial to the kind of certainty that pertains to real and ideal objects. Anticipation is not a certainty relating to objects, but a certainty relating to that to which objects appear. Anticipation is a way of certainty of Being-in-the-world. If we try to construe this kind of certainty along the lines of the certainty which relates to objects, we will fall prey to the mistake of treating that which constitutes as something constituted. This, in turn, nourishes the notion of the self or the "I" as a thing-like entity. Therefore, Heidegger claims, "the evidential character which belongs to the immediate givenness of ... the 'I,' must necessarily lag behind the certainty which anticipation includes" (BT, 310). While the former relates to the "I" as something given, i.e., as an object, the latter relates to the "I" as a subject and thus affords the philosopher a phenomenal basis on which to ground his investigation of the "I" without construing it as an object.

A fourth characterization of the existential conception of death is that its certainty is indefinite. It still remains unanswered how anticipation discloses this characteristic.

How does the anticipatory understanding project itself upon a possibility-for-Being which is certain and which is constantly possible in such a way the "when" in which the utter impossibility of existence becomes possible remains constantly indefinite? (BT, 310)

Recall that all understanding, anticipatory understanding included, is accompanied by situatedness. Anticipatory understanding can disclose the indefinite certainty of death, since it is accompanied by anxiety. Anxiety is *"the situatedness which can hold open the utter and constant threat to itself arising from Dasein's ownmost individualized Being"* (BT, 310).

In this situatedness, Dasein finds itself *face to face* with the "nothing" of the possible impossibility of its existence. Anxiety is anxious *about* the potentiality-for-Being of the entity so destined [des so bestimmten Seienden], and in this way it discloses the uttermost possibility. (BT, 310)

Hence, it is the very phenomenon that discloses the being of Dasein as care which also accounts for the possibility of understanding this being of Dasein as a whole. "Being-towards-death," Heidegger claims, "is essentially anxiety" (BT, 310). This kind of continuity is typical of what Heidegger does in BT. In Division One, he discusses phenomena whose legitimate appearance within a phenomenological endeavor is to be accounted for in Division Two, and in Division Two, we find that what justifies their appearance is what made us see them in the first place.

The phenomenon of anxiety is of pivotal importance for Heidegger's existential analytic. It justifies his description of the being of Dasein as care, it accounts for the possibility of seeing this phenomenon as a whole, and hence it accounts for the possibility of carrying out an existential analytic. However, Heidegger has not yet concluded his final pre-ontological confirmation. The "existentially 'possible' Being-towards-death remains, from the existentiell point of view, a fantastical exaction" (BT, 311).

The fact that an authentic potentiality-for-Being-a-whole is ontologically possible for Dasein, signifies nothing, so long as a corresponding ontical potentiality-for-Being has not been demonstrated in Dasein itself. (BT, 311)

Therefore, Heidegger claims, the "question of Dasein's authentic Being-a-whole and of its existential constitution still hangs in mid-air" (BT, 311). It has still not received the necessary phenomenal basis and it can be provided with such a foundation only if it can be attested in its existentiell possibility. Thus, authenticity must receive a phenomenal confirmation; it must refer to a possible mode of being Dasein, if it is to avoid being merely a construction. In other words, at this point we are at the very foundation of Heidegger's project.

6. AUTHENTICITY

Heidegger's discussion of Dasein's attestation of an authentic potentiality-for-Being is among the most impenetrable and, from a phenomenological point of view, seems to be the most speculative investigation carried out in BT. Nevertheless, Heidegger's existential analytic, and thus the fundamental ontological project as such, rests upon the possibility of having the authentic potentiality-of-Being revealed in its existentiell possibility by Dasein itself. Thus, this investigation is not one which can be bypassed on our way to the investigation of the full meaning of care. The reason for this is, as we have already noted, that the theory of wholes and parts plays such a central role in Heidegger's investigation of Dasein. If Heidegger cannot account for the appearance of the whole to which the existentials belong as moments, and not merely as an ontological possibility but also as an ontical existentiell possibility, his endeavor will be without phenomenal basis. Therefore, one must necessarily take this investigation seriously but also take it for what it is. Although Heidegger introduces terms like 'conscience,' 'call of conscience,' and 'guilt' this is not first and foremost an investigation of themes traditionally associated with psychology or theology. These terms are technical terms, and thus they do not reflect ordinary usage but rather correspond to the basic tenets of Heidegger's own project. Heidegger himself would claim that the difference between his treatment of conscience and that of a psychologist or a theologian is that his treatment is ontological. Thus, it would be different from the treatment carried out from the latter perspectives, but it would still be connected to it in the sense that an ontological investigation aims at working out the foundation of ontical interpretations.

This existential Interpretation is necessarily a far cry away from everyday ontical common sense, though it sets forth the ontological foundations of what the ordinary way of interpreting conscience has always understood within certain limits and has conceptualized as a 'theory' of conscience. (BT, 314)

In what follows, we attempt to pursue Heidegger's investigation of conscience in a systematic manner. Our objective will be to show how Heidegger provides the authentic Being-a-whole with an existentiell justification. We shall not so much discuss Heidegger's somewhat arcane language but instead try to see how his expressions conceptually follow from less arcane expressions concerning the being of Dasein.

One thing must be kept in mind as we set out to investigate Heidegger's notion of authenticity: authenticity is a modification of inauthenticity. Authenticity is not an ideal state of being from which Dasein falls or is driven at a certain point in life. Authenticity has a measure of primacy over inauthenticity in that it reveals the full meaning of the latter, but for this very reason it is not a kind of understanding that appears prior to and independently of our dealings with the world. In one sense we "have" this understanding, but as the condition of possibility of our productive everyday attitude, it remains hidden from the sight of everydayness. The objective of Heidegger is to turn this sight back on itself in order to transform this pre-ontological understanding of being into a full-fledged ontology. However, this must be done in accordance with the basic tenets of phenomenology. In order to avoid a constructive approach, one must provide every step of this process with a phenomenal basis. As we know, this is something of which Heidegger was well aware, indeed he goes to great pains in order to avoid violating this principle. His investigation of conscience is the last step of this process. If he can succeed uncovering the attestation of Being-a-whole phenomenologically, he has justified his approach and thus the discoveries of this approach, and is then free to go on to interpret the full meaning of Dasein's being as care.

In his investigation of conscience, Heidegger proceeds as follows. First he sets out to "trace conscience back to its existential foundations and structures and make it visible *as* a phenomenon of Dasein" (BT, 313). As a phenomenon of Dasein, conscience is not something present-at-hand. It "'*is*' only in Dasein's kind of Being, and it makes itself known as a Fact only with factical existence and in it" (BT, 313). Conscience is something that manifests itself only from time to time; it belongs to Dasein's being. According to Heidegger, "conscience gives us 'something' to understand; it *discloses*" (BT, 314).

If we analyze conscience more penetratingly, it is revealed as a *call* [*Ruf*] ... The call of conscience has the character of an *appeal* to Dasein by calling it to its ownmost potentiality-for-Being-itself; and this is done by way of summoning it to its ownmost Being-guilty. (BT, 314)

To this call, Heidegger maintains, there corresponds a possible hearing which "unveils itself as our *wanting to have a conscience* [*Gewissenhaben-wollen*]" (BT, 314). However, in this phenomenon there lies an existentiell choosing, this is "the choosing to choose a kind of Being-one's-Self which, in accordance with its existential structure, we call '*resoluteness*' [*Entschlossenheit*]" (BT, 314). Resoluteness designates a kind of being in which Being-a-whole is attested ontically. Admittedly, this sounds abstruse but let us nevertheless grant Heidegger the principle of charity and proceed to his actual analysis. It is our contention that the apparent incomprehensibility is more a matter of terminology than of content and that it reflects Heidegger's struggle with and attempt to distance himself from the language of the metaphysical tradition.

The first step of Heidegger's analysis consists in working out the existential ontological foundations of conscience. Conscience, Heidegger claims, is a phenomenon that gives us something to understand and thus "it belongs within the range of those existential phenomena which constitute the Being of *the* 'there' as disclosedness" (BT, 315). However, conscience is not merely one among many ways in which disclosure takes place. While Dasein's disclosedness discloses the world within which things can be apprehended, conscience designates a kind of disclosedness which discloses disclosure itself.

According to Heidegger, the structures of situatedness, understanding, discourse, and falling belong to disclosedness (which is the being of Dasein). Dasein is thrown understanding and what characterizes everyday Dasein is that this thrown understanding is under the spell of the One. Everyday Dasein is directed, not at its ownmost being, but at entities other than itself — that is, at entities within-the-world — and in virtue of that it is absorbed in the world and in the way in which the One has publicly interpreted things. There is nothing ungenuine about this inauthentic being. This is simply a description of Dasein's normal condition. When Dasein is directed at things in the world, it is not at the same time aware of the apriori structure of its ownmost being. The latter is precisely what orients Dasein away from itself towards what is other.

Heidegger makes this point several times throughout BT, but in the discussion of conscience he repeats it in a somewhat arcane fashion. According to Heidegger, the being under the spell of the One "is made possible existentially through the fact that Dasein ... can *listen* to Others" (BT, 315). But while listening to others one does not also listen to this listening, so to speak. When we are under the spell of the One, we do not also grasp the conditions of possibility of this being. Thus, Heidegger claims, by losing itself in the publicness Dasein "*fails to hear* [*überhört*] its own Self in listening to the they-self" (BT, 315). Although his manner of presentation is somewhat unfamiliar, what Heidegger is here emphasizing is that the everyday attitude is not tuned in to the apriori structures of its ownmost being but instead is directed towards what is other. If Dasein is to be brought back to its ownmost being, that is, to an understanding of what goes on when it is absorbed in the world, then it must "first be able to find itself — to find itself as something which has failed to hear itself, and which fails to hear in that it *listens away* to the One" (BT, 315-6). "This listening-away must get broken off; in other words, the possibility of another kind of hearing which will interrupt it, must be given by Dasein itself" (BT, 316). The reason Heidegger uses the term 'listen' is that discourse (*Rede*) is what articulates intelligibility. In presenting "being-in," the formal existential expression for the being of Dasein, Heidegger pointed out that "discourse is existentially equiprimordial with situatedness and understanding" (BT, 203). Discourse designates a third structural moment of Dasein. This moment is the very articulation of intelligibility. "That which can be Articulated in ... discourse, is what we have called 'meaning.' That which gets articulated as such in discursive Articulation, we call the 'totality-of-significations' [*Bedeutungsganze*]" (BT, 204). As we have seen, the "fundamental *existentialia* which constitute the Being of the 'there,' the disclosedness of Being-in-the-world, are situatedness and understanding" (BT, 203). However, discourse is a third phenomenon which plays a part in Dasein's constitutive activity in the sense that it articulates the disclosedness. "When the 'there' has been completely disclosed, its disclosedness is constituted by understanding, situatedness, and falling; and this disclosedness becomes Articulated by discourse" (BT, 400). According to Heidegger, discourse is "the basic signification of *logos*" (BT, 55). *Logos*, in turn, means "to make manifest [and to] let something be seen" (BT, 56). In PIA Heidegger refers to *legein* as that which "gives the being in its own self [and] the way in which *noein* is actualized" (PIA, 379). Thus, *logos* is the articulation of the founding sensuousness. It is an articulation of that which is already disclosed, but this articulation — this discourse — is equiprimordial with the fundamental existentials constituting disclosedness. Although it gets expressed in language, discourse is not reducible to language. "Vocal utterance," Heidegger claims, "is not essential for discourse" (BT, 316), rather discourse is "the existential-ontological foundation of language" (BT, 203). Discourse is already presupposed in any utterance in the sense that it is a giving of something to understand, but, Heidegger notes, "when fully concrete, discoursing (letting something be seen) has the character of speaking — vocal proclamation in words" (BT, 56).

> Factically, however, discourse expresses itself for the most part in language, and speaks proximally in the way of addressing itself to the 'environment' by talking about things concernfully. (BT, 400)

Language is what makes discoveredness possible. It shares a defining feature with Heidegger's notion of constitution — as this is developed in relation to his interpretation of Husserl — and with the notion of *praxis* as the "truthful safe-keeping-of-Being" — as this theme is developed in his interpretation of Aristotle. "Language makes manifest," Heidegger claims, but "it does not produce anything like discoveredness" (HCT, 262).

As we may recall, it is "the One that articulates the referential context of significance" (BT, 222). This is what Dasein "listens to" in its everyday dealings with the world. What characterizes this "listening-away" is precisely that it is not preoccupied with itself but rather with what is other. In other words, listening-away is not concerned with the listening itself but with what it is given to understand.

> Listening to ... is Dasein's existential way of Being-open as Being-with for Others. Indeed, hearing constitutes the primary and authentic way in which Dasein is open for its ownmost potentiality-for-Being. (BT, 206)

If Dasein is to be brought back to its ownmost being, this listening-away must be broken off and replaced with another kind of hearing, and the possibility for this must be provided for by Dasein itself. The listening-away can, Heidegger claims, be broken by a call "if that call ... arouses another kind of hearing which, in relationship to the hearing that is lost, has a character in every way opposite" (BT, 316). He continues, *"that which, by calling in this manner, gives us to understand, is the conscience"* (BT, 316).

Before we examine this claim, let us first have a look at Heidegger's investigation of the character of the call of conscience. What is talked about in the call of conscience is obviously Dasein itself, and its own self is what Dasein is called to in this call. However, what does it mean to say that Dasein calls itself, that Dasein "is *at the same time* the caller and the one to whom the appeal is made?" (BT, 320). Obviously, it is not a call in the sense of a vocal utterance. The voice of conscience is to be conceived as a "giving-to-understand." This "giving-to-understand" is a giving from Dasein to Dasein. It is a marginal experience in which Dasein is brought back from its inauthentic mode of being to face its ownmost being. *"Conscience manifests itself as the call of care*: the caller is Dasein, which, in its thrownness (in its Being-already-in), is anxious about its potentiality-for-Being" (BT, 322). Thus, conscience is a phenomenon of Dasein, it is the manifestation of care in anxiety. In this sense something is given to understand from Dasein to Dasein.

Now, as to what is heard by this appeal Heidegger maintains that *"conscience discourses solely and constantly in the mode of keeping silent"* (BT, 318). Taken strictly, Heidegger claims, nothing is said in this discourse. At first sight, this claim is hardly more comprehensible than the notion of Dasein calling itself. How can nothing be said and still something be given to us to understand? In approaching this apparent self-contradiction, we must remember that the terms 'silent' and 'nothing' are technical terms and thus have a very specific meaning in Heidegger's thinking. Firstly, nothing is said in the call in the sense that when "the call gives us a potentiality-for-Being to understand, it does not gives us one which is ideal and universal" (BT, 326). In this call, Dasein does not appear to itself in the way an object appears to a subject. Secondly, nothing is said in the call in the sense that it is "notness" (*Nichtheit*) that is given us to understand.

According to Heidegger, in the call of conscience Dasein is addressed as being-guilty. Being-guilty, in turn, is ontologically defined as being the basis for a void or a nothingness. He says, "we define the formally existential idea of the 'Guilty!' as 'Being-the-basis for a Being which has been defined by a 'not' - that is to say, as *'Being-the-basis of a nullity'"* (BT, 329). Dasein's being the basis for a nullity is, however, not a lack in the sense that it can be eliminated through improvement. It does not refer to something that is lacking in Dasein, in comparison with an ideal mode of being, nor does it refer to something that in any way is negative. This being-the-basis of a nullity refers to the very being of Dasein; it is a "notness" that belongs to the existential meaning of the structural moments of Dasein.

In relation to Dasein's facticity, there is present a "notness" in the sense that "Dasein is something that has been thrown; it has been brought into its 'there,' but *not* of its own accord" (BT, 329). Dasein has been delivered over to its "that it is and has to be," but not by itself. As existing, Dasein is never prior to its existence, it is always already "projecting itself upon possibilities into which it has been thrown" (BT, 330). This basis for its potentiality-for-Being is something existence itself has not laid the basis for, but rather something from which it projects itself upon possibilities.

> The Self, which as such has to lay the basis for itself, can *never* get that basis into its power; and yet, as existing, it must take over Being-a-basis ... It is never existent *before* its basis, but only *from it* and *as this basis*. Thus "Being-a-basis" means *never* to have power over one's ownmost Being from the ground up This "*not*" belongs to the existential meaning of "thrownness." (BT, 330)

In this sense there is something in the being of Dasein of which Dasein cannot get command. This "notness" is something that belongs to the existential meaning of this structural moment. Nullity is constitutive for Dasein's being as thrownness.

As is the case with thrownness, there is likewise an essential nullity belonging to the existential projection. In projecting itself upon possibilities, the process of actualizing a possibility is by the same token an annihilation of other possibilities qua possibilities. "[I]n having a potentiality-for-Being [Dasein] always stands in one possibility or another: it constantly is *not* other possibilities, and it has waived these in its existentiell projection" (BT, 331). Thus, nullity is constitutive for what Heidegger refers to as existence, understanding, and projection, that is, for Dasein's being-free for its existentiell possibilities. "Freedom ... *is* only in the choice of one possibility — that is, in tolerating one's not having chosen the others and one's not being able to choose them" (BT, 331). An essential nullity is not only present in the structural moments thrownness and projection. The whole to which these existentials belong as moments is also permeated by nullity. As thrown projection, Heidegger claims, "*care itself, in its very essence, is permeated with nullity through and through*" (BT, 331). Care is permeated by nullity in the sense that everyday Dasein is inauthentic. In its actual being, the being whose being is defined as care covers its ownmost being, and it does so necessarily. Hence, care nullifies itself as it unfolds as Being-in-the-world.

Thus, in the call of conscience Dasein is addressed as guilty, which, as we have seen, implies that Dasein is disclosed to itself as thrown projection, that is, as care. In anxiety care reveals itself to itself. "Uncanniness brings this entity face to face with its undisguised nullity, which belongs to the possibility of its ownmost being" (BT, 333). We have discussed the claim that Dasein calls itself and that what it is given to understand is its ownmost being. But what about the hearing that must correspond to such a call? Obviously, most of the time Dasein does not hear this call. Recall that everydayness is characterized precisely by a "listening-away." In everydayness Dasein does not focus upon its ownmost being, rather this being is attuned to the world. We do not see our seeing or hear our hearing. In other words, we do not take notice of the conditions of possibility for having a world when we have a world. The apriori structures of our being necessarily withdraw in this involvement. If they did not, if what characterized the apriori structures of our being was that they focused back on themselves, we would not have a world. This is what Heidegger emphasizes in BT. For the most part we do not see our having a world when we have a world. But there are specific experiences in which this "having a world" is lit up and thus provides us with a phenomenal basis for investigating the nature of this being.

When in anxiety, Dasein is brought face to face with its ownmost potentiality-for-Being, Dasein gives itself something to understand but this must be heard. According to Heidegger, "the hearing which corresponds to such a call would be a *taking cognizance* of the Fact that one is 'guilty'" (BT, 333). This is, however, not a matter of loading guilt upon oneself but rather of choosing itself.

Understanding the call is choosing; but it is not a choosing of conscience, which as such cannot be chosen. What is chosen is *having*-a-conscience as Being-free for one's ownmost Being-guilty. "*Understanding the appeal*" means "*wanting to have a conscience.*" (BT, 334)

Understanding the call of conscience is a matter of Dasein's choosing itself as being guilty, that is, of choosing itself as a being whose being is care. This is not a question of Dasein choosing its being, it is rather a matter of understanding this being properly. Undeniably, there is a profound Kierkegaardian influence on Heidegger in his discussion of choosing itself, but with the one important difference that Heidegger secularizes Kierkegaard. Whereas for Kierkegaard there is a need for the Christian to escape the leveling of the present age and become an individual self, Heidegger's focus is purely ontological. There is nothing ungenuine about inauthentic everyday self-understanding, but in order to understand this understanding we cannot be under the spell of this very understanding. Understanding the call of conscience and thus choosing oneself as guilty, is a matter of understanding correctly what is lit up in anxiety. Dasein must not interpret this phenomenon as it interprets other things in the world. In that case, Dasein would not appreciate what is given in anxiety but would rather cover it up by construing the self as a thing-like entity.

7. RESOLUTENESS

Let us now consider the existential structure of the authentic potentiality-for-Being, that is, how this "wanting to have a conscience" by which Dasein understands the appeal of conscience and thus understands its ownmost being is constituted. "Wanting to have a conscience is, as an understanding of oneself in one's ownmost potentiality-for-Being, a way in which Dasein has been *disclosed*" (BT, 342). Disclosedness is constituted by situatedness and understanding, and the latter "implies projecting oneself in each case upon one's ownmost factical possibility of having the potentiality-for-Being-in-the-world" (BT, 342). To this understanding there corresponds the situatedness of anxiety by reason of which Dasein is exposed to its ownmost being in the first place and thus by reason of which Dasein can project itself upon this being. This theme brings us to the third structural moment of disclosedness which is discourse. There are two ways in which Dasein can react towards anxiety, by fleeing in the face of it — thus fleeing in the face of its ownmost being — or by being ready for the anxiety. Obviously, an authentic potentiality-for-Being precludes the former. Flight from one's ownmost being is the defining feature of inauthenticity. Thus, the discourse of the readiness for anxiety is of a different nature than the one that defines everydayness. In this discourse, Heidegger maintains, there "is no corresponding counter-discourse in which, let us say, one talks about what the conscience has said, and pleads one's cause" (BT, 342). This is not because this discourse is suppressive but because, "in hearing this call understandingly, one denies oneself any counter-discourse ... because this hearing has appropriated the content of the call unconcealedly" (BT, 342).

In the call one's constant Being-guilty is represented, and in this way the Self is brought back from the loud idle talk which goes with the common sense of the "one." Thus the mode of Articulative discourse which belongs to wanting to have a conscience, is one of *reticence*. (BT, 342)

What Heidegger is on to here is not as arcane as it may sound. In fact, his position follows entirely from his previous investigations. It suffices to keep in mind the full technical meaning of his terms. Keeping silent is, Heidegger claims, an essential possibility of discourse. Discourse has nothing to do with vocal utterances, discourse is the giving of something to be understood. It is the very actualization of possibilities. Discourse, or *logos*, is the actualization of the founding sensuousness. Likewise, reticence has nothing to do with not making any sounds. Rather, this term seems to refer to not actualizing possibilities. In abstaining from giving the call of conscience an "as-what" — which is what everyday discourse does, Dasein avoids treating care as something present-at-hand. But keeping silent is still a possibility of discourse — and thus of care. Accordingly, discourse has a presence in reticence. However, this presence is not one in which discourse withdraws as it points to another being in its uncovered "as-what." This presence is one in which discourse announces itself and hence also illuminates the being of Dasein. This authentic disclosedness discloses the meaning of disclosedness.

The disclosedness of Dasein in wanting to have a conscience, is thus constituted by anxiety as situatedness, by understanding as a projection of oneself upon one's ownmost Being-guilty, and by discourse as reticence. This distinctive and authentic disclosedness, which is attested in Dasein itself by its conscience — *this reticent self-projection upon one's ownmost Being-guilty, in which one is ready for anxiety — we call "resoluteness"* [*Entschlossenheit*]. (BT, 343)

By systematically tracing the development of Heidegger's treatment of Dasein's justification of an authentic potentiality-for-Being, we have shown that there is at least an immanent consistency in his line of reasoning, however arcane it may sound. But at this point we might be tempted to ask what it all means? Firstly, it is our contention that this section of BT is an extremely important part of Heidegger's overall project. What forces him to undertake it is the fact that Husserl's theory of wholes and parts is imperative for his endeavor. He must make use of this approach in order to provide an account of subjectivity without advocating a notion of a detachable and essentially worldless thing-like entity. He does this by introducing a new kind of subjectivity which is not a thing that is not in the world, but a Being-in-the-world that is not a thing. These hyphens commit Heidegger to the theory of wholes and parts, because every element in the basic state of Dasein is a moment, just as the existentials in Dasein's being are moments. However, one cannot introduce moments without introducing a whole, and if the moments are to have an ontological status, so must the whole.

Secondly, in this analysis Heidegger struggles with the very foundation of phenomenology, particularly his own interpretation of it which requires him to provide a phenomenal basis for every step in the development of an ontology. Admittedly, the introduction of anxiety as a marginal experience in which Dasein is thrown face to face with its ownmost being and of resoluteness as a response in which this mode of being is welcomed might be criticized as nothing but an artificial construction on Heidegger's part in order to comply with his own demands in regard to pre-ontological confirmation. Heidegger would emphasize that his analysis is a phenomenological one and that it does not aim at providing an interpretation of anxiety that conforms to the terminology and scientific standards of psychology. Rather, his aim is to disclose anxiety as it shows itself before scientific inquiry. According to Heidegger, "the phenomenology of history and nature promises to disclose reality as it shows itself *before* scientific inquiry, as the reality which is already given to it" (HCT, 2). In response to the accusation of inventing anxiety as an experience in which we are thrown face to face with our ownmost being, Heidegger can legitimately call attention to an experience in which we find ourselves confronted with the indefinite certainty of death. What we are referring to are those experiences in which something takes hold of us to which we cannot give meaning but in which a certain "nothingness," for lack of a better word, nevertheless announces itself.

According to Heidegger, resoluteness involves a holding on to the anxiety and thus is an example of resoluteness which, in the sense that it is an activity at all is the activity of not distorting what is given us to understand. This is an activity in the sense that it is an act, but resoluteness is not compatible to those everyday activities in which we choose to actualize some possibilities and not others. When retrospectively commenting on the concept of resoluteness, Heidegger remarks that "[t]he resoluteness intended in *Being and Time* is not the deliberate action of a subject, but the opening up of [Dasein], out of its captivity in that which is, to the openness of being."[2] Thus, resoluteness is not the choice of a deliberating subject situated outside the possibilities of which it must choose one to actualize. Resoluteness is not a matter of actualizing anything at all, that is, it is not a *poietic* activity. Resoluteness is not productive, it is a *praxis* in which the guiding sight of everyday activity itself is properly seen.

> Resoluteness, as *authentic Being-one's-Self*, does not detach Dasein from its world, nor does it isolate it so that it becomes a free-floating "I." And how should it, when resoluteness is authentic disclosedness, is *authentically* nothing else than *Being-in-the-world*? (BT, 344)

Thus, resoluteness is not the act of an originally worldless subject deliberately freeing itself from its unfortunate absorption in the world. Rather, resoluteness is an intuition in which the being of Dasein announces itself and what it says is that "[w]henever a 'there' is disclosed, its whole Being-in-the-world — that is to say, the world, Being-in, and the Self which, as an 'I am,' this entity is — is disclosed with equal primordiality" (BT, 343). With the

---

[2] In "The Origin of the Work of Art," in *Poetry, Language, Thought* (New York: Harper & Row, 1971), 67.

concept of resoluteness Heidegger thus introduces a way in which the *poietic* seeing of everydayness itself can be properly seen.

The objective of this chapter has been to delineate Heidegger's attempt to provide a phenomenal basis for his determination of the concept of care and his account of how this phenomenon can be seen as a whole. We have proceeded from the question of the possibility of a primordial totality in which, as Heidegger points out, the whole of which the structural moments are parts cannot be reached by adding together these moments. The very definition of an entity as a moment presupposes the prior appearance of a whole. In discussing the phenomenon of anxiety, Heidegger justifies his description of such a whole, the phenomenon of care. But this phenomenon seems to preclude the possibility of its being seen as a whole.

In order to ensure the possibility of bringing the wholeness of Dasein into view, thus ensuring the possibility of carrying out an existential analytic, Heidegger introduced the phenomenon of death. He claims that a proper phenomenological analysis of this phenomenon shows that death is essentially tied to the notion of wholeness of the being we ourselves are; he adds that this should be understood as a being-towards rather than as an end of existence. In Being-towards-death, there lies an existentiell potentiality-for-Being-a-whole, as long as this possibility is not covered up. Although everyday Dasein flees in the face of death there is a way in which Dasein can choose itself as guilty, and thus hold on to what is revealed in anxiety. Heidegger refers to this response to anxiety as resoluteness. Thus, resoluteness is the full meaning of disclosedness. Having provided a phenomenal basis for Being-a-whole, Heidegger can go on to investigate its temporal constitution.

CHAPTER IX

TEMPORALITY

The essential problematic of Heidegger's fundamental ontology is the question of the meaning of being in general. However, in order to work out this question we must, Heidegger claims, first "make a being — the inquirer — perspicuous in his own Being" (BT, 27). The objective of the existential analytic is to provide a "concrete understanding of the basic constitution of Dasein" (BT, 358). The existential analytic is a twofold process. The first step consists of the preparatory analysis of Dasein carried out in Division One. The outcome of this analysis is that "the totality of Being-in-the-world as a structural whole has revealed itself as care" (BT, 274). The transition to the second step is carried out in the first chapters of Division Two, which provide a phenomenal basis for seeing this phenomenon as a whole. Having done so, Heidegger can go on to the second step of his existential analytic which is to "exhibit its concrete temporal constitution" (BT, 384). This will show, Heidegger claims, that "Temporality makes possible the unity of existence, facticity, and falling, and in this way constitutes primordially the totality of the structure of care" (BT, 376). Temporality is what holds care together as a whole and thus is also what gives the full meaning of the being of Dasein.

The subject of time was discussed by Heidegger already quite early in his career. For instance, in 1915 he offered a lecture in Freiburg on the topic of "The Concept of Time in Historical Studies."[1] In PIA, in 1922, he introduces the concept of time in relation to his interpretation of Aristotle, and in July, 1924, he delivered a lecture to the Marburg Theological Society under the title "The Concept of Time."[2] A year later, in the summer semester 1925, the Marburg lecture course HCT appeared in which Heidegger gives the first major presentation of his own philosophical thought that inaugurates major themes of BT. However, the concept of time is, despite of the title, only

---

[1] "Der Zeitbegriff in der Geschichteswissenschaft," published in 1916. Also made available in Martin Heidegger, *Frühe Schriften* (Frankfurt am Maim: Vittorio Klostermann, 1972), 355 - 375. Translated by H.S. Taylor and H.W. Uffelman in the *Journal of the British Society for Phenomenology* 9, 1978.

[2] "Der Begriff der Zeit," translated by W. McNeill (Cambridge: Blackwell, 1992). Hereafter CT.

briefly touched upon in this lecture, and both the 1922 introduction to the proposed book on Aristotle and the 1924 paper offer a more thorough investigation of this concept. HCT is not the only draft of BT, and decidedly not the first. There are at least three drafts of BT. Each exhibits an important influence upon Heidegger's thinking. In PIA, the basic concepts of BT are presented through an interpretation of Aristotle; in CT, the basic concepts of BT are presented through a discussion of the concept of time; and in HCT, the basic concepts are introduced through a discussion of the fundamental discoveries of Husserlian phenomenology. What these three drafts share is that they all introduce a new concept of time as essential to an investigation of Dasein.

In this chapter, we approach Heidegger's interpretation of Dasein's temporality by first discussing how this concept is developed in Heidegger's commentaries on certain philosophers and how it determines his interpretation of others. In the first section, we investigate his notion of temporality as it emerges in his discussion of Aristotle, and we relate this to his discussion of temporality in CT. In the second section, we shall have a look at Heidegger's introduction of temporality in his discussion of Kant and the transcendental power of imagination, and we intend to relate this back to our investigation of the original synthetic unity of apperception in Chapter IV. In the third section, we shall have a brief look at Husserl's analysis of internal time-consciousness. Husserl was the first to offer an extensive analysis of the concept of subjective time, and this analysis undoubtedly exercised a great influence upon Heidegger's thinking. Although this analysis was not published before 1928 (incidently, Heidegger was credited as the editor although the true editor in fact was Edith Stein), Heidegger was familiar with the text years ahead of its publication. For instance, in HCT from 1925, it is referred to in his treatment of the early development of phenomenological research.[3] We are, however, not about to claim that Heidegger simply took over this analysis from Husserl. Our objective is simply to set the stage for an approach to Heidegger's own investigation of temporality.

Heidegger mentions in his description of the decisive discoveries of Husserl's phenomenology — intentionality, categorial intuition, and the original sense of the apriori — that they are indispensable for a proper investigation of time. "Only in this way can '*time*' be brought into view phenomenologically. Only in this way is the possibility given for an orderly procedure in the analysis of time as it shows itself" (HCT, 27). Thus, even if he did not take over Husserl's analysis of time, it is still a matter of fact that it was the decisive discoveries of Husserl's phenomenology that lead him to a

[3] HCT, 92. Here Heidegger claims that Husserl's investigations of internal time consciousness "are in part published in his later works." These are works which Heidegger knew very well.

phenomenological concept of time. Of course, these are the same discoveries that lay at the foundation of Husserl's analysis of time consciousness.

Having established this basis for Heidegger's investigation of temporality, we shall go back to his analysis in Division Two of BT and discuss how he works his way from the concept of resoluteness to the notion of temporality as the ontological meaning of care.

1. THE TRADITIONAL THEORY OF TIME AND THE TEMPORALITY OF *PRAXIS*

As early as the 1915 lecture on "The Concept of Time in Historical Studies," Heidegger suggests a distinction between two different notions of time that is central to his thought throughout the period of fundamental ontology and quite possibly throughout his entire career. On the one hand, there is the notion of time operative in the natural sciences; on the other, there is the notion of time employed in historical research. Later, this distinction is presented as the one between the traditional philosophical, as well as the everyday conception of time, and a more original concept of time developed by Heidegger himself in BT and related lectures. The latter works approach time as something which belongs to and defines the being of Dasein. Thus, Heidegger not only distinguishes between subjective and objective time, but, as opposed to our everyday understanding of time, he claims that the latter is founded on the former. This is a very radical claim which has to be properly understood before it can be challenged. In what follows, we try to clear away the most obvious ways in which Heidegger's claim might be misunderstood.

Firstly, Heidegger's intention is not to prove that certain explanations of time are erroneous and thus replace them with his own theory of time. He is not trying to replace an objective theory of time with a subjective theory. He is merely saying that the traditional notion of time is not the most original one in the sense that it must be founded on another concept of time. In other words, Heidegger is not trying to replace the traditional notion of time, rather he is trying to justify it. Secondly, when using the term 'subjective' in reference to Heidegger's concept of primordial time, which admittedly is something of which Heidegger would strongly disapprove, we use this term simply as a neutral reference to the being we ourselves are. Heidegger's term for this being is Dasein but, as we have repeatedly pointed out, there are places where Heidegger clearly indicates that this concept designates a new way of interpreting what was traditionally known as the subject. Thus, to refer to Heidegger's notion of time as subjective is simply to say that this more original conception of time is one in which time is understood as something belonging to the being of Dasein, or, more accurately, as constituting the full ontological meaning of care.

So far, we have been referring to the traditional philosophical concept of time and to Heidegger's conception of primordial time without providing any further explanation as to what characterizes and distinguishes these notions of time. We know that the latter belongs to the being of Dasein and that the former is to be founded upon this more original concept of time, but we have yet to point out their distinctive characters. According to Heidegger, the traditional philosophical understanding of time has its origin in Aristotle's definition of time in the *Physics*. Since Aristotle, time has been conceived of as a phenomenon that is to be treated by the philosophy of nature. Heidegger translates Aristotle's definition of time as follows: "'For this is time: that which is counted in the movement which we encounter within the horizon of the earlier and the later'" (BT, 473).[4] Both in the traditional philosophical, as well as in the ordinary understanding of time the principle of time as something that is counted has prevailed since Aristotle's treatment of time. What gets counted according to this understanding is a series of "nows."

[F]or the ordinary understanding of time, time shows itself as a sequence of "nows" which are constantly 'present-at-hand,' simultaneously passing away and coming along. Time is understood as a succession, as a 'flowing stream' of "nows," as the 'course of time.' (BT, 474)

Thus, the traditional understanding of time sees time as something that is constructed out of "nows," and accordingly all its parts can be reduced to "nows." The future is a now that is not yet, the past is a now that is no more, and the present is a now that is. This notion of time Heidegger refers to as world-time (*Weltzeit*), and world-time is what the ordinary experience of time knows.

According to Heidegger, there is nothing wrong with this understanding of time. The problem is merely that this is not the most original conception of time. A major reason for making such a claim is that this traditional understanding of time in fact points to a more original understanding of time.

Although, proximally and for the most part, the ordinary experience of time is one that knows only 'world-time,' it always gives it a *distinctive* relationship to 'soul' and 'spirit,' even if this is still a far cry from a philosophical inquiry oriented explicitly and primarily towards the 'subject.' (BT, 479)

As evidence for this claim Heidegger calls attention to passages in Aristotle and St. Augustine. From Aristotle's *Physics* he quotes: "'But if nothing other

---

[4] Heidegger's own translation of Aristotle's *Physics*, 219b 1 ff.

than the soul or the soul's mind were naturally equipped for numbering, then if there were no soul, time would be impossible'" (BT, 479n).[5] From St. Augustine he quotes a passage from the *Confessions*:

'Hence it seemed to me that time is nothing else than extendedness; but of what sort of thing it is an extendedness, I do not know; and it would be surprising if it were not an extendedness of the soul itself.' (BT, 479n)[6]

Both these passages indicate that the world-time itself, if properly understood, in fact introduces a more original understanding of time as "subjective."

In CT, Heidegger introduces world-time in relation to Einstein's theory of relativity, whose basic thesis he presents in the following condensed manner: "Time ... is nothing. It persists merely as a consequence of the events taking place in it. There is no absolute time, and no absolute simultaneity either" (CT, 3). In relation to Einstein's theory of relativity, Heidegger emphasizes that one must not overlook the positive side of this theory while focusing only upon its destruction of absolute time. The positive side of Einstein's theory is that it underscores a position indicated in Aristotle in the above quotation, namely that "time is that within which events take place" (CT, 3). Thus, again we see that a thorough investigation of world-time in fact demonstrates that this notion of time cannot account for itself but rather points to a more original conception of time which is essentially linked to subjectivity. However, neither Einstein nor Aristotle ever arrived at this original conception of time — but the latter provides Heidegger with distinctions that enable him to develop such a conception.

Let us recall Heidegger's interpretation of Aristotelian terms in PIA, and his designation of Dasein's disclosedness as *phronesis*, that is, as a *praxis*. The fundamental difference between *poiesis* and *praxis* concerns the distinction between potentiality (*dynamis*) and actuality (*energeia*). While in *poiesis* the actuality is external to potentiality in the sense that the actuality of the activity finds its completeness in something that falls outside of the activity, in what is fabricated, the relation between actuality and potentiality is entirely different in the case of *praxis*. In *praxis* the end of, or completeness of, the activity does not fall outside of it, rather it is included in the activity itself. To see is also at the same time to have seen, likewise to understand is to have understood.

The way Aristotle characterizes *praxis* as an activity whose end or completeness is included in the activity itself seems to introduce a notion of temporality that is different from his definition of time in the *Physics*. If to

[5] Heidegger's own translation of Aristotle's *Physics*, 223a 25.
[6] Heidegger's own translation of *Confessions* XI, 26.

see is also at the same time to have seen, and to think is to have thought, it follows that the past and the future are included in the present instead of being a now that is no more and a now that is not yet. The temporality of *praxis* introduces a "thicker" present in the sense that this activity includes in itself its own future. Likewise, since to understand is to have understood, the past is included in the present, rather than being merely over. Hence, we have a present that essentially includes past and future, as opposed to the traditional theory of time where the present excludes past and future. Admittedly, this is not something that is worked out by Aristotle as a different notion of time, but his treatment of *praxis* does make suggestions to this effect.

It is not unreasonable to assume that Heidegger's investigation of temporality as something that belongs to the being of Dasein and his claim that the everyday notion of temporality is founded upon this original concept of time arises in part out of his interpretation of Aristotle. We have ascertained that Heidegger's distinction between discoveredness and disclosedness is an ontological reappropriation of Aristotle's distinction between *poiesis* and *praxis* that especially attends to the hierarchical relationship between these activities suggested by Aristotle. Given the fact that Dasein's being is disclosedness, it is highly possible that the temporality of *praxis* is what becomes the temporality of Dasein in Heidegger's existential analysis.

In PIA, the discussion of *phronesis* as the "truthful safe-keeping-of-Being" (as disclosedness) is succeeded by a brief discussion of the temporality of *phronesis* that certainly points in this direction. Heidegger introduces this discussion by claiming that "the concrete interpretation shows how the being which is *kairos* constitutes itself in *phronesis*" (PIA, 382). This assertion introduces a term that is central to Heidegger's notion of temporality in BT, namely *kairos*, or, more accurately, its German translation *Augenblick*. In BT, this term is translated either 'moment' or 'moment of vision' while the translator of PIA uses the term 'moment-of-insight.' For obvious technical reasons, 'moment' is not a very felicitous translation and 'moment of vision' seems a little stilted. Thus, we settle for the less ethereal 'moment-of-insight,' although *kairos* (*Augenblick*) connotes temporally in a way that is not so obviously captured by this translation. Admittedly, in a non-technical use, 'moment' does signify a now or a being-present, but this is not the way we have used this term so far. Below we shall see that the technical sense of 'moment' does have a temporal meaning.

According to Heidegger, then, it is the being which is moment-of-insight which constitutes itself in *phronesis* and thus in disclosedness.

Phronesis is possible as a discussing, a solicitous and considerative [kind of] *phronesis*, only because it is primarily an *aisthesis*, i.e., it is in the end a simple over-view of the moment-of-insight [*Augenblick*]. (PIA, 381)

In other words, disclosedness is possible only because it is an *aisthesis* (a founding sensuousness) and thus in the end "a simple over-view of the moment-of-insight." Hence, the true meaning of disclosedness is that of being a moment-of-insight. The being which becomes uncovered in the *alethenein* of *phronesis* is, Heidegger claims, "something which exists as *not yet* such and such Being" (PIA, 381-2).

As "not yet such and such," and in fact as the That-with-respect-to-which of concern, it is at the same time *already* such and such, as the That-with-respect-to-which of concrete readiness-for-dealings, whose constitutive illumination is determined by *phronesis*. (PIA, 382)

Heidegger continues,

[t]he "not-yet" and the "already" are to be understood in their "unity, i.e., they are to be understood on the basis of a primordial given-ness, a given-ness for which the "not-yet" and the "already" are determinate explicata. (PIA, 382)

Hence, it seems that the notion of temporality according to which past and future constitute a unity is inherent in the concept of *phronesis* in the sense that this temporal unity constitutes *phronesis*. This is a notion of time that is essentially different from the traditional understanding of time according to which the temporal phases exclude each other. Parts that are missing — like a now that is not yet and a now that is no more — cannot make up a unity. Thus, the unity of "not-yet" and "already" Heidegger is referring to is a notion where temporality is treated as an absolute *concretum*.

2. THE TEMPORALITY OF TRANSCENDENTAL APPERCEPTION

Although Heidegger situates the development of the traditional theories of time between Aristotle and himself, he finds in Kant an exception from this tradition in the sense that a different notion of temporality is suggested, although by no means fully worked out, in Kant's first critique. For instance, in the preface to the fourth edition of KPM, Heidegger claims that while preparing for a lecture course on Kant's First Critique that was held the winter semester 1927/28, he came to see in Kant a representative for his own approach. "[M]y attention was drawn to the chapter on Schematism, and I glimpsed therein a connection between the problem of Categories, that is, the problem of Being in traditional Metaphysics and the phenomenon of time" (KPM, xv). Likewise, in the lecture course *Logik. Die Frage nach der*

Wahrheit,[7] Heidegger portrays Kant as his predecessor on the topic of the original concept of time.

In this section, we investigate this source of influence in some detail. It will, however, not be our goal to provide an in-depth analysis of Heidegger's voluminous interpretation of Kant. That is clearly a project in its own rights. Nor do we intend even to provide a conclusive study of Heidegger's interpretation of the Kantian notion of temporality. Our objective will be merely to indicate Heidegger's reading of Kant, and textually we limit ourselves to certain fragments of Heidegger's discussion of the transcendental deduction and to his discussion of the temporal character of the transcendental power of imagination in KPM.

Before we begin this inquiry, let us briefly recall our investigation of the original synthetic unity of apperception discussed in Chapter IV. In presenting Heidegger's concept of existence, we made a detour to Sartre and Kant in order to indicate the kind of position Heidegger was advocating. Dasein is, qua existence, directed towards itself. However, this is not a kind of self-directedness where consciousness is aware of itself as an object. Dasein understands itself, not through introspection, but through its involvement with the world. Hence, Heidegger's concept of existence does not suggest an ego inhabiting consciousness, of which consciousness is aware prior to its involvement with the world. As we may recall, in TE Sartre discusses the tension within phenomenology as to whether consciousness actually contains an ego or whether it is simply a spontaneity transcending towards objects, and he shows that if one inserts an ego into consciousness, consciousness, as phenomenology defines it, will be destroyed. According to Sartre, given the phenomenological definition of consciousness as intentional, it follows that consciousness can only be aware of itself "*in so far as it is consciousness of a transcendent object*" (TE, 40). He adds that this consciousness of consciousness "is not *positional*, which is to say that consciousness is not for itself its own object" (TE, 41). It is our contention that Heidegger's concept of existence advocates, and must necessarily do so, the same position in regard to self-awareness and, moreover, that this position in fact is preceded by Kant in his distinction between synthetic and analytic unity of apperception. In maintaining that "the synthetic unity of apperception is [the] highest point" (Kant, B134n) Kant makes a claim to the effect that the reflection 'I think' through which "I represent to myself the analytic unity" (Kant, B134n) presupposes a prior unity, the synthetic unity of apperception. This claim along with Kant's identification of the synthetic unity of apperception with "understanding itself" (Kant, B134n) indicates a notion of pure or original apperception that bears strong resemblance to

---

[7] See GA 21, 200, 400.

what Sartre calls non-positional awareness. The claim that apperception is a non-positional awareness of the activity of thinking would entail that self-consciousness is consciousness, not of *a* self, but of *it*self.

Thus, it is our argument that there is a kinship between Heidegger and Kant on the interpretation of self-consciousness. Evidence in favor of this can be found in Heidegger's interpretation of the temporality of transcendental power of imagination. However, whereas we based our claim upon an inquiry into the B-Deduction, we shall now see that Heidegger focuses solely upon the A-Deduction. Heidegger's interest in the A-Deduction derives from the fact that in this deduction the transcendental apperception is related to the power of imagination. According to Kant, "the transcendental unity of apperception ... relates to the pure synthesis of imagination, as an *a priori* condition of [its] possibility" (Kant, A118). And Heidegger emphasizes the following passage in KPM:

Thus the principle of the necessary unity of the pure (productive) synthesis of the power of imagination, prior to apperception, is the ground for the possibility of all knowledge, especially of experience. (KPM, 54)[8]

At this point he asks,

[w]hat does the expression "prior to" apperception mean here? Does Kant want to say that the pure synthesis precedes Transcendental Apperception in the order of the grounding of the possibility of pure knowledge? (KPM, 54)

Heidegger acknowledges that this would seem to be in keeping with the notion of apperception presupposed by the pure synthesis of imagination, but this concession is merely a rhetorical introduction to the real subject matter. As we know, for a phenomenologist the status of the apriori is of vital importance. In our analysis of Heidegger's interpretation of this concept in Chapter III, we saw that he distinguished between the traditional sense of the apriori and the phenomenological sense of the apriori. What characterized the latter was that it was prior in the way a whole is prior to its moments. Thus, the phenomenological sense of the apriori does not allow for an apriori phenomenon to precede what it grounds in the sense that it might appear prior to and independent of it. In this way, Heidegger seeks to interpret Kant's notion of the apriori status of pure synthesis. Thus, in response to his above questions concerning the apriori status of this phenomenon Heidegger asks, "does the 'prior to' have yet another meaning?" (KPM, 54). And he answers,

[i]n fact, Kant uses the "prior to" in a way that first gives the whole statement the

---

[8] This is a passage from Kant, A118.

decisive structural sense, to the effect that in it the interpretation which was attempted first would indeed simultaneously be included with it. (KPM, 54)

In other words, the power of imagination does not introduce a phenomenon that appears prior to transcendental apperception in the sense that it precedes the latter. Although in some passages Kant seems to indicate precisely something like this,[9] in other passages he strongly suggests that the term 'prior to' should not be understood in terms of one object appearing prior to and independently of another. Instead, Heidegger emphasizes, if the 'prior to' in relation to transcendental apperception and the pure power of imagination is understood properly, then "the character of the structural unity of Transcendental Apperception and the pure power of imagination first comes to light" (KPM, 54). Thus, according to Heidegger, the apriori character of the transcendental power of imagination consists in its unifying the transcendental apperception by being "the mediator between Transcendental Apperception and time" (KPM, 55).

Now, let us leave Heidegger's analysis and try to relate it to the outcome of our own investigation of aspects of the B-Deduction. According to Kant "the *analytic* unity of apperception is possible only under the presupposition of a certain *synthetic* unity" (Kant, B133). In the following footnote, he adds that "the synthetic unity of apperception is ... [the] highest point ... [and] this faculty of apperception is the understanding itself" (B134n). Thus, in Kant, as in Heidegger, understanding is the ultimate condition of possibility for objectivity. But what is the nature of understanding? The reason Heidegger favors the A-Deduction is that in this version of the transcendental deduction Kant discusses the nature of the synthesis, whereas in the second edition's version little is said about the synthesis of the manifold. The reason for this change is that Kant's discussion in the A-Deduction was conceived as a psychologically oriented explanation of the nature of the synthesis. However, the principles of phenomenology enables Heidegger to detect in the A-Deduction an investigation of subjectivity highly related to his own approach — which is anything but psychologistic.[10]

In what follows we shall have a closer look at Heidegger's interpretation

[9] Cf. A287.

[10] In many ways the distinction between the A-Deduction and the B-Deduction inaugurates the distinction between the phenomenological and the analytic rejection of psychologism introduced around the turn of the century. Whereas the latter insisted on a rigid distinction between being-true and being-taken-to-be-true, the former took upon itself to provide this rigid distinction with an account of how objectivity is correlated to and grounded in subjective intuitions without thereby reducing it to a psychological phenomenon. Thus, it is our contention that, just as the A-Deduction provides the full meaning of the B-Deduction, so too does phenomenology provide the full meaning of the rejection of psychologism introduced by Frege, the father of analytic philosophy.

of the synthesis in the A-Deduction. We shall see that on Heidegger's interpretation the transcendental power of imagination has a temporal constitution that highly resembles the temporal constitution of the being of Dasein, of care. Although Kant treats the phenomenon of time in the Transcendental Aesthetic, Heidegger concentrates solely on the Transcendental Analytic in his discussion of Kant's notion of temporality. This is because he understands the transcendental power of imagination as the origin of pure, sensible intuition, and he grounds this by first pointing out that "time 'flows continually' as the pure succession of the sequence of nows [and] pure intuition intuits this succession unobjectively" (KPM, 118–9). According to Heidegger, "[i]ntuition means the taking-in-stride of what gives itself. Pure intuition, in the taking-in-stride, gives itself that which is capable of being taken in stride" (KPM, 119). However, Heidegger points out, "it is easily seen that the pure intuition of the pure succession of nows cannot be the taking-in-stride of a presence [*Anwesenden*]" (KPM, 119). If that were the case, one would only be able to intuit the present now and not a sequence of nows.

Indeed, strictly speaking, in the mere taking-in-stride of a "present moment" [*eines "Gegenwärtigen"*] it is not possible to intuit a single now insofar as it has an essentially continuous extension in its having-just-arrived and its coming-at-any-minute. (KPM, 119)

In other words, in pure intuition there is a looking-at, a looking-ahead, and a looking-back which in fact constitute the threefold character of the transcendental power of imagination. Hence, it also follows that the sequence of nows is not time in its originality. On the contrary, Heidegger maintains, "the transcendental power of imagination allows time as sequence of nows to spring forth, and as this letting-spring-forth it is therefore original time" (KPM, 120). Having established why Heidegger chooses to proceed directly to the Transcendental Analytic in his treatment of temporality, we shall now see how he unfolds the inner temporal character of the transcendental power of imagination and thus the synthetic unity of apperception.

There is one problem with Heidegger's granting primacy to the transcendental power of imagination and that is the fact that such a primacy seems at first sight not to be in keeping with the text. According to Kant, "receptivity can make knowledge possible only when combined with spontaneity" (Kant, A97).

Now this spontaneity is the ground of a threefold synthesis which must necessarily be found in all knowledge; namely, the *apprehension* of representations as modifications of the mind in intuition, their *reproduction* in imagination, and their *recognition* in a concept. (Kant, A97–8)

Hence, it seems to follow that, as Heidegger puts it, "the power of imagination is just one element among others and that it is in no way the root of intuition and concept" (KPM, 121). But, he points out, at the same time this systematic approach to pure knowledge also seems to indicate a more original ground. It might be, Heidegger argues, that the three modes of synthesis are three in number because there happen to be three elements belonging to the structure of pure knowledge. Maybe there are "three modes of synthesis because time appears in them and because they express the threefold unity of time as present, having-been, and future?" (KPM, 121). Obviously, in this context the question mark has a rhetorical status — this is clearly the view to which Heidegger subscribes. Hence, according to Heidegger, the three modes of synthesis points to a more original unity of temporal moments, and working out this temporality will enable us to see that "the power of imagination represents not just one faculty among others, but rather their mediating center" (KPM, 121).

[T]he working-out of the inner temporal character of the three modes of synthesis should produce the ultimate, decisive proof for the fact that the interpretation of the transcendental power of imagination as the root of both stems [sensibility and understanding] is not only possible, but also necessary. (KPM, 121–2)

However, one must, Heidegger maintains, keep in mind that the three modes of synthesis are moments of a whole. Although he does not use the terminology of the theory of wholes and parts when making this claim, he emphasizes the necessity of keeping the right entity in view as a whole.

[I]t is worth noting that the proper goal of interpretation of the three modes of synthesis — even if it is not always formulated clearly enough and in advance — lies in demonstrating their intrinsic and essential belonging-together in the essence of pure synthesis as such. (KPM, 122)

Thus, it is pure synthesis as such that makes up the whole. This means that the three modes of synthesis are not three different syntheses but rather that "synthesis as such has the character of either apprehension or reproduction or recognition" (KPM, 122).

According to Heidegger, the synthesis of apprehension in intuition refers to "that which offers the 'present in general'" (KPM, 223) and, he continues, this activity is time-forming. What is apprehended in intuition "contains" manifoldness. Quoting from Kant, Heidegger states that this can never "be represented as such a manifold ..., if the mind does not differentiate time in the sequence of one impression upon another" (KPM, 122).[11] Hence, it follows that in order to be able to encounter a being present in the now, which

---

[11] From Kant A99.

is what empirical intuition is concerned with, "our mind must already be saying constantly and in advance "now and now and now"" (KPM, 122–3). Thus, Heidegger claims, "[t]he pure, apprehending synthesis does not first take place within the horizon of time, but instead it forms precisely the like of the now and the sequence of nows" (KPM, 123).[12] On this interpretation, then, it follows that "the pure synthesis of apprehension in itself has a temporal character" (KPM, 123).

However, although he has ascertained the temporal character of the pure synthesis of apprehension, Heidegger has yet to establish the identity between this time-forming activity and the transcendental power of imagination. In order to do so, he quotes a passage in which Kant seems to suggest something to that effect. "It is thus an active faculty in us for the synthesis of his manifold which we call imagination, and its immediate action on perceptions I call apprehension" (Kant, A120).[13] As Heidegger sees it, in this passage Kant claims that apprehension is a mode of the transcendental power of imagination, and hence it also follows that the latter "has in itself a pure temporal character" (KPM, 123). Thus, the forming of the now and the sequence of nows is a mode of the transcendental power of imagination.

This interpretation requires, however, the possibility of maintaining some kind of distinction between imagination as a mode of synthesis, and the transcendental power of imagination. As a mode of synthesis, imagination is introduced as reproductive.

The "mind" can represent ... something previously perceived, even "without the presence of the object." Such making-present however, or as Kant says "imagination," presupposes that the mind has the possibility of bringing forth again representationally the being represented earlier in order to represent it in a more actual unity with the being directly perceived from time to time. (KPM, 124)

Thus, imagination is the reproduction of something already perceived, and

---

[12] While scholars like R. Makkreel, *Imagination* (Chicago: The University of Chicago Press, 1990), 25, and R. Morrison, "Kant, Husserl, and Heidegger on Time and the Unity of 'Consciousness,'" *Philosophy and Phenomenological Research*, 1978, Vol. 39, 183, argue that Heidegger, by making this claim, in fact confuses the difference between synthesis and synopsis, others, like F. Schalow, *The Renewal of the Heidegger-Kant Dialogue* (Albany: State University of New York Press, 1992), 73, and C.M. Sherover, *Heidegger, Kant and Time* (Bloomington: Indiana University Press, 1971), 221, argue that Heidegger does not so much superimpose his own view on Kant as he brings out the full scope of Kantian philosophy. It falls beyond our intent to discuss the legitimacy of Heidegger's interpretation of Kant, but we are inclined to agree with the latter. It is our contention that the fundamental discoveries of phenomenology enable Heidegger to develop Kantian themes in a manner that clarifies Kant's insights.

[13] This is R. Taft's (the translator of KPM) translation of this passage. It is more in keeping with the German text than is the original English translation of Kant.

this "bringing forth again" is a synthesis in the sense that the already perceived, the "what was," is unified with the "what is." Heidegger adds that the "reproducing synthesis ... can only unify if the mind does not 'loose from thought' what is brought-forth-again" (KPM, 124).[14] Thus, the synthesis necessarily implies the ability to retain what has already been experienced. Since that which has already been experienced belongs to the realm of earlier experiences, it follows that there is a temporal distinction involved in such an ability. It can only be done if "the mind 'differentiates time,' and thereby has in view such [temporal distinctions] as *'earlier'* and *'at that time"* (KPM, 124).

Hence, if empirical synthesis in the mode of reproduction is thereby to become possible, the no-longer-now *as such* must in advance and prior to all experience have been brought forth again and unified with the specific now. (KPM, 124)

Here, Heidegger seems to indicate a distinction between empirical synthesis in the mode of reproduction and its condition of possibility, which is that "the now-longer-now *as such* must in advance and prior to all experience have been brought forth again and unified with the specific now" (KPM, 124). While the former belongs to empirical imagination, the latter, Heidegger claims, belongs to the pure power of imagination. Thus, this distinction takes care of the necessary distinction between imagination as a mode of synthesis and the transcendental power of imagination. Moreover, it introduces the no-longer into the very structure of synthesis.

However, the outcome of this interpretation is the seemingly self-contradictory concept of productive reproducing. While the pure power of imagination is considered productive, the structural concept of imagination is by its very nature reproductive. Heidegger is aware of this apparent paradoxical notion of pure reproduction as productive reproducing but, nevertheless, in response to the question as to whether pure reproduction is a productive' reproducing he says, "[i]n fact, it forms the possibility of reproduction in general, namely, due to the fact that it brings the horizon of the earlier into view and holds it open as such in advance" (KPM, 124). Pure reproduction (transcendental power of imagination) is productive in the sense that it forms (produces) the possibility of reproduction. Thus, the notion of productive reproduction should not evoke the notion of an object with mutually exclusive features. In this case productive and reproductive are not equiprimordial phenomena; rather the latter is a moment of the former. But then it also follows that pure reproduction, productive reproducing, is not something that temporally precedes, or appears independently of, reproduction in general. Rather it forms the space of appearance for the

---

[14] The quoted section is from Kant, A102.

latter by being the having-been-ness as such.

Pure synthesis in the mode of reproduction forms having-been-ness [*Gewesenheit*] as such. But this says: the pure power of imagination, with regard to this mode of synthesis, is time-forming. (KPM, 124-5)

Pure reproduction does not attend to something experienced earlier, something that would fall under the realm of reproductive synthesis; rather, pure reproduction "opens up in general the horizon of the possible attending-to, the having-been-ness, and so it 'forms' this 'after' as such" (KPM, 125). Hence, just as the forming of the now and the sequence of nows is a mode of the transcendental power of imagination, so is the forming of the having-been-ness, and, quoting Kant, Heidegger maintains that these are bound up in an essential unity.

Pure reproduction is essentially unified with the pure synthesis of intuition as that which forms the present. "The synthesis of apprehension is thus inseparably bound up with the synthesis of reproduction," for every now is now already just-arrived. (KPM, 125)[15]

Having ascertained the unity of the forming of the now and the having-been in the pure power of imagination, Heidegger goes on to investigate the third structural moment of this apriori unity: the synthesis of recognition in a concept. If it is the case that Heidegger's temporal approach to the three modes of synthesis is legitimate, one should expect to find in relation to this synthesis a notion of the future. However, Heidegger is fully aware that this is not something that is entirely obvious as one starts reading Kant's investigation. As a matter of fact, he admits, Kant "opposes in the sharpest terms the 'I think' in particular and reason in general to all time-relations" (KPM, 126). In a passage in the Transcendental Dialectic, which Heidegger quotes, this is unambiguously spelled out. "Pure reason, as a faculty which is merely intelligible, is not subject to the form of time or, consequently, to the conditions of the succession of time" (KPM, 126).[16] But the claim that pure reason is not subject to time does not necessarily preclude its being time-forming. The former means that it does not have the temporality of an object, that is, it is not something with coordinates in time. We shall see that, on Heidegger's interpretation pure reason is nevertheless intrinsically temporal.

Heidegger begins his investigation of the synthesis of recognition in a concept by noticing how Kant proceeds to this synthesis from synthesis in the mode of reproduction. He quotes: "Without consciousness of the fact

---

[15] In quotation marks: Kant, A 102.
[16] Kant A551, R. Taft's translation.

that what we are thinking is the same as what we thought an instant before, all reproduction in the series of representations would be in vain" (KPM, 126).[17] Hence, it follows, Heidegger claims, that the "reproductive synthesis should effect and maintain what it brings forth in unity with the being which is revealed directly in perception" (KPM, 126). However, the question remains as to what guides this process.

[W]hen the mind again returns from its going-back into the past, when it returns again to the directly present being in order to set the former in unity with the latter, who then tells it about what it previously abandoned, so to speak, with the fulfillment of the visualization? (KPM, 126)

Thus, the unity between the synthesis of reproduction and apprehension seems not yet to be fully accounted for; instead, they threaten to explode the whole of which they are structural parts into individual representations. Without a guiding sight, we seem to be left with two representations, one which is introduced by the synthesis of reproduction and which must be set into unity with one that is directly at hand. Thus, Heidegger asks, "what is the unity of apprehending intuition and reproducing imagination to be if what they want to present as unified and the same is, so to speak, placeless?" (KPM, 126–7).

Does this place first come to be created ... after the achievement of a perception and the recollection connected to it ... Or are these two ways of synthesis already oriented in advance towards the being as something which has presence in sameness? (KPM, 127)

In the case of the former, it would follow that the modes of synthesis in fact designate different syntheses rather than being modes of one and the same synthesis, which, in fact, would be the end of the notion of pure knowledge as a unity of pure intuition, pure imagination, and pure understanding. Thus, Heidegger goes on to claim that the two ways of synthesis are not unified by yet another synthesis, but instead are "already oriented in advance toward the being as something which has presence in sameness" (KPM, 127). They are so oriented because at the ground of both modes of synthesis, thus directing them, a "unifying (synthesis) of the being with respect to its sameness is already found" (KPM, 127).

This synthesis of the same, i.e., the holding of the being before us as one which is the same, Kant calls — and justly so — the synthesis "in concepts," for the concept is

---

[17] Kant, A103. R. Taft's translation.

indeed the representing unity which as selfsame "applies to many." (KPM, 127)[18]

In other words, the synthesis of recognition in a concept, the third synthesis, is in a way the first. This synthesis, Heidegger maintains, is aptly referred to by Kant as a reconnoitering.

It explores in advance and is "watching out for" what must be held before us in advance as the same in order that the apprehending and reproducing synthesis in general can find a closed circumscribed field of beings within which they can attach to what they bring forth and encounter, so to speak, and take them in stride as beings. (KPM, 127)

However, just as empirical reproduction presupposes the possibility of a bringing-forth-again, which is formed by pure reproduction, so does empirical recognition presuppose pure recognition, that is, a forming of the possibility of reconnoitering. This, Heidegger claims, implies the forming of "the horizon of being-able-to-hold something-before-us [*Vorhaltbarkeit*] in general" (KPM, 127), which, in turn, implies the temporal distinction of future. "As pure, its exploring is the original forming of this preliminary attaching [*Vorhaften*], i.e., the future. Thus, the third mode of synthesis also proves to be one which is essentially time-forming" (KPM, 127). Thus, although at the outset the synthesis of recognition seemed to resist any association with temporality, Heidegger has succeeded in exhibiting, not only the temporal character of the third synthesis, but also the priority of this mode of synthesis over apprehension and reproduction and hence "the most original essence of time, i.e., that it is developed primarily from the future" (KPM, 128). But, again, this priority is not of a kind that allows the former to appear independently of the latter; on the contrary, it is still a mode of synthesis, and hence it essentially belongs with apprehension and reproduction.

At this point, Heidegger sees himself as having proved the inner time-character of the transcendental power of imagination, and from this he concludes as follows:

If the transcendental power of imagination, as the pure, forming faculty, in itself forms time — i.e., allows time to spring forth — then we cannot avoid the thesis stated above: the transcendental power of imagination is original time. (KPM, 128)

We may add that if that is the case and it also holds that the analytic unity of apperception presupposes the synthetic unity of apperception, and that

---

[18] As a ground for this interpretation Heidegger quotes Kant, A 103: "For this *one* consciousness {representing this unity as conceptual representing} is what unifies the manifold, which is intuited again and again and which is then also reproduced, into one representation." R. Taft's translation; Heidegger's insertion of parenthesis.

original apperception is essentially related to the transcendental power of imagination, it follows that synthetic unity of apperception, that is, understanding itself, is a temporal unity. In other words, it follows that the ego or the self or the "I" does not have the identity of an object — temporality is the lifestyle of the ego, not spatiality. The transcendental "I" or ego has a horizon structure and is spread out in a matter of time. In the last part of this chapter, we shall see that this is also the definition of Dasein, but before we inquire into the analysis of temporality in BT, let us first have a look at another source of influence, namely Husserl's analysis of the temporality of the transcendental ego.

3. HUSSERL ON THE TEMPORALITY OF ABSOLUTE CONSCIOUSNESS

Although Heidegger portrays Kant as an advocate of his own conception of primordial time, and thus as his predecessor, and although he does not make any references to Husserl's analysis of time at all in BT,[19] he was undoubtedly familiar with this analysis and was aware that his own notion of time is highly related to that of Husserl. In what follows, we shall have a look at this possible Husserlian influence upon Heidegger.

Since there is no textual evidence to be found in Heidegger's writings concerning the importance of Husserl's analysis of temporality for his own analysis of time, we will have to approach this via other Husserlian concepts of which Heidegger admits to making use. In the introduction, we mentioned that those discoveries referred to by Heidegger as the decisive discoveries of Husserl's phenomenology — intentionality, categorial intuition, and the original sense of the apriori — are considered by him as indispensable for a proper investigation of time.[20] These discoveries, however, presuppose the theory of wholes and parts — incidently a theory to which Heidegger refers in a footnote wherein he discusses the "not-yet" character of Dasein's being. Thus, it seems as if Heidegger in fact holds the theory of wholes and parts to be of fundamental importance for his own investigation of temporality. A terminological survey of Heidegger discussion of temporality seems to support such a claim.

---

[19] He makes one discrete reference to time in relation to Husserl in a footnote towards the end of BT (note xxiii in Chapter Four of the second division). Here, Heidegger refers to Husserl's description of the phenomenon of sensory perception as temporal, but this is a reference to LI and not to Husserl's analysis of time. Another place Husserl is mentioned in relation to time is in a footnote that occurs during a discussion of the "not-yet" character of Dasein's being. Again, Heidegger does not refer to Husserl's analysis of time but, interestingly enough, to his theory of wholes and parts (note iii in Chapter One of the second division).

[20] Cf. HCT, 27.

As we have seen, the objective of Division Two of BT is to reformulate the structural moments of Dasein as temporal moments in order to account for their possibility of creating a unity. According to Heidegger, it is temporality that grounds the unity of Dasein's being.

> Temporality makes possible the unity of existence, facticity, and falling, and in this way constitutes primordially the structure of care. The moments of care [*Die Momente der Sorge*] have not been pieced together [*zusammengestückt*] cumulatively any more than temporality itself has been put together 'in the course of time' ["*mit der Zeit*"] out of the future, the having been, and the present. (BT, 376; translation altered)

Thus, it seems that temporality itself is a whole constituted of the temporal moments future, past, and present. In HCT, Heidegger maintains that in the "two structural moments of being-ahead-of-itself and already-being-involved-in, there is a puzzling character which is peculiar to care ... and [which] is nothing other than *time*" (HCT, 295). Likewise, in BP Heidegger talks about the "structural moments of expressed time" (BP, 261), "time-moment" (BP, 264), "how ... structural moments belong essentially to time" (BP, 264), and the "structural moments of now-time" (BP, 268). Hence, it seems quite obvious that the theory of wholes and parts is at least terminologically present in Heidegger's analysis of time. Given the importance of this theory for Heidegger's overall project, it is not unreasonable to assume that this is not merely a terminological presence.

This will become quite obvious if we analyze the distinction between world-time and primordial time suggested by Heidegger. As we remember, Heidegger introduces the ordinary conception of time as an endless series of "nows."

> [F]or the ordinary understanding of time, time shows itself as a sequence of "nows" which are constantly 'present-at-hand,' simultaneously passing away and coming along. Time is understood as a succession, as a 'flowing stream' of "nows," as the 'course of time.' (BT, 474)

According to this view, the phases or parts of time mutually exclude each other. The past is a now that is no more, the future is a now that is not yet, and the present is a now that is. Thus, the phases or parts of world-time present themselves as pieces, that is, as parts that can appear independently of one another. Not so with what Heidegger refers to as original time. According to the original concept of time, the phases or parts of time permeate each other to the point where they cannot appear independently of one another. In other words, the parts of original time present themselves as moments.

However, not only does Heidegger with this concept of original temporality implicitly make use of the theory of wholes and parts, but he also holds that the very distinction between pieces and moments is a temporal distinction. What characterizes pieces is that they can appear temporally independently of each other, that is, before and after one another. Moments, on the other hand, are parts that cannot appear temporally independent of each other. They are parts in the sense that they are distinct, but they cannot appear before or after one another.

Now, if it is the case that the theory of wholes and parts is the very foundation of Husserlian phenomenology, then it also follows that it is the foundation of Husserl's analysis of time. In other words, it seems that the same theory that founds Husserl's investigation of time also permeates Heidegger's investigation of this phenomenon. It should come as no surprise, then, that the outcome of these investigations seems to be quite similar. It is our contention that even if Heidegger does not refer to Husserl's phenomenology of the consciousness of internal time, and, indeed, even if he was not influenced by this specific investigation (which, we may add, is highly unlikely), there is still textual evidence suggesting that Heidegger was influenced by what in fact produced this investigation. We may therefore conclude that Heidegger's theory is at least on the same track as that of Husserl. For this reason, we find it important to introduce Husserl's phenomenology of the consciousness of internal time before we proceed to Heidegger's analysis of temporality.

The concept of intentionality situates consciousness in the world without thereby reducing it to *res extensa*. Given the fact that objects and objectivity are considered correlates to subjective acts, it follows that subjectivity itself — as a condition of possibility of these acts — cannot be given as an object in the world. This subjectivity is a transcendental subjectivity. It is our argument that although this is a distinction not explicitly attended to in LI, it is nevertheless implicit in Husserl's distinctions between pieces and moments. His claim that, although independent in one sense, the former is not independent in the sense that it can be torn out of the unity of consciousness, fully suggests the presence of a transcendental perspective in Husserl's early phenomenology.

Husserl's analysis of time[21] brings this tacit transcendentalism to the fore

---

[21] Husserl, *On the Phenomenology of the Consciousness of Internal Time*, translated by J.B. Brough (Dordrecht, Boston, London: Kluwer Academic Publishers, 1991), hereafter PCT. *Zur Phänomenologie des inneren Zeitbewusstseins*, The Hague, 1966. Husserl's analysis of time was originally carried out in the years following the publication of LI but it did not appear before 1928. Husserl also worked out two other manuscripts dedicated to the theme of time — the "Bernauer" or "L" manuscripts from the early twenties and "C" manuscripts from the late twenties and early thirties — but they both remain unpublished.

as it presents a dimension referred to as absolute consciousness. Whereas in LI the central distinctions were kept within the frame of inner temporal objects, Husserl's writings on time introduce a distinction that goes beyond this sphere by describing the transcendence of retentional and protentional awareness in inner time. We shall also see that instead of time being just another object constituted in the thematic field of transcendental subjectivity, it is structurally associated with the latter.

The purpose of this section is not to provide an accurate in-depth presentation of Husserl's analysis of time but rather to outline briefly the way in which he temporalizes the condition of possibility of objectivity.[22] According to phenomenological orthodoxy as presented by Husserl, to be is to be constituted, and that also applies to time. Objective time is constituted time and the parts of a temporal object are the now-phase, the coming phase, and the just-elapsed phase. Hence, the givenness of temporal properties presupposes subjective acts. In this sense, subjectivity, instead of having coordinates in time like an object, in fact coordinates time. However, there is more to subjectivity than being merely the totality of acts. Not only are the objective correlates of straightforward acts of perception temporal objects. The acts themselves are also temporal objects, but these are, as opposed to transcendent temporal objects, inner temporal objects. The latter are the correlates of acts of reflection, and hence it follows that the set of inner temporal objects does not provide an exhaustive description of subjectivity. This dimension of reflection introduces a surplus which transcends the notion of immanence introduced in LI. It is a new dimension of nonobjective immanence which Husserl calls absolute consciousness and which is a condition of possibility of all forms of reflection. Although an intentional act can appear as an inner temporal object, it would be a mistake to claim that it originates in the flux of inner temporal objects — an object cannot constitute another object. An intentional act must have a non-objective origin, and this origin is a non-objective immanence whose structure makes possible the emergence of inner temporal objects. In order to further qualify these two different notions of immanence, it will be helpful to distinguish between a sequential and a non-sequential concept of temporality. While the former characterizes the temporality of inner temporal objects, the latter characterizes the temporality of absolute consciousness.

Husserl distinguishes between objective time, subjective time, and the absolute flow of inner time-consciousness. These are related to one another

[22] There are numerous studies of Husserl's investigation of internal time-consciousness. This outline is especially indebted to the view J.B. Brough presents in his article "The Emergence of an Absolute Consciousness in Husserl's Early Writings on Time-Consciousness," *Man and World* V, 1972, 298–326, and in the introduction to his translation of PCT.

in an abstract-concrete chain leading to an absolute *concretum* which is absolute consciousness. Since the appearance of a transcendent object presupposes the givenness of that to which an appearance can appear, that is, an act, it follows that subjective time (inner temporal objects), is a *concretum* for objective time. However, given the fact that acts are precisely inner temporal objects, it also follows that these are, although concrete in relation to transcendent objects, still abstract in another direction. Inner temporal objects are abstract in relation to the absolute flow of inner time-consciousness. This latter *concretum* in an absolute *concretum*. Thus, the final absolute *concretum* in Husserl's phenomenology is a temporally constituted unity.

As we pointed out above, given the fact that one can experience inner temporal objects through reflection, it follows that these do not provide an exhaustive description of subjectivity. There seems to be a surplus which transcends the sphere of immanence constituted by inner temporal objects, and this surplus is the sens*ing*, the experienc*ing*. In other words, the surplus is the activity itself which is what emerges if one approaches an act not as something already constituted, i.e., as an inner temporal object, but as an act, as constitut*ing*. Indeed, for an act to be an inner temporal object it must already be an act. Thus, the entities constituting the set of inner temporal objects, that is, objective immanence, and those that constitute non-objective immanence are in a sense the same phenomena, but differently regarded. In the case of the former, the acts are regarded qua objects; in the case of the latter, the acts are regarded qua acts.

Husserl discerns these phenomena by distinguishing between the temporality of an inner temporal object and the temporal dimension of absolute consciousness. Whereas the former has temporal phases such as "now," "just-past," and "not-yet," the latter is a whole consisting of the three temporal moments primal impression, retention, and protention. Although the latter moments are temporal structures, they make up a non-sequential temporality. They are correlated to the temporal phases in the sense that impression relates to the "now" phase, retention to the "just-past" phase and protention to the "not-yet" phase, but this correlation differs from ordinary correlations in that one cannot use the language of sequential temporality in order to describe it. As moments of a whole, the retentional-impressional-protentional constituents include rather than exclude each other, but one cannot say that they are simultaneous without making an incoherent appeal to sequential temporality. The structural make-up of the condition of possibility of sequential temporality cannot itself be described in terms of sequential temporality. Nor can one say that primal impression is simultaneous with the now-phase, that retention is just-past primal impression or that protention is not-yet to be. The retentional-impressional-protentional consciousness simply make up the framework — the primal flux — within which sequential temporality can take place. This framework cannot itself be sequential, and it would be a mistake to locate the sequential temporal phases on the same level as the temporal moments of absolute consciousness that make up this framework.

Thus, although Husserl refers to the retentional-impressional-protentional primal flux as the "living present," this is not an entity that is present "now." This is a retentional-impressional-protentional presence within which sequential time can make itself manifest as an essential moment of objective correlates.

4. ANTICIPATORY RESOLUTENESS

Heidegger introduces his investigation of temporality with a discussion which in fact recapitulates the analysis of chapters one and two of the second division of BT. The issue of pre-ontological confirmation is yet to be fully resolved. Before he can attempt to lay bare the temporal constitution of, and hence the full meaning of Dasein as an absolute *concretum*, he must be able to provide a phenomenal basis for such an endeavor. And that amounts to calling attention to a situation in which this full meaning announces itself.

As we indicated above in our brief treatment of Husserl's analysis of time, the difference between the sphere of objective immanence and non-objective immanence was that in the case of the latter the acts are approached as acts, that is, as sens*ing*, as experienc*ing*. However, it could be argued that this notion in fact does not make a whole lot of sense. It is one thing to claim that we can reflect on our acts, thus turning previous acts into inner objects; it is another to suggest that we can reflect on reflection without turning it into an object. Admittedly, we can infer from the fact that we can reflect on our thoughts to the notion of a non-objective immanence, but this is an approach that is not acceptable for phenomenology. Phenomenology is a descriptive enterprise, and hence it cannot very well introduce an inferential argument at the very foundation of accounting for its own possibility. It has to provide a phenomenal basis and Heidegger is very much aware of this requirement. Heidegger saw clearly the necessity of providing every step in the development of an ontology with a pre-ontological confirmation. The concept of anticipatory resoluteness is the last stop in that regard. *"Temporality gets experienced in a phenomenally primordial way in Dasein's authentic Being-a-whole, in the phenomenon of anticipatory resoluteness"* (BT, 351). Anticipatory resoluteness is a way in which

Dasein's potentiality-for-Being-a-whole has existentiell authenticity and thus in this situation "temporality gets experienced in a phenomenally primordial way" (BT, 351).

We have already discussed the terms 'anticipation' and 'resoluteness' but we have not treated them together as one concept. In order to do this, let us first briefly recall our previous discussion of each term. 'Anticipation' is a technical term which was introduced in relation to the possibility of an authentic Being-towards-death. Anticipation does not tend towards actualization but rather to a coming closer to it as a possibility — and thus away from it as something actual. According to Heidegger, the "*closest closeness which one may have in Being towards death as a possibility, is as far as possible from anything actual*" (BT, 306-7). Anticipation designates this kind of being towards; it leaves the possible as possible and the more thoroughly it is grasped as a possibility "the more purely does the understanding penetrate into it *as the possibility of the impossibility of any existence at all*" (BT, 307).

Death, as possibility, gives Dasein nothing to be 'actualized,' nothing which Dasein, as actual, could itself *be*. It is the possibility of the impossibility of every way of comporting oneself towards anything, of every way of existing. (BT, 307)

Thus, Heidegger maintains, "Being-towards-death is the anticipation of a potentiality-for-Being of that entity whose kind of Being is anticipation itself" (BT, 307). "Anticipation turns out to be the possibility of understanding one's *ownmost* and uttermost potentiality-for-Being — that is to say, the possibility of *authentic existence*" (BT, 307). While the term 'anticipation' designates what authentic Being-towards-death amounts to, the term 'resoluteness' is more oriented towards an existentiell attestation of such a being.

Let us briefly recall Heidegger's argument. The project of existential analytic presupposes the possibility of bringing Dasein's being into the view as a whole. This, in turn, presupposes the possibility of Being-a-whole, and this, Heidegger claims, finds its true expression in Being-towards-death. As we have just seen, anticipation designates this Being-towards-death. Now, at this stage we are, so to speak, still at a conceptual stage in the analysis of authenticity. We have yet to enter the realm of existentiell attestation. Instead, we have ascertained what, if possible, authenticity would have to be like. With the introduction of the term 'resoluteness' we enter this realm. As we may recall from the analysis in the previous chapter, Heidegger calls attention to a marginal experience which exhibits the structure of anticipation described in relation to Being-towards-death. This being is a "holding on to anxiety" which Heidegger terminologically designates as wanting to have conscience. Wanting to have conscience, in turn, is an existentiell choosing referred to as resoluteness. Thus, resoluteness is not something in addition to anticipation, and hence anticipatory resoluteness is not the addition or connection of two different ways of being. Rather, resoluteness is the appearance of anticipation. Thus, Heidegger says, "only *as anticipating* does resoluteness become a primordial Being towards Dasein's ownmost potentiality-for-Being" (BT, 354). He concludes:

We have now shown that anticipation is not just a fictitious possibility which we have forced upon Dasein; it is a *mode* of an existentiell potentiality-for-Being that is attested in Dasein — a mode which Dasein exacts of itself, if indeed it authentically understands itself as resolute. Anticipation 'is' not some kind of free-floating behavior, but must be conceived as *the possibility of the authenticity of that resoluteness which has been attested in an existentiell way — a possibility hidden in such resoluteness, and thus attested therewith.* (BT, 357)

Now, even if he has succeeded in providing the possibility of Being-a-whole with a phenomenal basis, Heidegger emphasizes that it would be impossible to transform this into a theoretical proof. Indeed, such an attempt would be a misunderstanding. What is brought to the fore is the condition of possibility for any kind of intentional directedness, practical as well as theoretical, and hence the latter, intentional directedness, cannot be appealed to in order to prove the former. Thus, a pre-ontological confirmation is not the construction of a proof; it is a descriptive articulation of a pre-ontological understanding of our being.

With the articulation of the phenomenon of anticipatory resoluteness, Heidegger considers the task of providing his existential analytic with the necessary foundation to have succeeded. Thus, he can now proceed and inquire into the full meaning of care.

In its anticipatory resoluteness, Dasein has now been made phenomenologically visible with regard to its possible authenticity and totality. The hermeneutical Situation which was previously inadequate for interpreting the meaning of the Being of care, now has the required primordiality. (BT, 358)

The hermeneutical situation Heidegger refers to is the one outlined in the introduction to the second division of BT which emphasized the seemingly impossible task of giving an account of the being of a being whose being is care. Existential analysis seemed to preclude the possibility of grasping Dasein's being as a whole precisely by introducing the very notion of Dasein's being as care. In other words, the outcome of existential analysis seemed to suggest the impossibility of such an endeavor. Heidegger's approach to this problem is an attempt, not to escape it or explain it away, but in fact to make it a part of the project of existential analytic. Existential analytic thus attempts to face the fundamental problem of transcendental philosophy by taking seriously the circular nature of seeking to understand understanding. It does so by approaching it by way of evidence rather than inference and, hence, it faces the following problem: by its very nature everyday understanding is destined to misunderstand itself, and yet there must be possible to call attention to a situation in which understanding sees itself and understands itself. Anxiety represents the kind of marginal experience in which understanding announces itself to itself, and anticipatory resoluteness is the response that holds on to what is given to understand. According to Heidegger, in the case of the latter, understanding has fallen victim to violence in the sense that it has been cut off from the world and forced back on itself, but this violence is not one that has its origin in a worldless subject. Firstly, as we may recall, Heidegger himself retrospectively pointed out that, "the resoluteness intended in *Being and Time* is not the deliberate action of a subject,"[23] and, secondly, that which Dasein is forced back on is Being-in-the-world and what brought it there is precisely Being-in-the-world. The possibility of anticipatory resoluteness is a marginal experience in which the being of Dasein announces itself, and it announces itself as something of which Dasein already has an understanding. Hence, the project of existential analytic adopts, rather than escapes, the circularity and makes it an essential part of Dasein's being. According to the project of existential analytic, Dasein has a circular being and the challenge is to leap into this circle.

To deny the circle, to make a secret of it, or even to want to overcome it, means finally to reinforce this failure [the misunderstanding of understanding]. We must rather endeavor to leap into the 'circle,' primordially and wholly, so that even at the start of the analysis of Dasein we make sure that we have a full view of Dasein's circular Being. (BT, 363)

According to Heidegger, trying to do away with the circle is exactly what characterizes the traditional misunderstanding of Dasein. This approach leave us with a static thing-like entity which is either conceived of as an object in the world or as something that has to get hooked up with the world. In both cases, Heidegger claims, "we have 'presupposed' not too much, but *too little*" (BT, 363).

Anticipatory resoluteness has cleared up the hermeneutical situation by providing a way into the circle, and by doing so it has justified the existential analytic by virtue of which we could arrive at this concept in the first place. We have thus seen, Heidegger points out, that "the care-structure does not speak *against* the possibility of Being-a-whole but is the *condition for the*

---

[23] In "The Origin of the Work of Art", in *Poetry, Language, Thought*, 67.

possibility of such an existentiell potentiality-for-Being" (BT, 365). At this point, Heidegger considers the task of providing the necessary phenomenal basis to have been completed. He can now go back to the concept of care and inquire about the full meaning of the being of Dasein and thus account for the unity of this phenomenon. He initiates this endeavor by asking "[h]ow are we to conceive this unity? How can Dasein exist as a unity in the ways and possibilities of its Being which we have mentioned?" (BT, 365). He answers:

Manifestly, it can so exist only in such a way that it *is itself* this Being in its essential possibilities — that in each case *I* am this entity. The 'I' seems to 'hold together' the totality of the structural whole. In the 'ontology' of this entity, the 'I' and the 'Self' have been conceived from the earliest times as the supporting ground (as substance or subject). (BT, 365)

Again we see that, on the one hand, Heidegger associates the entity holding together the unity with the 'I' and, on the other hand, he wants to disassociate it from what has traditionally been known as the subject. We have repeatedly argued that Heidegger's intent is not to do away with subjectivity as such but rather to reinterpret the subjective perspective and do away with a notion of subjectivity that is in conflict with the phenomena. The notion of subjectivity Heidegger rejects is the notion of a thing-like entity whose apriori status has exiled it in to worldlessness. This notion of the subject as a thing that is not in the world is replaced with a Being-in-the-world that is not a thing. According to this interpretation of the being we ourselves are, it follows, Heidegger maintains, that "'I'-hood and Selfhood must be understood *existentially*" (BT, 365). That is, the self or the 'I' is not to be understood as a thing-like entity given prior to the world, but rather as something which appears as that to which appearances appear. Understanding the self existentially implies approaching it from the definition of Dasein as existence, according to which the self is neither a thing-like entity contained in consciousness, nor something other than the act in the sense that it can appear independently of it. Rather, the self is the act qua act, the actualiz*ing* in itself, and not some additional entity. Hence, the relation between self and care is not one in which care is founded upon the self, but neither is it so that the concept of self-constancy is secondary to the concept of care. The distinction between care and "I"-hood or selfhood is instead comparable to Kant's distinction between synthetic and analytic unity of apperception. The latter presupposes the former, and the former gives the full meaning of the latter.

Care does not need to be founded in a Self. But existentiality, as constitutive for care, provides the ontological constitution of Dasein's Self-constancy, to which there belongs, in accordance with the full structural content of care, its Being-fallen factically into non-Self-constancy. (BT, 370)

Thus, it is care that provides the ontological constitution of Dasein's self-constancy. By virtue of having this constitution everyday Dasein is not directed towards its own constitution but rather away from itself towards what is other. It is precisely the constitution of the peculiar self-constancy belonging to Dasein that turns it away from its ownmost being towards objects. Dasein's way of having itself is thus not a matter of being directed at this self, but away from it. In short, Dasein is non-positionally aware of itself.

5. TEMPORALITY

Heidegger introduces his discussion of the meaning of care by clarifying what the term 'meaning' signifies in this context. This term occupies an enormously significant place in Heidegger's fundamental ontology whose expressed goal is precisely to pose and answer the question of the meaning of being. The first step of this endeavor is the existential analytic which seeks to work out the question concerning the meaning of the being who grasps meaning, that is, the being we ourselves are. We are now about to reach the summit in regard to this objective in the sense that temporality is to be introduced as the ontological meaning of care.

According to Heidegger, in his investigation thus far the term 'meaning' has been has been encountered "in connection with the analysis of understanding and interpretation" (BT, 370).

[A]ccording to that analysis, meaning is that wherein the understandability [*Verstehbarkeit*] of something maintains itself — even that of something which does not come into view explicitly and thematically. "Meaning" signifies the "upon-which" [*das Woraufhin*] of a primary projection in terms of which something can be conceived in its possibility as that which it is." (BT, 370-1)

Since a projection is always a disclosing of possibilities, it follows that the laying bare of the "upon-which" in fact is a disclosing of a condition of possibility. In other words, the term 'meaning' in the context of the meaning of care refers to the condition of possibility of care. This, in turn, implies inquiring into what constitutes this being as Being-a-whole.

We already know that the phenomenon of care is constituted by the following equiprimordial structural moments: understanding, situatedness, and discourse. However, what has yet to be disclosed is what holds these together. Care is not merely a heap composed of pieces, it is a whole and what makes it a whole is not yet another part. The parts of the structural whole care are moments, and hence it follows that what constitutes this whole as a whole ontologically precedes the appearance of these parts. In other words, what constitutes this whole as a whole also gives the full meaning of its moments. Thus, the inquiry into the meaning of care is in fact an investigation of what constitutes this whole as a unity.

When we inquire about the meaning of care, we are asking *what makes possible the totality of the articulated structural whole of care, in the unity of its articulation as we have unfolded it*. (BT, 371)

When, in anticipatory resoluteness Dasein faces its ownmost being, this authentic Being-a-whole is characterized by a *"Being-towards* one's ownmost, distinctive potentiality-for-Being" (BT, 372). This is, Heidegger claims, only possible on the basis of a certain kind of temporality.

This letting-itself-*come-towards*-itself in that distinctive possibility which it puts up with, is the primordial phenomenon of the *future as coming towards*" (BT, 372). ... If either authentic or inauthentic *Being-towards-death* belongs to Dasein's Being, then such Being-towards-death is possible only as something *futural* [als *zukünftiges*].(BT, 372–3)

However, in this context the term 'future' or 'futural' should not be understood sequentially and thus as something that is not yet now. According to Heidegger, by the term 'futural' "we do not here have in view a 'now' which has *not yet* become 'actual' and which sometimes *will be* for the first time" (BT, 373). The term 'futural' should be understood, not as a not yet now, but as something Dasein is. Dasein *is* essentially a coming towards itself, and only for that reason is anticipation possible. Hence, this non-sequential notion of future as being-futural is the full meaning of the structural moment understanding or existentiality.

However, by being a being-towards its ownmost being it also follows that "anticipatory resoluteness understands Dasein in its own essential Being-guilty" (BT, 373). This understanding amounts to taking over something one already is in the sense that in anticipatory resoluteness Dasein is what it already was. In other words, anticipatory resoluteness, as a coming towards itself, implies an aspect of past, of having been. But, as was the case with future, this notion of past cannot be understood sequentially. Just as the future had to be understood in terms of being-futural, so must the past be understood in terms of something Dasein is.

Taking over thrownness, however, is possible only in such a way that the futural Dasein can *be* its ownmost 'as-it-already-was' — that is to say, its 'been' [*sein "Gewesen"*]. Only in so far as Dasein *is* as an "I-*am*- as-having-been," can Dasein come towards itself futurally in such a way that it comes back. (BT, 373)

Thus, having-been designates a way in which Dasein is rather than something Dasein is no longer. Moreover, it is intrinsically related to being futural in the sense that the latter implies the former. "The character of 'having been' arises," Heidegger claims, "in a certain way, from the future" (BT, 373).

However, not only does anticipatory resoluteness disclose Dasein as coming back to itself futurally; by doing so resoluteness also "brings itself into the Situation by making present" (BT, 374).

The character of "having been" arises from the future, and in such a way that the future which "has been" (or better, which "is in the process of having been") releases itself from the Present. (BT, 374)

Thus, in anticipatory resoluteness Dasein presents to itself its ownmost being. That is, it presents its own presencing nature and the latter discloses itself as a unity of being-futural and having been. Heidegger designates this unity as temporality (*Zeitlichkeit*) and, he concludes,

[o]nly in so far as Dasein has the definite character of temporality, is the authentic potentiality-for-Being-a-whole of anticipatory resoluteness, as we have described it, made possible for Dasein itself. *Temporality reveals itself as the meaning of authentic care.* (BT, 374)

Heidegger goes to great lengths to assure that 'temporality' is a technical term and thus should not be confused with an ordinary conception of time and the corresponding temporal phases of past, present, and future. The same holds for conceptions of time as subjective, objective, transcendent, and immanent. According to Heidegger, then, temporality is radically different from the ordinary conception of time, according to which time is an infinite series of nows. Heidegger seems to make a distinction that closely resembles the one Husserl makes between the living present and the realm of inner temporal objects and transcendent temporal objects. Both distinguish between a non-objective immanence on the one hand and temporal objects on the other, and both maintain that the former has a non-sequential temporal constitution. Moreover, both agree that sequential temporality is a derivative phenomenon which has its origin in non-objective immanence which, in accordance to Heidegger's terminology, is constituted by temporality. Thus, it is our contention that Heidegger's concept of Dasein and Husserl's concept of absolute consciousness have the same temporal constitution. This kinship will become even clearer as we investigate more thoroughly the constitution of Dasein.

Heidegger distinguishes between inauthentic and authentic temporality.[24] Although the former is considered a genuine phenomenon it is still a derivative one. Again, we see that Heidegger does not consider what is inauthentic less genuine. What distinguishes inauthenticity from authenticity is simply that while the former cannot account for itself, the latter can. That is, the latter can account for the former. Hence, an authentic phenomenon is not something radically different from and independent of its inauthentic counterpart; it is simply what provides the full meaning of the latter.

It has been Heidegger's systematic approach throughout BT to proceed from our actual directedness towards the world — including things, other human beings and, indeed, our own self — to the meaning of this directedness. The meaning here pertains to what accounts for, or what constitutes, the directedness. This is what the interplay between the ontical and the ontological amounts to in Heidegger's phenomenology, and this interplay is structured according to the relation between *abstracta* and *concreta*. Every step in BT has taken its point of departure in an ontical phenomenon and has then proceeded to an ontological level, which has always been a whole of which the original ontical phenomenon is a moment and thus which can account for it. We have seen this procedure carried out in relation to the two constituting ontological entities of modern metaphysics: subjects and objects; *res cogitans* and *res extensa*. Just as an object cannot account for itself but must be understood from the point of view of Being-in-the-world, so too is the concept of subject traced back to Being-in-the-world. The phenomenon of Being-in-the-world, in turn, finds its expression in Dasein's existence, whose meaning is care, and, as we have seen, whose meaning again is temporality. At this point, we have reached the last stage of the existential analytic. Temporality is the final *concretum*.[25]

Now, even if temporality is a *concretum* for care it does not thereby follow that we have discovered yet another phenomenon residing beyond care. Rather temporality brings out the full meaning of care. Thus, temporality has in fact been in view all along, although not thematically.

Dasein's totality of Being as care means: ahead-of-itself-already-being-in (a world) as Being-alongside (entities encountered within-the-world). When we first fixed this

---

[24] Husserl does the same in his analysis of the consciousness of internal time. The distinction between a proper (*Eigentlich*) and a nonproper (*Uneigentlich*) is discussed throughout this analysis. See, for instance, PCT, 5, 9, 17, 57, 219, 248, 276.

[25] By claiming that temporality is the final and absolute *concretum* we are not forcing a specific terminology, and thereby also its content, upon Heidegger. Admittedly, Heidegger does not claim that temporality is an absolute *concretum*, but his dependence upon the theory of wholes and parts is so obvious that we feel we can legitimately apply its terminology on Heidegger even when he does use it himself. It is hard to see what distinguishes Heidegger's notion of a primordial phenomenon from an absolute *concretum*.

articulated structure, we suggested that with regard to this articulation the ontological question must be pursued still further back until the unity of the totality of this structural manifoldness has been laid bare. *The primordial unity of the structure of care lies in temporality.* (BT, 375)

Heidegger emphasizes the non-sequential nature of temporality, thus distinguishing it from the traditional and derivative concept of time. For instance, the ahead-of-itself is grounded in future, but future in this context does not designate something that is not yet now. The same goes for the "already" which, although grounded in the past, does not signify something "no longer now."

If the expressions 'before' and 'already' were to have a time-oriented [*zeithafte*] signification such as *this* [not yet and no longer] (and they can have this signification too) then to say that care has temporality would be to say that it is something which is 'earlier' and 'later,' 'not yet' and 'no longer.' Care would then be conceived as an entity which occurs and runs its course 'in time.' (BT, 375)

Accordingly, care would be reduced to something present-at-hand and hence it could not account for its own unity. If the structural moments "ahead-of" and "already" are conceived of as grounded in a sequential or linear "not yet" and "no longer" then they would cease to be moments. Sequentially understood the "not yet" and the "no longer" are mutually exclusive, and thus they cannot be defined as moments. For moments are defined precisely as the opposite, as mutually inclusive. Such an interpretation would sabotage the entire existential analytic and would reintroduce the impossible choice of modern metaphysics: either you situate subjectivity outside the world in order to rescue freedom and knowledge, at the cost of having to explain how this subjectivity ever gets hooked up with the world, or you leave subjectivity within the world, at the expense of having no means to distinguish it from other entities within the world. In the case of the former, knowledge and freedom seem to be ideally possible, but hardly in this world; in the case of the latter, they are impossible in any world. This choice is exactly what phenomenology seeks to get beyond. Temporality — in Heidegger's technical meaning of this term — is what ultimately grounds this endeavor.

Thus, the structural moment "ahead-of" is before or futural in a nonsequential sense of this term; it designates, not something that is not yet, but something which Dasein in every case is.

The 'before' and the 'ahead' indicate the future as of a sort which would make it possible for Dasein to be such that its potentiality-for-Being is an issue. Self-projection upon the 'for-the-sake-of-oneself' is grounded in the future and is an essential characteristic of *existentiality. The primary meaning of existentiality is the future.* (BT, 375-6)

Likewise, the structural moment "already-in" has a temporal meaning that is non-linear. That is, the "already-in" implies the past, but not as something that is no longer now, but as something which Dasein is.

> Only because care is based on the character of "having been," can Dasein exist as the thrown entity which it is. 'As long as' Dasein factically exists, it is never past [*vergangen*], but it always is indeed as already having *been*, in the sense of the "I *am*-as-having-been." And only as long as Dasein is, *can* it *be* as having been. (BT, 376)

Thus, Heidegger claims, "the primary existential meaning of facticity lies in the character of "having been"" (BT, 376).

The full meaning of the structural moments of existentiality and facticity, then, is indicated by the temporal terms 'before' and 'already.' These are intrinsically bound together in the sense that they do not appear independently of one another. In anticipatory resoluteness, this temporal meaning of the structural moments of care discloses itself as a unity. Resoluteness is futural in the sense that it is a Being-towards-death through which Dasein's ownmost being is disclosed, but this is by the same token a "having been" in the sense that in authentic Being-towards-death Dasein is what it already was. However, we have yet to indicate the temporality of the third structural moment of care, the being-alongside (*sein-bei*) which falls.

In anticipatory resoluteness, Dasein is given to understand its ownmost being, that is, it has "brought itself back from falling, and has done so precisely in order to be more authentically 'there' in 'the moment of *insight*' [*Augenblick*]" (BT, 376). This moment of insight is a seeing and thus the adequate temporal expression is "present." But this is a presence which is not a now-phase. What is given to understand in anticipatory resoluteness is not an object; what is given to understand is understanding itself, that is, the act qua act. What is made present in anticipatory resoluteness is presencing itself; what appears is appearance, and this appears as the original amalgamation of "being futural" and "having been." In the moment of insight, understanding appears to itself in a manner which discloses that it is always already its own end, and hence has the structure of temporality.

> Temporality makes possible the unity of existence, facticity, and falling, and in this way constitutes primordially the totality of the structure of care. The moments of care have not been pieced together cumulatively any more than temporality itself has been put together 'in the course of time' [*"mit der Zeit"*] out of future, the having been, and the Present. (BT, 376)

Again, we see that Heidegger emphasizes the nature of the structural moments as moments and thus the whole — care — as an original, or apriori whole, that is, as something that is not pieced together. Only as temporality is such a whole possible.

Temporality has a measure of primacy over care in the sense that it provides the full meaning of the latter, but temporality is not something that can appear prior to Dasein. Rather, temporality is "the primordial '*outside-of-itself*' *in and for itself*" (BT, 377).

We therefore call the phenomena of the future, the character of having been, and the Present, the "*ecstases*" of temporality. Temporality is not, prior to this, an entity which first emerges from *itself*; its essence is a process of temporalizing in the unity of ecstases. (BT, 377)

The term 'ecstasis' (*Ekstase*) has its origin in the Greek *ekstasis*, whose root-meaning is standing (*stasis*) out or outside (*ek*), and it also has the same root as existence. Existence, as we remember, is a relating to one's own being which essentially implies a standing out in, or being-in, the world, and ecstases designate the structural aspects, or moments, of this standing out.

According to Heidegger, the being of Dasein is care. Care finds its meaning in temporality, and temporality is constituted by the three non-sequential temporal ecstases the future, the having been, and the present. The latter are moments of temporality which, in turn, is the only absolute *concretum*. It is difficult to detect a radical difference between this interpretation of Dasein and Husserl's notion of absolute consciousness. It is our contention that Heidegger's concept of Dasein and Husserl's concept of absolute consciousness simply have the same temporal constitution. They both designate non-objective immanence and both have the temporality of *phronesis*. The most conspicuous difference seems to be the fact that Heidegger provides his analysis with the necessary pre-ontological confirmation, and that is a very significant difference. Heidegger goes to great lengths to comply with the phenomenological demand for phenomenal basis and is quite possibly the phenomenologist who takes most seriously the full meaning of the decree *zu den Sachen Selbst*. Each step of the existential analysis has been accompanied by a pre-ontological confirmation, each structural moment has been provided with the appearance of a *concretum*, which in turn has been justified by another *concretum*. The ultimate *concretum* of Division One was the concept of care, which announced itself in anxiety, the ultimate *concretum* of Division Two is temporality, and this final *concretum* announces itself with anticipatory resoluteness. The latter *concretum* provides the full meaning of the *concretum* disclosed in the preparatory fundamental analysis of Division One.

At this stage of his existential analysis, Heidegger starts going the opposite direction in order to show that temporality is not merely a product of authenticity but in fact is the full meaning of Dasein's being both in its authentic and inauthentic modes of existence. Indeed, temporality is indifferent between the former and the latter.[26] The difference between authenticity and inauthenticity is not temporality; the difference is simply that the former brings to the fore the full meaning of the latter, which is temporality.

6. REPEATING THE EXISTENTIAL ANALYSIS

The investigation of subjectivity differs from any other kind of investigation in that the entity investigated is precisely the entity investiga*ting*. And if it is the case that the former has a specific structure, this structure is already had by the latter. In other words, for an investigation of the being of human being it would follow that the method used and the ontology sought in fact are one and the same. Furthermore, the former is not justified until the latter is disclosed. This sets up a hermeneutical situation from which the philosopher cannot, and therefore should not, try to escape. Heidegger is aware of this, and he is aware to the point that it is reflected in the very architecture of BT.

If temporality is the full meaning of the being of Dasein, one could inquire as to why Heidegger waits so long before he introduces it, or at least why he introduces a notion of the being of Dasein in Division One that is not the final one. Care cannot account for itself, rather it finds its full meaning in temporality. The reason for this cautious step-by-step process is the consideration mentioned above. Although temporality provides the full meaning of Dasein's being as care, Heidegger could not simply have introduced it at the end of his analysis of everydayness. At this stage of the analysis, he could not methodologically account for this insight. Temporality could only be introduced as it announces itself, and that does not take place in everydayness. The farthest one gets at the stage of everydayness is that everyday Dasein is not the whole story but in fact hides its ownmost being from itself. Towards the end of the first division this being is disclosed as care, but after confirming the possibility of care knowing itself is it possible to go on to investigate the full meaning of this phenomenon. This is done as Heidegger returns to the structures discussed in the first division and discloses their temporal status.

In what follows, we shall have a brief look at Heidegger's discussion of

[26] This point is well taken by W.D. Blattner, "Existential Temporality in *Being and Time* (Why Heidegger is not a Pragmatist)," *Heidegger: A Critical Reader*, Edited by H. Dreyfus and H. Hall (Cambridge: Blackwell, 1992), 99–129.

the intrinsic temporality of all the basic phenomena introduced in the first division. Although Heidegger carries out this investigation in great detail, we limit ourselves to a more general presentation of his argument. Our objective is to show that originary temporality is not reserved for authenticity but in fact is indifferent with regard to authenticity and inauthenticity. This is clearly indicated as Heidegger systematically distinguishes between authentic and inauthentic temporality in relation to the phenomena discussed. Heidegger takes his point of departure in a discussion of the temporality of disclosedness and thus of the existentials understanding, situatedness, falling, and discourse. The temporal interpretation of these existentials has already been suggested; what is now considered is their relation to inauthentic time. In the case of understanding, we have indicated that its temporal structure is ahead of, or being futural. "The future makes ontologically possible an entity which is in such a way that it exists understandingly in its potentiality-for-Being. Projection is basically futural" (BT, 385). In referring to authentic future, Heidegger reserved the term 'anticipation,' but, by claiming that "factically, Dasein is constantly ahead of itself, but inconstantly anticipatory with regard to its existentiell possibility" (BT, 386), he acknowledges that the temporality of Dasein is not exhausted by anticipation. Anticipation is rather a mode of future in which Dasein sees itself in its ownmost being. Another, and far more common mode of future, is inauthentic future and this "future has the character of *awaiting*" (BT, 386). Inauthentic future is the future of everyday understanding where Dasein is oblivious to its ownmost being. We shall refrain from a more detailed analysis of Heidegger's description of the concept of awaiting and simply conclude that originary temporality is a condition of the possibility of this understanding, just as it is a condition of possibility for understanding this understanding.

In relation to the structural moment situatedness, Heidegger presents a somewhat similar argument in the sense that he introduces both inauthentic and authentic having been. However, this is done by investigating the temporality of fear and anxiety, where the former represents inauthentic temporality and the latter authentic temporality. According to Heidegger, moods are impossible except on the basis of temporality, but they can "have different sources with regard to their own temporalization in the temporality of care" (BT, 395). "Anxiety springs from the *future* of resoluteness, while fear springs from the lost Present, of which fear is fearfully apprehensive, so that it falls prey to it more than ever" (BT, 395). Regarding the temporality of fear, Heidegger says that it "is a forgetting which awaits and makes present" (BT, 392), and this takes "its orientation from what we encounter within-the-world" (BT, 392). However, although the temporality of fear is one that is inauthentic, this does not alter the fact that fear, qua situatedness, temporalizes itself primarily in having been. It just does so in a way that forgets its ownmost being. The temporality of anxiety, on the other hand, springs from the future of resoluteness, and hence it "brings one back to the pure 'that-it-is' of one's ownmost individualized thrownness" (BT, 394). However, Heidegger points out, "both fear and anxiety, as modes of situatedness, are grounded primarily in *having been*" (BT, 395). That is, both inauthentic and authentic situatedness is grounded in temporality.

The third structural moment of care is falling. Like understanding and situatedness, it has its existential meaning in a primary ecstasis.

Just as understanding is made possible primarily by the future, and moods are made possible by having been, the third constitutive moment in the structure of care — namely, *falling* — has its existential meaning in the *Present*. (BT, 396-7)

Now falling is by definition inauthentic. Hence, there is no such thing as an authentic falling. But Heidegger still distinguishes between inauthentic and authentic Present, where the former is referred to as 'making-present' and the latter 'moment of insight.' Inauthentic Present or making-present is what characterizes everydayness, and in this mode of being Dasein remains temporal in the sense of awaiting and being forgetful, that is, making-present is a synthesis of inauthentic future and inauthentic having been. The temporality of the moment of insight, on the other hand, is characterized by resoluteness and anticipation and this synthesis constitutes an authentic Present.

Now, let us summarize Heidegger's temporal repetition of the existential analysis.

Understanding is grounded primarily in the future (whether in anticipation or awaiting). Situatednesses temporalize themselves primarily in having been (whether in repetition or in having forgotten). Falling has its temporal roots primarily in the Present (whether in making-present or in the moment of insight). (BT, 401)

Hence, here we see clearly that Heidegger distinguishes between the moments of originary temporality, which are future, having been, and present, and its authentic and inauthentic modes, which are *anticipation* and *awaiting* for understanding, *repetition* and *having forgotten* for situatedness, and *moment of insight* and *making-present* for present. Moreover, this originary temporality presents itself as a unity of its temporal moments. In the temporal interpretation of understanding, situatedness, and falling, one does not only come up against a primary ecstasis, which is future, having been, and present, respectively, but one also comes up against temporality as a whole.

All the same, understanding is in every case a Present which 'is in the process of having been.' All the same, one's situatedness temporalizes itself as a future which is 'making present.' And all the same, the Present 'leaps away' from a future that is in the process of having been, or else is held on to by such a future. (BT, 401)

Thus, Heidegger concludes,

we can see that *in every ecstasis, temporality temporalizes itself as a whole; and this means that in the ecstatical unity with which temporality has fully temporalized itself currently, is grounded the totality of the structural whole of existence, facticity, and falling — that is, the unity of the care-structure.* (BT, 401)

Hence, we see that originary temporality — the ecstatical unity of temporality — is what makes both inauthentic everyday existence and authentic existence, which is the seeing of the former, possible. Thus, as Heidegger puts it, "the ecstatical unity of temporality ... is the condition for the possibility that there can be an entity which exists as its 'there'" (BT, 401).

In the remainder of this chapter, Heidegger goes on to discuss the temporality of other central concepts of the first division such as circumspection, readiness-to-hand, and presence-at-hand, but we shall refrain from any further inquiry into the repetition of the existential analysis. Our basic objective has been fulfilled in the sense that we have shown that originary temporality is indifferent with regard to authentic and inauthentic modes of existence and thus that originary temporality provides the full meaning of both. Authenticity refers to a mode of being in which the basic temporality of everydayness is brought to the fore, and not to a kind of being that is radically other than everyday Being-in-the-world.

7. TEMPORALITY AND EGOLOGY

Inherent in the phenomenological analysis of time and the attempt to temporalize the subjective perspective there is a danger of collapsing the egological project and thus exploding the central topic of phenomenology. This danger becomes more and more apparent for every decade that passes after the publication of Husserl's LI. As it advances from early Husserl to late Husserl, from early Heidegger to late Heidegger, and beyond,[27] the original

---

[27] The best known advocate for the "beyond" is Jacques Derrida. In *Speech and Phenomena* (Evanston: Northwestern University Press, 1973) Derrida on the one hand attacks Husserl for invoking traditional concepts of Western metaphysics to serve as the axiomatic foundation for phenomenology, namely the interpretation of being as presence. But, according to Derrida, unlike most of the tradition, Husserl's phenomenology also contains elements that can be turned against his project, and he proceeds to use Husserl's own

anti-psychologism of phenomenology has tipped over into radical historicism. The attempt to give a non-reductive account of subjectivity has yielded a new kind of reductionism. At this point we seem to have analyzed ourselves back to where we started. What we lack is exactly what Husserl tried to add to philosophy: a theory of subjectivity that accounts for its fundamental transcendence without thereby psychologizing the world or objectifying the subject, that is, without confusing the distinction between the subjective and objective domain.

The central question concerning the relation between the temporalization of the subjective perspective and the egological project concerns the status of temporality. If it is the case that temporality constitutes the ego, in what sense is the former prior to the latter? Put differently, in what sense is the horizon prior to the agent? Is this priority a matter of one entity appearing independently and ahead of another so that the context or horizon is independent of the subjective perspective, or is it apriority in which the prior entity is not construed as appearing independently of what it grounds, but rather provides the full meaning of the ego? In other words, are we, by temporalizing the subjective perspective, replacing one constituting entity — the ego — with another — time or history — or is it rather that time and history brings to the fore the full meaning of the ego? In the case of the former, the ego loses its primordial status and is reduced to a more or less unresisting placeholder within a temporal framework, in the case of the latter it simply follows that the ego has a horizonal structure.

According to Husserl's original analysis of time, the temporalization of the subjective perspective does not undermine the egological project because temporality originates in the living present.[28] Although the living present has a temporal make-up, temporality is not thereby prior to it. Rather, these temporal structures are what they are by virtue of being moments of this whole. Thus, it is our contention that when Husserl introduces temporality as the final absolute *concretum*, he is not thereby suggesting that temporality is a phenomenon that can appear prior to and independently of subjectivity.

analysis of temporality in order to undermine an essential distinction in Husserlian phenomenology. It falls beyond our intent to discuss this analysis, but the end of the story is that Derrida sees the temporalization of subjectivity as collapsing the egological project, thus doing away with the essential balance between the subjective and objective domain so central to phenomenology. For a thorough discussion of Derrida's interpretation of Husserlian temporality which grounds this approach, see for instance R. Cobb-Stevens, "Derrida and Husserl on Retention," *Analecta Husserliana*, XIX, Edited by A.-T. Tymieniecka, Dordrecht, 1985, 367-381.

[28] It falls beyond our intent to discuss to what extent this characterizes Husserl's view throughout his career. Apparently, in his later writings on time, in the C manuscripts, he makes certain suggestions to the effect that time is considered something pre-egological, but our interest is directed solely at the Husserl that influenced Heidegger's Marburg-philosophy.

However, by introducing temporality on this level of the analysis Husserl does open the door for an interpretation according to which the ego is secondary to a pre-egological temporal phenomenon.

Now the question remains as to where Heidegger's project finds itself on this issue, that is, whether Heidegger in fact inaugurates a collapse of the egological project or merely redefines subjectivity in a phenomenological manner. It is our contention that the latter is what characterizes Heidegger's project at least throughout the Marburg-period. Admittedly, and as we have repeatedly pointed out in this inquiry, there are numerous passages in Heidegger's writings where he specifically maintains that his concept of Dasein challenges the traditional notion of subjectivity, but it is our conviction that the notion of subjectivity he challenges is the one introducing the subject-object dichotomy. Heidegger does not try to do away with subjectivity as such, nor does he try to do away with objectivity; he tries to do away with the dichotomy. And the tools for such an endeavor are the basic tenets of phenomenology, such as the theory of wholes and parts, intentionality, categorial intuition, and the phenomenological sense of the apriori.

Nevertheless, Heidegger is ambiguous when it comes to the relation between Dasein and temporality. Towards the end of the Marburg-period he uses a terminology that seems to suggest that Dasein is replaced by history or horizon as the source-point of constitution. However, we argue that such an interpretation would not be in keeping with the general approach of Heidegger's existential analytic. It would simply prevent Heidegger from using the principles of phenomenology that are so central to his arrival at the concepts of care and thus of temporality. In other words, if temporality is considered a pre-egological source of constitution, Heidegger simply could not account for how he arrived at the concept of temporality in the first place.

While the early Heidegger's analysis of time makes it clear that original time is something that belongs to the subjective perspective, the terminology towards the end of the Marburg-period seems to be on the verge of suggesting that originary temporality is something other than Dasein. As we have noted above, in both PIA and CT Heidegger refers to original temporality as something essentially linked to subjectivity and *praxis*. Likewise, in the conclusion of HCT he states that "Dasein ... temporalizes" (HCT, 319) thus making it clear that the temporalization of subjectivity does not break with the egological project. And in his temporal interpretation of the transcendental power of imagination, it is quite clear that, although temporality constitutes the synthesis of the manifold, it can only have the character it has in relation to this synthesis. This view is certainly also fully present in BT;

indeed, it is this way temporality is originally presented. But in Division Two of BT, Heidegger nevertheless seems to refer to time in a way that suggests that time is somehow prior to Dasein. i.e., a pre-egological source. For instance, he says that "temporality temporalizes" (BT, 377), and he summarizes his position in BT with the statement, "time is primordial as the temporalizing of temporality, and as such it makes possible the Constitution of the structure of care" (BT, 380). In other words, Heidegger seems to indicate that temporality is a kind of pre-egological entity that makes Dasein possible. Now, does Heidegger inaugurate a collapse of the egological project with these remarks, or are they in fact proper ways in which to express a Heideggerian egology? We argue in favor of the latter, and we shall do so by examining the four theses by means of which Heidegger himself summarizes the outcome of his investigation of primordial temporality. These theses make it clear that, although prior to Dasein, temporality is not something other than Dasein. Rather, temporality is prior to Dasein in the phenomenological sense of this term, that is, temporality brings out the full meaning of Dasein and by doing so it in fact cements the primordial status of this entity. Now, before we proceed let us first quote Heidegger's summary of the concept of originary temporality.

Time is primordial as the temporalizing of temporality, and as such it makes possible the Constitution of the structure of care. Temporality is essentially ecstatical. Temporality temporalizes itself primordially out of the future. Primordial time is finite. (BT, 380)

The first thesis seems to claim that the constitution of care is made possible by a prior phenomenon which is temporality. However, the question remains as to the sense in which this phenomenon is prior to care. Concerning the nature of temporalizing, Heidegger makes the following claim:

Temporalizing does not signify that ecstases come in a 'succession.' The future is *not later* than having been, and having been is *not earlier* than the Present. Temporality temporalizes itself as a future which makes present in the process of having been. (BT, 401)

Thus, the temporalization of temporality is always the appearance of a whole and there is simply no way that temporality can appear that way prior to Dasein. As something separated from subjectivity, time is precisely not a whole; non-subjective time does not exhibit that distinctive character. Hence, the first thesis does not claim that temporality is a pre-egological or a pre-Dasein phenomenon; rather it makes a claim to the effect that to be Dasein is to appear as this kind of a temporal whole. The constitution of Dasein as being ahead-of and already-there is made possible by its having a distinctive temporal nature.

In response, one could legitimately ask why Heidegger claims that temporality temporalizes itself instead of saying that Dasein temporalizes. If we have a look at a claim made in HCT, we will, however, find that there is not necessarily a difference between these claims.

Not "time is" but "Dasein qua time temporalizes its being." Time is not something that is found outside somewhere as a framework for world events. Time is even less something which whirs away inside consciousness. It is rather that which makes possible the being-ahead-of-itself-in-already-being-involved-in, that is, which makes possible the being of care. (HCT, 319–20)

In other words, since the meaning of Dasein's being is time, there is really no difference in saying that temporality temporalizes or Dasein temporalizes; in both cases it means "*Dasein qua time temporalizes its being.*" Thus, not only is it the case that time provides the full meaning of Dasein, it also works the opposite way: there is no time without Dasein.

This is further underscored by the second and third thesis. By claiming that "temporality is essentially ecstatical [and] temporality temporalizes itself primordially out of the future," Heidegger obviously claims that time can be in that way only as an essential part of an act-structure. It is very difficult, if not impossible, to see how temporality can have these features disengaged from Dasein. And lastly, the fourth thesis concerning primordial time as finite firmly establishes that time is not a pre-egological phenomenon. Only in relation to Dasein can time be finite. Hence, we can conclude that Heidegger's temporalization of Dasein does not collapse the egological project. On the contrary, it establishes the full meaning of a phenomenological notion of subjectivity.

The conclusion of the existential analytic as we know it appears with the exhibition of the temporal constitution of Dasein. At this point, Heidegger provides the full meaning of the concept of Dasein in the sense that he exhibits how the structural moments of existence, facticity, and falling can appear as a unified whole. In this chapter, we have suggested several sources of influence upon Heidegger's notion of temporality. We have pointed out how Heidegger saw the traditional theory of time in fact pointing to a more primordial concept of time; we have seen how he interpreted Kant's power of imagination on a temporal basis, and we have briefly investigated Husserl's analysis of internal time consciousness. All of these influences are present in Heidegger's development of the temporal constitution of Dasein. Obviously, Heidegger was influenced by Husserl, who in fact was the first to offer a systematic development of a non-objective and non-psychological notion of temporality, but the insight Heidegger seeks to communicate through this temporalization goes all the way back to the Aristotelian notion of *praxis*. As we pointed out in Chapter VII, the Aristotelian distinction between *poiesis* and *praxis* is at the very foundation of Heidegger's existential analytic. The being of Dasein is *praxis*. Temporality, in Heidegger's sense of this term, is simply what characterizes this activity.

CONCLUSION

The objective of this investigation has been to interpret Heidegger's existential analysis and our argument has been that this analysis designates a phenomenological interpretation of subjectivity. What characterizes this phenomenon is that it is essentially related to itself and that it is a condition of possibility for the appearance of entities. In other words, what characterizes the phenomenological concept of subjectivity does not depart from the traditional modern interpretation of the same phenomenon in regard to its distinctive character. The difference between the phenomenological concept of subjectivity and the traditional modern conception of subjectivity concerns location. Whereas the latter typically is introduced as a worldless thing-like entity, the former is presented as a Being-in-the-world that is not a thing. But the basic principles of phenomenology allow the relocation of subjectivity in the world without eliminating the peculiarity of subjectivity. Dasein is both a subject and in the world which means that its being related to its own being and its appearance as the condition of possibility of appearances takes place in the world.

This introduces us to a new kind of transcendental subjectivity. It is transcendental in the sense that it is a condition of possibility for appearances. Dasein has a measure of primacy over world, but this condition of possibility or primacy is not a matter of construction. In order to construct something one has to appear ahead of and independently of what is constructed — just as the craftsman appears temporally ahead of what he builds — but this is not the way Dasein is prior to the world. If that were the case Dasein would have to be worldless, which, in turn, would be nothing but an oxymoron: a Being-in-the-world cannot be worldless. Dasein still has a primacy over the world in the sense that there is no world without Dasein, but this primacy is non-constructive. Dasein is prior to the world the way a whole is prior to its moments; it is ontologically prior, not ontically prior. In this sense Dasein designates a phenomenological transcendental subjectivity, this is the notion of subjectivity one arrives at if one take one's point of departure from the basic principles of phenomenology.

The strength of Heidegger's existential analytic is his emphasis on pre-ontological confirmation. It may very well be that for the most part there is nothing really new in Heidegger apart from his investigations of Aristotle, Kant, and Husserl, and that his genius was in the way he synthesized the insights of these thinkers. But on the topic of pre-ontological confirmation Heidegger seems to transcend both Aristotle, Kant, and Husserl. Admittedly, it would be anachronistic to impose the requirement of pre-ontological confirmation upon Aristotle, but when it comes to modern philosophers such as Kant and Husserl this is an entirely legitimate demand. This kind of foundation seems to be alien to Kantian analysis in that his approach is conceptual, but we think that Heidegger's investigation provides Kantian analysis with a basis more solid than can be provided conceptually. With regard to Husserl, we would suggest that Heidegger's emphasis on pre-ontological foundation is the only area in which he really transcends Husserl. The need for such a basis clearly follows from the basic tenets of phenomenology, and Husserl was obviously aware of the necessity of providing it, but Heidegger does so in a much more systematic manner. In short, at times Heidegger seems to be a more thorough phenomenologist than Husserl.

Having justified his endeavor phenomenally, Heidegger goes on to investigate the full meaning of this entity that is both related to its own being and appears as the condition of possibility for appearances, and which does it in the world, and the answer is temporality. Dasein is a temporally constituted subjectivity and in so being it seems to be closely related to Husserl's concept of absolute consciousness. Temporality, as the meaning of Dasein and absolute consciousness, as the meaning of Husserl's transcendental ego, have the exact same constitution. They are both constituted out of non-sequential temporal moments and both entities appear as the final absolute *concretum*.

BIBLIOGRAPHY

Allison, H. *Transcendental Idealism, An Interpretation and Defense* (New Haven and London: Yale University Press, 1983).
Arendt, H. *The Human Condition* (Chicago & London: The University of Chicago Press, 1958).
Aristotle. *The Complete Works of*, The Revised Oxford Translation, edited by J. Barnes (New Jersey: Princeton University Press, 1984).
Bast, R.A. *Handbuch zum Textstudium von Martin Heideggers 'Sein und Zeit'* (Stuttgart: Frommann-Holzboog, 1980).
Bell, D. *Husserl* (London and New York: Routledge, 1990).
Benhabib, S. *The Reluctant Modernism of Hannah Arendt* (London: Sage Publications, 1996).
Bernasconi, R. "The Fate of the Distinction Between *Praxis* and *Poiesis*," *Heidegger Studies* 2, 1986, 111–139.
Bernet, R. "Husserl and Heidegger on Intentionality and Being," *Journal of the British Society for Phenomenology*, Vol. 21, May 1990, 136–152.
—."Is the Present Ever Present? Phenomenology and the Metaphysics of Presence," translated by W. Brown, *Research in Phenomenology*, Vol. XII, 1982, 85–112.
Bernsen, N.O. *Heidegger's Theory of Intentionality*, translated by H. Vøhtz (Odense: Odense University Press, 1986).
Blattner, W. "The Concept of Death in *Being and Time*," *Man and World* 27, 1994, 49–70.
Brandom, R. "Heidegger's Categories in Being & Time," *The Monist*, Vol. 66, July 1983, 387–404.
Brogan, W. "Heidegger's Interpretation of Aristotle: The Finitude of Being," *Research in Phenomenology*, Vol. XIV, 1984, 249–258.
Brough, J. "The Emergence of an Absolute Consciousness in Husserl's Early Writings on Time-Consciousness," *Man and World*, V, 1972, 298–326.
—."Husserl and the Deconstruction of Time," *Review of Metaphysics* 46, March 1993, 503–536.
Buren, J.v. *The Young Heidegger: Rumor of the Hidden King* (Bloomington: Indiana University Press, 1994).
—.Editor, *Reading Heidegger from the Start, Essays in His Earliest Thought* (Albany: State University of New York Press, 1994).
Canovan, M. *Hannah Arendt: A Reinterpretation of Her Political Thought* (Cambridge: Cambridge University Press, 1992).

—."Socrates or Heidegger? Hannah Arendt's Reflections on Philosophy and Politics," *Social Research*, Vol. 57, No.1, Spring 1990, 135-165.
Caws, P. *Sartre* (London: Routledge & Kegan Paul, 1979).
Chisholm, R. Editor, *Realism and the Background of Phenomenology* (New York: The Free Press, 1960).
Cobb-Stevens, R. *Husserl and Analytic Philosophy* (Dordrecht, Boston, London: Kluwer Academic Publishers, 1990).
—.*James and Husserl: The Foundations of Meaning* (The Hague: Martinus Nijhoff, 1974).
—."Derrida and Husserl on Retention," *Analecta Husserliana*, Vol. XIX, edited by A.-T. Tymieniecka, Dordrecht, 1985, 367-381.
—."Being and Categorial Intuition," *Review of Metaphysics*, Vol. XXLIV, No. 1, September 1990, 43-66.
—."Hermeneutics without Relativism: Husserl's Theory of Mind," *Research in Phenomenology*, Vol. XII, 1982, 127-148.
—."Transcendental and Empirical Dimensions in Husserl's Phenomenology" *Continental Philosophy in America*, edited by J. Silverman, J. Sallis, and T.M. Seebohm (Pittsburgh: Duquesne University Press, 1983).
Dahlstrom, D. "Heidegger's Kantian Turn: Notes to his Commentary on the *Kritik der reinen Vernunft*," *Review of Metaphysics* 45, December 1991, 329-361.
Deely, J. *The Tradition Via Heidegger* (The Hague: Martinus Nijhoff, 1971).
d'Entrèves, M.P. *The Political Philosophy of Hannah Arendt* (London and New York: Routledge, 1994).
Derrida, J. *Speech and Phenomena, And Other Essays on Husserl's Theory of Signs*, translated by D.B. Allison (Evanston: Northwestern University Press, 1973).
—.*Margins of Philosophy*, translated by A. Bass (Chicago: The University of Chicago Press, 1982).
Dreyfus, H. *Being-in-the-world, A Commentary on Heidegger's Being & Time, Division 1* (Cambridge and London: The MIT Press, 1991).
—."Holism and Hermeneutics," *Review of Metaphysics*, 34, September 1980, 3-23.
—.Editor, *Husserl, Intentionality, and Cognitive Science* (Cambridge: MIT Press, 1982).
—.Editor, *Heidegger: A Critical Reader*, Cambridge (Oxford and Cambridge: Blackwell, 1992).
Elliston, F. Editor, *Heidegger's Existential Analytic* (The Hague: Mouton Publishers, 1978).
Fine, K. "Part-whole," in *The Cambridge Companion to Husserl*, edited by B. Smith and D. Woodruff Smith (New York and Cambridge: Cambridge University Press, 1995), 463-485.
Flynn, B.C. "From Finitude to the Absolute: Kant's Doctrine of Subjectivity," *Philosophy Today*, Winter 1985, 284-301.
Føllesdal, D. "Husserl and Heidegger on the Role of Actions in the Constitution of the World," in *Essays in honor of Jaakko Hintikka*, 365-378, edited by E. Saa-

rinen (Dordrecht: Reidel, 1979), 356-378.

—."Husserl's Notion of Noema," *Journal of Philosophy* 66, 1969, 680-687.

Guignon, C. *Heidegger and the Problem of Knowledge* (Indianapolis: Hackett Publishing Company, 1983).

—."On Saving Heidegger from Rorty," *Philosophy and Phenomenological Research*, Vol. XLVI, March 1986, 401-417.

—."Philosophy after Wittgenstein and Heidegger," *Philosophy and Phenomenological Research*, Vol. 1, June 1990, 649-672.

—.Editor, *The Cambridge Companion to Heidegger*, (New York and Cambridge: Cambridge University Press, 1993).

Haar, M. *Heidegger and the Essence of Man*, translated by W. McNeill (Albany: State University of New York Press, 1993).

Hammond, M. *Understanding Phenomenology* (Cambridge: Blackwell, 1991).

Hannay, A. *Human Consciousness* (London and New York: Routledge, 1990).

Hansen, P. *Hannah Arendt: Politics, History and Citizenship* (Cambridge: Polity Press, 1993).

Haugland, J. "Heidegger on Being a Person," *Noûs*, Vol. XVI, March 1982, 15-26.

—."Dasein's Disclosedness," *The Southern Journal of Philosophy*, Supplement, Vol. XXVIII, 1989, 51-73.

Heidegger, M. *Being and Time*, translated by Macquarrie & Robinson (Oxford: Basil Blackwell, 1980); *Sein und Zeit* (Tübingen: Max Niemeyer Verlag, 1957).

—.*The Basic Problems of Phenomenology*, translated by A. Hofstadter (Bloomington: Indiana University Press, 1988); *Die Grundprobleme der Phänomenologie*, Gesamtausgabe Band 24 (Frankfurt am Main: Vittorio Klostermann, 1975).

—.*History of the Concept of Time: Prolegomena*, translated by T. Kisiel (Bloomington: Indiana University Press, 1985); *Prolegomena zur Geschichte des Zeitbegriffs*, Gesamtausgabe Band 20 (Frankfurt am Main: Vittorio Klostermann, 1979).

—.*The Metaphysical Foundations of Logic*, translated by M. Heim (Bloomington: Indiana University Press, 1984); *Metaphysische Anfangsgründe der Logik im Ausgang von Leibniz*, Gesamtausgabe Band 26 (Frankfurt am Main: Vittorio Klostermann, 1978).

—.*The Question Concerning Technology and Other Essays*, translated by W. Lovett (New York: Harper & Row, 1977).

—.*On Time and Being*, translated by J. Stambaugh (New York: Harper & Row, 1972).

—.*Kant and the Problem of Metaphysics*, translated by R. Taft (Bloomington: Indiana University Press, 1990); *Kant und das Problem der Metaphysik, Vierte, erweiterte Auflage* (Frankfurt am Main: Vittorio Klostermann, 1973).

—.*Poetry, Language, Thought*, translated by A. Hofstadter (New York: Harper & Row, 1971).

—."Phenomenological Interpretation with Respect to Aristotle: Indication of the Hermeneutical Situation," translated by M. Baur, *Man and World* 25, 1992,

355-393.
—.*Basic Writings*, edited by D.F. Krell (San Francisco: Harper, 1977).
—.*Frühe Schriften*, Gesamtausgabe Band 1 (Frankfurt am Main: Vittorio Klostermann, 1978).
—.*Platon: Sophistes*, Gesamtausgabe Band 19 (Frankfurt am Main: Vittorio Klostermann, 1992).
—. *Logik. Die Frage nach der Wahrheit*, Gesamtausgabe Band 21 (Frankfurt am Main: Vittorio Klostermann, 1976).
—.*Grundbegriffe der antiken Philosophie*, Gesamtausgabe Band 22 (Frankfurt am Main: Vittorio Klostermann, 1993).
—.*Phänomenologische Interpretation von Kants Kritik der reinen Vernunft*, Gesamtausgabe Band 25 (Frankfurt am Main: Vittorio Klostermann, 1977).
—.*Einleitung in die Philosophie*, Gesamtausgabe Band 27 (Frankfurt am Main: Vittorio Klostermann, 1996).
—.*Phänomenologische Interpretationen zu Aristoteles, Einführung in die phänomenologische Forschung*, Gesamtausgabe Band 61 (Frankfurt am Main: Vittorio Klostermann, 1985).
—.*Ontologie (Hermeneutik der Faktizität)* Gesamtausgabe Band 63 (Frankfurt am Main: Vittorio Klostermann, 1988).
—.*Vier Seminare* (Frankfurt am Main: Vittorio Klostermann, 1977).
Henrich, D. *Identität und Objektivität, Eine Untersuchung über Kants transzendentale Deduktion* (Heidelberg: Carl Winters Universitäts-Verlag, 1976).
Herrmann, F.W.v. *Subjekt und Dasein* (Frankfurt am Main: Vittorio Klostermann, 1974).
—.*Der Begriff der Phänomenologie bei Heidegger und Husserl* (Frankfurt am Main: Vittorio Klostermann, 1981).
—.*Heideggers "Grundprobleme der Phänomenologie"* (Frankfurt am Main: Vittorio Klostermann, 1991).
Hopkins, B.C. *Intentionality in Husserl and Heidegger* (Dordrecht, Boston, London: Kluwer Academic Publishers, 1992).
Husserl, E. *Logical Investigations*, translated by J. Findlay (New York: Humanities Press, 1970); *Logische Untersuchungen* (Tübingen: Max Niemeyer, 1968).
—.*The Idea of Phenomenology,* translated by W. P. Alston and G. Nakhnikian (The Hague: Martinus Nijhoff, 1964); *Die Idee der Phänomenologie*, edited by W. Biemel, Husserliana II (The Hague: Martinus Nijhoff, 1950).
—.*Ideas Pertaining to a Pure Phenomenology and to a Phenomenological Philosophy - First Book*, translated by F. Kersten (The Hague: Martinus Nijhoff, 1982); *Ideen zu einer reinen Phänomenologie und phänomenologischen Philosophie. Buch I.* Edited by K. Schuhmann, Husserliana III (The Hague: Martinus Nijhoff, 1976).
—.*Experience and Judgment*, translated by J.S. Churchill and K. Ameriks (Evanston: Northwestern University Press, 1973); *Erfahrung und Urteil*, edited by L. Landgrebe, Second edition (Hamburg: Claassen Verlag, 1954).
—.*Formal and Transcendental Logic*, translated by D. Cairns (The Hague:

Martinus Nijhoff, 1969); *Formale und transzendentale Logik. Versuch einer Kritik der logischen Vernunft*, edited by P. Janssen, Husserliana XVII (The Hague: Martinus Nijhoff, 1974).

—.*Cartesian Meditations, An Introduction to Phenomenology*, translated by D. Cairns (The Hague: Martinus Nijhoff, 1960); *Cartesianische Meditationen und Pariser Vorträge*, edited by S. Strasser, Husserliana I (The Hague: Martinus Nijhoff, 1950).

—.*On the Phenomenology of the Consciousness of Internal Time*, translated by J.B. Brough (Dordrecht, Boston London: Kluwer Academic Publishers, 1991); *Zur Phänomenologie des inneren Zeitbewusstseins*, edited by R. Boehm, Husserliana X (The Hague: Martinus Nijhoff, 1966).

—.*Erste Philosophie, Zweiter Teil: Theorie der phänomenologischen Reduktion*, edited by R. Boehm, Husserliana VIII (The Hague: Martinus Nijhoff, 1959).

—.*Ideen zu einer reinen Phänomenologie und phänomenologische Philosophie. Zweites Buch: Phänomenologische Untersuchungen zur Konstitution*, edited by W. Biemel, Husserliana IV (The Hague: Martinus Nijhoff, 1952).

—.*Phänomenologische Psychologie,* edited by W. Biemel, Husserliana IX (The Hague: Martinus Nijhoff, 1962).

Höffe, O. *Immanuel Kant*, translated by M. Farrier (Albany: State University of New York Press, 1994).

Kant, I. *Critique of Pure Reason*, translated by N. Kemp Smith (Toronto: Macmillan, 1965).

Kaufmann, W. Editor, *Existentialism from Dostoevsky to Sartre* (New York: Meridian Books, 1957).

Kisiel, T. Editor, *Reading Heidegger from the Start, Essays in His Earliest Thought* (Albany: State University of New York Press, 1994).

—."Why the First Draft of *Being and Time* Was never Published," *Journal of the British Society for Phenomenology*, Vol. 20, No. 1, January 1989 3-22.

—."On the Way to *Being and Time*; Introduction to the Translation of Heidegger's *Prolegomena zur Geschichte des Zeitbegriffs, Research in Phenomenology*, Vol. XV, 1985, 193-226.

Kockelmans, J.J. Editor, *A Companion to Martin Heidegger's "Being and Time"* (Washington, D.C.: University Press of America, 1986).

Lampert, J. "Husserl's Theory of Parts and Wholes: The Dynamic of Individuating and Contextualizing Interpretation—*Übergehen, Abheben, Ergänzungsbedürftigkeit*," *Research in Phenomenology*, Vol. XIX, 1989, 195-212.

Madison, G.B. Editor, *Working Through Derrida* (Evanston: Northwestern University Press, 1993).

Macann, C. Editor, *Critical Heidegger* (London and New York, 1996).

Makkreel, R.A. "The Genesis of Heidegger's Phenomenological Hermeneutics and the Rediscovered 'Aristotle Introduction' of 1922," *Man and World* 23, 1990, 305-320.

Marx, W. *Heidegger and the Tradition*, translated by T. Kisiel and M. Greene, (Evanston: Northwestern University Press, 1971).

Merlan, P. "Time Consciousness in Husserl and Heidegger," *Philosophy and*

Phenomenological Research, 8, 1947/48, 23-53.
Mohanty, J.N. "Consciousness and Existence: Remarks on the Relation between Husserl and Heidegger," *Man and World* 11, 1978 324-335.
—.*The Possibility of Transcendental Philosophy* (Dordrecht: Martinus Nijhoff, 1985).
Morrison, R.P. "Kant, Husserl, and Heidegger on Time and the Unity of 'Consciousness,'" *Philosophy and Phenomenological Research*, Vol. 39, No. 2, December 1978, 182-198.
Mulhall, S. *On Being In the World: Wittgenstein and Heidegger on Seeing Aspects* (London and New York: Routledge, 1990).
Murray, M. *Heidegger and Modern Philosophy* (New Haven and London: Yale University Press, 1978).
—."Husserl and Heidegger: Constructing and Deconstructing Greek Philosophy," *Review of Metaphysics* 41, March 1988, 501-518.
—."A Note on Wittgenstein and Heidegger," *The Philosophical Review*, 83, 1971, 501-503.
Okrent, M. "Heidegger and Davidson (and Haugland)," *The Southern Journal of Philosophy*, supplement, Vol. XXVIII, 1989, 75-81.
—.*Heidegger's Pragmatism, Understanding, Being, and the Critique of Metaphysics* (Itacha and London: Cornell University Press, 1988).
Olafson, F. *Heidegger and the Philosophy of Mind* (New Haven and London: Yale University Press, 1987).
—.*What is a Human Being? A Heideggerian View* (Cambridge: Cambridge University Press, 1995).
—.Owens, W.D. "Heidegger and the Philosophy of Language," *Auslegung*, Vol. VIV, No.1, 1987, 49-66.
Pöggeler, O. *Martin Heidegger's Path of Thinking*, translated by D. Magurshak and S. Barber (Atlantic Highlands N.J.: Humanities Press International, 1987).
—.*Neue Wege mit Heidegger* (Freiburg/München: Verlag Karl Alber, 1992).
Richardson, J. *Existential Epistemology, Heidegger's Critique of the Cartesian Project* (Oxford: Clarendon Press, 1986).
Richardson, W. *Heidegger - Phenomenology Through Thought* (The Hague: Martinus Nijhoff, 1963).
Rosen, S. *The Limits of Analysis* (New Haven and London: Yale University Press, 1984).
—.*The Question of Being. A Reversal of Heidegger* (New Haven and London: Yale University Press, 1993).
Römpp, G. "Truth and Interpersonality: An Inquiry into the Argumentative Structure of Heidegger's Being & Time," *International Philosophical Quarterly*, Vol. XXIX, December 1989, 429-447.
Sallis, J. Editor, *Reading Heidegger* (Bloomington: Indiana University Press, 1993).
Sartre, J-P. *The Transcendence of the Ego, An Existentialist Theory of Consciousness*, translated by F. Williams and R. Kirkpatrick (New York: Hill and Wang, 1960).

Schalow, F. *The Renewal of the Heidegger-Kant Dialogue* (Albany: State University of New York Press, 1992).

Schürmann, R. *Heidegger On Being and Acting. From Principles to Anarchy*, (Bloomington: Indiana University Press, 1990).

Schwabe-Hansen, E., *Forholdet mellom transcendental og konkret subjektivitet i Edmund Husserls fenomenologi* (Oslo, 1985).

Seebohm, T.M. "Reflexion and Totality in the Philosophy of E. Husserl," *Journal of the British Society for Phenomenology*, Vol. 4, No. 1, January 1973, 20-30.

Sheehan, T.J. "The 'Original Form' of Sein und Zeit: Heidegger's *Der Begriff der Zeit*," *Journal of the British Society for Phenomenology*, Vol. 10, No. 2, May 1979, 78-83.

Sherover, C.M. *Heidegger, Kant, and Time* (Bloomington: Indiana University Press, 1971).

Simons, P.M. *Parts: A Study in Ontology* (Oxford: Clarendon Press, 1982).

—."The Formalization of Husserl's Theory of Parts and Wholes," in *Parts and Moments: Studies in Logic and Formal Ontology*.

Smith, B. *Parts and Moments: Studies in Logic and Formal Ontology* (Munich: Philosophia, 1982).

Sokolowski, R. *Husserlian Meditations* (Evanston: Northwestern University Press, 1974).

—."The Logic of Wholes and Parts in Husserl's *Investigations*" *Philosophy and Phenomenological Research*, XXVIII, 1968, 537-553.

—."The Structure and Content of Husserl's *Logical Investigations*," *Inquiry*, XIV, 1971, 318-347.

—."Husserl's Concept of Categorial Intuition," *Phenomenology and the Human Sciences*, XII, 1981, 127-141.

—.*The Formation of Husserl's Concept of Constitution* (The Hague: Martinus Nijhoff, 1970).

—.Editor, *Edmund Husserl and the Phenomenological Tradition: Essays in Phenomenology* (Washington D.C.: Catholic University of America Press, 1988).

Spiegelberg, H. *The Phenomenological Movement* (Dordrecht, Boston, London: Kluwer Academic Publishers, 1994).

Stewart, R.M. "The Problem of Logical Psychologism for Husserl and the Early Heidegger," *Journal of the British Society for Phenomenology*, Vol. 10, No. 3, October 1979, 184-193.

Taminiaux, J. *Heidegger and the Project of Fundamental Ontology*, translated & edited by M. Gendre (Albany: State University of New York Press, 1991).

—.*Dialectic and Difference: Modern Thought and the Sense of Human Limits*, edited by R. Crease and J.T. Decker (Atlantic Highlands, N.J.: Humanities Press International, 1985).

—."*Poiesis* and *Praxis* in Fundamental Ontology," *Research in Phenomenology*, Vol. XVII, 1987, 137-169.

Villa, D.R. *Arendt and Heidegger, The Fate of the Political* (Princeton: Princeton University Press, 1996).

Watson, S. "Heidegger, Rationality, and the Critique of Judgment," *Review of Metaphysics* 41, March 1988, 461–499.
Wittgenstein, L. *Culture and Value,* translated by P. Winch (Oxford: Blackwell, 1980).
—.*Philosophical Investigations*, translated by G.E.M. Anscombe (Oxford: Basil Blackwell, 1958).
Øverenget, E. *Heidegger's Concept of Dasein* (Oslo, 1992).
—."Heidegger and Arendt: Against the Imperialism of Privacy," *Philosophy Today*, Winter, 1995, 430–444.
—."The Presence of Husserl's Theory of Wholes and Parts in Heidegger's Phenomenology," *Research in Phenomenology*, Vol. XXVI, 1996, 171–197.

INDEX

Ability-to-be, 114, 143, 244
Absolute concretion, 14, 19, 98, 104
Abstraction, 44, 66
Abstractum, 13, 14, 17, 30, 31, 53, 82, 100, 128, 131, 212, 227; *Abstracta*, 17, 73, 82, 100, 173, 192, 300
Accentuation, 24, 63, 104
Act of identification, 44, 49, 51
Action, 3, 5, 108, 118, 143, 179, 180, 200-202, 204-206, 219, 223, 224, 226, 268, 282, 295
Aletheia, 130, 131, 227, 229
Allison, H., 151, 153
Anticipation, 16, 256, 257, 293, 294, 298, 305, 306
Anticipatory resoluteness, 292, 294, 295, 298, 299, 302, 303
Anxiety, 6, 33, 233, 236, 237, 239-241, 243, 245, 252-254, 258, 263, 265-269, 295, 303, 305, 306
Appearances, 3, 15, 73, 75, 76, 78, 80, 85, 99, 101, 109, 138, 204, 205, 229, 296, 313, 314
Apperception, 5, 11, 140, 141,145-147, 149-155, 157-159, 161, 166, 199, 230, 243, 271, 276-280, 287, 296; Analytic unity of a., 5, 11, 140, 145, 153, 154, 157-159, 166, 199, 230, 277, 279, 287,296; Synthetic unity of a., 5, 11, 140, 141, 146, 151, 154, 155, 158, 159, 199, 230, 243, 271, 277-280, 287; Transcendental a., 147, 153, 161, 276, 278, 279
Apprehension, 24, 48, 50, 51, 54, 59-64, 66-70, 82, 83, 85, 88-90, 111, 157, 189, 213, 280-282, 284

Appresentation, 172
Apriori, 4, 5, 7, 8, 11-13, 17, 18, 21, 22, 32, 33, 35, 36, 47, 71-78, 80-84, 91-93, 98-104, 106, 137, 138, 164, 165, 167, 170, 176, 193, 196, 197, 209, 223, 228, 229, 231, 235, 238, 239, 261, 265, 271, 278, 279, 284, 287, 296, 302, 309
Apriori necessity, 7, 11, 12, 17, 32, 33
Apriorism, 8, 47, 72-75, 91, 97, 104, 123, 196
Aquinas, T., 225
Arendt, H., 199-205, 219, 222, 223
Aristotle, 6, 19, 34, 68, 100, 199, 205-208, 223-225, 227, 228, 262, 270, 271, 273-276, 314
Articulation, 43, 63, 64, 83, 84, 130-133, 206, 262, 294, 298, 301
Assertion, 16, 43, 51, 55, 56, 58, 60, 80, 125, 128-132, 170, 174, 217, 275
Augustine, 274
Authenticity, 199, 200, 207, 209, 211, 213-216, 222, 223, 230, 238, 239, 258, 259, 292-294, 300, 304, 305, 307
Being-a-whole, 6, 233, 243-247, 251, 252, 254, 257-260, 269, 292-295, 297-299
Being-in-the-world, 2, 22-24, 28, 30-33, 99, 101, 103, 107, 115, 117, 119-121, 125, 140, 165-167, 174, 175,192-194, 198-200, 207, 212, 214, 215, 218, 233, 238-243, 246, 247, 251, 252, 255, 257, 262, 265, 267, 270, 295, 296, 300, 307, 313

323

Being-towards-death, 6, 33, 237, 245-248, 252-256, 258, 269, 293, 298, 302
Being-with-Others, 220
Bergson, H., 48
Blattner, W., 304
Bracketing, 89, 95, 111, 163
Breakdown, 4, 125, 165, 182-184, 186, 237
Brentano, F., 210, 211
Call of conscience, 260, 263, 265-267
Care, 22-24, 33, 107, 123, 136-140, 143, 144, 160, 162, 164, 165, 220, 232, 233, 236, 237, 242-245, 247, 251-254, 258-260, 263, 265, 267, 269, 270, 272, 273, 280, 283, 288, 294-304, 306, 307, 309-311
Categorial intuition, 4, 5, 8, 34-36, 42-48, 52-54, 58, 61-65, 70-78, 82, 83, 95, 96, 98, 102, 104, 127, 128, 165, 167-174, 196-198, 207, 222, 228, 239, 271, 287, 309; Categorial acts, 36, 41-44, 48, 58-62, 65, 67-71, 73, 77, 95, 96, 167, 169, 170; Acts of ideation, 36, 43, 48, 61, 62, 65, 67, 68, 76, 96; Acts of synthesis, 36, 43, 44, 48, 61, 62, 65-68, 96
Categorial object, 43, 64
Circumspection, 124-126, 179-181, 185, 187, 188, 190, 195, 212, 226, 230, 255, 307
Cobb-Stevens, R., 308
Cognition, 42, 119, 121, 122, 127, 128, 142, 162, 163, 176, 178-180, 208
Complex objects, 10, 60
Comportment, 57, 74-76, 81, 82, 108, 109, 114, 116, 122-126, 128, 140-143, 148, 166
Concreteness, 27-29, 235, 245
Concretum, 12-15, 17, 28, 30, 31, 51, 53, 80-82, 84, 98-102, 104, 123, 128, 131, 137, 138, 173, 192, 193, 198, 200, 207, 209, 212, 224, 227, 228, 232, 233, 244, 254, 276, 290-292, 300, 303, 308, 314; Absolute *c.*, 15, 17, 28, 31, 80, 81, 84, 99-101, 104, 138, 173, 192, 193, 198, 232, 233, 244, 254, 276, 290-292, 300, 303, 308, 314; *Concreta*, 13-15, 17, 73, 82, 100, 101, 131, 138, 300
Condition of possibility, 3, 6, 7, 44, 119, 122, 123, 127, 129, 137, 143, 151, 158, 163, 170, 185, 202, 207, 212, 228, 231, 244, 260, 283, 289-291, 294, 297, 305, 313, 314
Conscience, 6, 259-261, 263, 265-267, 293
Consciousness, 3, 7, 11-17, 19, 32, 36, 37, 45, 56, 57, 66, 72, 75, 84-98, 101, 102, 104, 106, 108, 109, 111, 112, 125, 126, 138-142, 144-166, 209, 210, 212, 213, 216, 271, 272, 277, 278, 285-287, 289-292, 296, 299, 303, 311, 314; Pure c., 84, 90, 91, 93, 94, 96, 97, 101, 104; Self-c., 3, 11, 104, 108, 125, 126, 139-142, 145, 150-152, 154, 155, 161, 163, 164, 166, 212, 213, 278; Unity of c., 7, 12, 16, 17, 19, 32, 101, 147-149, 289
Constitution, 5, 6, 23-25, 28, 29, 32, 47, 48, 61, 68, 71-73, 78, 84, 92, 93, 98, 104, 106, 112, 115, 119, 121, 124, 128, 131, 135, 138, 141, 162, 163, 166-170, 175, 196-198, 200, 204, 211, 217, 218, 222, 227, 235, 238, 245, 258, 262, 269, 270, 280, 292, 296, 297, 299, 303, 309-311, 314
Construction, 60, 82, 83, 167, 170, 181, 185, 233, 234, 239, 243, 268, 294, 313
Daseinsanalytik, 4, 8, 19, 27, 33, 98
Death, 6, 33, 146, 148, 233, 237, 245-258, 268, 269, 293, 298, 302
Demise, 250, 255
Derrida, J., 307
Descartes, R., 56, 74, 75, 93, 113, 141,

160, 161
Disclosedness, 2, 5, 22, 107, 119, 125, 129, 131, 168, 170, 172-175, 193-200, 206, 207, 219, 222-224, 226, 230, 232, 238, 243, 255, 261, 262, 266-269, 274-276, 305
Discourse, 32, 131-135, 139, 261-263, 266, 267, 297, 305
Discoveredness, 129, 168, 172-175, 193-198, 200, 206, 207, 219, 222-224, 230, 262, 275
Dreyfus, H., 101, 108, 117, 134, 176, 187, 304
Ecstasis, 306, 307
Ego, 2, 84, 108, 112, 126, 140,144-147, 149, 158-161, 199, 212-214, 216, 277, 287, 308, 314; Transcendental e., 144, 146, 147, 149, 159, 287
Egology, 5, 141, 144-148, 158-160, 217, 307, 310
Eidetic abstraction, 66
Empirical self, 146
Empty intention, 38, 49
Episteme, 225, 226
Epoché, 89, 145, 157
Equipment, 29, 169, 175-197, 212, 219, 222, 223
Essence, 3, 12, 14, 17, 23, 32, 33, 69, 86, 87, 96, 104, 110, 112-114, 116, 124, 127, 140-142, 144, 162-167, 177, 178, 180, 193, 194, 200, 232, 244, 265, 281, 286, 303
Essentia, 112, 163, 208
Everydayness, 5, 6, 31, 109-111, 134, 135, 175, 176, 181, 182, 190, 191, 209, 212, 214-216, 218, 221, 222, 231, 232, 236-241, 251-254, 260, 265, 266, 269, 304, 306, 307
Evidence, 4, 20, 22, 36, 38, 48-51, 53, 54, 69, 99, 128-131, 144, 151, 152, 173, 176, 182, 197, 225-227, 273, 278, 287, 289, 295; Psychologistic notion of e., 49
Existence, 2-6, 10, 14, 17, 22, 23, 32, 40, 45, 66, 67, 89, 90, 96, 105, 106, 112-118, 120, 122-125, 131, 133-138, 140-144, 146, 147, 157, 158, 161-167, 194, 197, 198, 200, 204, 209, 212-215, 218, 232, 240, 244, 247, 251, 252, 256-258, 260, 264, 269, 270, 277, 288, 293, 296, 300, 302-304, 307, 311
Existentia, 113
Existential, 2-6, 19, 20, 23, 26, 32, 106, 107, 115, 116, 118-124, 126, 127, 130-132, 134-137, 139, 163, 165, 190, 200, 204, 205, 207, 209, 211, 218, 220-222, 225, 226, 231, 232, 234-237, 239, 241-245, 247, 250-252, 254-264, 266, 269, 270, 275, 293-295, 297, 300-304, 306, 307, 309, 311-313
Existential analysis, 135, 275, 294, 303, 304, 306, 307
Existentialism, 101, 163, 237
Existentiell, 118, 238, 239, 241, 245, 247, 252, 253, 257-260, 264, 269, 292-295, 305
Factical, 108, 119, 136, 137, 190, 195, 211, 214, 242, 243, 246, 260, 266
Facticity, 23, 118, 119, 122, 139, 164, 242, 251, 252, 264, 270, 288, 302, 307, 311
Falling, 1, 23, 62, 63, 91, 93, 97, 131, 134, 139, 160, 169, 185, 203, 222, 238-240, 242, 244, 251-253, 261, 262, 270, 288, 302, 305-307, 311
Fear, 24, 77, 108, 239, 240, 253, 305, 306
Fleeing, 237, 238, 240, 252, 253, 266
Føllesdal, D., 163, 164
Founded acts, 37, 41, 46, 58, 61, 62, 65, 68, 71, 78, 95, 167, 223
Founding acts, 61, 95, 165
Frege, G., 1, 279
Fundamental ontology, 6, 100, 175, 199, 205, 206, 215, 224, 231, 235, 244, 270, 272, 297
Generality, 68, 70, 95-97, 106, 138

INDEX

Guignon, C., 107, 108, 117, 133
Guilt, 6, 265
Haugland, J., 107
Hegel, G.W.F., 161
Henrich, D., 152
Hermeneutical, 130, 131, 206, 294, 295, 304
Herrmann, F.W.v., 30
Höffe, O., 152
Husserl, E., 1, 2, 6-21, 25-27, 33-46, 49, 55, 57-59, 61, 62, 64, 65, 69, 71-73, 76, 77, 79, 80, 85, 86, 88-91, 93, 94, 97, 100, 101, 104, 106, 107, 111, 112, 128, 138, 139, 145-149, 158, 159, 163, 164, 166, 169, 171-173, 175, 176, 182, 197, 198, 210, 211, 239, 262, 271, 282, 287, 289-292, 299, 307, 308, 311, 314
Ideal object, 35, 67
Idealism, 1, 17, 18, 30, 56, 68, 69, 83, 151, 169; Empirical i., 17, 30; Transcendental i., 151
Immanence, 37, 50, 75, 85-87, 89, 90, 92, 143, 147, 290-292, 299, 303
Impression, 70, 196, 282, 291
Inauthenticity, 199, 200, 207, 209, 211, 213-216, 221-223, 230, 238, 241, 259, 266, 300, 304, 305
Individuality, 90, 95, 96, 106, 138
Intentio, 51, 53, 76, 81, 82, 84, 226-228
Intentional fulfillment, 38, 48
Intentionality, 8, 17, 30, 35-37, 45, 47, 49-51, 53, 56, 57, 59-61, 66, 72, 73, 75, 78, 80-84, 87-89, 91, 93, 95, 97, 102, 104, 106, 108, 109, 132, 133, 137, 143, 147, 148, 162, 163, 166, 175, 176, 212, 213, 228, 271, 287, 289, 309
Intentionality in its apriori, 73, 78, 81, 82, 84, 91, 104, 106, 176, 228
Intentum, 51, 53, 76, 81, 82, 84, 227, 228
Interpretation, 1, 2, 4, 5, 9, 11, 16, 21, 23, 26, 29, 30, 35, 36, 49, 50, 52, 54, 59, 61, 65, 73-75, 78, 79, 95-97, 99, 101-104, 106-109, 112-115, 125, 128-131, 137, 138, 146-148, 150, 152, 154, 155, 157, 159, 161, 162, 171, 174, 182, 186, 203, 206, 208, 217-219, 222, 225, 226, 232-237, 247, 250, 251, 253, 254, 259, 262, 268, 270, 271, 274, 275, 277-284, 286, 296, 301, 303, 305-309, 313
Introspection, 52, 122, 124, 140, 143, 144, 193, 197, 198, 277
Intuition, 4-6, 8, 16, 34-36, 38-40, 42-48, 52-54, 58, 60-65, 68, 70-78, 82, 83, 95, 96, 98, 102, 104, 127, 128, 152, 165, 167-174, 186, 196-198, 207, 210, 222, 228, 231, 236, 237, 239, 243, 269, 271, 280-282, 284, 285, 287, 309; Sensuous i., 35, 71; Simple i., 65; Straightforward i., 171, 172
James, W., 65
Kairos, 275
Kant, I., 5, 6, 8, 9, 11, 13, 17, 18, 44, 45, 56, 70, 75, 79, 93, 103, 126, 140, 141, 144-147, 150-161, 166, 199, 204, 212-214, 243, 271, 276-287, 314
Kierkegaard, S., 237, 266
Legein, 229, 262
Logos, 227, 262, 267
Mental content, 12, 13, 77
Mill. J.S., 144
Mineness, 2, 215, 216, 218, 230-232
Moment, 11-14, 26, 27, 29, 32, 39, 41, 42, 44, 52, 53, 56, 57, 60, 64, 69, 76, 90, 100, 102, 115, 124, 131, 135, 144, 155, 157, 171, 189, 199, 212, 228, 233, 234, 236, 245, 247-249, 251, 252, 262, 264, 266, 267, 269, 275, 276, 284, 292, 298, 300-303, 305, 306
Moment-of-insight, 275, 276
Mood, 116-121
Multi-level intuition, 58

Natural attitude, 15, 28, 85, 88, 95, 110, 111, 163
Noein, 229, 262
Nominalism, 66, 69
Non-positional awareness, 5, 141, 151, 153, 155-157, 165, 166, 214, 230, 231, 256, 278
Non-sequential temporality, 291
Nous, 225, 229
Nullity, 264, 265
Objectification, 40, 64, 77
Objective correlates, 17, 38-40, 46, 64, 73, 76, 85, 86, 90, 98, 172, 290, 292
Objectivity, 3, 5, 17, 39, 40, 44, 60-70, 74, 76, 77, 80, 87, 89, 92, 93, 95-97, 121, 126, 127, 167-173, 225, 226, 228, 257, 279, 289, 290, 309
Okrent, M., 141, 142, 162, 175, 176
Ontical, 28, 29, 31, 100, 109, 110, 121, 126, 128, 129, 137, 138, 160, 189, 190, 195, 211, 215, 217, 218, 236-239, 250, 251, 258, 259, 300
Ontological, 6, 7, 23, 27-29, 31-33, 35, 39, 48, 66, 69, 71, 74, 80, 82, 108-110, 112, 117, 120-122, 124, 126, 129-131, 135-137, 160, 161, 164, 168-170, 176, 178, 181-187, 190, 195, 199, 205, 206, 211, 214, 215, 217, 220, 230-237, 239-245, 250-254, 256, 258-260, 262, 266-268, 272, 273, 275, 292, 294, 296, 297, 300, 303, 314
Ontological difference, 35, 71, 74, 122, 126, 169, 170
Opacity, 149
Perception, 36-46, 48-50, 52, 54-64, 82, 85, 86, 88-90, 92, 95, 98, 126, 143, 168, 169, 171, 172, 178, 197, 207, 213, 222, 228, 285, 287, 290; Supersensuous p., 36, 41, 42; Unity of p., 44
Phenomenalism, 70
Phenomenological attitude, 15, 28, 88, 95, 211

Phenomenological reduction, 4, 73, 78, 89-91, 94-97, 104, 106, 107, 111, 112, 135; Eidetic reduction, 90, 93-95, 97, 104, 110; Transcendental reduction, 16, 90, 95, 104, 111, 135, 138, 165, 181, 186, 237
Phenomenology, 1-4, 7-9, 13-16, 18, 19, 22, 26, 30, 34, 36, 39, 40, 42, 44, 46, 47, 49, 56, 60, 65-67, 69-73, 75, 78-85, 87, 91, 93-98, 102, 104, 106, 117, 138, 140, 141, 145-147, 149, 152, 158, 160, 171, 175, 182, 197, 205, 206, 209-213, 217, 223, 244, 245, 260, 268, 270-272, 277, 279, 282, 287, 289, 291, 292, 300, 307-309, 313, 314; Transcendental p., 7, 13-16, 22, 98, 102, 245
Phronesis, 224-226, 230-232, 255, 274-276, 303
Pieces, 10, 11, 14, 17-20, 22, 24, 25, 39, 63, 86, 99, 136, 187, 188, 234, 242, 248, 249, 288, 289, 297
Poiesis, 5, 180, 199, 200, 205-209, 212, 219, 220, 222-225, 230, 274, 275, 312
Poietic activity, 216, 217, 221, 223, 230, 268
Polis, 201, 202
Potentiality-for-Being, 123, 135, 136, 237-242, 244, 245, 247, 251-253, 256-258, 260, 263-267, 292-294, 299, 301, 305
Praxis, 5, 180, 199, 200, 205-207, 216, 223-226, 230, 231, 262, 268, 272, 274, 275, 309, 311, 312
Presence-at-hand, 183, 184, 188, 205, 207, 209, 212, 240, 307; Present-at-hand, 113, 126, 127, 162, 183, 185, 188, 189, 196, 208, 209, 212, 214, 216, 217, 219, 220, 237, 247, 249, 255, 257, 260, 267, 301
Presencing, 42, 171, 299, 302
Pre-ontological, 33, 110, 112, 130, 137, 181-183, 185, 186, 211, 215, 231, 232, 236, 237, 243-245, 253, 258,

260, 268, 292, 294, 303, 314; Pre-ontological confirmation, 33, 112, 130, 137, 181, 182, 185, 212, 231, 232, 236, 237, 243, 244, 253, 258, 268, 292, 294, 303, 314; Phenomenal basis, 1, 4, 6, 125, 130, 134, 232, 233, 236, 239, 241, 244-247, 252, 254, 257-260, 265, 268-270, 292, 294, 296, 303

Plato, 19, 26

Primary presence, 171-173, 197, 198, 207

Projection, 124, 125, 131, 132, 135, 264, 265, 267, 297, 305

Protention, 291

Psychological sphere, 9, 11, 31, 57, 59, 77

Psychologism, 1, 7, 18, 32, 69, 91, 97, 144, 175, 279, 308

Rationalism, 60, 62, 69, 77

Readiness-to-hand, 178, 179, 183, 184, 186-189, 191, 193, 205, 209, 240, 307; Ready-to-hand, 129, 178, 179, 182-193, 195-197, 207, 219, 240, 242, 248, 249, 255

Real object, 40, 43, 46, 59, 60, 66, 86

Realism, 7, 17, 29, 32, 45, 68, 69, 169, 203; Transcendental Realism, 29, 45, 203

Reference, 8, 9, 15, 19, 25, 35, 57, 69, 75, 90, 92, 94, 101, 102, 106, 132, 145, 148, 177, 186-189, 191, 206, 222, 228, 272, 287

Referential whole, 29, 169, 177, 187, 191

Reflection, 21, 40, 52, 56, 57, 85, 86, 88-92, 109, 119, 120, 122, 140, 141, 143, 144, 146, 148, 150, 154, 156-158, 165, 166, 175, 193, 198, 213, 214, 277, 290-292

Res cogitans, 1, 30, 31, 102, 161, 300

Res extensa, 31, 161, 289, 300

Resoluteness, 260, 266, 268, 269, 272, 292, 294, 295, 298, 299, 302, 303, 305, 306

Retention, 291, 308

Richardson, W., 30, 117

Rickert, H., 49

Sartre, J.P., 5, 101, 126, 140, 141, 144-163, 166, 212, 214, 216, 277, 278

Schalow, F., 282

Seebohm, T., 9

Seinsfrage, 8, 27, 33-35, 47, 48, 63, 71, 98

Self, 3, 5, 6, 11, 14, 16, 23, 30, 31, 43-45, 72-74, 81, 86, 87, 94, 104, 108, 113, 114, 116, 122-126, 133-137, 139-146, 150-157, 159-167, 180, 193, 194, 198-200, 202, 211-218, 220-222, 226, 230-232, 238, 244, 257, 260-264, 266-269, 277, 278, 283, 287, 296, 297, 300, 301; S.-comportment, 114, 116, 125, 140-143, 166; S.-directedness, 3, 5, 108, 113, 114, 123, 125, 135, 140-142, 161-163, 166, 198, 277; S.-reflection, 122, 140, 143, 144, 193, 198, 214

Sensualism, 70

Sensuous object, 37

Sensuousness, 69, 70, 126-128, 228, 262, 267, 276

Sherover, C.M., 282

Simple object, 59, 62, 69

Simple objects, 63, 69, 70

Situatedness, 32, 107, 116-122, 131, 135, 137, 139, 236, 239, 252, 258, 261, 262, 266, 267, 297, 305-307

Sokolowski, R., 7, 15, 42

Solipsism, 241

Sophia, 225, 230

Spontaneity, 45, 70, 140, 145, 149, 151, 152, 154, 155, 277, 280

Stumpf, C., 10, 11

Subjective perspective, 1, 11-13, 18, 31, 57, 83, 91, 98, 103, 161, 296, 307-309

Subjectivity, 1-6, 13-15, 19, 29-31, 57, 69, 72, 73, 75, 77, 101, 103, 106,

108-110, 112, 113, 120, 138, 160, 161, 164, 165, 173, 175, 200, 203, 204, 212, 217, 267, 274, 279, 289-291, 296, 301, 304, 307-311, 313, 314

Taminiaux, J., 44, 205, 206, 224

Techne, 225, 226

Temporality, 3, 6, 23, 25, 27, 32, 33, 102, 107, 139, 147, 149, 159, 162, 232, 245, 270-272, 275-278, 280, 281, 284, 286-292, 297-312, 314

Temporality of absolute consciousness, 290

The One, 2, 12, 34, 40, 44, 49, 51, 62, 86, 93, 120, 122-124, 141, 144, 149, 175, 187, 200, 204, 206, 209, 216, 219, 221-223, 225, 226, 235, 237, 253, 256, 257, 261, 263, 266, 272, 294, 296, 299, 307, 309

Thrownness, 118-120, 124, 252, 263, 264, 298

Totality of equipment, 29, 177, 180, 187, 188, 192

Traditional interpretation of time, 49

Traditional theory of time, 272, 275, 311

Transcendence, 1, 37, 50, 85, 87, 89, 140, 147, 290, 308

Transcendental field, 146, 158, 159

Transcendental knowledge, 18, 72

Transcendental power of imagination, 271, 279-284, 286, 287

Transcendental turn, 13, 15, 16, 18, 19, 72, 100

Translucency, 149

Truth, 1, 30, 38, 42, 49-54, 56; Scholastic definition of t., 50, 51, 53, 129, 226, 227, 129-131, 148, 156, 164, 226-230

Uncanniness, 241, 252

Understanding, 2, 3, 5, 6, 28, 32-34, 45, 53, 65, 70, 72-74, 77, 81, 93, 94, 98, 100, 102, 107, 109-112, 115, 116, 120-133, 135-137, 139, 140, 142-144, 154, 155, 158, 163, 169, 171, 173, 179, 188, 190, 193, 194, 206, 209-217, 220-222, 224-226, 230, 232, 235, 238, 239, 243-245, 248, 250, 253-262, 264-267, 270, 272-274, 276, 279, 285, 287, 288, 294-298, 302, 305, 306

Vita activa, 201, 203

Wanting to have a conscience, 260, 267

Wholes and Parts, 4, 7-9, 13, 15, 16, 18-20, 22-28, 32, 33, 39, 59, 64, 71, 73, 78, 79, 82, 86, 91, 94, 97-99, 104, 123, 128, 165, 167, 171, 173, 177, 211, 212, 223, 232, 233, 239, 242, 248, 259, 267, 281, 287-289, 300, 309

Wittgenstein, L., 133

World, 1-3, 5, 7, 11, 14, 15, 22-24, 28-33, 37, 41, 66, 69, 71, 75-77, 82, 85-90, 93, 99, 101, 103, 104, 107-123, 125-127, 129, 130, 132-138, 140-144, 146, 147, 158-160, 162-168, 170, 174-176, 180, 182, 184-195, 197-204, 206-208, 212-215, 217-224, 231-233, 235, 237-243, 246, 247, 249, 251, 252, 255-257, 259, 261, 262, 265-270, 273, 274, 277, 288-290, 295, 296, 300, 301, 303, 307, 308, 311, 313, 314

Worldless subject, 101, 103, 108, 141, 143, 175, 219, 269, 295

Worldlessness, 87, 101, 103, 296

Worldliness, 103, 104, 120, 126, 128, 168, 169, 174, 175, 182, 183, 186, 187, 189-192, 197, 200, 204

Zu den Sachen selbst, 16, 303

Phaenomenologica

1. E. Fink: *Sein, Wahrheit, Welt.* Vor-Fragen zum Problem des Phänomen-Begriffs. 1958   ISBN 90-247-0234-8
2. H.L. van Breda and J. Taminiaux (eds.): *Husserl et la pensée moderne / Husserl und das Denken der Neuzeit.* Actes du deuxième Colloque International de Phénoménologie / Akten des zweiten Internationalen Phänomenologischen Kolloquiums (Krefeld, 1.-3. Nov. 1956). 1959   ISBN 90-247-0235-8
3. J.-C. Piguet: *De l'esthétique à la métaphysique.* 1959   ISBN 90-247-0236-4
4. *E. Husserl: 1850-1959.* Recueil commémoratif publié à l'occasion du centenaire de la naissance du philosophe. 1959   ISBN 90-247-0237-2
5/6. H. Spiegelberg: *The Phenomenological Movement.* A Historical Introduction. 3rd revised ed. with the collaboration of Karl Schumann. 1982
    ISBN Hb: 90-247-2577-1; Pb: 90-247-2535-6
7. A. Roth: *Edmund Husserls ethische Untersuchungen.* Dargestellt anhand seiner Vorlesungsmanuskripte. 1960   ISBN 90-247-0241-0
8. E. Levinas: *Totalité et Infini.* Essai sur l'extériorité. 4th ed., 4th printing 1984
    ISBN Hb: 90-247-5105-5; Pb: 90-247-2971-8
9. A. de Waelhens: *La philosophie et les expériences naturelles.* 1961
    ISBN 90-247-0243-7
10. L. Eley: *Die Krise des Apriori in der transzendentalen Phänomenologie Edmund Husserls.* 1962   ISBN 90-247-0244-5
11. A. Schutz: *Collected Papers, I.* The Problem of Social Reality. Edited and introduced by M. Natanson. 1962; 5th printing: 1982
    ISBN Hb: 90-247-5089-X; Pb: 90-247-3046-5
    Collected Papers, II see below under Volume 15
    Collected Papers, III see below under Volume 22
12. J.M. Broekman: *Phänomenologie und Egologie.* Faktisches und transzendentales Ego bei Edmund Husserl. 1963   ISBN 90-247-0245-3
13. W.J. Richardson: *Heidegger. Through Phenomenology to Thought.* Preface by Martin Heidegger. 1963; 3rd printing: 1974   ISBN 90-247-02461-1
14. J.N. Mohanty: *Edmund Husserl's Theory of Meaning.* 1964; reprint: 1969
    ISBN 90-247-0247-X
15. A. Schutz: *Collected Papers, II.* Studies in Social Theory. Edited and introduced by A. Brodersen. 1964; reprint: 1977   ISBN 90-247-0248-8
16. I. Kern: *Husserl und Kant.* Eine Untersuchung über Husserls Verhältnis zu Kant und zum Neukantianismus. 1964; reprint: 1984   ISBN 90-247-0249-6
17. R.M. Zaner: *The Problem of Embodiment.* Some Contributions to a Phenomenology of the Body. 1964; reprint: 1971   ISBN 90-247-5093-8
18. R. Sokolowski: *The Formation of Husserl's Concept of Constitution.* 1964; reprint: 1970   ISBN 90-247-5086-5
19. U. Claesges: *Edmund Husserls Theorie der Raumkonstitution.* 1964
    ISBN 90-247-0251-8
20. M. Dufrenne: *Jalons.* 1966   ISBN 90-247-0252-6
21. E. Fink: *Studien zur Phänomenologie, 1930-1939.* 1966   ISBN 90-247-0253-4
22. A. Schutz: *Collected Papers, III.* Studies in Phenomenological Philosophy. Edited by I. Schutz. With an introduction by Aaron Gurwitsch. 1966; reprint: 1975
    ISBN 90-247-5090-3

Phaenomenologica

23. K. Held: *Lebendige Gegenwart.* Die Frage nach der Seinsweise des transzendentalen Ich bei Edumund Husserl, entwickelt am Leitfaden der Zeitproblematik. 1966
ISBN 90-247-0254-2
24. O. Laffoucrière: *Le destin de la pensée et 'La Mort de Dieu' selon Heidegger.* 1968
ISBN 90-247-0255-0
25. E. Husserl: *Briefe an Roman Ingarden.* Mit Erläuterungen und Erinnerungen an Husserl. Hrsg. von R. Ingarden. 1968   ISBN Hb: 90-247-0257-7; Pb: 90-247-0256-9
26. R. Boehm: *Vom Gesichtspunkt der Phänomenologie* (I). Husserl-Studien. 1968
ISBN Hb: 90-247-0259-3; Pb: 90-247-0258-5
For *Band II* see below under Volume 83
27. T. Conrad: *Zur Wesenslehre des psychischen Lebens und Erlebens.* Mit einem Geleitwort von H.L. van Breda. 1968   ISBN 90-247-0260-7
28. W. Biemel: *Philosophische Analysen zur Kunst der Gegenwart.* 1969
ISBN Hb: 90-247-0263-1; Pb: 90-247-0262-3
29. G. Thinès: *La problématique de la psychologie.* 1968
ISBN Hb: 90-247-0265-8; Pb: 90-247-0264-X
30. D. Sinha: *Studies in Phenomenology.* 1969
ISBN Hb: 90-247-0267-4; Pb: 90-247-0266-6
31. L. Eley: *Metakritik der formalen Logik.* Sinnliche Gewissheit als Horizont der Aussagenlogik und elementaren Prädikatenlogik. 1969
ISBN Hb: 90-247-0269-0; Pb: 90-247-0268-2
32. M.S. Frings: *Person und Dasein.* Zur Frage der Ontologie des Wertseins. 1969
ISBN Hb: 90-247-0271-2; Pb: 90-247-0270-4
33. A. Rosales: *Transzendenz und Differenz.* Ein Beitrag zum Problem der ontologischen Differenz beim frühen Heidegger. 1970   ISBN 90-247-0272-0
34. M.M. Saraïva: *L'imagination selon Husserl.* 1970   ISBN 90-247-0273-9
35. P. Janssen: *Geschichte und Lebenswelt.* Ein Beitrag zur Diskussion von Husserls Spätwerk. 1970   ISBN 90-247-0274-7
36. W. Marx: *Vernunft und Welt.* Zwischen Tradition und anderem Anfang. 1970
ISBN 90-247-5042-3
37. J.N. Mohanty: *Phenomenology and Ontology.* 1970   ISBN 90-247-5053-9
38. A. Aguirre: *Genetische Phänomenologie und Reduktion.* Zur Letztbegründung der Wissenschaft aus der radikalen Skepsis im Denken E. Husserls. 1970
ISBN 90-247-5025-3
39. T.F. Geraets: *Vers une nouvelle philosophie transcendentale.* La genèse de la philosophie de Maurice Merleau-Ponty jusqu'à la 'Phénoménologie de la perception.' Préface par E. Levinas. 1971   ISBN 90-247-5024-5
40. H. Declève: *Heidegger et Kant.* 1970   ISBN 90-247-5016-4
41. B. Waldenfels: *Das Zwischenreich des Dialogs.* Sozialphilosophische Untersuchungen in Anschluss an Edmund Husserl. 1971   ISBN 90-247-5072-5
42. K. Schuhmann: *Die Fundamentalbetrachtung der Phänomenologie.* Zum Weltproblem in der Philosophie Edmund Husserls. 1971   ISBN 90-247-5121-7
43. K. Goldstein: *Selected Papers/Ausgewählte Schriften.* Edited by A. Gurwitsch, E.M. Goldstein Haudek and W.E. Haudek. Introduction by A. Gurwitsch. 1971
ISBN 90-247-5047-4

Phaenomenologica

44. E. Holenstein: *Phänomenologie der Assoziation*. Zu Struktur und Funktion eines Grundprinzips der passiven Genesis bei E. Husserl. 1972   ISBN 90-247-1175-4
45. F. Hammer: *Theonome Anthropologie?* Max Schelers Menschenbild und seine Grenzen. 1972   ISBN 90-247-1186-X
46. A. Pažanin: *Wissenschaft und Geschichte in der Phänomenologie Edmund Husserls*. 1972   ISBN 90-247-1194-0
47. G.A. de Almeida: *Sinn und Inhalt in der genetischen Phänomenologie E. Husserls*. 1972   ISBN 90-247-1318-8
48. J. Rolland de Renéville: *Aventure de l'absolu*. 1972   ISBN 90-247-1319-6
49. U. Claesges und K. Held (eds.): *Perspektiven transzendental-phänomenologischer Forschung*. Für Ludwig Landgrebe zum 70. Geburtstag von seiner Kölner Schülern. 1972   ISBN 90-247-1313-7
50. F. Kersten and R. Zaner (eds.): *Phenomenology: Continuation and Criticism*. Essays in Memory of Dorion Cairns. 1973   ISBN 90-247-1302-1
51. W. Biemel (ed.): *Phänomenologie Heute*. Festschrift für Ludwig Landgrebe. 1972
   ISBN 90-247-1336-6
52. D. Souche-Dagues: *Le développement de l'intentionnalité dans la phénoménologie husserlienne*. 1972   ISBN 90-247-1354-4
53. B. Rang: *Kausalität und Motivation*. Untersuchungen zum Verhältnis von Perspektivität und Objektivität in der Phänomenologie Edmund Husserls. 1973
   ISBN 90-247-1353-6
54. E. Levinas: *Autrement qu'être ou au-delà de l'essence*. 2nd. ed.: 1978
   ISBN 90-247-2030-3
55. D. Cairns: *Guide for Translating Husserl*. 1973   ISBN (Pb) 90-247-1452-4
56. K. Schuhmann: *Die Dialektik der Phänomenologie, I*. Husserl über Pfänder. 1973
   ISBN 90-247-1316-1
57. K. Schuhmann: *Die Dialektik der Phänomenologie, II*. Reine Phänomenologie und phänomenologische Philosophie. Historisch-analytische Monographie über Husserls 'Ideen I'. 1973   ISBN 90-247-1307-2
58. R. Williame: *Les fondements phénoménologiques de la sociologie compréhensive: Alfred Schutz et Max Weber*. 1973   ISBN 90-247-1531-8
59. E. Marbach: *Das Problem des Ich in der Phänomenologie Husserls*. 1974
   ISBN 90-247-1587-3
60. R. Stevens: *James and Husserl: The Foundations of Meaning*. 1974
   ISBN 90-247-1631-4
61. H.L. van Breda (ed.): *Vérité et Vérification / Wahrheit und Verifikation*. Actes du quatrième Colloque International de Phénoménologie / Akten des vierten Internationalen Kolloquiums für Phänomenologie (Schwabisch Hall, Baden-Württemberg, 8.-11. September 1969). 1974   ISBN 90-247-1702-7
62. Ph.J. Bossert (ed.): *Phenomenological Perspectives*. Historical and Systematic Essays in Honor of Herbert Spiegelberg. 1975.   ISBN 90-247-1701-9
63. H. Spiegelberg: *Doing Phenomenology*. Essays on and in Phenomenology. 1975
   ISBN 90-247-1725-6
64. R. Ingarden: *On the Motives which Led Husserl to Transcendental Idealism*. 1975
   ISBN 90-247-1751-5
65. H. Kuhn, E. Avé-Lallemant and R. Gladiator (eds.): *Die Münchener Phänomenologie*. Vorträge des Internationalen Kongresses in München (13.-18. April 1971). 1975
   ISBN 90-247-1740-X

Phaenomenologica

66. D. Cairns: *Conversations with Husserl and Fink.* Edited by the Husserl-Archives in Louvain. With a foreword by R.M. Zaner. 1975 ISBN 90-247-1793-0
67. G. Hoyos Vásquez: *Intentionalität als Verantwortung.* Geschichtsteleologie und Teleologie der Intentionalität bei Husserl. 1976 ISBN 90-247-1794-9
68. J. Patočka: *Le monde naturel comme problème philosophique.* 1976
    ISBN 90-247-1795-7
69. W.W. Fuchs: *Phenomenology and the Metaphysics of Presence.* An Essay in the Philosophy of Edmund Husserl. 1976 ISBN 90-247-1822-8
70. S. Cunningham: *Language and the Phenomenological Reductions of Edmund Husserl.* 1976 ISBN 90-247-1823-6
71. G.C. Moneta: *On Identity.* A Study in Genetic Phenomenology. 1976
    ISBN 90-247-1860-0
72. W. Biemel und das Husserl-Archiv zu Löwen (eds.): *Die Welt des Menschen - Die Welt der Philosophie.* Festschrift für Jan Patočka. 1976 ISBN 90-247-1899-6
73. M. Richir: *Au-delà du renversement copernicien.* La question de la phénoménologie et son fondement. 1976 ISBN 90-247-1903-8
74. H. Mongis: *Heidegger et la critique de la notion de valeur.* La destruction de la fondation métaphysique. Lettre-préface de Martin Heidegger. 1976
    ISBN 90-247-1904-6
75. J. Taminiaux: *Le regard et l'excédent.* 1977 ISBN 90-247-2028-1
76. Th. de Boer: *The Development of Husserl's Thought.* 1978
    ISBN Hb: 90-247-2039-7; Pb: 90-247-2124-5
77. R.R. Cox: *Schutz's Theory of Relevance.* A Phenomenological Critique. 1978
    ISBN 90-247-2041-9
78. S. Strasser: *Jenseits von Sein und Zeit.* Eine Einführung in Emmanuel Levinas' Philosophie. 1978 ISBN 90-247-2068-0
79. R.T. Murphy: *Hume and Husserl.* Towards Radical Subjectivism. 1980
    ISBN 90-247-2172-5
80. H. Spiegelberg: *The Context of the Phenomenological Movement.* 1981
    ISBN 90-247-2392-2
81. J.R. Mensch: *The Question of Being in Husserl's* Logical Investigations. 1981
    ISBN 90-247-2413-9
82. J. Loscerbo: *Being and Technology.* A Study in the Philosophy of Martin Heidegger. 1981 ISBN 90-247-2411-2
83. R. Boehm: *Vom Gesichtspunkt der Phänomenologie II.* Studien zur Phänomenologie der Epoché. 1981 ISBN 90-247-2415-5
84. H. Spiegelberg and E. Avé-Lallemant (eds.): *Pfänder-Studien.* 1982
    ISBN 90-247-2490-2
85. S. Valdinoci: *Les fondements de la phénoménologie husserlienne.* 1982
    ISBN 90-247-2504-6
86. I. Yamaguchi: *Passive Synthesis und Intersubjektivität bei Edmund Husserl.* 1982
    ISBN 90-247-2505-4
87. J. Libertson: *Proximity.* Levinas, Blanchot, Bataille and Communication. 1982
    ISBN 90-247-2506-2

Phaenomenologica

88. D. Welton: *The Origins of Meaning*. A Critical Study of the Thresholds of Husserlian Phenomenology. 1983 ISBN 90-247-2618-2
89. W.R. McKenna: *Husserl's 'Introductions to Phenomenology'*. Interpretation and Critique. 1982 ISBN 90-247-2665-4
90. J.P. Miller: *Numbers in Presence and Absence*. A Study of Husserl's Philosophy of Mathematics. 1982 ISBN 90-247-2709-X
91. U. Melle: *Das Wahrnehmungsproblem und seine Verwandlung in phänomenologischer Einstellung*. Untersuchungen zu den phänomenologischen Wahrnehmungstheorien von Husserl, Gurwitsch und Merleau-Ponty. 1983
ISBN 90-247-2761-8
92. W.S. Hamrick (ed.): *Phenomenology in Practice and Theory*. Essays for Herbert Spiegelberg. 1984 ISBN 90-247-2926-2
93. H. Reiner: *Duty and Inclination*. The Fundamentals of Morality Discussed and Redefined with Special Regard to Kant and Schiller. 1983 ISBN 90-247-2818-6
94. M. J. Harney: *Intentionality, Sense and the Mind*. 1984 ISBN 90-247-2891-6
95. Kah Kyung Cho (ed.): *Philosophy and Science in Phenomenological Perspective*. 1984 ISBN 90-247-2922-X
96. A. Lingis: *Phenomenological Explanations*. 1986
ISBN Hb: 90-247-3332-4; Pb: 90-247-3333-2
97. N. Rotenstreich: *Reflection and Action*. 1985
ISBN Hb: 90-247-2969-6; Pb: 90-247-3128-3
98. J.N. Mohanty: *The Possibility of Transcendental Philosophy*. 1985
ISBN Hb: 90-247-2991-2; Pb: 90-247-3146-1
99. J.J. Kockelmans: *Heidegger on Art and Art Works*. 1985 ISBN 90-247-3102-X
100. E. Lévinas: *Collected Philosophical Papers*. 1987
ISBN Hb: 90-247-3272-7; Pb: 90-247-3395-2
101. R. Regvald: *Heidegger et le problème du néant*. 1986 ISBN 90-247-3388-X
102. J.A. Barash: *Martin Heidegger and the Problem of Historical Meaning*. 1987
ISBN 90-247-3493-2
103 J.J. Kockelmans (ed.): *Phenomenological Psychology*. The Dutch School. 1987
ISBN 90-247-3501-7
104. W.S. Hamrick: *An Existential Phenomenology of Law: Maurice Merleau-Ponty*. 1987
ISBN 90-247-3520-3
105. J.C. Sallis, G. Moneta and J. Taminiaux (eds.): *The Collegium Phaenomenologicum. The First Ten Years*. 1988 ISBN 90-247-3709-5
106. D. Carr: *Interpreting Husserl*. Critical and Comparative Studies. 1987.
ISBN 90-247-3505-X
107. G. Heffernan: *Isagoge in die phänomenologische Apophantik*. Eine Einführung in die phänomenologische Urteilslogik durch die Auslegung des Textes der *Formalen und transzendenten Logik* von Edmund Husserl. 1989 ISBN 90-247-3710-9
108. F. Volpi, J.-F. Mattéi, Th. Sheenan, J.-F. Courtine, J. Taminiaux, J. Sallis, D. Janicaud, A.L. Kelkel, R. Bernet, R. Brisart, K. Held, M. Haar et S. IJsseling: *Heidegger et l'idée de la phénoménologie*. 1988 ISBN 90-247-3586-6
109. C. Singevin: *Dramaturgie de l'esprit*. 1988 ISBN 90-247-3557-2

Phaenomenologica

110. J. Patočka: *Le monde naturel et le mouvement de l'existence humaine.* 1988
    ISBN 90-247-3577-7
111. K.-H. Lembeck: *Gegenstand Geschichte.* Geschichtswissenschaft in Husserls Phänomenologie. 1988   ISBN 90-247-3635-8
112. J.K. Cooper-Wiele: *The Totalizing Act.* Key to Husserl's Early Philosophy. 1989
    ISBN 0-7923-0077-7
113. S. Valdinoci: *Le principe d'existence.* Un devenir psychiatrique de la phénoménologie. 1989   ISBN 0-7923-0125-0
114. D. Lohmar: *Phänomenologie der Mathematik.* 1989   ISBN 0-7923-0187-0
115. S. IJsseling (Hrsgb.): *Husserl-Ausgabe und Husserl-Forschung.* 1990
    ISBN 0-7923-0372-5
116. R. Cobb-Stevens: *Husserl and Analytic Philosophy.* 1990   ISBN 0-7923-0467-5
117. R. Klockenbusch: *Husserl und Cohn.* Widerspruch, Reflexion und Telos in Phänomenologie und Dialektik. 1989   ISBN 0-7923-0515-9
118. S. Vaitkus: *How is Society Possible?* Intersubjectivity and the Fiduciary Attitude as Problems of the Social Group in Mead, Gurwitsch, and Schutz. 1991
    ISBN 0-7923-0820-4
119. C. Macann: *Presence and Coincidence.* The Transformation of Transcendental into Ontological Phenomenology. 1991   ISBN 0-7923-0923-5
120. G. Shpet: *Appearance and Sense.* Phenomenology as the Fundamental Science and Its Problems. Translated from Russian by Th. Nemeth. 1991   ISBN 0-7923-1098-5
121. B. Stevens: *L'apprentissage des signes.* Lecture de Paul Ricœur. 1991
    ISBN 0-7923-1244-9
122. G. Soffer: *Husserl and the Question of Relativism.* 1991   ISBN 0-7923-1291-0
123. G. Römpp: *Husserls Phänomenologie der Intersubjektivität.* Und Ihre Bedeutung für eine Theorie intersubjektiver Objektivität und die Konzeption einer phänomenologischen Philosophie. 1991   ISBN 0-7923-1361-5
124. S. Strasser: *Welt im Widerspruch.* Gedanken zu einer Phänomenologie als ethischer Fundamentalphilosophie. 1991   ISBN Hb: 0-7923-1404-2; Pb: 0-7923-1551-0
125. R. P. Buckley: *Husserl, Heidegger and the Crisis of Philosophical Responsibility.* 1992   ISBN 0-7923-1633-9
126. J. G. Hart: *The Person and the Common Life.* Studies in a Husserlian Social Ethics. 1992   ISBN 0-7923-1724-6
127. P. van Tongeren, P. Sars, C. Bremmers and K. Boey (eds.): *Eros and Eris.* Contributions to a Hermeneutical Phenomenology. Liber Amicorum for Adriaan Peperzak. 1992   ISBN 0-7923-1917-6
128. Nam-In Lee: *Edmund Husserls Phänomenologie der Instinkte.* 1993
    ISBN 0-7923-2041-7
129. P. Burke and J. Van der Veken (eds.): *Merleau-Ponty in Contemporary Perspective.* 1993   ISBN 0-7923-2142-1
130. G. Haefliger: *Über Existenz: Die Ontologie Roman Ingardens.* 1994
    ISBN 0-7923-2227-4
131. J. Lampert: *Synthesis and Backward Reference in Husserl's Logical Investigations.* 1995   ISBN 0-7923-3105-2
132. J.M. DuBois: *Judgment and Sachverhalt.* An Introduction to Adolf Reinach's Phenomenological Realism. 1995   ISBN 0-7923-3519-8

Phaenomenologica

133. B.E. Babich (ed.): *From Phenomenology to Thought, Errancy, and Desire*. Essays in Honor of William J. Richardson, S.J. 1995　ISBN 0-7923-3567-8
134. M. Dupuis: *Pronoms et visages. Lecture d'Emmanuel Levinas*. 1996
　ISBN 0-7923-3655-0; Pb 0-7923-3994-0
135. D. Zahavi: *Husserl und die transzendentale Intersubjektivität*. Eine Antwort auf die sprachpragmatische Kritik. 1996　ISBN 0-7923-3713-1
136. A. Schutz: *Collected Papers, IV*. Edited with preface and notes by H. Wagner and G. Psathas, in collaboration with F. Kersten. 1996　ISBN 0-7923-3760-3
137. P. Kontos: *D'une phénoménologie de la perception chez Heidegger*. 1996
　ISBN 0-7923-3776-X
138. F. Kuster: *Wege der Verantwortung*. Husserls Phänomenologie als Gang durch die Faktizität. 1996　ISBN 0-7923-3916-9
139. C. Beyer: *Von Bolzano zu Husserl*. Eine Untersuchung über den Ursprung der phänomenologischen Bedeutungslehre. 1996　ISBN 0-7923-4050-7
140. J. Dodd: *Idealism and Corporeity*. An Essay on the Problem of the Body in Husserl's Phenomenology. 1997　ISBN 0-7923-4400-6
141. E. Kelly: *Structure and Diversity*. Studies in the Phenomenological Philosophy of Max Scheler. 1997　ISBN 0-7923-4492-8
142. J. Cavallin: *Content and Object*. Husserl, Twardowski and Psychologism. 1997
　ISBN 0-7923-4734-X
143. H.P. Steeves: *Founding Community*. A Phenomenological-Ethical Inquiry. 1997
　ISBN 0-7923-4798-6
144. M. Sawicki: *Body, Text, and Science*. The Literacy of Investigative Practices and the Phenomenology of Edith Stein. 1997　ISBN 0-7923-4759-5
145. O.K. Wiegand: *Interpretationen der Modallogik*. Ein Beitrag zur phänomenologischen Wissenschaftstheorie. 1998　ISBN 0-7923-4809-5
146. P. Marrati-Guénoun: *La genèse et la trace*. Derrida lecteur de Husserl et Heidegger. 1998　ISBN 0-7923-4969-5
147. D. Lohmar: *Erfahrung und kategoriales Denken*. 1998　ISBN 0-7923-5117-7
148. N. Depraz and D. Zahavi (eds.): *Alterity and Facticity*. New Perspectives on Husserl. 1998　ISBN 0-7923-5187-8
149. E. Øverenget: *Seeing the Self*. Heidegger on Subjectivity. 1998　ISBN 0-7923-5219-X

Previous volumes are still available

Further information about *Phenomenology* publications are available on request

Kluwer Academic Publishers – Dordrecht / Boston / London